Visual C++ 6: The Complete Reference

Chris H. Pappas and William H. Murray, III

Osborne/**McGraw-Hill**

Berkeley New York St. Louis San Francisco
Auckland Bogotá Hamburg London Madrid
Mexico City Milan Montreal New Delhi Panama City
Paris São Paulo Singapore Sydney
Tokyo Toronto

Osborne/**McGraw-Hill**
2600 Tenth Street
Berkeley, California 94710
U.S.A.

For information on translations or book distributors outside the U.S.A., or to arrange bulk purchase discounts for sales promotions, premiums, or fund-raisers, please contact Osborne/**McGraw-Hill** at the above address.

Visual C++ 6: The Complete Reference

.34567890 DOC DOC 90198765432109!

ISBN 0-07-882510-5

Publisher
  Brandon A. Nordin

Editor-in-Chief
  Scott Rogers

Acquisitions Editor
  Wendy Rinaldi

Project Editor
  Heidi Poulin

Editorial Assistant
  Debbie Escobedo

Technical Editor
  David Hodges

Copy Editor
  Dennis Weaver

Proofreaders
  Rhonda Holmes
  Karen Mead

Indexers
  Chris H. Pappas
  William H. Murray, III

Computer Designers
  Jani Beckwith
  Jean Butterfield
  Michelle Galicia

Illustrator
  Brian Wells

Series Design
  Peter Hancik

For Professor Morton Goldberg
Upon his retirement after more than 30 years of
dedicated teaching of mathematics.

Contents

Part II

Programming Foundations

15 Power Programming: Tapping Important C and C++ Libraries 479

Part III

Foundations for Object-oriented Programming in C++

Part IV

Windows Programming Foundations

Part V
Wizards

Introduction

This book was written with two main goals: To help you become more familiar with the Microsoft Visual C++ compiler package and to help those of you with different programming backgrounds become more proficient in C, C++, and 32-bit Windows programming. This is quite a task, even for a book containing hundreds of pages, but it was written with you in mind.

Our two major goals encompass a number of specific aims:

■ This book introduces the powerful programming tools provided in your Microsoft Visual C++ compiler package. These include the compiler, debugger, and various Windows 95, 98, and NT development tools. This book compliments your Microsoft reference manuals and online help to provide a quick start with each of the components in the compiler package.

■ Programmers need a thorough understanding of each programming language they intend to use. You will find that this book covers all the important programming concepts in the C, C++, and Windows languages, including the Microsoft Foundation Class Library (MFC). If you are a novice programmer, early chapters will help you build the solid foundation you need to write more sophisticated programs. For advanced programmers, early chapters will serve as a reference source and will introduce exciting C++ concepts.

■ You will learn how to debug program code and write programs that are free of syntax and logical programming errors.

■ You will gain an understanding of how procedural programming differs from object-oriented programming and how to develop simple OOPs programs.

■ You will explore the exciting world of Microsoft Windows programming. Chapters are devoted to helping you understand Windows concepts and how to write simple to intermediate programs.

We believe in teaching by example. We have made every effort to make each example in this book simple, complete, and bug-free. You can study these examples, alter them, and expand them into programs tailored to fit your needs.

This book will serve as a lasting reference to the Microsoft Visual C++ compiler and the tools it supports.

How This Book Is Organized

Chapters 1 through 4 introduce you to the programming tools contained in the Microsoft Visual C++ compiler package.

Chapters 5 through 15 teach the foundational programming concepts needed for the C and C++ languages. These are procedure-oriented chapters that teach traditional C and C++ programming concepts.

Chapters 16 through 19 give you a complete introduction to object-oriented programming with C++. Here you will find terminology, definitions, and complete programming examples to help you with your development of object-oriented programs.

Chapters 20 and 21 introduce you to Microsoft Windows 95, 98, and NT programming concepts and show you how to use the Microsoft Visual C++ compiler to develop applications that include GDI primitives, cursors, icons, menus, and dialog boxes. The applications in these chapters are traditional message-based programs.

Chapters 22 and 23 are devoted to programming with the Microsoft Foundation Class Library (MFC). By using the power of C++ classes, the MFC will shorten both your Windows application development cycle and your program length.

Chapters 24 and 25 continue working with the MFC and introduce powerful Wizards that will automatically generate program code for you. You'll also learn important OLE concepts and you'll use Wizards to build OLE applications.

The MFC and Wizard discussion continues with Chapter 26 where you'll be introduced to the concepts of ActiveX control design.

The last chapter of the book, Chapter 27, teaches the concepts for creating COM and DHTML documents with the Visual C++ compiler and associated wizards.

Finally, Appendix A provides you with an ASCII table, Appendix B lists interrupt parameters, and Appendix C discusses the fundamentals of dynamic link library (DLL) design.

How the Book's Material Was Developed

The material in this book was developed and tested on two Dell Pentium Pro computers running at 200MHz and on two Toshiba Tecra 730CDT computers running at 166MHz. All computers contained a minimum of 32MB of RAM. The computers were operated under Windows 95, 98, and NT.

The entire manuscript was prepared with Microsoft Word for Windows. All screen shots were taken with Collage, a Windows capture utility.

Part I

A Quick Overview of Visual C++

Visual
C++ 6

Chapter 1

The Visual C++ Compiler, Version 6

3

The new Microsoft Visual C++ provides you with a comprehensive, up-to-the-minute production-level development environment for developing all Windows 95/98 and Windows NT applications. Microsoft's Visual C++ version 6 ships in three different configurations: the Learning, the Professional, and the Enterprise Edition.

What's New for Visual C++ Version 6?

Microsoft Visual C++ version 6.0 provides new features such as AutoCompletion to facilitate coding, and Edit and Continue to optimize your debugging sessions. Other features support the Active Platform, such as Dynamic HTML and Active Document Containment. OLE DB Consumer and Provider Template Support and ADO Databinding are designed to help database and control developers who use MFC and ATL. These new features are detailed below.

The following discussion presents the purpose and special features of each edition. This text was prepared using the Enterprise Edition; however, all of the material covered (except where noted in the text) is portable to all three editions.

Learning Edition

Microsoft's Visual C++ Learning edition allows you to easily learn the C++ language while using the professional Visual C++ toolset. The Learning Edition contains all of the features of the Professional edition except code optimizations, the Profiler, and static linking to the MFC Library. This edition is the perfect choice for students and is priced low to make learning the C++ language affordable for a single individual. The license for the Learning Edition explicitly prohibits using the product to develop software for distribution.

Professional Edition

Microsoft's Professional Edition provides developers with the license to distribute programs developed under the Professional Edition, and additional horsepower by taking the Learning Edition and adding to it services and controls for Win32 platforms, including Windows 95/98 and Windows NT. These additions allow you to target the operating system's graphical user interface or console APIs.

New features added to the Professional Edition include the following:

- New C++ keywords, including **bool**, **explicit**, **false**, **mutable**, **true**, and **typename**, for improved C++ performance
- Use of **__declspec** to declare whether the specified storage-class attribute applies to a type or to a variable of a type
- Compiler support for COM files
- New compiler optimization options

- An updated AppWizard that automates the dialog class in a dialog-based application
- MFC asynchronous (URL) monikers (providing asynchronous application Internet communication)
- Active Documents (displayed either in the entire client window of a Web browser (e.g., Internet Explorer), or in an OLE container (e.g., Microsoft Word)
- Win32 Internet API (WinInet)—making the Internet an integral part of any application, simplifying Internet services FTP, HTTP, and gopher
- Active Template Library (ATL)
- C Runtime Library
- ANSI C++ Standard Library
- ERRLOOK—Look up system error messages

Enterprise Edition (Used for this Manuscript)

With the Enterprise Edition, you receive all of the capabilities provided by the Professional Edition plus the ability for developers to create and debug client/server applications for the Internet, or even an intranet. Microsoft's Enterprise Edition ships with additional tools for working with SQL databases and debugging SQL stored procedures. The Visual SourceSafe source-code control system simplifies developing in a team environment. Features unique to the Enterprise Edition include the following:

- Specialized Microsoft Transaction Server
- Visual Database Tools
- Extensive SQL data type support

Note   *Unless specifically mentioned, the applications in this book can be compiled with any version of the compiler. For example, the applications in Chapters 1 through 20 are standard command-line C or C++ applications that can be run under MS_DOS or in a compatibility box under Windows 95/98 or Windows NT. Likewise, the Windows applications developed in Chapter 25 will run under Windows 95/98 or Windows NT.*

These latest Visual C++ compiler releases incorporate many new and upgraded features. Some of the most important enhancements include support for the AT&T C++ 2.1 standard, precompiled headers, auto-inlining, and p-code (packed code).

The Microsoft Visual C++ compiler packages also provide tools for building Windows programs targeted for other platforms. Your code can even be leveraged for both Apple Macintosh and other RISC machines. The C++ compiler includes all the header files, libraries, and dialog and resource editors necessary to create a truly robust Windows application. Microsoft has also incorporated the resource editors for bitmaps, icons, cursors, menus, and dialog boxes directly into the integrated environment. And speaking of integration, new ClassWizards help you build OLE applications using the Microsoft Foundation Class (MFC) libraries in record time.

In this chapter you will learn about the various components of the C++ compiler, the system requirements, and recommendations for setting up the development environment. This chapter explains the Microsoft Visual C++ system and shows you how to fine-tune it to your particular needs.

Many of the subjects discussed in this chapter are dealt with in greater detail throughout the remainder of the book. For example, there are chapters on the Microsoft Foundation Class library, ClassWizards, OLE, and so on.

Recommended Hardware

This section provides hardware and software recommendations that will help you get the most out of the Microsoft Visual C++ compiler. Many of the suggestions are intended to improve overall system performance, while others are meant to make the product more enjoyable to use.

Minimum Hardware and Software Requirements

Microsoft's standard Visual C++ compiler package will operate on a wide range of Intel-based computers.

Note   *There are special versions of the Visual C++ compiler for the MIPS & DEC Alpha AXP and Macintosh systems.*

The following is a list of Microsoft's minimum hardware and software requirements necessary to run the 32-bit version of the Microsoft Visual C++ compiler package:

- Microsoft Windows 95/98 or Windows NT
- Microsoft Visual C++
- Intel 486 or greater
- 16 megabytes of RAM
- 800 × 600 or greater resolution display
- 20 megabytes free hard disk space
- A mouse or other pointing device
- InstallWizard is designed for a typical developer's computer, which means a Pentium® processor and 800 × 600 resolution or better. You can run InstallWizard on a 640 × 480 screen, but you may need to arrange the windows differently to see all the information.

Recommended Hardware and Software

Minimal hardware and software requirements are not always the optimal choice for ease of use, performance, and overall product enjoyment. We recommend the following system profile to optimize the development cycle of C and C++ programs:

- A Pentium based PC, running at 200MHz (or higher)
- 32 MB of RAM
- A 1-gigabyte hard disk space
- A Super VGA monitor
- One high-density floppy disk drive (3.5")
- One CD-ROM drive (for online documentation)
- Microsoft IntelliPoint Mouse

You will want a fast microprocessor that can handle the size and complexity of advanced Windows applications. Having a lot of memory maximizes the overall performance of both Microsoft Visual C++ and the Windows environment. (You can also obtain these performance enhancements by having a large amount of free disk space.)

Two operating systems are emerging as the new standard for 32-bit PC-based computers; Windows 95/98 or its more robust cousin Windows NT. If you have not upgraded to either Windows 95/98 or Windows NT, you should do so before installing your Microsoft C++ compiler package.

The improvements made to Windows 95/98 and Windows NT provide you with the features and performance necessary to create state-of-the-art Windows applications. As you develop these applications in a graphical environment, your eyes will appreciate Super VGA resolution monitors. Buy a monitor with as large a screen as possible.

A Typical Windows Installation

The Microsoft Visual C++ compiler package installs almost automatically. However, there are some questions that you will need immediate answers for. In this section we'll take a look at a typical installation for the 32-bit version of the compiler.

1. Run the SETUP.EXE program on your first Visual C++ diskette or CD-ROM, while operating under Windows 95/98 or Windows NT.

2. You will be given a choice of install options, such as: Typical, Custom, Minimum, or CD_ROM. The amount of hard disk space you must have depends upon the option you chose. We recommend a Typical installation. It is also possible to set which hard drive and/or subdirectory the installation will take place under.

3. You will be prompted for your Name, Organization and Product ID. Enter this information carefully.

4. At this point, files will be copied from your diskettes or CD-ROM to you hard disk. You can view the progress by watching the File Copy Process dialog box. This installation took over 20 minutes on a 200MHz Pentium machine using an 8x CD-ROM drive.

5. When all files have been installed, you will be prompted as to whether your configuration should be changed now or later. We recommend the first option—*make changes now and backup current version*.

6. You will receive a prompt to register environment variables. This is in the form of a checkbox, with the box already checked. At this time, accept the default: And Register the Environment Variables. By registering the environment variables, you will provide your compiler with important information about your system.

7. With the installation complete, reboot your entire system to allow all changes to go into effect.

Directories

Table 1-1 shows a typical subdirectory group for the Visual C++ compiler installation made in the MSVC subdirectory.

Location	Purpose
BIN	Executable files and build tools needed to build 32-bit applications
HELP	Help files
INCLUDE	C++ runtime and header files
LIB	C++ runtime and Win32 SDK libraries
MFC	Microsoft Foundation Class (MFC)
Library files	
OLE	Files for building OLE applications
PROJECTS	The subdirectory used to organize your development projects
TEMPLATES	Subdirectory used to organize object templates
SAMPLES	Sample programs

Table 1-1. *Important Visual C++ Subdirectories*

You will also find several README files located in the MSDEV subdirectory. These files are used to provide the latest release (and bug) information for the compiler.

Documentation

Visual C++ online documentation consists of Quick Reference and Books Online. Quick Reference allows you to quickly look up information while you program. Books Online is the documentation set for Visual C++ in online format. Every Quick Reference topic has a link to Books Online, where complete information is available.

Depending on which install option you choose, Visual C++ will set up Quick Reference files on your hard disk, while Books Online files may remain on the CD-ROM (Note: choose this install configuration if you need to conserve hard disk space). You can customize where to set up files or where to get information, or go directly to Books Online for context-sensitive (F1) help. Topics covered include the following:

- How to use Books Online
- User's guides
- Microsoft Foundation Classes (MFCs)
- Programming with the Microsoft Foundation Class library
- Class library reference
- MFC samples
- MFC technical notes
- C/C++
- Programming techniques
- C language reference
- C++ language reference
- Runtime library reference
- iostream reference
- Preprocessor reference
- C/C++ samples
- Win32 Software Development Kit (SDK)
- API 32 functions
- Win32s programmer's reference
- Windows Sockets
- OLE Software Development Kit (SDK)

The Development System

The Microsoft 32-bit Visual C++ compiler for Windows 95/98 and Windows NT incorporates new, fully integrated Windows development tools and a visual interface. For example, the debugging capabilities of Microsoft's original CodeView are now directly accessible from within the compiler's integrated debugger. The following sections list those stand-alone utilities that are now incorporated directly into the Microsoft Visual C++ compiler.

The New Integrated Debugger

Microsoft pulls the horsepower of its original CodeView debugger directly into the Visual C++ platform with its new integrated debugger. The debugger is accessed from the Debug menu. The integrated debugger allows you to execute programs in single steps, view and change variable contents, and even back out of code sections. You will find it to be a big help when programs compile but don't seem to perform as expected.

The New Integrated Resource Editors

These editors are accessed from the Resource menu. The resource editors allow you to design and create Windows resources, such as bitmaps, cursors, icons, menus, and dialog boxes. Resources allow you to create visually appealing user interfaces to your applications. In the next sections, we'll look at some specific information on two of the most popular resource editors.

The Dialog Box Editor

The Dialog Box editor is a slick graphical development tool that allows you to easily and quickly create professional-looking dialog boxes. The Dialog Box editor allows you to customize a dialog box's labels, framing, option and checkbox selections, text windows, and scroll bars.

The Dialog Box editor allows you to combine numerous controls into your custom dialog boxes. Controls combines a visual graphical representation of some feature with a predefined set of properties that you can customize. For example, checkboxes, radio buttons, and list boxes are all forms of Windows controls.

The Image Editors

The graphical image editors allow you to easily create custom bitmaps, icons, and cursors. A bitmap is a picture of something—for example, an exclamation point used in a warning message. An icon is a small color image used to represent an application when it has been minimized. Visual C++ even allows you to use an image editor to create custom cursors. For example, you could design a financial package with a cursor that looks like a dollar sign. Custom icons, cursors, and bitmaps can be saved with an

.RC file extension and used in resource script files. You'll learn how these resources are used in Chapters 20 through 23.

The Binary Editor

The Binary Editor allows you to edit a resource at the binary level in either hexadecimal or ASCII format. You can also use the Find command to search for either ASCII strings or hexadecimal bytes, and use regular expressions with the Find command to match a pattern. You should use the Binary Editor only when you need to view or make minor changes to custom resources or resource types not supported by the Microsoft Developer Studio environment.

The String Editor

A string table is a Windows resource that contains a list of IDs, values, and captions for all the strings of your application. For example, the status bar prompts are located in the string table. An application can have only one string table. String tables make it easy to localize your application into different languages. If all strings are in a string table, you can localize the application by translating the strings (and other resources) without changing source code.

Additional Tools

Additional Visual C++ tools that are integrated into the compiler's package are located under the Tools menu. These include Spy++, MFC Tracer, Control Wizard, AVI Editor, DataObject Viewer, and the ActiveX Control Test Container. You'll find the Spy++ utility a great help when working on 32-bit Windows applications.

ActiveX Control Test Container

The Test Container tool is an application designed by Microsoft that allows you to quickly test custom controls. Properties and features of the control can be altered while in the test container.

API Text Viewer

The API Text Viewer allows you to view constants, variables, declarations, and types that can be copies from API files into Visual Basic applications.

AVI Editor

The AVI Editor allows you to view, edit, and merge AVI files.

DataObject Viewer

The DataObject Viewer displays the list of data formats offered by ActiveX and OLE data objects created by the Clipboard or drag-and-drop operations.

DDE Spy

You use DDE Spy to track all messages.

DocFile Viewer

The DocFile Viewer displays the contents of a small compound file.

Error Lookup

This tool allows you to view a detailed analysis of an error message.

Heap Walk Utility

The HeapWalk utility enumerates the memory blocks in a specified heap.

Help Workshop

This tool provides the framework for navigating from application user interfaces to help contexts. Implementing further navigation within the Help file is the domain of help authoring rather than programming. The purpose of the utility is to describe the general process of authoring and editing Help topic files.

OLE Client, Tools, and View

The OLE Viewer displays the ActiveX and OLE objects installed on your computer and the interfaces they support. It also allows you to edit the registry and look at type libraries.

The Process Viewer

The Process Viewer allows you to quickly set and view all of the options necessary to track current processes, threads, and processor time-slicing. To start the Process Viewer, simply double-click on the Process Viewer icon in the Visual C++ group box.

The Process Viewer can help answer questions such as the following:

- How much memory does the program allocate at various points in its execution?
- How much memory is being paged out?
- Which processes and threads are using the most CPU time?
- How does the program run at different system priorities?
- What happens if a thread or process stops responding to DDE, OLE, or pipe I/O?
- What percentage of time is spent running API calls?

Resource Viewer

This tool allows you to access your project resources.

ROT Viewer

The ROT Viewer displays information about ActiveX and OLE objects currently existing in memory.

Spy++

Spy++ is a utility that gives a graphical view of the system's processes, threads, windows, and windows messages.

Stress Utility

The Stress application provides acquisition of system resources for low resource stress testing. The acquirable resources include the global heap, user heap, GDI heap, disk space, and file handles. Stress provides fixed-, random-, and message-dependent allocations of these resources. In addition, it provides several logging options to help locate and reproduce bugs.

MFC Tracer

MFC Tracer is a tool that allows the programmer to set the trace flags in AFX.INI. These Trace flags are used to define the category of Trace messages that are sent from the application to the debugging window. Tracer is thus a debugging tool. You'll want to use the MFC Tracer tool when you build MFC applications in Chapters 23 to 27.

UUID Generator

You use the UUID Generator to generate a universally unique identifier (UUID) that lets the client and server applications recognize each other.

WinDiff

The WinDiff utility is also found in the Visual C++ group. This tool allows you to graphically compare and modify two files or two directories. All of the options within WinDiff operate much like their counterpart commands in the Windows 95/98 Explorer or Windows NT File Manager.

ZoomIn

You can use the ZoomIn utility (ZOOMIN.EXE) to capture and enlarge an area of the Windows desktop.

 # Some New Tools and Utilities

The new Developer Studio has added many new and improved features to make it easier than ever to develop world-class applications. New additions include the ability to host Visual J++ 1.1 and Visual InterDev, as well as Visual C++ 6.0 and MSDN.

Automation and Macros

With Visual Basic Scripts you can automate routine or repetitive tasks. While macro recording allows for quick and easy authoring, the Developer Studio allows you to manipulate Studio components as objects, allowing you to automate tasks that include opening, editing, or closing documents, or sizing windows. You can also create integrated add-ins using Developer Studio's object model.

ClassView

The new improved ClassView now works with Java classes as well as C++ classes. You can create new classes using MFC, ATL, or your own classes. ClassView also now provides the ability to view and edit interfaces for COM objects implemented in MFC or ATL. You can also use folders to organize classes the way you want.

Customizable Toolbars and Menus

Developer Studio makes it easy to customize toolbars and menus to fit the way you work. For example, you can now do the following:

- Add a menu to a toolbar
- Add or delete menu commands or toolbar buttons
- Change a toolbar button into a menu command
- Clone a menu or toolbar button from one toolbar to another so it is always accessible
- Design new toolbars or menus
- Personalize an existing toolbar or menu
- Reassign a menu command, making it a toolbar button

Internet Connectivity

Viewing World Wide Web pages in Developer Studio is a snap with the all-new InfoViewer or your own registered web browser to view Microsoft on the Web. With a web address in the URL window, you can click the address to view the Web page. This feature allows Visual Studio users assurance of the latest breaking news, documentation, fixes, and/or upgrades as they become available.

Project Workspaces and Files

The new Developer Studio's flexible project system makes it easy to have a workspace with different project types. For example, you can create a workspace containing a Visual InterDev project *and* a J++ applet.

Note *Workspace files now have an extension DSW (formerly MDP). Project files now have the extension DSP (formerly MAK).*

There are now two Build files types: internal (DSP) and external (MAK). All DSP files are created when you create a new project within the Developer Studio environment or when you convert a project from a previous version. (Note: DSP files are not compatible with NMAKE.) You can create an external MAK file, compatible with NMAKE, by clicking Export Makefile on the Project menu.

Projects can now include active documents, such as spreadsheets and Word document files. You can even edit them without leaving Visual Studio's integrated development environment.

When you start a new workspace, the Developer Studio creates a file by the name, *YOURWORKSPACENAME.DSW*, (DSW), which is a new extension. Workspace files no longer include data specific to your local computer. At this point you may do the following:

- Add the workspace file to a previously defined source control project

- Copy a workspace from another computer or a network directory and open the workspace copy directly, without creating a new workspace file for your local computer

- Use resource editors

- Use the WizardBar with dialog boxes to hook up code to the visual elements of your program

Wizards

The new Microsoft Developer Studio incorporates many new Wizards, including Wizards for the new integrated Visual J++ and Visual InterDev packages (available if you have these packages installed). You can use these Wizards to create files, controls, and new types of projects.

Important Compiler Features

The Visual C++ compiler package contains many useful enhancements, new features, and options. The following sections introduce you to these improvements and briefly explain their uses.

p-code

p-code (short for "packed code") is geared toward optimizing code speed and size. p-code can significantly reduce a program's size and execution speed by as much as 60 percent. Better yet, all of this is accomplished simply by turning on the specific compiler option. This means that any code written in C or C++ can be compiled either normally or with p-code.

This technology compiles an application's source code into "interpreted object code," which is a higher-level and more condensed representation of object code. The process is completed when a small interpreter module is linked into the application.

The most efficient use of this technology does require some expertise, however. Since the interpreter generates object code at run time, p-code runs more slowly than native object code. With careful use of the #pragma directive, an application can generate p-code for space-critical functions and switch back to generating native code for speed-critical functions.

The best candidates for p-code generation are those routines that deal with the user interface, and because many Windows applications spend 50 percent of their time handling the user interface, p-code provides the optimum performance characteristics.

Precompiled Headers and Types

Visual C++ places generic types, function prototypes, external references, and member function declarations in special files called header files. These header files contain many of the critical definitions needed by the multiple source files that are pulled together to create the executable version of your program. Portions of these header files are typically recompiled for every module that includes the header. Unfortunately, repeatedly compiling portions of code can cause the compiler to slow down.

Visual C++ speeds up the compile process by allowing you to precompile your header files. While the concept of precompiled headers isn't new, the way that Microsoft has implemented the feature certainly is. Precompilation saves the state of an application's compilation to a certain point and represents the relationship that is set up between the source file and the precompiled header. It is possible to create more than one precompiled header file per source file.

One of the best applications of this technology involves the development cycle of an application that has frequent code changes but not frequent base-class definitions. If the header file is precompiled, the compiler can concentrate its time on the changes in the source code. Precompiled headers also provide a compile-time boost for applications with headers that comprise large portions of code for a given module, as often happens with C++ programs.

The Visual C++ compiler assumes that the current state of the compiler environment is the same as when any precompiled headers were compiled. The compiler will issue a warning if it detects any inconsistencies. Such inconsistencies could arise from a change in memory models, a change in the state of defined constants, or the selection of different debugging or code-generation options.

Unlike many popular C++ compilers, the Microsoft C++ compiler does not restrict precompilation to header files. Since the process allows you to precompile a program up to a specified point, you can even precompile source code. This is extremely significant for C++ programs, which contain most of their member function definitions in header files. In general, precompilation is reserved for those portions of your program that are considered stable; it is designed to minimize the time needed to compile the parts of your program under development.

The Microsoft Foundation Class Library

Windows applications are easy to use; however, they are not as easy to develop. Many programmers get waylaid by having to master the use of hundreds of Windows API functions required to write Windows applications.

Microsoft's solution to this steep learning curve is the object-oriented Foundation Classes library. The reusable C++ classes are much easier to master and use. The Microsoft Foundation Class (MFC) library takes full advantage of the data abstraction offered by C++, and its use simplifies Windows programming. Beginning programmers can use the classes in a "cookbook" fashion, and experienced C++ programmers can extend the classes or integrate them into their own class hierarchy.

The MFC library features classes for managing Windows objects and offers a number of general-purpose classes that can be used in both MS-DOS and Windows applications. For example, there are classes for creating and managing files, strings, time, persistent storage, and exception handling.

In effect, the Microsoft Foundation Class library represents virtually every Windows API feature and includes sophisticated code that streamlines message processing, diagnostics, and other details that are a normal part of all Windows applications. This logical combination and enhancement of Windows API functions has ten key advantages:

- *The encapsulation of the Windows API is logical and complete*   The MFC library provides support for all of the frequently used Windows API functions, including windowing functions, messages, controls, menus, dialog boxes, GDI (graphics device interface) objects (fonts, brushes, pens, and bitmaps), object linking, and the multiple document interface (MDI).

- *The MFC functions are easy to learn*   Microsoft has made a concerted effort to keep the names of the MFC functions and associated parameters as similar as possible to their Windows API parent classes. This minimizes the confusion for experienced Windows programmers wanting to take advantage of the simplified MFC platform. It also makes it very easy for a beginning Windows programmer to grow into the superset of Windows API functions when they are ready or when the application requires it.

- *The C++ code is more efficient*   An application will consume only a little extra RAM when using the classes in the MFC library. The execution speed of an MFC application is almost identical to that of the same application written in C using the standard Windows API.

■ *The MFC library offers automatic message handling*   The Microsoft Foundation Class library eliminates one frequent source of programming errors, the Windows API message loop. The MFC classes are designed to automatically handle every one of the Windows messages. Instead of using the standard **switch case** statements, each Window message is mapped directly to a member function, which takes the appropriate action.

■ *The MFC library allows self-diagnostics*   Incorporated into the MFC library is the ability to perform self-diagnostics. This means that you can dump information about various objects to a file and validate an object's member variables, all in an easily understood format.

■ *The MFC library incorporates a robust architecture*   Anticipating the much-needed ANSI C throw/catch standard, the Microsoft Foundation Class library already incorporates an extensive exception-handling architecture. This allows an MFC object to eloquently recover from standard error conditions such as "out of memory" errors, invalid option selection, and file or resource loading problems. Every component of the architecture is upward compatible with the proposed ANSI C recommendations.

■ *The MFC library offers dynamic object typing*   This extremely powerful feature delays the typing of a dynamically allocated object until run time. This allows you to manipulate an object without having to worry about its underlying data type. Because information about the object type is returned at run time, the programmer is freed from one additional level of detail.

■ *The MFC library can harmoniously coexist with C-based Windows applications*   The most important feature of the Microsoft Foundation Class library is its ability to coexist with C-based Windows applications that use the Windows API. Programmers can use a combination of MFC classes and Windows API calls within the same program. This allows an MFC application to easily evolve into true C++ object-oriented code as experience or demand requires. This transparent environment is possible because of the common naming conventions between the two architectures. This means that MFC headers, types, and global definitions do not conflict with Windows API names. Transparent memory management is another key component to this successful relationship.

■ *The MFC library can be used with MS-DOS*   The Microsoft Foundation Class library was designed specifically for developing Windows applications. However, many of the classes provide frequently needed objects used for file I/O and string manipulation. For this reason, these general-purpose classes can be used by both Windows and MS-DOS developers.

■ *The MFC library and wizards*   The Class and Control Wizards only create code compatible with the MFC. These dynamic program developers are a must when developing OLE applications.

Function Inlining

The Microsoft Visual C++ Compiler supports complete function inlining. This means that functions of any type or combination of instructions can be expanded inline. Many popular C++ compilers restrict inlining to certain types of statements or expressions—for example, the inline option would be ignored by any function that contains a **switch, while,** or **for** statement. The Visual C++ compiler allows you to inline your most speed-critical routines (including seldom-used class member functions or constructors) without restricting their content. This option is set from the Project menu by selecting Settings..., then the C/C++ folder, and finally Optimizations from the Category list.

Compiler Options

Microsoft Visual C++ compilers discussed in the book are global optimizing compilers that allow you to take advantage of several speed or code size options for every type of program development. In this section, we will discuss those options directly related to the 32-bit version 4.0 Microsoft C++ compiler. If you are using the 16-bit and/or 32-bit version 2.0 compiler, your options will be similar but located under different tabs.

The following compiler options allow you to optimize your code for executable size, speed, or build time. If you do not see an appreciable performance boost, it is possible that your test application does not contain enough code. All options are set from the Build menu by selecting the Settings menu item.

General

From the General tab, you can specify the use, or nonuse, of the Microsoft Foundation Class library. Output directories can also be given for intermediate and final C/C++ compiled files.

Debug

From the Debug tab, the location of the executable file can be specified along with the working directory, optional program arguments, and a remote executable path and filename. Additionally, by using the Category list, additional dynamic link libraries (DLLs) can be specified.

Custom Build

From the Custom Build tab, you can specify custom tools for use in building projects. This includes tools to run on the output file of the project configuration.

C/C++

The C/C++ tab allows you to select from the following categories: General, C++ Language, Code Generation, Customization, Listing Files, Optimizations, Precompiled Headers, and Preprocessor.

General

The General category permits the warning error level to be set, debug information to be specified, compiler optimizations to be set, preprocessor definitions to given, and project options listed.

C++ Language

The C++ Language category allows the representation method to be specified, exception handling to be set, runtime type information to be set, construction displacements to be set, and project options listed.

Code Generation

The Code Generation category allows the microprocessor to be targeted (80386 to Pentium), calling convention given, runtime library specified, and structure member alignment noted. Project options are, again, listed.

Customization

The Customization category allows the following items to be enabled or disabled:

- Language extensions
- Function-level linking
- Duplicate strings
- Minimal rebuild
- Incremental compilation
- Banner and information message suppression

Listing Files

The Listing Files category allows the generation of browse information. Additionally, the browse file destination can be set. Local variables can be allowed in the browse file. The file types can also be optionally set. Project Options are listed.

Optimizations

The Optimizations category allows various code optimizations to be set, such as speed, size, and so on. Inline function expansion can also be given. Project Options are listed.

Precompiled Headers

The Precompiled Headers category allows the use of precompiled header files. These are files with PCH extensions. Precompiled header files speed the compile and link process, but should be eliminated from your directory upon project completion because of their large size. Project Options are listed.

Preprocessor

The Preprocessor category allows preprocessor definitions to be given. It is also possible to add additional include directories (subdirectories containing header files) and ignore standard paths. Project Options are listed.

Link

The Link tab allows you to select from the following categories: General, Customization, Debug, Input, and Output.

General

From the General category, the name of the file and extension can be specified. Most frequently, the extension will be an EXE file extension. However, you'll learn how to develop applications with DLL and SCR file extensions in this text. Object/library modules can also be entered. These are very important for multimedia applications, where specific libraries are not assumed. The following items can also be included:

- Debug information
- Incremental linking
- Profiling
- Ignoring default libraries
- Map file generation

Customization

The Customization category allows the following items to be included:

- Incremental linking
- Program database
- Output file name
- Process message printing
- Startup banner

Debug

The Debug category allows the generation of a map file and debug information in various formats.

Input

The Input category allows the specification of object/library modules. Additionally, symbol references and MS-DOS stub filenames are displayed.

Output

The Output category allows the base address, entry point, stack allocation, and version information for the project to be set.

Resources

The Resource tab permits the resource file (usually a file with a RES file extension) to be given. Additional features include the language, resource include directories, and preprocessor definitions.

OLE Types

The OLE Types tab permits the output filename, the output header filename, preprocessor definitions, and startup banner to be specified.

Browse Info

The Browse Info tab allows the Browse info file name to be specified. Additionally, the browse info file and startup banner can be checked.

Chapter 2

A Quick Start Using the IDE

The Microsoft Visual C++ IDE is an integrated development environment that allows you to easily create, open, view, edit, save, compile, and debug all of your C and C++ applications. As an integral part of the Microsoft Development Studio, the C/C++ environment operates as a cohesive component within the entire Microsoft family of languages, including Visual Basic, and Visual J++. The advantage to this language development suite is the ease of learning and use provided by such a cohesive set of development features and tools. To a very large degree, except for the specific language's syntax, once you have learned one environment's features (for example, Visual C++), you automatically know how to use the others! With Microsoft Development Studio 's language integration, you can easily develop and combine multi-language source files into one program.

As do all of the Development Studio components, the Visual C++ IDE (integrated development environment) contains options for fine-tuning your work environment according to your personal preferences and to comply with application-specific hardware requirements. Many of the features discussed in the next sections are demonstrated in Chapter 3.

Starting the Visual C++ IDE

Launching the Visual C++ IDE is easy. If you are using a mouse, you can double-click on the Visual C++ icon, which is found in the Microsoft Visual C++ group. Figure 2-1 shows the initial screen for the Visual C++ IDE.

Accessing Context-Sensitive Help

Help for each Visual C++ IDE feature is easily accessed because all of the compiler's documentation is online. Tapping into this valuable resource is as simple as placing the cursor on the feature in question and pressing F1.

However, context-sensitive help is not restricted to Visual C++ IDE features. If you place the cursor on a C/C++ language construct and press F1, the help utility will automatically display a description of the construct's syntax, an explanation of its use, and often a clarifying, executable example.

This chapter is designed to give you a broad overview of each Visual C++ IDE option. Do not become discouraged by the number of features and options available. You can use the default settings of many of the Visual C++ IDE's capabilities, which makes it easy to get an application up and running.

As your experience grows and your application requirements increase in complexity, you will gradually gain hands-on experience with the more sophisticated capabilities of this powerful environment. While you are reading this chapter, take a pencil and check those Visual C++ IDE features that sound interesting to you. When the need arises to use one of these features, you can easily refer back to this section for an explanation of how to use the option.

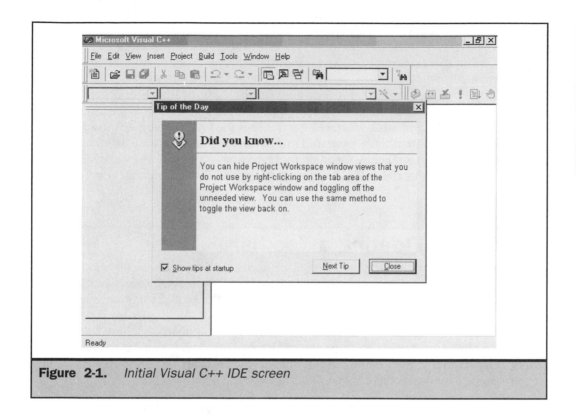

Figure 2-1. *Initial Visual C++ IDE screen*

Understanding Menus

Before beginning a discussion of each Visual C++ IDE feature, let us examine a few traits that all menu items have in common. For example, there are two ways to access menu items. The most common approach is to place the mouse pointer over the preferred option and click the left mouse button. The second approach is to use the underscored hot key. For example, you can access the File menu directly from the keyboard by simultaneously pressing the ALT key and the letter F.

Menu items can be selected using the same sequences described above, and there is often one additional way to select them. You can directly activate some menu items from anywhere within the integrated environment by using their specific hot-key combinations. If a menu item has this capability, the option's specific hot-key combination is displayed to the right of the menu item on the menu. For example, the first option listed on the File menu is New.... This option can be invoked immediately, avoiding the necessity of first selecting the File menu, simply by pressing CTRL-N.

Additional comments concerning menus: First, if a menu item is grayed, the integrated environment is alerting you to the fact that that particular option is currently unavailable. This means that the integrated environment is lacking some necessary prerequisite for that particular option to be valid. For example, the File menu's Save option will be grayed if the edit window is empty. The option knows that you cannot save something that does not exist, and it indicates this by deactivating and graying the Save command.

Second, any menu item followed by three periods, ..., indicates an option that, when selected, will automatically display a dialog box or a submenu. For example, the File menu's Open... command, when selected, causes the Open dialog box to appear.

Finally, you can activate some menu items by clicking on their associated buttons on the toolbars, which are below the main menu bar.

Let's look at the interesting IDE features that are usually available via a menu choice.

Docking or Floating a Toolbar

You can make the standard toolbar (found just under the Visual C++ title bar), or any other toolbar docked or floating. In docked mode, a toolbar is fixed to any of the four borders of the application window. You cannot modify the size of a toolbar when it is docked.

In floating mode, a toolbar has a thin title bar and can appear anywhere on your screen. A floating toolbar is always on top of all other windows. You can modify the size or position of a toolbar when it is floating.

To change a docked toolbar into a floating toolbar:

- Click (keep left mouse button depressed) on the title bar or to a blank area in the toolbar.
- Drag the toolbar away from the dock to any position you desire.

To dock a floating toolbar:

- Click (keep left mouse button depressed) on the title bar or to a blank area in the toolbar.
- Drag the toolbar to any of the four borders in the application window.

To position a floating toolbar over a docked toolbar:

- Click (keep left mouse button depressed) on the title bar or to a blank area in the toolbar.
- Depress the CTRL key, and drag the toolbar over any docking area within the application window.

The File Menu

The Visual C++ IDE File menu localizes the standard set of file manipulation
commands common to many Windows applications. Figure 2-2 shows the command
options available from the File menu.

New...

The New... menu item opens a new edit dialog box window. You usually begin any
new application at this point. The IDE automatically titles and numbers each window
you open. Numbering begins at 1, so your first window title will always be *xxx*1, your
second window title *xxx*2, and so on. The *xxx* is a label identifying the type of file you
are working with (code, project, resource, bitmap, binary, icon, or cursor).

If you have windows titled *xxx*1 through *xxx*6 open and then decide to close the
window titled *xxx*2, the next time you invoke the New... option that title (in this case,
*xxx*2) will not be reused. Windows automatically supplies the next higher number (for
this example, *xxx*7).

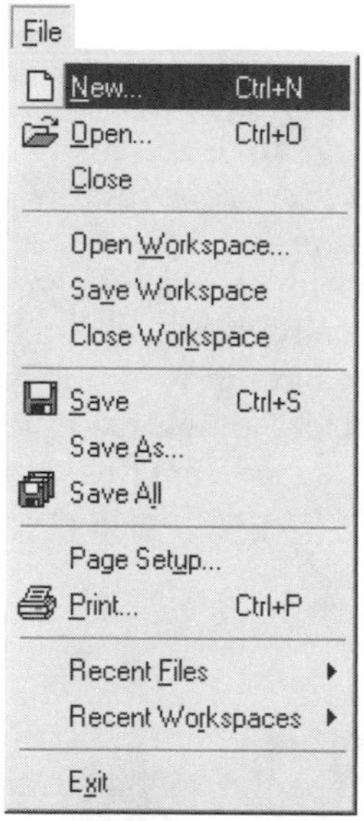

File		
New...	Ctrl+N	
Open...	Ctrl+O	
Close		
Open Workspace...		
Save Workspace		
Close Workspace		
Save	Ctrl+S	
Save As...		
Save All		
Page Setup...		
Print...	Ctrl+P	
Recent Files	▶	
Recent Workspaces	▶	
Exit		

Figure 2-2.   *The Visual C++ File menu*

The quickest way to open a new edit dialog box is to click on the leftmost button on the toolbar. This button has a picture of a file on it. You can invoke the New... option directly by clicking on this control.

Open...

Unlike New..., which opens an edit dialog box window for a previously nonexistent file, the Open... menu item opens a dialog box that requests information on a previously saved file. This dialog box is the standard Open File dialog box, which displays the default drive, path, and file search parameters, and allows you to select your own.

The dialog box has a timesaving feature that automatically remembers your preferences, using these as defaults each time you use the Open... command. Attempting to open an already opened file automatically invokes an audible alert and warning message. This useful reminder prevents you from accidentally opening two or more copies of the same file, editing only one of them, and then resaving the nonupdated version!

The second button from the left on the toolbar, which has a picture of a folder with an open arrow on it, can be used to invoke the Open... option directly.

Close

The Close menu item is used to close an open file. If you have multiple files opened, this command will close the *active* or *selected* window. You can tell which window is active by looking at the window's border. Active or selected windows have the keyboard and mouse focus and are displayed with your system's selected color preferences. These preferences usually include colored title bars and darker window borders. Inactive windows usually have grayed title bars and window borders.

If you accidentally attempt to close an unsaved file, do not worry. The integrated environment automatically protects you from this potentially devastating scenario by warning you that the file has not been previously saved, and it asks you if you want to save the file at this point.

Save

The Save menu item saves the contents of the currently selected or active window to the file specified. You can distinguish the previously saved contents of a window from the unsaved contents of a window by simply checking the window's title bar. If you see a default title, such as $xxx1$, you will know that the window's contents have never been given a valid filename and saved. Saving a previously unsaved file will automatically invoke the Save As... dialog box.

You can also use the Save button on the toolbar. The third from the left, this button has the image of a floppy disk on it. If a file was opened in read-only mode (see the description of the View | Properties command), the control's image will be grayed, indicating that the option is currently unavailable.

Save As...

The Save As... menu item allows you to save a copy of the active window's contents under a new name. If you are wondering why you might choose this option, here's a possible scenario. You have just finished a project. You have a working program. However, you would like to try a few changes. For the sake of security, you do not want to tweak the current version. By choosing the Save As... option, you can copy the file's contents under a new name, and then you can tweak the duplicate. Should disaster ensue, you can always go back to your original file.

Save All

If you have never written a C, C++, Windows 98/95, or Windows NT application, you will be stunned at the actual number of files involved in creating a project's executable file. The problem with the Save option is that it only saves the active window's contents. The Save All menu item saves every window's contents. If any window contains previously unsaved text, the Save All command will automatically invoke the Save As... dialog box, prompting you for a valid filename for each window.

Page Setup...

The most frequent use for the Page Setup... menu item is to document and format your hard copies. The Page Setup dialog box allows you to select a header and footer for each printed page, and you can use it to set the top, bottom, left, and right print margins.

Table 2-1 lists the formatting codes available for selecting the type of header and footer.

Print...

Obtaining a hard copy of the active window's contents is as simple as selecting the Print... menu item. The Print dialog box provides you with several options. First, you can choose between printing the entire window's contents or printing only selected text by clicking on the appropriate radio button. You can also select which printer to use and configure the selected printer by choosing the Setup option.

If you wish to print only a portion of a window's contents, you must first select the desired text. Selecting text is as simple as placing the mouse pointer on the first character in the text you want to print and holding the left mouse button down while you drag the mouse to the right and/or down through the text. This causes the selected text to be displayed in reverse video. When text is selected, the Print dialog box will

Formatting Code	Associated Use
&c	Center text
&d	Add current system date
&f	Use the file's name
&l	Left-justify text
&p	Add page numbers
&r	Right-justify text
&t	Add current system time

Table 2-1. *Page Setup Formatting Codes*

show the Print Range Selection radio button in normal type (not grayed), indicating the option's availability.

Recent File List

Right below the Print... menu item is a list of the most recently edited files. The nice feature about such lists (often called *history lists*) is that they are context sensitive. History lists save you time by remembering the last several items you have selected for a particular option. For this menu, the items remembered are previously opened files. The first time you use the Visual C++ IDE, this portion of the File menu is empty, because there is no history of opened files.

Recent Workspace List

The recent project list is immediately below the recent file list on the menu. This history list is similar to the recent file list, except that the recent project list contains only project files. To open any file, in either list, double-click the left mouse button on the selected item.

Exit

The Exit menu item allows you to quit the Visual C++ IDE. Do not worry if you have forgotten to save a window's contents before selecting Exit. The IDE will automatically display a warning message for each window containing unsaved text, allowing you to save the information before exiting.

The Edit Menu

Edit menu items allow you to quickly edit or search through an active window's
contents in much the same way you would with any standard word processor.
Figure 2-3 shows the Visual C++ IDE Edit menu with the Advanced pop-up menu.

Undo

The Undo menu item allows you reverse the most recent editing change you made.
You can also use the Undo option from the toolbar. The Undo option is the
left-pointing arrow on the toolbar. This is the seventh icon from the left on our system.

Redo

The Redo menu item allows you to reverse the action of the last Undo. Use this option
to reinstate a valid editing change that you thought was an incorrect change. The Redo
option can also be used from the toolbar. On the toolbar, the Redo option is the
right-pointing arrow. This is the eighth icon from the left on our system.

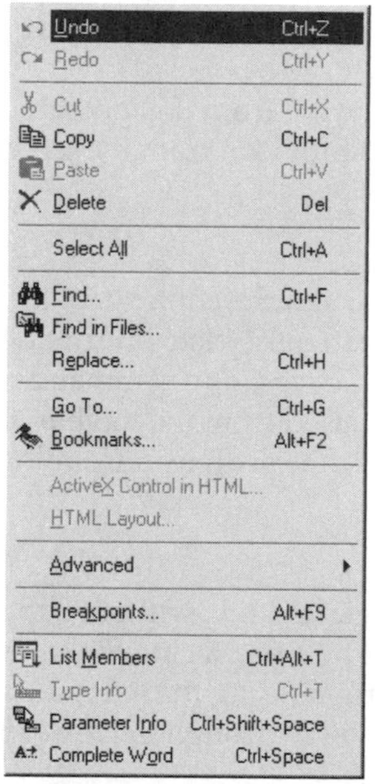

Figure 2-3.   *The Visual C++ Edit menu*

Cut

The Cut menu item copies the selected text in the active window to the Clipboard and then deletes the text from the active window. Selecting text is as simple as placing the mouse pointer on the first character in the text you want to cut and holding the left mouse button down while you drag the mouse to the right and/or down through the text. This causes the selected text to be displayed in reverse video.

The Cut command is often used in conjunction with the Paste command to move text from one location to another. When the cut text is placed on the Clipboard, all previous Clipboard contents are destroyed.

The Cut option can also be used from the toolbar. On the toolbar, the Cut option is the scissors icon. This is the fourth icon from the left on our system.

Copy

Like Cut, the Copy menu item places the selected text on the Clipboard. However, unlike Cut, Copy leaves the original selected text in place. A good use for this option would be to reproduce intricate code sequences or clarifying comments needed in multiple source files.

The Copy command is often used in conjunction with the Paste command to copy text from one location to another. When the copied text is placed on the Clipboard, all previous Clipboard contents are destroyed.

The Copy option can also be used from the toolbar. On the toolbar, the Copy option is the dual-page icon. This is the fifth icon from the left on our system.

Paste

The Paste menu item is used to insert the contents of the Clipboard at the current cursor location. The Clipboard can only paste information that has been previously placed on the Clipboard by the Cut or Copy command.

The Paste option can also be used from the toolbar. On the toolbar, the Paste option is the clipboard-page icon. This is the sixth icon from the left on our system.

Delete

The Delete menu item deletes selected text without copying the information to the Clipboard. Selecting text is as simple as placing the mouse pointer on the first character in the text you want to delete and holding the left mouse button down while you drag the mouse to the right and/or down through the text. This causes the selected text to be displayed in reverse video.

Even though deleted text is not copied to the Clipboard, you can still undo a Delete by choosing the Edit | Undo command.

Select All

The Select All menu item is used to select the entire contents of the active window for cutting, copying, or deleting.

Find...

The Find... menu item works very much like a standard word processor's search option. However, since the C/C++ language is case sensitive, the Find... command can be tailored to search for case-sensitive, case-insensitive, and whole-word-only matches. The Find dialog box also allows you to set the direction for the search (up or down) from the current cursor location.

One very useful and sophisticated Find... option that is not usually associated with any word processor's search capabilities is the Regular Expression option. Table 2-2 lists and describes the Regular Expression search pattern symbols that can be used in the Find What: window.

Pattern	Meaning
*	Substitutes for any number of characters
	Example: Data*1
	Finds: Data1, DataIn1, DataOut1
.	Substitutes for a single character
	Example: Data
	Finds: Data1, Data2, but not DataIn1
^	Starts a search at the beginning of a line for the string
	Example: ^do
	Finds: each line beginning with "do"
+	Substitutes for any number of characters preceding the string
	Example: +value
	Finds: i_value, fvalue, lng_value

Table 2-2.   *Regular Expression Search String Patterns*

Pattern	Meaning
$	Starts a search at the end of each line for the string
	Example: some_var_n);$
	Finds: each line ending with "some_var_n);"
[ ]	Starts a search of the given character subset
	Example: Data[A…Z]
	Finds: DataA not Data1
	Example: Data[1248]
	Finds: Data2 not Data3
\	Starts a search for strings where the preceding character must be exactly matched
	Example: Data[A…Zi\0…9]
	Finds: DataAi1 not DataDo3
\{\}	Starts a search for any sequence of characters placed between the braces
	Example: \{no\}*_answer
	Finds: answer, no_answer, nono_answer, nonono_answer

Table 2-2.   *Regular Expression Search String Patterns* (continued)

Find in Files...

Find in Files... is one of the most valuable tools you'll ever use once you understand its capabilities. Find in Files..., while identical in horsepower to Find..., adds one special advantage, the search has multiple-file scope! You may ask yourself, "Why would I ever need such a feature?" Here is why: If you are learning a new C/C++ language feature, use this option to scan for all programs containing it. If you are modifying a program, use Find in Files... to make certain you have caught all occurrences of the older syntax. If you are working on a large project, use Find in Files... to locate all of the code authored by a particular group or programmer. And remember, Find in Files... isn't just capable of searching one subdirectory, or one hard drive. Find in Files... can scan an entire network, intranet, or the Internet, tracking down any name, string, keyword, method, and much more.

Replace...

The Replace... menu item invokes the Replace dialog box, which allows you to replace text. Simply type in the string to search for, then type in the replacement string, and, finally, select from several matching criteria. Matching options include whole words only, case-sensitive or case-insensitive matches, and Regular Expressions (see the previous explanation).

Be careful when selecting the Replace All option, because this can have disastrous results. There are two things to remember when doing a replace: first, save the file *before* you invoke the command; second, if something goes wrong with the replace, remember that you can always use the Undo option.

Go To...

You can quickly move the cursor to a specified location within an active edit window with the Go To... menu item. Choosing this option invokes a Line dialog box that allows you to enter the line number for the line of code you wish to jump to. Entering a line number greater than the actual number of source code lines available causes the command to place the cursor at the bottom of the window's text file.

Bookmarks...

The Bookmarks... option allows you to set bookmarks to mark frequently accessed lines in your source file. Once a bookmark is set, you can use menu or keyboard commands to move to it. You can remove a bookmark when you no longer need it. You can use both named and unnamed bookmarks. Named bookmarks are saved between editing sessions. Once you create a named bookmark, you can jump to that location whether or not the file is open. Named bookmarks store both the line number and the column number of the location of the cursor when the bookmark was created. This location is adjusted whenever you edit the file. Even if you delete the characters around the bookmark, the bookmark remains in the correct location.

ActiveX Control in HTML... and HTML Layout...

These two options allow you to edit either an embedded HTML ActiveX control or the HTML layout itself.

Breakpoints...

The Breakpoints... option allows you to set breakpoints at specific locations, on selected data items, or on messages.

List Members

This feature displays a list of valid member variables or functions for the selected class or structure.

Type Info

The Type Info option displays a ToolTip containing the complete declaration for any identifier.

Parameter Info

This feature displays the complete declaration, including a parameter list, for the function to the left of the cursor. The parameter in bold indicates the next parameter required as you type the function.

Complete Word

The Complete Word option fills in the rest of your function or variable name for you. This can save you from having to repeatedly type long names.

 # View Menu

The View menu contains commands that enable you to change your view of the Query Designer (see Figure 2-4).

Script Wizard...

An easy way to get started with scripting is by using an HTML authoring tool like Microsoft ActiveX Control Pad. The ActiveX Control Pad is freely available for downloading from the authoring tools section in the Microsoft Site Builder Workshop, accessible through www.microsoft.com. You use the Script Wizard... option to begin the design of a VBScript or JavaScript. Once the Script Wizard... is launched, you first select the Default Script Language, next you Select an Event, Load, and then Insert Event.

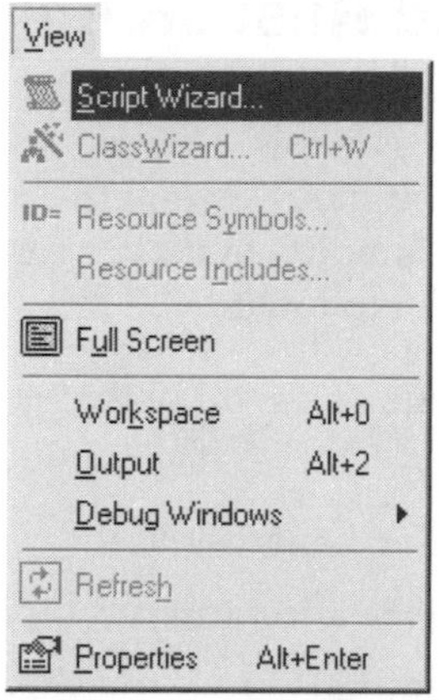

Figure 2-4.   *The Visual C++ View menu*

ClassWizard...

The Microsoft C++ ClassWizard makes it easier for you to do repetitive tasks such as creating new classes, defining message handlers, overriding MFC virtual functions, and gathering data from controls in a dialog box, form view, or record view. One very important note is that the ClassWizard only works with applications that use MFC classes, unlike ClassView and WizardBar, which work with MFC, ATL, or your own classes. Also, ClassView does not recognize classes unless they are registered in the ClassView database file. These are files with a *.CLW file extension. With ClassWizard, you can do the following:

- Attach Automation methods and properties when creating a new class
- Author new classes from many of the main framework base classes that handle Windows messages and recordsets
- Author new message-handling member functions
- Declare member variables that automatically initialize, gather, and validate data entered into dialog boxes or form views
- Delete message-handling member functions
- Map messages to functions associated with windows, dialog boxes, controls, menu items, and accelerators
- See which messages have message handlers already defined and jump to the handler program code
- Work with existing classes and type libraries

Resource Symbols... and Resource Includes...

You will quickly discover that as your programs grow in size and sophistication, so will the number of resources and symbols. This makes tracking an ever-increasing number of symbols scattered throughout several files difficult. The Resource Symbols... and Resource Includes... options simplify symbol management by offering a central tool through which you can do the following:

- Modify the name and value of a symbol that is not in use
- Define new symbols
- Remove a symbol if it is not being used
- Quickly locate the appropriate resource editor where the symbol is being used
- Scan existing symbol definitions to see the value of each symbol, a list of symbols being used, and the resources assigned to each symbol

Full Screen

If you are like most programmers, when it comes to intense code authoring and/or editing, you like to see as much code at one time as possible. The Full Screen option is ideal for these situations, allowing you to zoom your edit window (or any other window, e.g., help screens) for maximum viewing.

Workspace

Imagine a desktop development environment. You have editors, compilers, manuals, Post-Its, textbooks, phone messages, and e-mail scattered across your desk and monitor, all of it relating to the project at hand. Try and think of the Workspace option as an electronic secretary trying to organize some of this information. The Workspace option opens the Workspace view (usually the upper-left portion of your screen), giving you instant access to the current classes, files, resources, and reference manuals most recently accessed. Switching layouts is as simple as clicking on the tabs found at the bottom of the Workspace view.

Output

The Output menu item brings the Output window to the foreground. The Output window contains progress reports on build, compile, and link processes, and it displays any generated warning or error messages.

Debug Windows

Choosing this option pops up a menu providing access to various integrated debugger options including: Watch Window, Register Window, Call Stack, Memory, Variables, and Disassembly Code.

Refresh

You use Refresh to repaint and update the currently active view pane in a similar manner to how pressing F5 in the Windows Explorer repaints and updates its contents.

Properties

If applicable, the Properties command displays current file statistics such as date created, file size, file type, editing characteristics, and much more, depending on the file's type.

 # Insert Menu

The Insert menu accesses a list of commands for including new files, resources, or objects into your workspace (see Figure 2-5).

New Class...

When you select this option, the IDE creates a new MFC, ATL, or generic class. The New Class dialog appears, in which you define the class name and the base class. It creates a header file and an implementation file for the class.

Resource...

This option allows you to add one of several resources to your workspace, including Accelerator, Bitmap, Cursor, Dialog, Icon, Menu, String Table, Toolbar, and Version identifier.

Insert

New Class...
New Form...
Resource...   Ctrl+R
Resource Copy...

Into HTML   ▶
File As Text...

New ATL Object...

Figure 2-5.   *The Visual C++ Insert menu*

Resource Copy...

Visual C++ allows you to copy resources while changing the resource's language, its property condition, or both. When you create or copy a resource with a different language or condition, this is displayed after the symbol name in the Project window. The Language identifies the language used for text in the resource. The Property Condition is a symbol that identifies a condition under which this copy of the resource is used.

Note	*You can also copy from a template.*

Into HTML

The Into HTML option allows you to insert resources to enhance a web page.

File As Text...

Usually used to add source code, the File As Text... option first asks you to name the new file, and then launches a clean edit window ready for text input. (This command requires an open edit window and inserts the file at the current position.)

New ATL Object...

The New ATL Object... allows you to add an Active Template Library class to your worskspace. ATL objects are a set of template-based C++ classes that allow you to easily create small, fast component object model (COM) objects. They provide special support for key COM features, including stock implementations of IUnknown, IClassFactory, IClassFactory2, and IDispatch; dual interfaces; standard COM enumerator interfaces; connection points; tear-off interfaces; and ActiveX controls. ATL code can be used to create single-threaded objects, apartment-model objects, free-threaded model objects, or both free-threaded and apartment-model objects.

Project Menu

The Project menu commands enable you to manage all of your open projects.

Note	*The Data Connection command is added to the Add to Project submenu when Microsoft Visual Database Tools is active—Data Connection launches the Select Data Source dialog box so that you can add a data connection to your current database project. See Figure 2-6.*

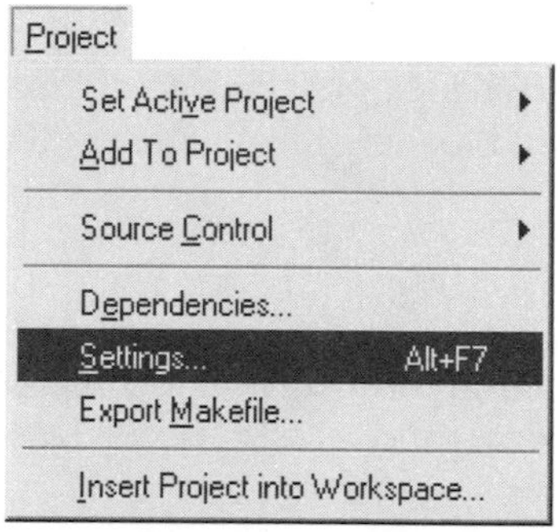

Figure 2-6.   *The Visual C++ Project menu*

Set Active Project

In advanced program development, there comes a time where it is best to break a large project down into subprojects. A subproject establishes a dependency of one project on another in a hierarchical fashion. Subprojects are used in Visual C++ projects, for example, when a project builds an executable program that depends on a static library. If the static library is a subproject of the project that builds the executable program, then the library will be updated before the executable program is built. The Set Active Project option determines which project or subproject is currently active.

Add to Project

You use this option whenever you wish to add a file to a project. The file is added to a specified project, and to all project configurations in that project. For instance, if you have a project named myFirstProj, with Debug and Release configurations, and an additional project configuration named myFinalProj based on the Release configuration, adding a file adds it to all those project configurations. If you add files from directories above the project workspace directory, Microsoft Developer Studio uses absolute paths in the filenames for those files in the project's DSP file. Because of the absolute paths, it is difficult to share the project (DSP) file.

Source Control

This provides options for managing project files in a source-controlled project. This submenu appears only if you have installed a source control program such as Visual SourceSafe.

Dependencies

In advanced program design, where a project is made up of several subprojects, you use the Dependencies command to view this hierarchical relationship.

Settings...

The Settings command opens up a very sophisticated dialog box, allowing you to totally define your projects configuration settings, from classes used, to C/C++ compiler options, to link options, browse, OLE types, resources, browse settings, and build options.

Export Makefile...

The Export Makefile option stores all the information required to build the project and can be used from the command line. Makefiles define the same project build settings you set in the Developer Studio environment.

Insert Project into Workspace...

This option inserts a project into your workspace. However, this might be slightly confusing without the following comparison between what a project is and how it differs from a workspace. A project workspace is the area defined that contains your projects and their configurations. A project is defined as a configuration and a group of files that produce a program or final binary file(s). On the other hand, a workspace can contain multiple projects, even projects of different types (for instance, Microsoft Visual C++).

Build Menu

The options in the Build Menu provide access to the IDE features that are involved in actual code generation, debugging, and running your program (see Figure 2-7).

Compile

Choosing this option instructs the IDE to compile the active window's contents. Compiling in this sense is asking the environment to check the syntax of the active file—for example, C or C++ source code.

Build

Typical C/C++ programs are comprised of many files. Some of these files may be supplied by the compiler, the operating system, the programmer, or even third-party

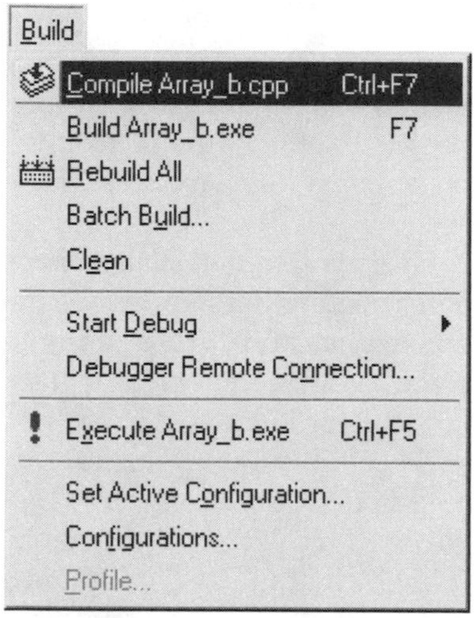

Figure 2-7.   *The Visual C++ Build menu*

vendors. It can get even more complicated if the project's files are created by several programming teams. Because there can be so many files, and because the compile process can take a very long time, the Build menu item becomes an extremely useful tool. Build examines all of the files in the project and then compiles and links only those dependent files displaying dates and times more recent than the project's executable file.

One decision you must make when selecting Build is whether the resulting file is to include debugging information (Debug mode) or not (Release mode). These modes are selected from the Project | Settings... menu item. Once you have a program up and running, you should usually choose a Build without the Debug option, since inclusion of the information makes the resulting executable file unnecessarily large.

If the Build process detects any syntax errors, either nonfatal warnings or fatal errors, these are displayed in the Output window. Use the Next Error or Previous Error menu items to search forward or backwards through this list.

If you have the toolbar visible, you can use the sixth button from the right to invoke Build. This button has a picture that looks like a bucket with two dark-colored, downward-pointing arrows on it.

Rebuild All

The only difference between Build and Rebuild All is that Rebuild All ignores the dates of all of a project's files and painstakingly compiles and links all of them.

Imagine the following scenario. Your company, for the sake of economy, has decided to go without any systems maintenance personnel. This decision, coupled with the seasonal time change, system down time, and so on, results in your discovery that the systems on your network all have different system clock settings. Because of this, newly created files are being stamped with the previous day's date! Choosing the Build option in this case could leave these current, updated files out of the final executable file. However, by choosing Rebuild All, you avoid any date/time stamp checks, creating an executable file that truly reflects the current state of all included files.

If the Rebuild All process detects any syntax errors, either nonfatal warnings or fatal errors, these are displayed in the Output window. Use the Next Error or Previous Error menu items to search forward or backwards through this list.

If you have the toolbar visible, you can use the fifth button from the right to invoke Rebuild All. This button has a picture that looks like a bucket with three light-colored, downward-pointing arrows on it.

Batch Build...

This option is similar to the Build menu item except that it builds multiple project targets.

Clean

With the Clean command you can easily remove all files from the intermediate directories in any project configuration in your project workspace. Removing the files forces the development environment to build these files if you subsequently click the Build command.

Update All Dependencies...

Choosing this option instructs the IDE to read the compiler-generated dependencies and to scan non-C/C++ source files for dependencies. Therefore, the dependency information for C/C++ files will not reflect any changes made since the last build.

Start Debug

Unlike a full-speed program execution, this option instructs the IDE to begin executing your program line by line, or up to any set breakpoint.

Debugger Remote Connection...

After you have configured a connection on both ends, you can begin remote debugging by choosing this option.

Execute

Once you have built your project with 0 errors, the Execute command allows you to run the program at full speed.

Set Active Configuration...

With large projects being combinations of many subprojects, you need to instruct the Build or Rebuild command as to which project's executable needs creation. The Set Active Configuration... command performs this task.

Configurations...

The Configurations... option allows you to add or remove configurations from the active build cycle. For example, you may have begun with only a debug configuration and now wish to add a release version.

Profile...

This option is only available under the Professional and Enterprise Editions. Before using the profiler, you must build the current project with profiling enabled. If you want to perform function profiling only in the current project, you only need to enable profiling for the linker. If you want to do line profiling, you also need to include debugging information.

You use the Profiler to examine the runtime behavior of your programs. The Profiler allows you to determine which sections of your code are working efficiently by producing information showing areas of code that are not being executed or that are taking a long time to execute.

Tools Menu

The Tools menu accesses commands that enable you to work with your query. The Tools menu commands as described below apply to the Query Designer (see Figure 2-8).

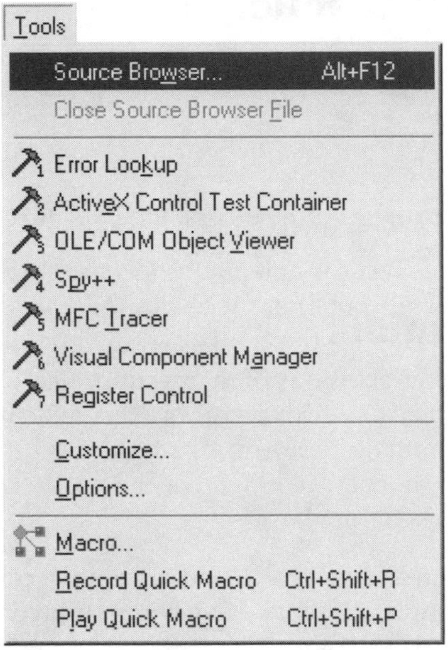

Figure 2-8. *The Visual C++ Tools menu*

Source Browser...

You use this option to browse your information files. You can instruct the compiler to create an SBR file for each object file (OBJ) it compiles. When you build or update your browse information file, all SBR files for your project must be available on disk. To create an SBR file with all possible information, specify Generate Browse Info in the Project Settings dialog box (or /FR). To create an SBR file that doesn't contain local symbols, specify Generate Browse Info, and then check Exclude Local Variables from Browse Info (/Fr on the compiler command line). If the SBR files contain local symbols, you can still omit them from the BSC file by using BSCMAKE's /El option.

Close Source Browser File

This closes the currently active *.SBR file.

Error Lookup

You use the Error Lookup command to retrieve a system error message or module error message based on the value entered. This option retrieves the error message text automatically if you drag and drop a hexadecimal or decimal value from the Developer Studio debugger or other OLE-enabled application. You can also enter a value either by typing it in or pasting it from the Clipboard and clicking Look Up. The accelerator keys for Copy (CTRL-C), Cut (CTRL-X) and Paste (CTRL-V) work for both the Value and Error Message boxes if you first highlight the text.

ActiveX Control Test Container

This command launches the Test Container application, shipped with Visual C++. The program is an ActiveX control container for testing ActiveX controls. Test Container allows the control developer to test the control's functionality by changing its properties, invoking its methods, and firing its events. In addition, Test Container can display logs of data-binding notifications and provides facilities for testing ActiveX control's persistence functionality.

OLE/COM Object Viewer

The OLE/COM Object Viewer displays the ActiveX and OLE objects installed on your computer and the interfaces they support. It also allows you to edit the registry and look at type libraries.

Spy++

The Spy++ option activates a Win32-based utility that gives you a graphical view of the system's processes, threads, windows, and window messages. The Spy++ utility provides a toolbar and hyperlinks to help you work faster. Spy++ also allows you to refresh the active view, supplies a Window Finder Tool to make spying easier, and provides a Font dialog box to customize view windows.

MFC Tracer

To help debug windows programs, MFC provides the MFC Tracer command. This will display, to a debugging output window or console, messages about the internal operation of the MFC library as well as warnings and errors if something goes wrong in your application.

Visual Component Manager

The main screen of Visual Component Manager features a toolbar to select commonly used commands and three panes for viewing the databases, folders and subfolders, and individual items stored by Visual Component Manager. These elements are briefly described next.

Register Control

OLE controls, like other OLE server objects, can be accessed by other OLE-aware applications. This is achieved by registering the control's type library and class. You use the Register Control command for this purpose.

Customize...

The Customize... menu item selects the Customize dialog box, which allows you to add, delete, and customize tools used by the Tools menu. Additional options allow you to assign shortcut keys to various commands.

Options...

The Options... menu item brings up the Options submenu, which offers commands that allow you to customize the Visual C++ IDE itself or modify how your application is developed. If you are a first-time user of Microsoft Visual C++, feel free to examine the contents of the Options submenu. However, until you fully understand the ramifications of changing install defaults, look but do not touch. Many of the changes that can be made at this level have global effects, and an incorrectly set option can literally halt all further application development.

Macro... / Record... / Play...

You use this option to create VBScript macros. The macros are procedures you write in the Visual Basic Scripting Edition language. With VBScript macros, you can simplify your work in Developer Studio. For example, in a macro you can combine several commands, speed up routine editing, or automate a complex series of tasks.

Window Menu

With the possible exception of the Docking View command, you will see that the remaining Window Menu options are similar to those found in all standard Windows products (see Figure 2-9).

New Window

The New Window command provides one of the many ways to begin entering and editing a new file.

Split

The Split option places a four-quadrant pane over the Edit view, allowing you to determine both a horizontal and vertical split point.

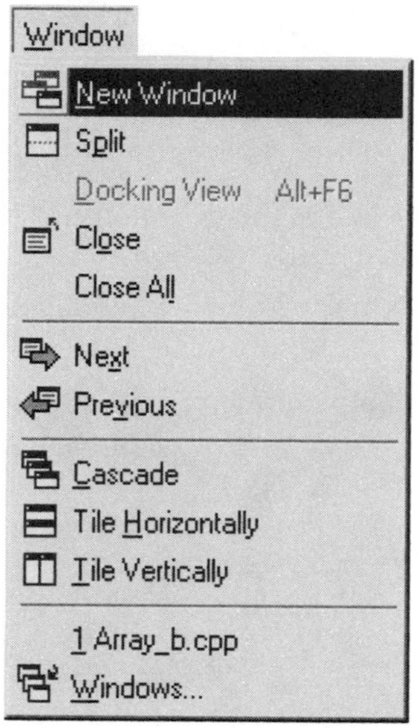

Figure 2-9.   *The Visual C++ Window menu*

Docking View

A dockable toolbar can be attached, or docked, to any side of its parent window, or it
can be detached, or floated, in its own miniframe window. Not all views are dockable,
but if the active window is, for example, the Workspace view, this is one method for
docking and undocking the pane.

Close

This closes the active window. You are prompted if the window's contents have not
been previously saved.

Close All

This closes all open windows. The IDE prompts you if any of the individual files have
not been previously saved before actually closing and deleting their contents.

Next

Rather than clicking on a window to make it active, you can choose the Window |
Next command to cycle through all open window contents.

Previous

This is similar to the Next command, only it works in reverse.

Cascade

This displays all open windows in a manner similar to a splayed deck of cards. This allows for easy viewing of window titles.

Tile Horizontally

This tiles open windows with a wide but squat configuration. It is best used for source code viewing.

Tile Vertically

This tiles open windows with a tall and narrow configuration. It is best used for hierarchy analysis.

History List

This is a dynamic list of open windows, by name, allowing you to make the highlighted window active.

 # Help Menu

The Help menu begins with the standard online documentation Contents and Search options and then diverges into several new help features—for example, the Documentation home page (see Figure 2-10).

Contents and Search... / Index

These standard online documentation navigation controls provide the expected access to Microsoft's extensive online documentation.

Use Extension Help

This toggles the extension help option.

Documentation Home Page

The Documentation Home Page command takes you to the highest-level page for the currently active help topic. It is similar to choosing the first page of a chapter that begins with an overview outline. Documentation Home Page topics are hot-links to topic-specific help files.

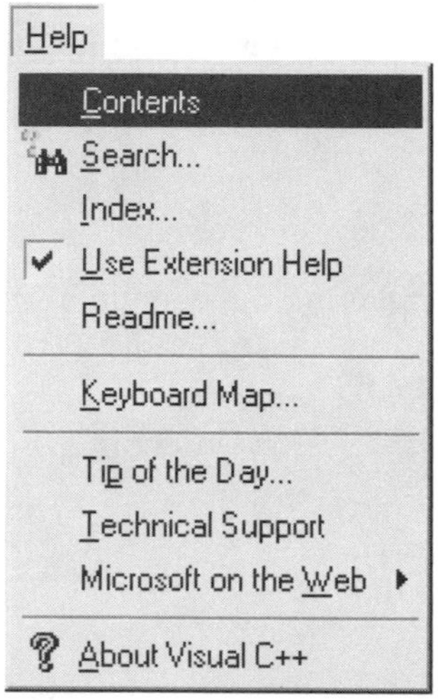

Figure 2-10.   *The Visual C++ Help menu*

Readme...

This displays the README file.

Tip of the Day... and Technical Support

These two options speak for themselves.

Microsoft on the Web

This option is active if your computer can connect to the World Wide Web; it allows you to view web pages through the InfoViewer. Web access is available from the following locations in Developer Studio:

- A URL address in a source window
- Hypertext jumps in the InfoViewer Topic window
- Microsoft on the Web on the Help menu
- The Current URL box on the InfoViewer toolbar

You should take any steps necessary to prepare your computer to connect to the World Wide Web. For example, you must have the appropriate communications hardware installed, be connected to a telephone jack or other communications line, and be properly configured. You must establish access to the World Wide Web through some Internet service provider. If you are working within a corporate network with a security firewall, you need to take the necessary steps to communicate with other computers beyond the firewall.

About Visual C++

This is a standard About box displaying the version, product ID, and installed component ID numbers.

Chapter 3

Writing, Compiling, and Debugging Simple Programs

The Visual C++ component of the Microsoft Developers Studio, just like any new state-of-the-art development environment, can on first encounter be a very intimidating product. While the initial window seems straightforward, as soon as you begin peeking and poking around submenus and their related dialog windows, you can easily become overwhelmed by the options and apparent complexity of this new world.

You see, developing a multitasking, object-oriented, GUI (graphical user interface), multimedia, Internet-aware application really is no easy task (that is, if you had to do all of this from ground zero). However, today's language development environments automate the code generation for the majority of these goals. This text is designed to give you both a thorough understanding of the C and C++ Languages and experience in today's number one development environment (i.e., Microsoft's Visual C++), while learning the logic, constructs, and tools necessary to develop state-of-the-art programs.

This chapter is designed to give you hands-on experience with those commands needed to create, edit, save, compile, and debug simple programs. At this point, if you haven't done so already, you may want to take out a highlighting pen. Since the integrated environment offers so many ways to initiate each operation, you might want to highlight the text where you see the method that you prefer. For example, some people prefer to use keyboard commands, while others like the point-and-click mouse/menu interaction.

Starting the Developer Studio

In Chapter 2, you learned that starting the Visual C++ IDE (integrated development environment) is easy. If you are using a mouse, you can double-click on the Visual C++ icon, which is found in the Microsoft Visual C++ group.

Alternatively, you can access the Windows menu system by doing the following numbered steps:

1. Simultaneously pressing CTRL-ESC;

2. Enter **P** for Programs group;

3. Followed by repeated presses of the CURSOR-DOWN key until the Microsoft Visual C++ Group is highlighted;

4. Next, pressing the RIGHT-ARROW cursor key;

5. Followed by repeated presses of the CURSOR-DOWN key until the Microsoft Visual C++ program is highlighted;

6. Then pressing the ENTER key!

(Here's the first opportunity to highlight your personal preference!) Use the method you prefer, and start Microsoft Visual C++ now.

Creating Your First Program

The first thing you need to do before you enter a program is open a new file. From the File menu, choose the New... menu item. This option opens the New dialog box shown in Figure 3-1.

This dialog box is used to select the type of file you wish to create. For our example, click on the Win32 Console Application. Once you have given the project a name, the Visual Development Studio presents you with the Application options seen in Figure 3-2.

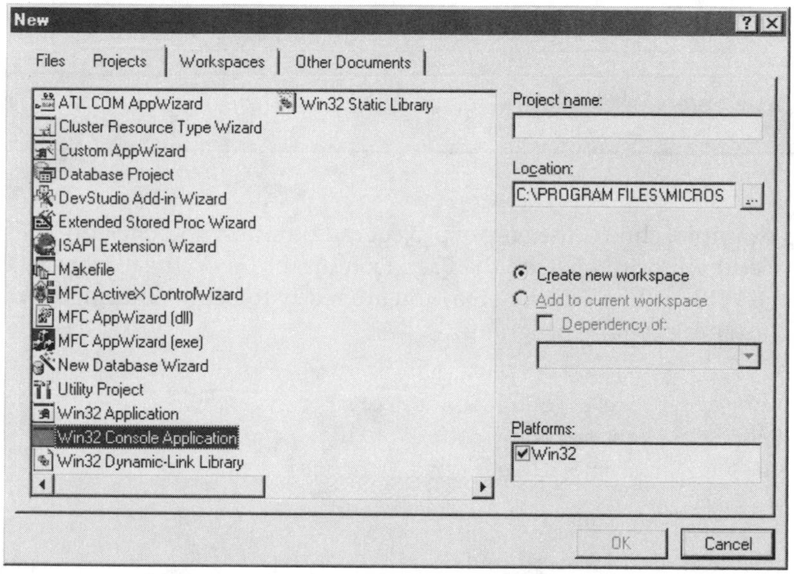

Figure 3-1.   *The New dialog box allows the programmer to start a new program*

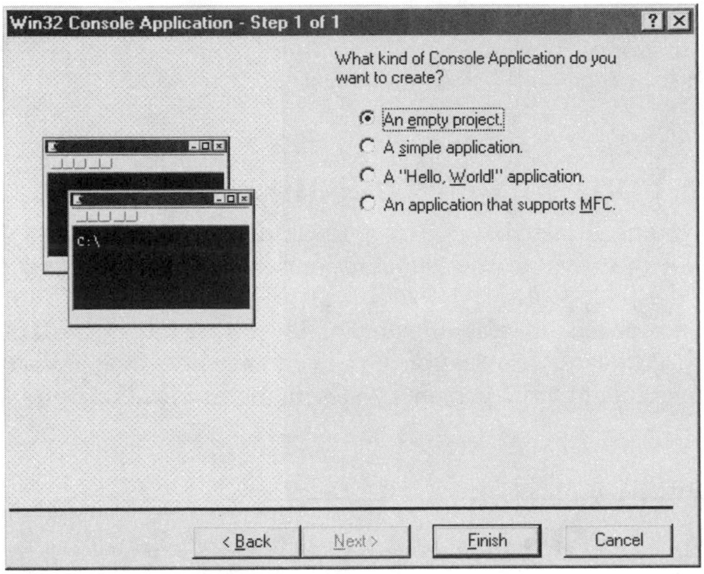

Figure 3-2. *Selecting a Win32 Console Application type*

For this example, choose the empty project radio button and click on Finish. To open a clean edit window, click on the Page icon (first icon on the extreme left of the Edit Toolbar). With a clean editing area, you are ready to begin entering a program. Enter the following example program:

```
/* NOTE: This program contains errors    */
/* entered for the purpose of teaching    */
/* you how to use the Integrated Debugger! */

#include <stdio.h>

/* The following symbolic constant is used to
   dimension the array */
#define SIZE 5

/* Function Prototype   */
void print_them(int offset,char continue,int iarray[SIZE]);
```

```
void main( void )
{
  int offset;          /* array element selector    */
  int iarray[SIZE];    /* integer array             */
  char continue = 0;   /* used to hold user's response */

/* First function call prints variables "as is"     */
  print_them(offset,continue,iarray);

/* Welcome message and input of user's response      */
  Printf(\n\nWelcome to a trace demonstration!");
  printf("\nWould you like to continue (Y/N) ");
  scanf("%c",continue);

/* User-input of new integer array data              */
  if(continue == 'Y')
    for(offset=0; offset < SIZE; offset++) {
      printf("\nPlease enter an integer: ");
      scanf("%d",&iarray[offset]);
    }

/* Second function call prints user-entered data     */
  print_them(offset,continue,iarray);

}

/* Function outputs the contents of all variables    */
void print_them(int offset, char continue, int iarray[SIZE])
{
  printf("\n\n%d",offset);
  printf("\n\n%d",continue);
  for(offset=0; offset < SIZE, offset++)
    printf("\n%d",iarray[offset]);
}
```

Enter the program exactly as you see it. If you are familiar with the C language, you will notice that there are errors in the program. Do not correct them. The errors were placed there specifically to give you hands-on experience with various features of the integrated environment.

Editing Source Code

One of the main reasons for the success of Microsoft Windows is the graphical user interface (GUI). Windows 98/95 has introduced a modified GUI, but one that is intuitive to the experienced Windows user. A consistent user GUI means that when a particular feature appears in two different applications—for example, a Windows word processor and the Visual C++ IDE editor—that feature usually has the same menu and keyboard commands, in the same locations, in both applications.

This means that even if you have never used the Visual C++ IDE editor, you should find that correcting mistakes or moving to the end of a line, the beginning of a line, or the bottom of the edit window is just as easy and familiar as it is in your favorite Windows word processor.

Here are some helpful tips for working with the Visual C++ IDE editor. To move quickly through a line, hold down the CTRL key while pressing the left or right cursor key. This causes the edit cursor to move to the right or the left (depending on the cursor key pressed) one whole word at a time. (A word is defined as anything delimited by a blank space or punctuation.)

To delete an entire word instead of a single character, place the cursor on the space before or after the word to be deleted and press either CTRL-DELETE (to delete the word to the right) or CTRL-BACKSPACE (to delete the word to the left).

To allow for the maximum amount of editing workspace, the horizontal and vertical scroll bars can be turned off (see Tools | Options). If you chose this option, the mouse cannot be used to scroll the window, either horizontally or vertically. For this reason, you need to know two key combinations: CTRL-PAGE UP, which moves you to the top of a program; and CTRL-END, which moves you to the bottom of a program. How are you doing with that highlighter?

Perhaps you are wondering why we have made no mention of the horizontal movement keyboard equivalents. There is a reason: Most professionally written code fits within the standard monitor's 80-column width. This makes for easy reading and code debugging—since each line of code is completely visible, there can be no hidden bugs in column 95.

Saving Files

There is usually a major conflict between you and the compiler. You think that you write flawless code, while the compiler believes otherwise. If that insult is not bad enough, there's the linker's impression of your algorithmic genius. However, the final blow to your ego comes from the microprocessor itself, which, after being passed an executable file filtered by both the compiler and the linker, chokes on your digital instructions.

Although disagreements between you and the compiler or the linker are not catastrophic, disagreements between you and the microprocessor are. So, here's the moral to this story: Save your file before you compile, before you link, and definitely before you try to run a program. Many a sad story has been told of a programmer who runs an unsaved file, crashes the application or the system, and then has to reenter the entire program.

If you have not already done so, save the example program you are working with. You can do so by either clicking on the third button from the left on the toolbar (the picture on this button looks like a 3 1/2-inch floppy disk), using the File | Save command, or pressing CTRL-S.

The first time you save a file, the IDE will present you with a Save dialog box. Save this file under the name ERROR.C.

Figure 3-3 shows the edit window as it looks just before the file is saved. After the file is saved, the title in the title bar will show the saved file's name.

Creating the Executable File

Most Windows 3.x, Windows 98/95, and Windows NT programs contain many files. Initially, however, most simple C/C++ programs start with just one file, the main( ) C/C++ file. As you become a more experienced programmer, this introductory approach will prove to be inefficient.

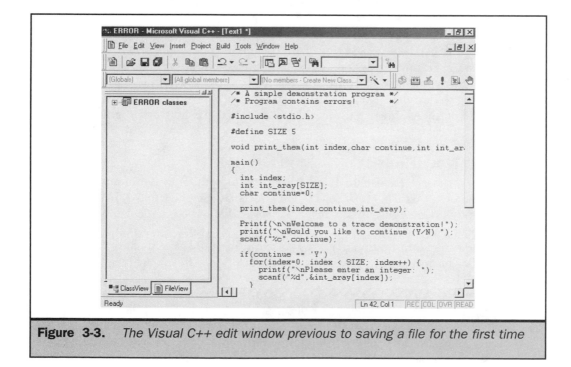

Figure 3-3. *The Visual C++ edit window previous to saving a file for the first time*

As your understanding of C/C++ and Windows application development increases, you will begin to break your solutions into multiple, logically related C/C++ files. To these you will add your own header files (header files have an h file extension). By the time you reach the end of this book, you will be creating applications with source code files, header files, resource files, and so on.

So, even though the sample program contains just a single file, the following sections explain the steps necessary to build a fully formed C/C++ application under Windows.

Using Workspaces

Before you can compile a typical C/C++ program, the Visual C++ IDE needs to be informed of the names of all of the C/C++ and resource files needed to create the executable file. In the past, this process was typically done in a *make* file (make files have a .MAK file extension).

Make files are text files that follow a special syntax that details file dependencies. In other words, the syntax of the make file defines the files that must be present and compiled before the target file can be used in another phase of the compile or link process. By the way, due to the sophistication of this process, it is no longer called "compiling and linking." The word now used to describe these steps is "building."

Traditionally, make files had to be executed from the command line by a stand-alone utility program known as NMAKE. Microsoft has streamlined this entire process in the Visual C++ compiler by including a substitute utility called the Project utility. This utility can be accessed from within the IDE.

Whereas a programmer previously had to create a separate *.MAK text file and run the NMAKE utility, the Project utility now allows you to achieve the same result without having to quit the Visual C++ IDE. The Project utility creates, edits, and uses make files with a *.MAK file extension. What's even better is that creating the project file is an easy process.

Starting a New Project

To create a new project, choose the File | New... menu item. This command opens up the New File dialog box. This time select the Projects tab (see Figure 3-4). After you have selected this item, you will see the New Project dialog box, which is the first step in creating a project file.

The first piece of information that the Project utility requires is a name for the project file. The name of your project file is important, since this is the label that will be used to name the final executable file.

Many first-time C/C++ programmers are surprised that the name of the program's executable file does not match the name of the source file containing the main( ) or WinMain( ) function. Remember, all project files must have a *.MAK file extension, but their actual name may be different from your source code files. For our sample program, use the project file name ERROR.MAK.

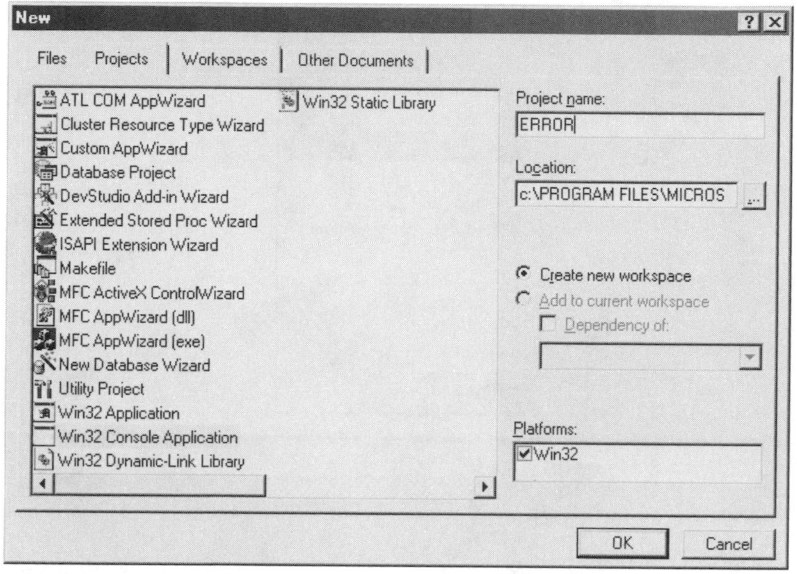

Figure 3-4.   *The New Projects dialog box is used to create a new project file*

The second piece of information required is the project type. Options include dynamic link libraries (DLLs) and various executable formats. For this example, the Win32 Console Application option should be selected.

If you place an entry in the Location: category, this option instructs the Visual C++ IDE to automatically create a new subdirectory for your new project.

A fourth option involves the project's target platform. For the 32-bit version of the Visual C++ compiler, the Win32 option is active. Figure 3-3, shown earlier, holds information for a completed sample project file. To accept this information, click on the OK button.

Adding Files to a Project

Once a new project file is defined, the Project utility allows you to easily add files. Figure 3-5 shows the Add Files to Project... menu item highlighted. Accessing this pop-up menu is as simple as clicking the right mouse button within the FileView.

Selecting this option opens a standard File Manager window, allowing you to easily locate and then include all of the files necessary to create the executable program. One note about the types of included files: Header files (files with .H file extensions) are *not* inserted into a project's file list. Header files are incorporated directly into the build process by **#include** preprocessor statements.

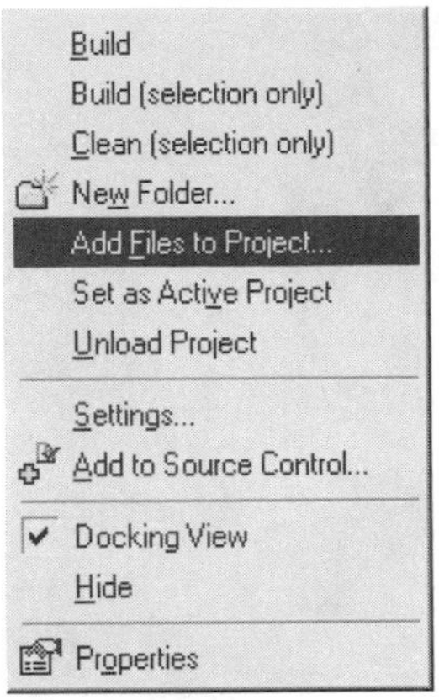

Figure 3-5. *The Add Files to Project menu item*

The Insert Files into Project dialog box (see Figure 3-6) is very similar to the standard Windows File dialog box. It allows you to select a default drive and path, and it automatically lists the target path's filenames. For our sample program, simply double-click on the ERROR.C filename in the File name: list. This will automatically insert the filename into the project file.

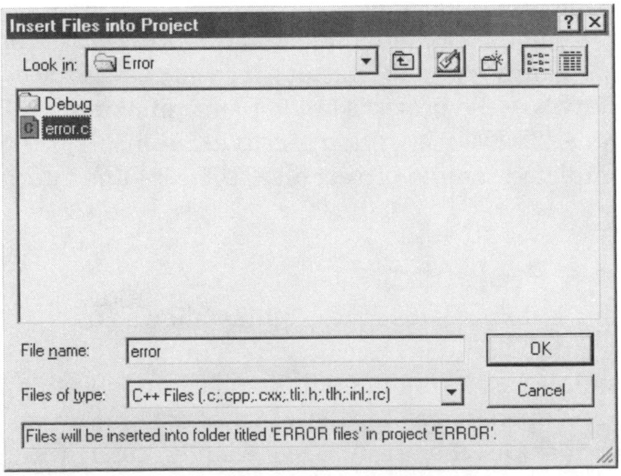

Figure 3-6. *Adding the file ERROR.C to the project*

If this were a more fully formed project file, such as one that would be used for Windows application development, at this point you would continue to select files needed by the project. For our sample program, however, one file will do. At this point you are ready to formally end the project file's definition by clicking on the OK button.

Choosing Build or Rebuild All

Now that the project file has been created, you are ready to instruct the IDE to create the executable file. Remember, under Visual C++ this process is called a *build*.

Figure 3-7 shows the Build menu with the Rebuild All command highlighted.

In Chapter 2, you learned that the only difference between the Build and Rebuild All commands is that Rebuild All does not check the dates of any of the files used by the project. This command always recompiles and links every file in the project.

Because a poorly maintained system can have inaccurate internal clock settings, it is always safest to choose the Rebuild All option for small applications. Now, activate the build process by clicking on the Rebuild All command or pressing ENTER when the command is highlighted.

Debugging Programs

If your program contains syntax errors, executing a Build or Rebuild All command automatically opens the compiler output message window, as seen at the bottom of the screen in Figure 3-8.

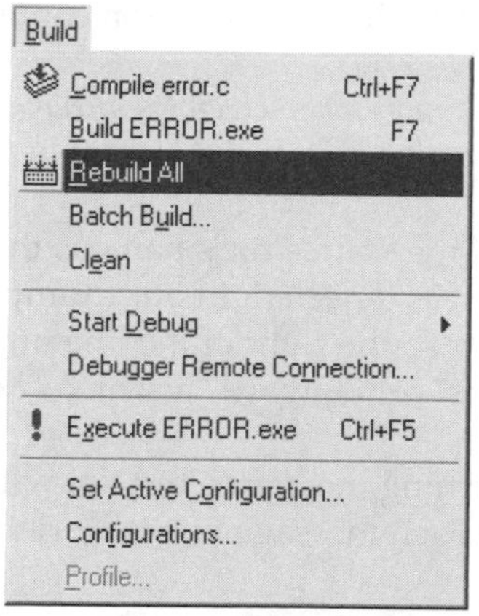

Figure 3-7. *The Rebuild All menu item will compile and link this new application*

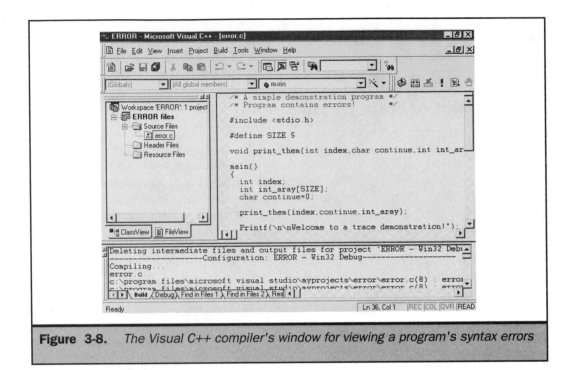

Figure 3-8. *The Visual C++ compiler's window for viewing a program's syntax errors*

Each message begins with the source file's name, which for this example is
C:\Program Files\DevStudio\MyProjects\Error\ERROR.C. This filename is
important, because the typical Windows application contains many source files.

Note *You will probably have your monitor's screen resolution set high enough to actually
view the entire error or warning messages described in the following text.*

Immediately to the right of the source file's name is the line number, in parentheses,
in which the warning or error was detected. In our example, the first error message
was generated on line eight (8). To the right of the line number is a colon, followed
immediately by the word "error" or the word "warning," which is then followed by
the associated error number.

Programs can run with warning messages, but not with error messages. The last
piece of information found on each message line is a brief description of the detected
syntax error.

Differences Between Warning and Error Messages

Warning messages might flag the use of a standard C/C++ automatic rule. For
example, an automatic rule might be invoked when having a **float** value automatically

truncated when assigning it to an integer variable. This does not mean that the code was written incorrectly, only that the statement is using some sort of behind-the-scenes feature of C/C++.

For example, all of the functions prototyped in MATH.H have formal arguments of the type **double** and return the type **double**. If your program passes to one of these functions an argument of the type **float**, the compiler will generate a warning. This warning will inform you that a conversion is taking place from the type **float** to the type **double** as the argument is pushed onto the call stack.

You can remove many warning messages by overriding automatic language defaults. You can do this by placing in the foreground those operators or functions designed to perform the behind-the-scenes operation. The example-warning message described in the preceding paragraph would be removed by doing an explicit cast of the argument from the type **float** to the type **double**.

Your First Unexpected Bug

The first error message, shown earlier in Figure 3-8, shows what might happen when you are using a new language for the first time. Here, the programmer tried to give a variable the name of a reserved, or language, keyword. If you are using a programming language that you *are* familiar with, you will probably not have this problem.

In C/C++, the word **continue** is a reserved, or language, keyword. In the sample program, the variable's name was chosen for self-documenting, readability reasons; however, it bumped into a language restriction. Chapter 6 contains a table (Table 6-1) of these reserved words for you to refer to when initially creating your source code.

Viewing Output and Source Windows

Once you have viewed your list of warning and error messages, you will want to switch back to the edit window to make the necessary code changes. You can select the edit window by either clicking on the mouse inside the edit window itself or by going to the Window menu and clicking on the filename, ERROR.C. Using whichever approach you prefer (has the highlighter dried out yet?), make the edit window the topmost window.

Using Find and Replace

There will be times when you will want to quickly locate something within your program. You could do this by bringing down the Search | Replace... dialog box, but the Visual C++ IDE provides a quicker option. If you look closely at the toolbar in Figure 3-9, you will see the word "continue" in the Quick Find list box.

To use Quick Find, simply click the left mouse button anywhere within the control's interior and type the label you want to find. Quick Find can now be activated by pressing ENTER. Figure 3-9 shows the results of this action. The first occurrence of the *continue* variable is highlighted.

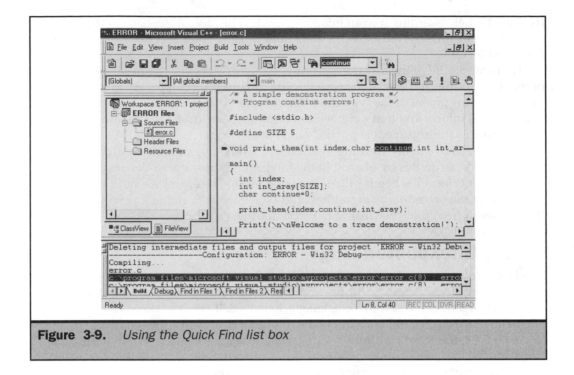

Figure 3-9.   *Using the Quick Find list box*

This approach is fine for locating first occurrences, but in our case it is inefficient because we need to locate all occurrences of the *continue* variable. For this reason, the Edit | Replace... dialog box, shown in Figure 3-10, is a better choice.

The easiest way to use Replace... is to first place the cursor on the word to search for *before* you invoke the Edit | Replace... option. If you follow this sequence, the word being searched for will be automatically entered into the Find what: list when you invoke the command.

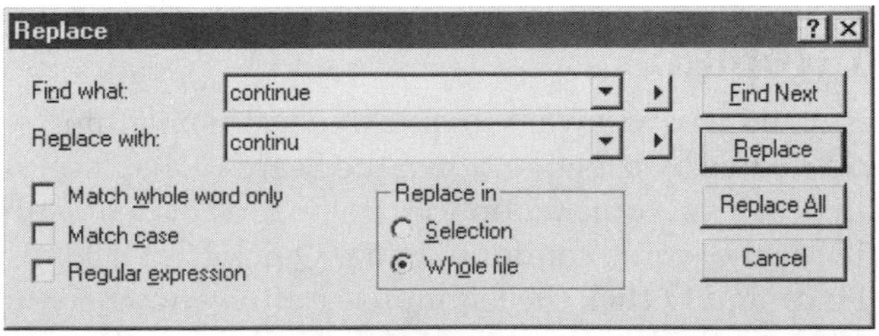

Figure 3-10.   *Using the editor's Edit | Replace option*

In Figure 3-10, you saw this approach used by first placing the cursor on the variable *continue*, which was highlighted in the previous figure. Practice this sequence and see if you can get your screen to appear like the one in Figure 3-10.

For our sample program, we want the variable that is currently named *continue* to still be readable, but it needs to be spelled differently than the reserved word. At this point, you need to manually enter the word "**continu**" into the Replace dialog box's Replace with: list.

Notice that this dialog box contains many of the standard word processor search-and-replace options, such as the ability to match whole words and designate case sensitivity. If you are new to the C/C++ language, you will be surprised to find out that C/C++ is case sensitive. For this reason, variables named *TOTAL* and *total* are treated as different variables.

One word of advice: Before you perform any search-and-replace operation, save the file. This will allow you to easily recover from a disastrous pattern match. Another approach is to use the Edit | Undo command. However, if your Undo buffer is not sufficiently large to hold all the changes the search-and-replace operation made, Undo might not be able to restore your whole program.

Now that you have entered the proper information into the Replace dialog box, you are ready to execute the replacement. However, there is one problem. The program contains the output statement "\nWould you like to continue (Y/N)". If you were to choose the Replace dialog box option of Replace All, your output statement would have a spelling error in it, because a Replace All would misspell the word "continue" in the program's screen output. For this reason, click now on the Find Next button.

Using Replace Options

The Replace dialog box presents you with several search options. Find Next searches for the search string's next occurrence. Replace inserts the substitute string. The Replace All option races through your code without interruption, finding and replacing the targeted text.

In this example, you need to repeatedly choose Replace, followed by Find Next, until you have replaced every use of the variable *continue* with the new spelling, *continu*. Remember, do not change the spelling of the word "continue" in the printf( ) statement.

Shortcuts to Switching Views

Earlier you saw that switching between the output message window and the edit window required some keyboard or mouse gymnastics. There is an easier way to get these two windows to interact. But first, if you are following the example development cycle, you need to stop and rebuild your program. If you made all of the necessary *continu* substitutions described previously, your output message window should look like the one in Figure 3-11.

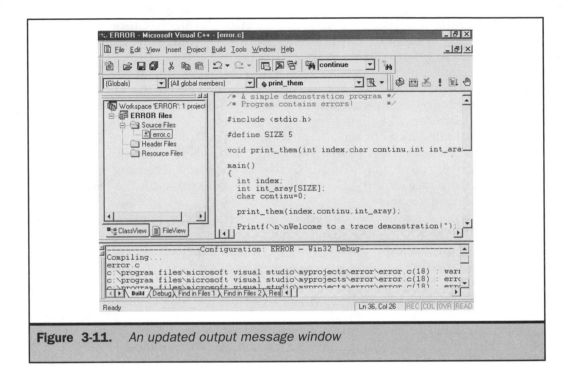

Figure 3-11.   *An updated output message window*

The improved way to interact with these two windows is very straightforward. First, place the cursor on the warning or error message of interest. For our example, pick the first message in the new output message window:

```
warning C4013: 'Printf' undefined;...
```

Now press ENTER. Voilà! The integrated environment automatically switches to the edit window and automatically highlights the suspicious code segment (with an arrow), as shown in Figure 3-12.

Useful Warning and Error Messages

When you learn a new language, you actually encounter two major learning curves. First, there's the time it takes to learn the syntax and nuances of the new language itself. But the second, more subtle learning curve involves understanding this new environment's help, warning, and error messages. In other words, you have to learn how this new compiler processes source code.

The good news is that the Visual C++ compiler produces some of the most accurate messages ever produced by any language environment. In our example, the compiler adroitly detected the misuse of a language keyword, **continue**.

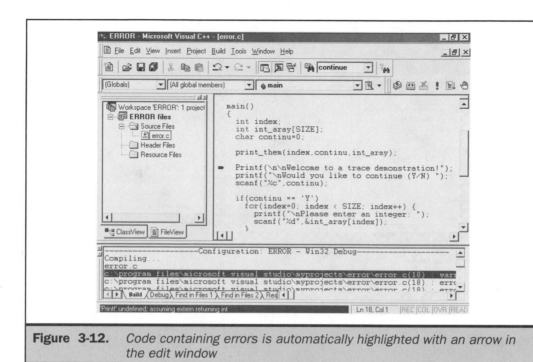

Figure 3-12. *Code containing errors is automatically highlighted with an arrow in
the edit window*

As you now know, C/C++ is case sensitive. Once again, the compiler correctly
detected an error. The function printf( ), supplied with your compiler, was defined in
all lowercase letters. Because this function was accidentally entered with an uppercase
"P", the compiler was unable to locate a matching library function Printf( ). With this
word highlighted in the edit window, make the edit change by replacing the uppercase
"P" with its lowercase equivalent. Don't forget to save your file.

More Work with the Debugger

At this point, the program is ready for another attempt at building an executable file.
Return to the Project menu and select the Rebuild All menu item. Figure 3-13 shows
the updated output messages.

Do you remember how to easily switch to the edit window and automatically locate
the illegal escape sequence identified in the error message? (All you need to do is place
the cursor on the error message and press ENTER.)

As it turns out, the same statement that contained the misspelled printf( ) function
has a second error. In C/C++, all format strings must begin with a double quote. Edit
the line by placing a double quote (") after the opening parenthesis in the printf( )
function—that is, after printf(.

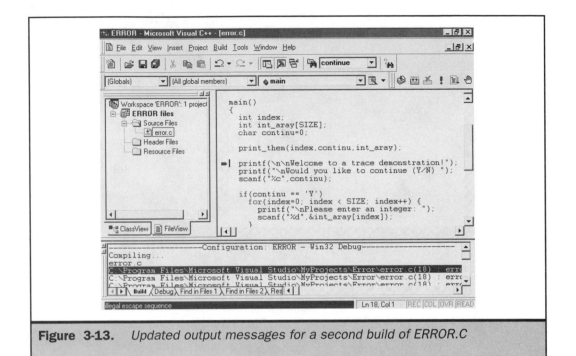

Figure 3-13.   *Updated output messages for a second build of ERROR.C*

Make sure that your first printf( ) statement matches the one in Figure 3-14. Now, save the file and attempt another rebuild. Figure 3-14 shows the third updated output message window.

Our last error message was

```
syntax error : missing ';' before ')'
```

Place the cursor on the message and press ENTER. In the C/C++ language, unlike in Pascal, a semicolon is considered to be a statement terminator, not a statement separator. For this reason, the second statement within the **for** loop expression needs a terminating semicolon, not a comma. Change the comma after the constant SIZE to a semicolon, save the file, and execute a Rebuild All once again.

Success? According to the output message window, you should now have no warnings and no errors, and the Rebuild All command has successfully generated the executable file, ERROR.EXE.

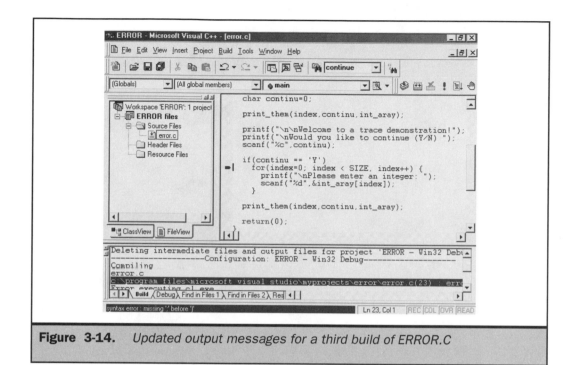

Figure 3-14. *Updated output messages for a third build of ERROR.C*

Note *At this point, if your compiler's errors and warnings message window does not show 0 errors and 1 warning (you can ignore this), you have inadvertently added a few typos of your own. Simply retrace your steps and edit the necessary code statements.*

Running Your First Program

To run a program after you have completed a successful Build or Rebuild All operation, simply click on the Project menu's Execute command. If you do this with the sample program, and enter a **Y** when asked if you would like to continue, your screen should display something like the following:

```
-858993460
```

```
0

-858993460

-858993460

-858993460

-858993460

-858993460


Welcome to a trace demonstration!

Would you like to continue (Y/N) y
```

Figure 3-15 illustrates what happens after you type the **Y** and press ENTER.

Using the Integrated Debugger

The sample program's output begins by dumping the uninitialized contents of the array. It then asks if you want to continue. A Y (yes) answer logically indicates that you

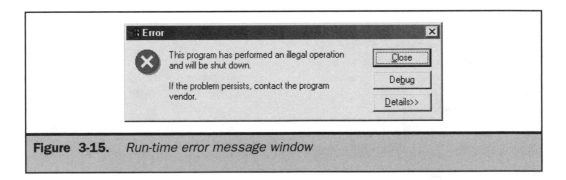

Figure 3-15. *Run-time error message window*

would now like to fill the array with your own values and then reprint the array's contents to the screen.

In this sample execution, you responded with a Y. However, if you examine the program's output, you can easily see that you were never prompted for input. In addition, the array's contents have not been changed, as evidenced by the duplicated output.

In other words, although you have a program that appears to be syntactically correct—there are no syntax errors—the application fails to perform as expected. These types of errors are called *logical* errors. Fortunately, the Visual C++ IDE integrated debugger has several features ready to come to your rescue.

Although the integrated debugger has many features, you will regularly use only a small subset of the commands. Basically, a debugger provides two powerful capabilities. First, it allows you to execute your program line by line, instead of at full speed. Second, it allows you to examine the contents of any variable at any point in your program.

When used correctly, these capabilities allow you to quickly locate an offending line of code. Unfortunately, the debugger does not automatically correct the code. (So, for the moment, your job security as a programmer is still not threatened!)

The Subtle Differences Between Step Into and Step Over

Figure 3-16 shows the Start Debug menu. When you start the debugger, usually by pressing F11, a Debug Toolbar appears. Two of the more frequently used buttons

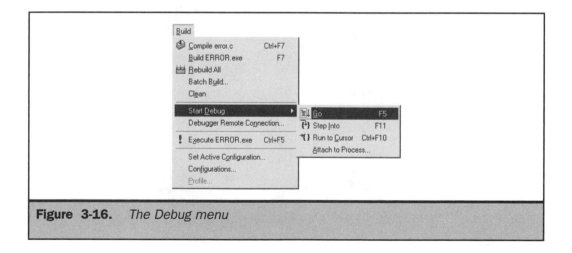

Figure 3-16.   *The Debug menu*

represent the options Step Into (fifth button from the left on the Debug Toolbar) and Step Over (sixth button). Both commands execute your program line by line.

The appearance of the edit window is different if you are using either one of these commands. When you are debugging a program using Step Into or Step Over, the integrated debugger highlights the line of code *about* to be executed.

The only difference between Step Into and Step Over occurs when the statement about to be executed is a function call. If you select Step Into on a function call, the debugger jumps to the function header and continues debugging the code inside the function. If you select Step Over on a function call, the debugger executes the associated function at full speed and then returns to the statement following the function call. You should use this command whenever you are debugging a program that incorporates previously tested subroutines.

Using either Step command, invoke the command three times. Figure 3-17 shows the sample program as it will appear after you have invoked Step Into or Step Over three times.

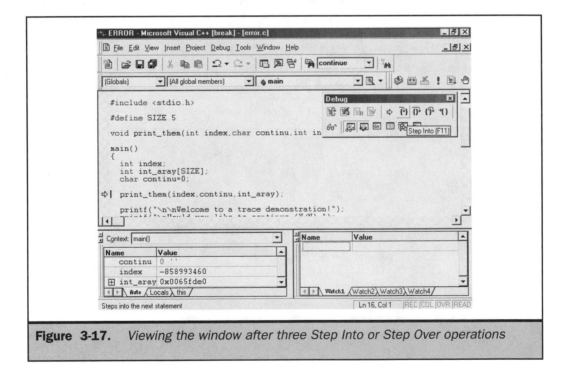

Figure 3-17.   *Viewing the window after three Step Into or Step Over operations*

As you can see from Figure 3-17, the single-step arrow (also called a trace arrow) is positioned next to the call to the print_them( ) function.

For now, we want to execute the function at full speed. To do this, choose the **Step Over** command now. If you watch closely, you will notice that the function executes and the trace arrow stops on the first printf( ) statement. So far, so good. Now press F10 three times, until the trace arrow stops on the scanf( ) statement.

At this point, you need to switch to the program's execution window. You can do this by pressing the ALT-TAB key combination. (You may need to use this key combination several times, depending on the number of tasks you have loaded.) When you are in ERROR's window, as shown in Figure 3-18, answer the question "Would you like to continue (Y/N)" with a **Y** and press ENTER.

The integrated debugger immediately responds with the error message shown in Figure 3-19.

This message relates to the scanf( ) statement just executed. See if you understand enough of the C language to figure out what the problem is.

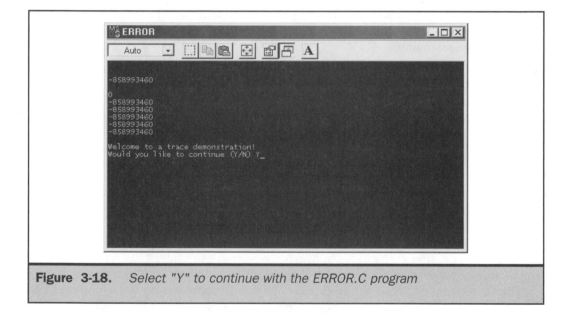

Figure 3-18.   *Select "Y" to continue with the ERROR.C program*

Figure 3-19. *The debugger reports an error*

The problem relates to the incorrect use of the scanf( ) function. The scanf( ) function expects to receive the address of a memory location to fill. Examine this statement:

```
scanf("%c",continu);
```

As you can see, this statement does not provide an address. The solution is to place the address operator (**&**) in front of the variable *continu*. Correct the statement so that it looks like this statement:

```
scanf("%c",&continue);
```

Save the change and execute a Rebuild All.

Advanced Debugging Techniques

You can think of a breakpoint as a stop sign for the integrated debugger. Logically, breakpoints tell the debugger that all statements prior to the breakpoint are OK, so the debugger shouldn't waste time single-stepping through them.

The easiest way to set a breakpoint is to click on the breakpoint control, which you can do if the toolbar is visible. This button is the second from the right on the toolbar. The picture on it resembles a hand signaling "stop."

The Breakpoint button is a toggle. If the line that the cursor is on when you click on the button does not contain a breakpoint, the command sets one. If the line that the cursor is on already has a breakpoint set, the command removes it. You can set as many breakpoints as you need by repeating this sequence. The Go command, when selected, will always run your program from the current line up to the next break point.

For the sample program, you know that all statements prior to the scanf( ) function call are OK. You have just edited this line and are now interested in seeing if the new statement works properly. For the sake of efficient debugging, you are going to set a break point on line 26, at the scanf( ) function.

Figure 3-20 illustrates another approach to setting breakpoints: using the Edit_ | Breakpoints... command.

This menu item opens up the Breakpoints dialog box. The default breakpoint type is Break at Location. All you need to do is type in the line number in the Location: box. For our example, this is line 20. (If your scanf( ) statement is on a different line number,

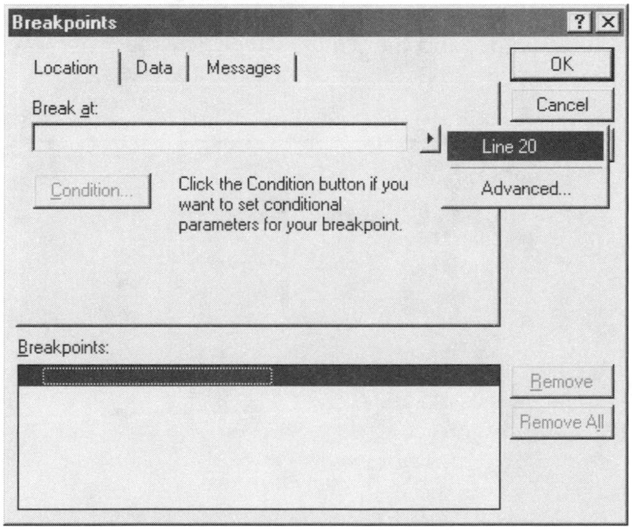

Figure 3-20.   *Setting breakpoints*

possibly because there are extra blank lines in the source code, enter your source file's line number for the scanf( ) statement.) Now choose the OK button.

Using Breakpoints

To debug a program at full speed up to, but not including, the breakpoint, you can use the Debug | Go menu item, as shown in Figure 3-21.

Assuming that you have the previously described breakpoint set, invoke the Go command. (Either select the command with the mouse, use the keyboard to access the command via the menus, or press F5.) Notice that the trace arrow speeds quickly to the statement containing the scanf( ) function call and then stops.

Once the debugger stops at a breakpoint, you can return to single-stepping through the program or even pause to examine a variable's contents. For now, we are interested in seeing if the syntax change made to the scanf( ) statement works. Choose the Step Over option, switch to the program's execution window, type an uppercase **Y**, and press ENTER. (You want Step Over so the debugger doesn't attempt to step into the scanf( ) function. Stepping in will prompt for location of the SCANF.C file. If you Cancel this, then you're in disassembly and the window won't be ready to accept input, etc.)

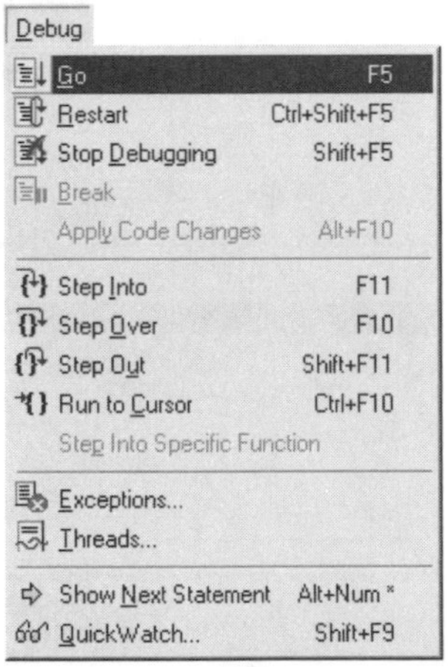

Figure 3-21. *Running a program at full speed with breakpoints*

Success! The integrated debugger no longer flags you with warning message windows. However, does this really mean that the code problem is fixed? The simplest way to answer this question is to examine the current contents of the variable *continu*.

An Introduction to QuickWatch

The QuickWatch... command opens up the QuickWatch dialog box, which allows you to instantaneously view and modify the contents of a variable. The fastest way to put a variable in the QuickWatch window is to place the cursor on the variable in your source code and press SHIFT-F9. If you do this with the sample program, you will see a QuickWatch dialog box similar to the one in Figure 3-22.

Now that you know that the contents of *continu* are correct, you can run the program at full speed to the end, using the Debug | Go command, as shown in Figure 3-23.

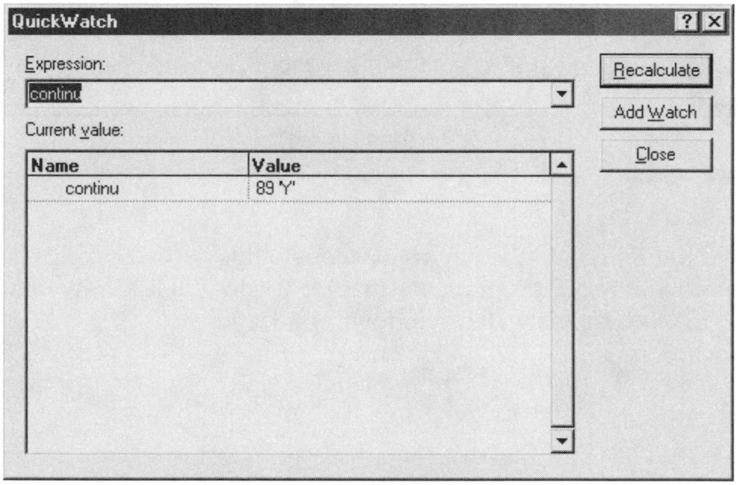

Figure 3-22. *A QuickWatch window*

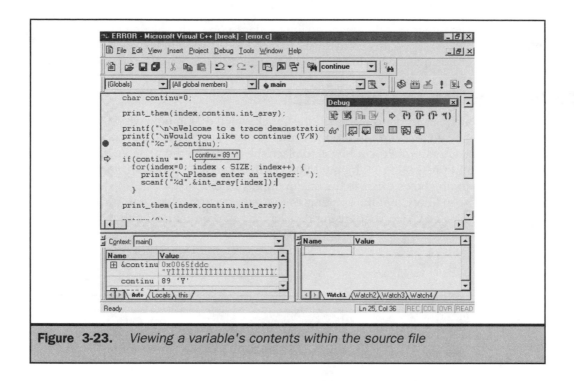

Figure 3-23. *Viewing a variable's contents within the source file*

What's Coming?

In this chapter, you rehearsed the day-to-day commands necessary to create, edit, save, build, and debug a simple C program. In Chapter 4, you will learn about programming issues specific to more sophisticated Windows applications.

Chapter 4

Advanced Visual C++ Features

The Microsoft Visual C++ compiler includes several advanced tools that are useful for program development. This chapter examines the creation of bitmaps, cursors, and icons from within the Visual C++ integrated development environment (IDE), and it discusses several stand-alone utilities, such as Books Online, Spy++, Process Viewer, and WinDiff.

As you begin developing programs in C, C++, and Windows, you will find that the Visual C++ compiler helps you locate syntax errors during the build (compile and link) operation. Syntax errors are often the easiest errors to fix because of the detailed help provided by the online help facilities. However, just because an application is free of syntax errors does not mean that it will perform as expected.

Perhaps you wanted to print the time to the screen, but it didn't show up; or perhaps you wanted to see a file in a particular format, but you got it in another format. Maybe the screen was supposed to have a blue background with a white figure drawn on it, but what you got was a white screen and a white figure—kind of difficult to see. It may even be a performance issue: The program runs correctly when it is the only application loaded, but it crashes if more than one program is running. All of these situations fall outside the scope of simple syntax errors. Advanced development tools are needed to correct these problems.

This chapter introduces you to the tools designed to help locate these types of problems. You will learn the purpose of each tool and how to use it. As you work through the programming examples later in this book, you will find these tools very useful.

Custom Icons, Cursors, and Bitmaps

Customizing a Windows application with your own icons, cursors, bitmaps, and dialog boxes is easy with Microsoft's Visual C++ IDE. The Visual C++ IDE is not just a compiler. It is also an easy-to-use, powerful resource editor.

Creating Bitmap Resources

This section teaches you how to use the Visual C++ IDE to draw a bitmap. All other graphic figures, such as icons and cursors, can be created in a similar manner.

The Visual C++ IDE allows you to design device-independent color bitmap images. These bitmaps are functionally device independent with respect to resolution. The image file format allows you to create a bitmap that always looks the same, regardless of the resolution of the display on which it appears.

For example, a single bitmap might consist of four definitions (DIBs): one designed for monochrome displays, one for CGAs, one for EGAs, and one for VGAs. Whenever the application displays the bitmap, it simply refers to it by name; Windows automatically selects the icon image that is best suited to the current display.

Figure 4-1 shows the initial Visual C++ IDE window. The first step you must take to create an application resource such as a bitmap is to click on the Insert | Resource... menu item.

The resulting dialog box, shown in Figure 4-2, shows the drop-down list that displays the kinds of resources available. Because we want to create a bitmap, click on the Bitmap resource. Simply press ENTER to confirm your selection.

Creating a bitmap with the Visual C++ resource editor is just about as easy as creating a picture with Windows Paintbrush. The Visual C++ resource editor first presents you with a blank bitmap grid and the Drawing Tools toolbar.

You use the toolbar to select the brush size, the brush color, and various drawing modes, such as fills and predefined shapes. Figure 4-3 shows a completed bitmap.

To set a resource's properties, begin by pressing ALT-ENTER. This step displays the particular resource's Properties dialog box. Figure 4-4 shows the Bitmap Properties dialog box with the details of the bitmap's width, height, colors, filename, and save compressed properties.

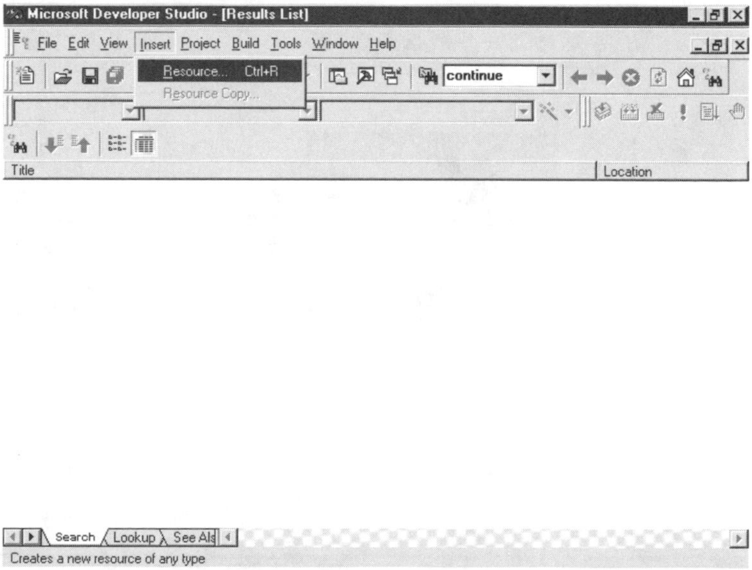

Figure 4-1.   *Preparing to create a new resource*

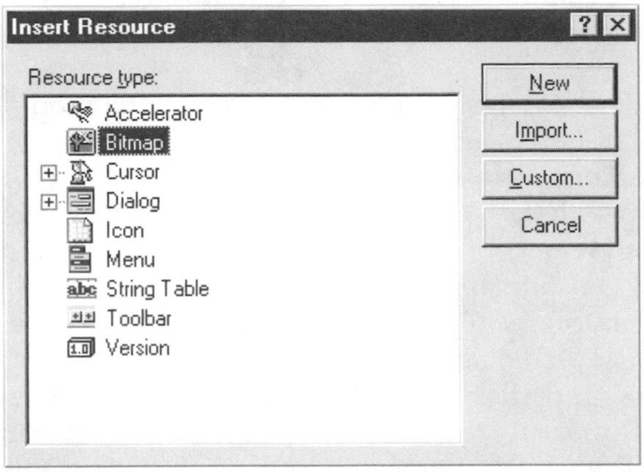

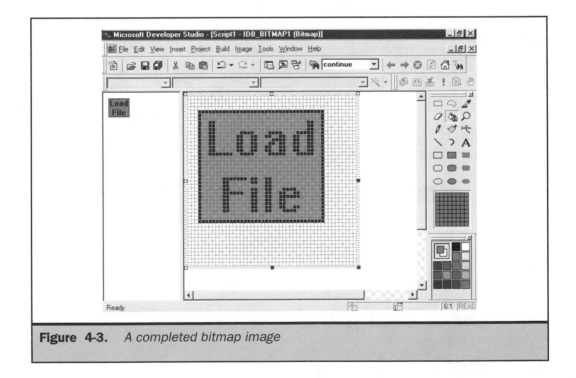

Figure 4-2. *Selecting a bitmap resource from the list box*

Figure 4-3. *A completed bitmap image*

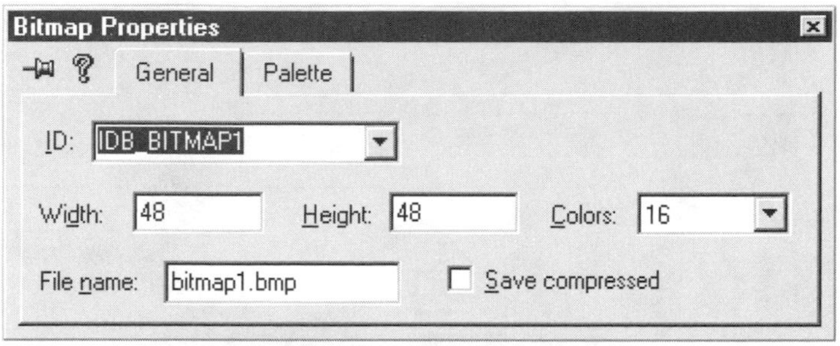

Figure 4-4.   *Viewing the Bitmap Properties dialog box*

Creating Dialog Box Resources

The initial steps required for creating a dialog box resource are identical to those described previously for creating a bitmap resource. First, choose the kind of resource you wish to create; refer to Figure 4-2, shown earlier. However, this time, select the Dialog option.

Figure 4-5 shows a completed dialog box, the dialog box Objects toolbox (on the right side of the screen), and the Text Properties dialog box.

The Objects toolbox allows you to place a variety of controls in your dialog box design. These include (starting at the top and proceeding from left to right, not including the "arrow" selection control): Bitmap, Label, Edit box, Group Box, Button, Checkbox, Radio button, Combo box, List box, Horizontal scroll bar, Vertical scroll bar, Spin, Progress, Slider, Hot key, List Control, Tree Control, Tab Control, Animate, Rich Edit, Date Time, Month Calendar, IP Address, Custom, and Extended Combo box.

Figure 4-5, shown earlier, shows the company name label object selected. The Properties dialog box is brought to the foreground simply by double-clicking on the label object itself. This is a convenient alternative to returning to the main resource window. Each kind of control has its own set of properties.

The Cursor's Hotspot Editor

A cursor resource differs slightly from a bitmap or an icon resource in that it can contain a hotspot. A cursor's hotspot represents the part of the image that registers the cursor's screen coordinates.

Creating a cursor involves the same initial steps used for creating bitmaps and dialog boxes. This process is started by first selecting the Insert I Resource... menu item

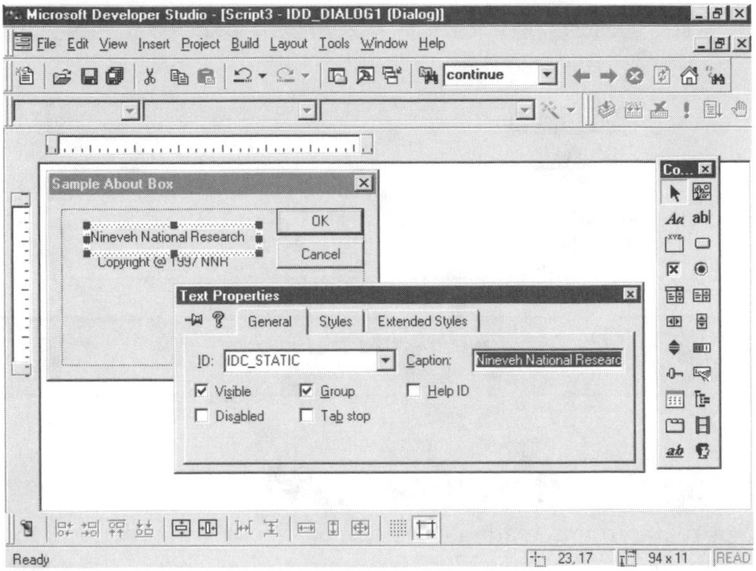

Figure 4-5.   *A completed dialog box*

command, and then choosing the cursor resource. Figure 4-6 shows a finished cursor design resembling a stylized UP arrow.

A cursor's hotspot is set by first clicking on the hotspot button to the right of the Hotspot: label in the Design toolbar. Once you have clicked on the button, simply move the mouse pointer into the cursor's bitmap design and click on the appropriate cell.

Books Online

Books Online (found either in the Visual C++ IDE Help menu or in the Visual C++ group) has an easy-to-use graphical interface that allows you to access hundreds of pages of Microsoft magazine and book articles. Figure 4-7 shows the initial Books Online window. (Your window might look different, depending on the latest update supplied with your compiler.)

Notice that each entry has a closed-book icon followed by the book's title. Take a moment to study the previous figure, making a mental note of those books you feel you might need to refer to in the near future. Part of doing an efficient topic search, such as looking up keywords or C/C++ topics, involves knowing the type of information that is available.

A QUICK OVERVIEW OF
VISUAL C++

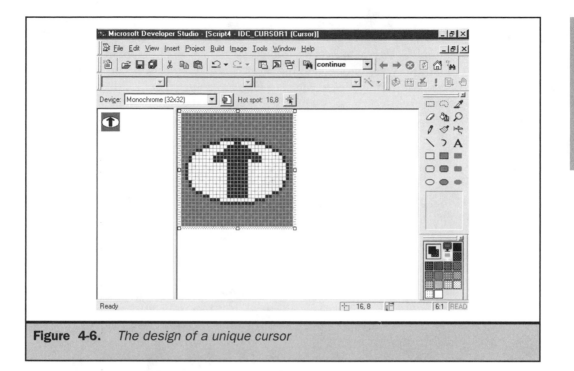

Figure 4-6.   *The design of a unique cursor*

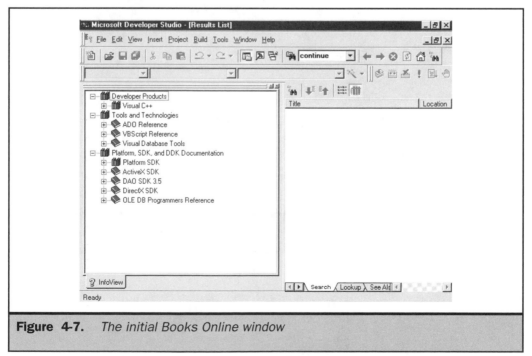

Figure 4-7.   *The initial Books Online window*

Beginning a Topic Search from the Contents Window

One way to do a topic search is to first double-click on the book title you are interested in. Figure 4-8 illustrates what happens to the Books Online window when you double-click on the *What's New | What's New For Visual C++ Version 6.0* book title.

When you double-click on a book's title, the graphical display of the Books Online dialog box changes. First, the closed-book icon to the left of the book's title turns into an open book. Listed underneath the title is an expanded drop-down list of associated titles.

Notice that the subtitle's icon changes to an open book. Listed underneath this subtitle are all the names for the pages or chapters available. At this point, once you have found a page or chapter of interest, simply double-click on the item's title. Figure 4-9 shows the Visual C++ home page.

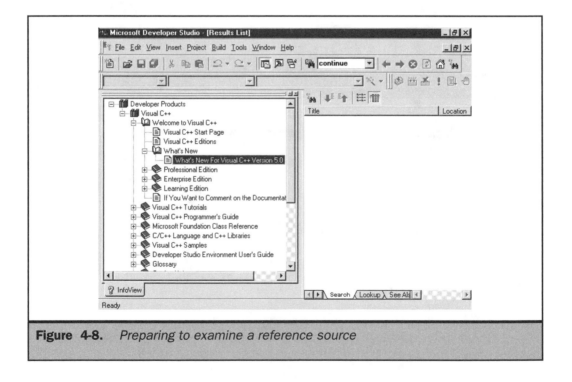

Figure 4-8.   *Preparing to examine a reference source*

A QUICK OVERVIEW OF VISUAL C++

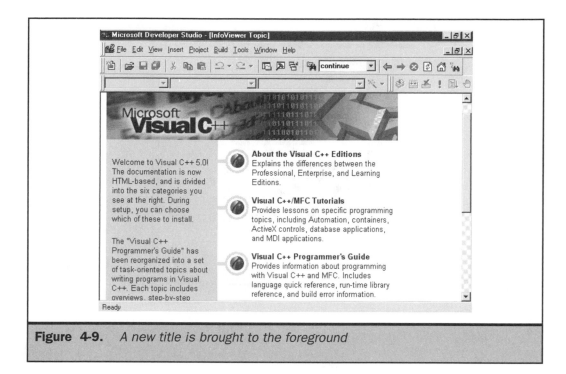

Figure 4-9.   *A new title is brought to the foreground*

Beginning a Topic Search Using Search

A second approach to executing a search begins with double-clicking on the Help | Search button. When you select this option, the dialog box presents you with a standard Windows Search dialog box, shown in Figure 4-10. This figure shows the dialog box set up to begin a search on Visual C++ System Requirements category features.

Simply select the List Topics button to update the workspace to show the requested topic.

Printing Help Topics

Although it is definitely true that Books Online and its associated views make for efficient searches, the utility pair may leave your eyes crossed. Besides, what if you want some hardcopy documentation, or you want to further analyze something after your system is shut down? For these and other reasons, many people still prefer reading a printed page over staring endlessly at a computer monitor.

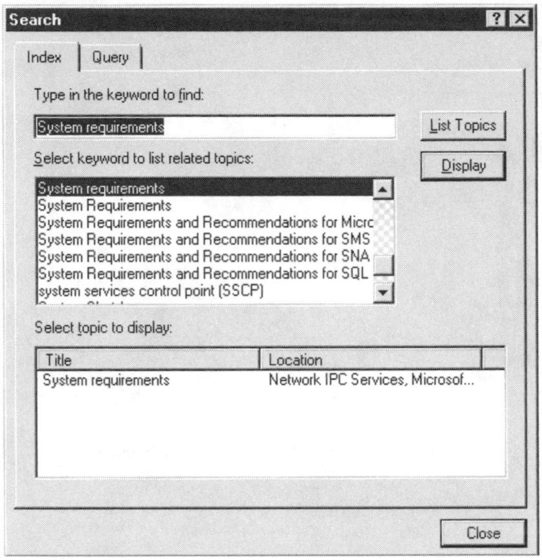

Figure 4-10.   *Preparing to search for a topic*

Books Online uses a straightforward approach to document printing. Simply use the File | Print Topic command. Books Online will print the topic that is displayed in the active window when this command is selected.

Selective Printing of Help Topics

Often you will not need to print an entire topic, especially if the selected title is an entire chapter. By choosing the Edit | Copy command, you can decide which portions of a topic to print.

First, select the portion of the help text that you want to print. You select text by placing the mouse pointer inside the text window at the beginning of the text you want to select, holding down the left mouse button, and dragging the mouse until it highlights (shows in reverse video) the desired text.

Clicking the Edit | Copy button completes the operation. Copy places the information on the Windows Clipboard. Clipboard contents can be pasted into any Windows-based word processor for printing and editing.

Debugging and Testing

The following sections explain the use of Microsoft's debugging and testing utilities. These utilities are used to locate an application's logical errors or errors that are generated when the application is executed simultaneously with other programs.

Spy++

Spy++ is one of the most dynamic tools shipped with Microsoft Visual C/C++. This utility allows you to "spy" on one or all of the currently loaded Windows applications. This utility's Window option allows you to view each application's name, class, module, parent, display window's rectangular screen coordinates, window style (for example, WS_CHILD), and window ID number.

Spy++ also lets you view the messages being sent throughout the environment. There are nine check boxes that allow you to predefine the reported message types:

Mouse	Input	System
Window	Init	Clipboard
Other	DDE	Non-Client

Generated output can be displayed in synchronous or asynchronous mode and sent to a Spy++ window, a file, or to COM1 for remote debugging.

Figure 4-11 shows the Spy++ Message Options dialog box with window selection data entered.

After you have selected the types of windows you want to watch, you use the Window menu to decide if these messages are to be watched for one window only or for all windows.

Process Viewer

Figure 4-12 shows a sample Process Viewer window. The Process Viewer dialog box allows you to quickly set and view all of the options necessary to track current processes, threads, and processor time-slicing.

To start the Process Viewer, simply double-click on the PView icon in the Visual C++ group. The Process Viewer can help you answer questions such as:

- How much memory does the program allocate at various points in its execution, and how much memory is being paged out?
- Which processes and threads are using the most CPU time?

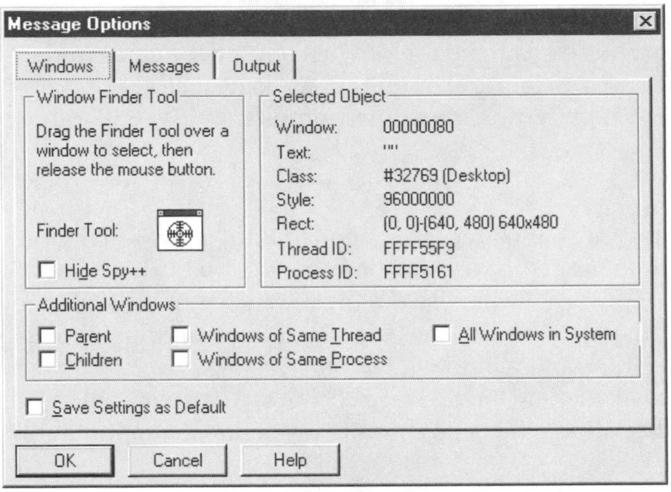

Figure 4-11. *Spy++'s Message Options dialog box*

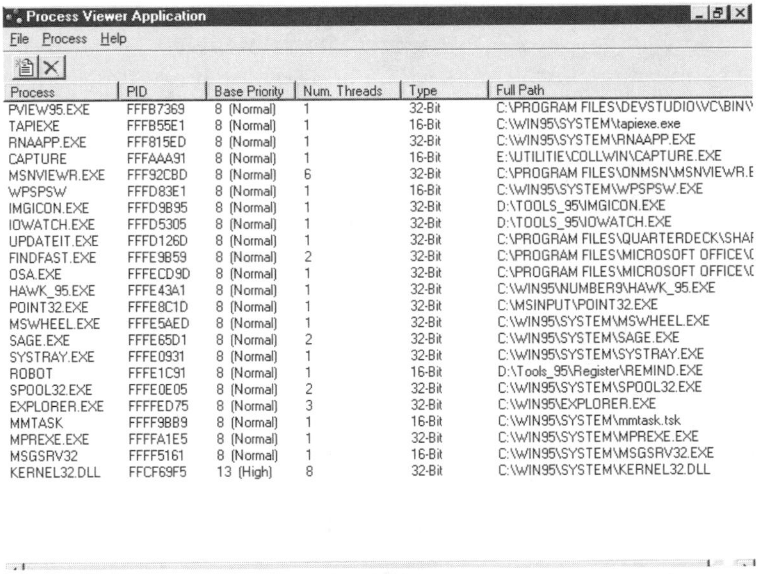

Process	PID	Base Priority	Num. Threads	Type	Full Path
PVIEW95.EXE	FFFB7369	8 (Normal)	1	32-Bit	C:\PROGRAM FILES\DEVSTUDIO\VC\BIN\
TAPIEXE	FFFB55E1	8 (Normal)	1	16-Bit	C:\WIN95\SYSTEM\tapiexe.exe
RNAAPP.EXE	FFF815ED	8 (Normal)	1	32-Bit	C:\WIN95\SYSTEM\RNAAPP.EXE
CAPTURE	FFFAAA91	8 (Normal)	1	16-Bit	E:\UTILITIE\COLLWIN\CAPTURE.EXE
MSNVIEWR.EXE	FFF92CBD	8 (Normal)	6	32-Bit	C:\PROGRAM FILES\ONMSN\MSNVIEWR.E
WPSPSW	FFFD83E1	8 (Normal)	1	16-Bit	C:\WIN95\SYSTEM\WPSPSW.EXE
IMGICON.EXE	FFFD9B95	8 (Normal)	1	32-Bit	D:\TOOLS_95\IMGICON.EXE
IOWATCH.EXE	FFFD5305	8 (Normal)	1	32-Bit	D:\TOOLS_95\IOWATCH.EXE
UPDATEIT.EXE	FFFD126D	8 (Normal)	1	32-Bit	C:\PROGRAM FILES\QUARTERDECK\SHAI
FINDFAST.EXE	FFFE9B59	8 (Normal)	2	32-Bit	C:\PROGRAM FILES\MICROSOFT OFFICE\(
OSA.EXE	FFFECD9D	8 (Normal)	1	32-Bit	C:\PROGRAM FILES\MICROSOFT OFFICE\(
HAWK_95.EXE	FFFE43A1	8 (Normal)	1	32-Bit	C:\WIN95\NUMBER9\HAWK_95.EXE
POINT32.EXE	FFFE8C1D	8 (Normal)	1	32-Bit	C:\MSINPUT\POINT32.EXE
MSWHEEL.EXE	FFFE5AED	8 (Normal)	1	32-Bit	C:\WIN95\SYSTEM\MSWHEEL.EXE
SAGE.EXE	FFFE65D1	8 (Normal)	2	32-Bit	C:\WIN95\SYSTEM\SAGE.EXE
SYSTRAY.EXE	FFFE0931	8 (Normal)	1	32-Bit	C:\WIN95\SYSTEM\SYSTRAY.EXE
ROBOT	FFFE1C91	8 (Normal)	1	16-Bit	D:\Tools_95\Register\REMIND.EXE
SPOOL32.EXE	FFFE0E05	8 (Normal)	2	32-Bit	C:\WIN95\SYSTEM\SPOOL32.EXE
EXPLORER.EXE	FFFFED75	8 (Normal)	3	32-Bit	C:\WIN95\EXPLORER.EXE
MMTASK	FFFF9BB9	8 (Normal)	1	16-Bit	C:\WIN95\SYSTEM\mmtask.tsk
MPREXE.EXE	FFFFA1E5	8 (Normal)	1	32-Bit	C:\WIN95\SYSTEM\MPREXE.EXE
MSGSRV32	FFFF5161	8 (Normal)	1	16-Bit	C:\WIN95\SYSTEM\MSGSRV32.EXE
KERNEL32.DLL	FFCF69F5	13 (High)	8	32-Bit	C:\WIN95\SYSTEM\KERNEL32.DLL

Figure 4-12. *A typical Process Viewer window*

■ How does the program run at different system priorities?

■ What happens if a thread or process stops responding to DDE, OLE, or pipe I/O?

■ What percentage of time is spent running API calls?

Caution *Since the Process Viewer lets you modify the status of processes running on your system, you can stop processes and potentially halt the entire system. Make sure that you save edited files before running the Process Viewer.*

WinDiff

The WinDiff utility, found in the Visual C++ group, allows you to graphically compare and modify two files or two directories. All of the options within WinDiff operate in a manner similar to those commands found in the File Manager.

Figure 4-13 shows a WinDiff dialog box with selections made to begin the process of locating the first file to be compared.

	WinDiff: scanning	_ 8 x
	File Edit View Expand Options Mark Help	
	Comparing... d:\aol30 : e:\aol30	Abort
1	.\aol.cnt	identical
2	.\aol.exe	identical
3	.\aol.fts	only in e:\aol30
4	.\aol.gid	only in e:\aol30
5	.\aol.hlp	identical
6	.\aol.ini	identical
7	.\aolmac.vxd	identical
8	.\aolndi.dll	identical
9	.\aolphx.exe	identical
10	.\cfx2032.dll	identical
11	.\compver.bin	only in e:\aol30
12	.\diag.dat	only in e:\aol30
13	.\doorbell.wav	only in e:\aol30
14	.\doorslam.wav	only in e:\aol30
15	.\dosgame.exe	only in e:\aol30
16	.\drop.wav	identical
17	.\dunzip.dll	only in e:\aol30
18	.\dunzipnt.dll	identical
19	.\filedone.wav	identical
20	.\goodbye.wav	identical
21	.\gotmail.wav	identical
22	.\goto.ini	identical
23	.\im.wav	identical
24	.\imglib.dll	identical
25	.\insmac16.dll	identical
26	.\insmac32.dll	identical

Figure 4-13.   *A WinDiff dialog box*

What's Coming?

In this chapter you have learned the fundamentals of using Microsoft's development and debugging tools. Unless you are already an advanced user, you will probably not need to use these tools until you reach the latter portion of this book.

The next chapter gives a formal introduction to the C/C++ language. The chapter looks at the early development of the C language up to its current state-of-the-art components.

Part II

Programming Foundations

Chapter 5

C and C++ Programming

C and C++ Foundations

Beginning with this chapter, you will explore the origins, syntax, and usage of the C and C++ languages. A study of C's history is worthwhile because it reveals the language's successful design philosophy and helps you understand why C and C++ may be the languages of choice for years to come. Before you proceed, you should be comfortable with both the Microsoft Visual C and C++ development environments. By now you should have installed the package, configured it to your personal requirements, and practiced using the compiler and the integrated debugger.

C Archives

Our archeological dig for the origins of the C language begins with a discussion of the UNIX operating system, since both the system and most of the programs that run on it are written in C. However, this does not mean that C is tied to UNIX or any other operating system or machine. The UNIX/C co-development environment has given C a reputation for being a *system programming language* because it is useful for writing compilers and operating systems. C is also very useful for writing major programs in many different domains.

The UNIX OS was originally developed in 1969 on what would now be considered a small DEC PDP-7 at Bell Laboratories in Murray Hill, New Jersey. UNIX was written entirely in PDP-7 assembly language. By design, this operating system was intended to be "programmer friendly," providing useful development tools, lean commands, and a relatively open environment. Soon after the development of UNIX, Ken Thompson implemented a compiler for a new language called B.

At this point it is helpful to examine the origins and history behind Ken Thompson's B language, a direct predecessor to C. Following is a comprehensive C lineage:

Language	Origins/Inventor
Algol 60	Designed by an international committee in early 1960
CPL	(Combined Programming Language) Developed at both Cambridge and the University of London in 1963
BCPL	(Basic Combined Programming Language) Developed at Cambridge by Martin Richards in 1967
B	Developed by Ken Thompson, Bell Labs, in 1970
C	Developed by Dennis Ritchie, Bell Labs, in 1972

Then, in 1983, the American National Standards Institute (ANSI) committee was formed for the purpose of creating ANSI C—a standardization of the C language.

Algol 60 was a language that appeared only a few years after FORTRAN was introduced. This new language was more sophisticated and had a strong influence on the design of future programming languages. Its authors paid a great deal of attention to the regularity of syntax, modular structure, and other features usually associated with high-level structured languages. Unfortunately, Algol 60 never really caught on in the United States. Many say this was due to the language's abstractness and generality.

The inventors of CPL (Combined Programming Language) intended to bring Algol 60's lofty intent down to the realities of an actual computer. However, just as Algol 60 was hard to learn and difficult to implement, so was CPL. This led to its eventual downfall. Still clinging to the best of what CPL had to offer, the creators of BCPL (Basic Combined Programming Language) wanted to boil CPL down to its basic good features.

When Ken Thompson designed the B language for an early implementation of UNIX, he was trying to further simplify CPL. He succeeded in creating a very sparse language that was well suited for use on the hardware available to him. However, both BCPL and B may have carried their streamlining attempts a bit too far; they became limited languages, useful only for dealing with certain kinds of problems.

For example, no sooner had Ken Thompson implemented the B language than a new machine, called the PDP-11, was introduced. UNIX and the B compiler were immediately transferred to this new machine. While the PDP-11 was a larger machine than its PDP-7 predecessor, it was still quite small by today's standards. It had only 24K of memory, of which the system used 16K, and one 512K fixed disk. Some thought was given to rewriting UNIX in B, but the B language was slow because of its interpretive design. There was another problem as well: B was word oriented, but the PDP-11 was byte oriented. For these reasons, work was begun in 1971 on a successor to B, appropriately named C.

Dennis Ritchie is credited with creating C, which restored some of the generality lost in BCPL and B. He accomplished this through a shrewd use of data types while maintaining the simplicity and direct access to the hardware that were the original design goals of CPL.

Many languages developed by a single individual (C, Pascal, Lisp, and APL) contain a cohesiveness that is missing from those created by large programming teams (Ada, PL/I, and Algol 60). It is also typical for a language written by one person to reflect the author's field of expertise. Dennis Ritchie was noted for his work in systems software—computer languages, operating systems, and program generators.

Given Ritchie's areas of expertise, it is easy to understand why C is a language of choice for systems software design. C is a relatively low-level language that allows you to specify every detail in an algorithm's logic to achieve maximum computer efficiency. But C is also a high-level language that can hide the details of the computer's architecture, thereby increasing programming efficiency.

C vs. Older High-level Languages

At this point, you may be asking, "How does C compare to other programming languages?" A possible continuum is shown in Figure 5-1. If you start at the bottom of the continuum and move upward, you go from the tangible and empirical to the elusive and theoretical. The dots represent major advancements, with many steps left out. Early ancestors of the computer, like the Jacquard loom (1805) and Charles Babbage's "analytical engine" (1834), were programmed in hardware. The day may well come when we will program a machine by plugging a neural path communicator into a socket implanted into the temporal lobe (language memory) or Broca's area (language motor area) of the brain's cortex.

The first assembly languages, which go back to the original introduction of electronic computers, provide a way of working directly with a computer's built-in instruction set and are fairly easy to learn. Because assembly languages force you to think in terms of hardware, you had to specify every operation in the machine's terms. Therefore, you were always moving bits into or out of registers, adding them, shifting register contents from one register to another, and finally storing the results in memory. This was a tedious and error-prone endeavor.

The first high-level languages, such as FORTRAN, were created as alternatives to assembly languages. High-level languages were much more general and abstract, and they allowed you to think in terms of the problem at hand rather than in terms of the computer's hardware.

Unfortunately, the creators of high-level languages made the fallacious assumption that everyone who had been driving a standard, so to speak, would prefer driving an automatic. Excited about providing ease in programming, they left out some necessary

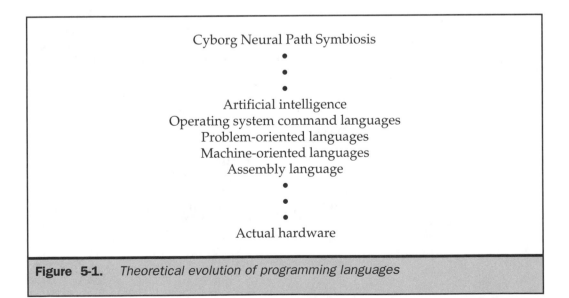

Figure 5-1.   *Theoretical evolution of programming languages*

options. FORTRAN and Algol are too abstract for systems-level work; they are *problem-oriented languages,* the kind used for solving problems in engineering, science, or business. Programmers who wanted to write systems software still had to rely on their machine's assembler.

In reaction to this situation, a few systems software developers took a step backward—or lower, in terms of the continuum—and created the category of *machine-oriented languages.* As you saw in C's genealogy, BCPL and B fit into this class of very low-level software tools. These languages were excellent for a specific machine but not much use for anything else; they were too closely related to a particular architecture. The C language is one step above machine-oriented languages but still a step below most problem-solving languages. C is close enough to the computer to give you great control over the details of an application's implementation, yet far enough away to ignore the details of the hardware. This is why the C language is considered at once a high- and a low-level language.

Advantages of C

Every computer language you use has a definite look to its source code. APL has its hieroglyphic appearance, assembly language its columns of mnemonics, and Pascal its easily read syntax. And then there's C. Many programmers encountering C for the first time will find its syntax cryptic and perhaps intimidating. C contains very few of the friendly English-like syntax structures found in many other programming languages. Instead, C presents the software engineer with unusual-looking operators and a plethora of pointers. New C programmers will soon discover a variety of language characteristics whose roots go back to C's original hardware/software progenitor. The following sections highlight the strengths of the C language.

Optimal Code Size

There are fewer syntax rules in C than in many other languages, and it is possible to write a top-quality C compiler that will operate in only 256K of total memory. There are actually more operators and combinations of operators in C than there are keywords.

Terse Set of Keywords

The original C language, as developed by Dennis Ritchie, contained a mere 27 keywords. The ANSI C standard has added several reserved words. Microsoft C/C++ further enhances the instruction set and brings the total Microsoft C/C++ keyword count to over 70.

Many of the functions commonly defined as part of other programming languages are not included in C. For example, C does not contain any built-in input and output capabilities, nor does it contain any arithmetic operations (beyond those of basic addition and subtraction) or string-handling functions. Since any language missing these capabilities is of little use, C provides a rich set of library functions for input/output, arithmetic operations, and string manipulation. This agreed-upon library set is so commonly used that it can almost be seen as part of the language itself.

One of the strengths of C, however, is its loose structure, which enables you to recode these functions easily.

Lightning-fast Executables

The C code produced by most compilers tends to be very efficient. The combination of a small language, a small run-time system, and the fact that the language is close to the hardware makes many C programs run at speeds close to their assembly language equivalents.

Limited Type Checking

Unlike Pascal, which is a strongly typed language, C treats data types somewhat more loosely. This is a carryover from the B language, which was also a loosely typed language. This looseness allows you to view data in different ways. For example, at one point in a program, the application may need to see a variable as a character and yet, for purposes of uppercasing (by subtracting 32), may want to see the same memory cell as the ASCII equivalent of the character.

Top-down Design Implementations

C contains all of the control structures you would expect of a modern-day language. This is impressive when you consider C's 1971 incubation period, which predated formal structured programming. For loops, **if** and **if-else** constructs, **case** (switch) statements, and **while** loops are all incorporated into the language. C also provides for the compartmentalization of code and data by managing their scope. For example, C provides local variables for this purpose and calls-by-value for subroutine data privacy.

Modular Structure

C supports *modular programming*, which is the concept of separate compilation and linking. This allows you to recompile only the parts of a program that have been changed during development. This feature can be extremely important when you are developing large programs, or even medium-size programs on slow systems. Without support for modular programming, the amount of time required to compile a complete program can make the change, compile, test, and modify cycle prohibitively slow.

Transparent Interface to Assembly Language

There is a well-defined method for calling assembly language routines from most C compilers. Combined with the separation of compilation and linking, this makes C a very strong contender in applications that require a mix of high-level and assembler routines. C routines can also be integrated into assembly language programs on most systems.

Bit Manipulation

Often in systems programming, it is necessary to manipulate objects at the bit level. Naturally, with C's origins so closely tied to the UNIX operating system, the language provides a rich set of bit-manipulation operators.

Pointer Data Types

One of the features an operating system requires of a language is the ability to address specific areas of memory. This capability also enhances the execution speed of a program. The C language meets these design requirements by using pointers (discussed in Chapter 10). While it is true that other languages implement pointers, C is noted for its ability to perform pointer arithmetic. For example, if the variable *student_record_ptr* points to the first element of an array *student_records*, then *student_record_ptr + 1* will be the address of the second element of *student_records*.

Extensible Structures

All arrays in C are one-dimensional. Multidimensional arrangements are built from combinations of these one-dimensional arrays. Arrays and structures (records) can be joined in any manner desired, creating database organizations that are limited only by the programmer's ability. Arrays are discussed in more detail in Chapter 9.

Memory Efficient

For many of the same reasons that C programs tend to be fast, they tend to be very memory efficient. The lack of built-in functions saves programs from having to carry around support for functions that are not needed by that application.

Cross-platform Portability

Portability is a measure of the ease of converting a program running on one computer or operating system to another computer or operating system. Programs written in C are among the most portable in the modern computer world. This is especially true in the mini- and microcomputer worlds.

Powerful Library Routines

There are many commercial function libraries available for all popular C compilers. Libraries are available for graphics, file handling, database support, screen windowing, data entry, communications, and general support functions. By using these libraries, you can save a great deal of development time.

Disadvantages of C

There are no perfect programming languages. Different programming problems require different solutions. It is the software engineer's task to choose the best language for a project. On any project, this is one of the first decisions you need to make, and it is nearly irrevocable once you start coding. The choice of a programming language can also make the difference between a project's success and failure. The following sections cover some of the weaknesses of the C language to give you a better idea of when to use and when not to use C for a particular application.

Limited Type Checking!

The fact that C is not strongly typed is one of its strengths, but it is also one of its weaknesses. Technically, *typing* is a measure of how closely a language enforces the use of variable types. (For example, integer and floating-point are two different types of numbers.) In some languages, it is illegal to assign one data type to another without invoking a conversion function. This protects the data from being compromised by unexpected roundoffs.

As discussed earlier, C will allow an integer to be assigned to a character variable, and vice versa. What this means to you is that you are going to have to properly manage your variables. For experienced programmers, this will present no problem. However, novice program developers may want to remind themselves that this can be the source of side effects.

A *side effect* in a language is an unexpected change to a variable or other item. Because C is not a strongly typed language, it gives you great flexibility to manipulate data. For example, the assignment operator (=) can appear more than once in the same expression. This flexibility, which you can use to your advantage, means that expressions can be written that have no clear and definite value. Restricting the use of the assignment and similar operators, or eliminating all side effects and unpredictable results, would have seriously lessened much of C's power and appeal as a high-level assembly language.

Limited Run-time Monitors

C's lack of checking in the run-time system can cause many mysterious and transient problems to go undetected. For example, the run-time system would not warn you if your application exceeded an array's bounds. This is one of the costs of streamlining a compiler for the sake of speed and efficiency.

C Is Not for Children!

C's tremendous range of features—from bit manipulation to high-level formatted I/O—and its relative consistency from machine to machine have led to its acceptance in science, engineering, and business applications. It has directly contributed to the wide availability of the UNIX operating system on computers of all types and sizes.

Like any other powerful tool, however, C imposes a heavy responsibility on its users. C programmers need to acquire a discipline very quickly, adopting various rules and conventions in order to make their programs understandable both to themselves, long after the programs were written, and to others trying to analyze the code for the first time. In C, programming discipline is essential. The good news is that it comes almost automatically with practice.

American National Standards Institute—ANSI C

The ANSI (American National Standards Institute) committee has developed standards for the C language. This section describes some of the significant changes suggested and implemented by the committee. Some of these changes are intended to increase the flexibility of the language, others to standardize features previously left to the discretion of the compiler implementor.

Previously, the only standard available was the book *The C Programming Language* by B. Kernighan and D. Ritchie (Prentice-Hall, Murray Hill, NJ: 1988). This book was not specific on some language details, which led to a divergence among compilers. The ANSI standard strives to remove these ambiguities. Although a few of the proposed changes could cause problems for some previously written programs, they should not affect most.

The ANSI C standard provides an even better opportunity than before to write portable C code. The standard has not corrected all areas of confusion in the language, however, and because C interfaces efficiently with machine hardware, many programs will always require some revision when they are moved to a different environment. The ANSI committee that developed the standard adopted as guidelines some phrases that collectively have been called the "spirit of C." Some of those phrases are:

- Trust the programmer.
- Don't prevent the programmer from doing what needs to be done.
- Keep the language small and simple.

Additionally, the international community was consulted to ensure that ANSI (American) standard C would be identical to the ISO (International Standards Organization) standard version. Because of these efforts, C is the only language that effectively deals with alternate collating sequences, enormous character sets, and multiple user cultures. Table 5-1 highlights just some of the areas the ANSI committee addressed.

From C to C++ and Object-oriented Programming

Simply stated, C++ is a superset of the C language. C++ retains all of C's strengths, including its power and flexibility in dealing with the hardware/software interface; its low-level system programming; and its efficiency, economy, and powerful expressions. However, C++ brings the C language into the dynamic world of object-oriented programming and makes it a platform for high-level problem abstraction, going beyond even Ada in this respect. C++ accomplishes all of this with a simplicity and support for modularity similar to Modula-2, while maintaining the compactness and execution efficiency of C.

Feature	Standardized
Data types	(four); character, integer, float point, and enumeration.
Comments	(/*) opening, (*/) closing; proposed —(//) anything to symbol's right is ignored by the compiler.
Identifier length	31 characters to distinguish uniqueness.
Standard identifiers and header files	An agreed-upon minimum set of identifiers and header files necessary to perform basic operations such as I/O.
Preprocessor statements	The # in preprocessor directives can have leading white space (any combination of spaces and tabs), permitting indented preprocessor directives for clarity. Some earlier compilers insisted that all preprocessor directives begin in column one.
New preprocessor directives	**#if** defined (expression) **#elif** (expression)
Adjacent strings	The committee decided that adjacent literal strings should be concatenated. For example, this would allow a **#define** directive to extend beyond a single line.
Standard libraries	The proposed ANSI standard specifies a basic set of system-level and external routines, such as read( ) and write( ).
Output control	An agreed-upon set of escape codes representing formatting control codes such as newline, new page, and tabs.
Keywords	An agreed-upon minimum set of verbs used to construct valid C statements.
sizeof( )	The committee agreed that the sizeof( ) function should return the type *size_t*, instead of a possibly system-limiting variable of size integer.
Prototyping	The committee agreed that all C compilers should handle programs that do/do not employ prototyping.

Table 5-1. *ANSI C Recommendations*

Feature	Standardized
Command line arguments	In order for the C compiler to properly handle command-line arguments, an agreed-upon syntax was defined.
Void pointer type	The **void** keyword can be applied to functions that do not return a value. A function that does return a value can have its return value cast to **void** to indicate to the compiler that the value is being deliberately ignored.
Structure handling	Structure handling has been greatly improved. The member names in structure and union definitions need not be unique. Structures can be passed as arguments to functions, returned by functions, and assigned to structures of the same type.
Function declarations	Function declarations can include argument-type lists (function prototyping) to notify the compiler of the number and types of arguments.
Hexadecimal character constants	Hexadecimal character constants can be expressed using an introductory \x followed by from one to three hexadecimal digits (0-9, a-f, A-F). For example, 16 decimal = \x10, which can be written as 0x10 using the current notation.
Trigraphs	*Trigraphs* define standard symbol sequences that represent those characters that may not be readily available on all keyboards. For example, (??<) can be substituted for the more elaborate ({) symbol.

PROGRAMMING FOUNDATIONS

Table 5-1. *ANSI C Recommendations* (continued)

This new hybrid language combines the standard procedural language constructs familiar to so many programmers and the object-oriented model, which you can exploit fully to produce a purely object-oriented solution to a problem. In practice, a C++ application can reflect this duality by incorporating both the procedural programming model and the newer object-oriented model. This biformity in C++ presents a special challenge to the beginning C++ programmer; not only is there a new language to learn, but also a new way of thinking and problem solving.

C++ Archives

Not surprisingly, C++ has an origin similar to C's. While C++ is somewhat like BCPL and Algol 60, it also contains components of Simula 67. C++'s ability to overload operators and its flexibility to include declarations close to their first point of application are features found in Algol 60. The concept of subclasses (or derived classes) and virtual functions is taken from Simula 67. Like many other popular programming languages, C++ represents an evolution and refinement of some of the best features of previous languages. Of course, it is closest to C.

Bjarne Stroustrup, of Bell Labs, is credited with developing the C++ language in the early 1980s. (Dr. Stroustrup credits Rick Mascitti with the naming of this new language.) C++ was originally developed to solve some very rigorous event-driven simulations for which considerations of efficiency precluded the use of other languages. C++ was first used outside Dr. Stroustrup's language group in 1983, and by the summer of 1987, the language was still going through a natural refinement and evolution.

One key design goal of C++ was to maintain compatibility with C. The idea was to preserve the integrity of millions of lines of previously written and debugged C code, the integrity of many existing C libraries, and the usefulness of previously developed C tools. Because of the high degree of success in achieving this goal, many programmers find the transition to C++ much simpler than when they first went from some other language, such as FORTRAN, to C.

C++ supports large-scale software development. Because it includes increased type checking, many of the side effects experienced when writing loosely typed C applications are no longer possible.

The most significant enhancement of the C++ language is its support for object-oriented programming (OOP). You will have to modify your approach to problem solving to derive all of the benefits of C++. For example, objects and their associated operations must be identified and all necessary classes and subclasses must be constructed.

Object Code Efficiency

What follows is an example of how an abstract data object in C++ can improve upon an older language's limited built-in constructs and features. For example, a FORTRAN software engineer may want to keep records on students. You could accomplish this with multiple arrays of scalar data that represent each set of data. All of the arrays are necessarily tied together by a common index. Should there be ten fields of information on each student, ten array accesses would have to be made using the same index location in order to represent the array of records.

In C++, the solution involves the declaration of a simple object, *student_database*, that can receive messages to *add_student*, *delete_student*, *access_student*, or *display_student* information contained within the object. The manipulation of the *student_database* object can then be performed in a natural manner. Inserting a new record into the *student_database* object becomes as simple as this:

```
student_database.add_student(new_recruit)
```

Assuming the *student_database* object has been appropriately declared, the add_student( ) function is a method suitably defined in the class that supports *student_database* objects, and the *new_recruit* parameter is the specific information that is to be added. Note that the class of objects called *student_database* is not a part of the underlying language itself. Instead, the programmer extends the language to suit the problem. By defining a new class of objects or by modifying existing classes (creating a subclass), a more natural mapping from the problem space to the program space (or solution space) occurs. The biggest challenge comes in truly mastering this powerful enhancement.

Subtle Differences Between C and C++

The following sections detail the minor (non-object-oriented) enhancements to the C language.

Comment Syntax

C++ introduces the comment to end-of-line delimiter //. However, the comment brackets /* and */ can still be used.

Enumerated Variables

The name of an enumeration is a type name. This streamlines the notation by not requiring the qualifier enum to be placed in front of the enumeration type name.

Structure Versus Classes

The name of a structure or class is a type name. This class construct does not exist in C. In C++, it is not necessary to use the qualifier struct or class in front of a structure or class name.

Block Scope

C++ permits declarations within blocks and after code statements. This feature allows you to declare an identifier closer to its first point of application. It even permits the loop control variable to be declared within the formal definition of the control structure, as shown here:

```
// C++ point-of-use variable declaration
   for(int index = 0; index < MAX_ROWS; index++)
```

Scope Resolution Operator

You use the new scope qualifier operator :: to resolve name conflicts. For example, if a function has a local declaration for a variable *vector_location* and there exists a global variable *vector_location*, the qualifier *::vector_location* allows the global variable to be accessed within the scope of the local function. The reverse is not possible.

The const Specifier

You can use the **const** specifier to lock the value of an entity within its scope. You can also use it to lock the data pointed to by a pointer variable, the value of the pointer address, or the values of both the pointer address and the data pointed to.

Anonymous Unions

Unions without a name can be defined anywhere a variable or field can be defined. You can use this ability for the economy of memory storage by allowing the sharing of memory among two or more fields of a structure.

Explicit Type Conversions

You can use the name of a predefined type or user-defined type as a function to convert data from one type to another. Under certain circumstances, such an explicit type conversion can be used as an alternative to a cast conversion.

Unique Function Capabilities

C++ will please many a Pascal, Modula-2, and Ada programmer because it permits the specification by name and type for each function parameter inside the parentheses next to the function name. For example:

```
void * dupmem(void *dest, int c, unsigned count)
{
   .
   .
   .
}
```

The equivalent C interface, under the ANSI standard, would look exactly the same. In this case, C++ influenced the ANSI standards committee.

The C++ translator will perform type checking to ensure that the number and type of values sent into a function when it is invoked match the number and type of the formal arguments defined for the function. A check is also made to ensure that the function's return type matches the variable used in the expression invoking the function. This type of parameter checking is missing in most C systems.

Overloading Functions

In C++, functions can use the same names if you use the specifier overload, and each of the overloaded functions can be distinguished on the basis of the number and type of its parameters.

Default Parameter Values

You can assign **default** values to trailing sets of C++ function parameters. In this case, the function can be invoked using fewer than the total number of parameters. Any missing trailing parameters assume their default values.

Varying-Length Argument Lists

You can define C++ functions with an unknown number and type of parameters by employing the ellipsis (...). When you use this feature, parameter type checking is suppressed to allow flexibility in the interface to the function.

Reference Argument Types

Through the use of the ampersand operator (&), a formal function parameter can be declared as a reference parameter. For example:

```
int i;
increment(i);

  .
  .
  .

void increment(int &variable_reference)
{
   variable_reference++;
}
```

Because &*variable_reference* is defined as a reference parameter, its address is assigned to the address of *i* when increment( ) is invoked. The value of *i* that is sent in is incremented within function increment( ) and returned to variable *i* outside of function increment( ). It is not necessary for the address of *i* to be explicitly passed into function increment( ), as it is in C.

Inline Functions!

You can use the inline specifier to instruct the compiler to perform inline substitution of a given function at the location where the function is invoked.

The new and delete Keywords

The **new** and **delete** operators that are introduced by C++ allow for programmer-controlled allocation and deallocation of heap storage.

void Pointers

In C++, the type **void** is used to indicate that a function returns nothing. Pointer variables can be declared to point to **void**. They can then be assigned to any other pointer that points to an arbitrary base type.

Major Differences Between C and C++

The most significant major enhancement to C involves the concept of object-oriented programming. The following sections briefly explain all of the C++ enhancements that make object-oriented programming possible.

Class Constructs and Data Encapsulation

The class construct is the fundamental vehicle for object-oriented programming. A class definition can encapsulate all of the data declarations, the initial values, and the set of operations (called *methods*) for data abstraction. Objects can be declared to be of a given class, and messages can be sent to objects. Additionally, each object of a specified class can contain its own private and public sets of data representative of that class.

The struct Class

A *structure* in C++ is a subset of a class definition and has no private or protected sections. This subclass can contain both data (as is expected in ANSI C) and functions.

Constructors and Destructors

Constructor and destructor methods are used to guarantee the initialization of the data defined within an object of a specified class. When an object is declared, the specified initialization constructor is activated. Destructors automatically deallocate storage for the associated object when the scope in which the object is declared is exited.

Messages

As you have seen, the object is the basic fabric of OOP. You manipulate objects by sending them messages. You send messages to objects (variables declared to be of a given class) by using a mechanism similar to invoking a function. The set of possible messages that can be sent to an object is specified in the class description for the object. Each object responds to a message by determining an appropriate action to take based on the nature of the message. For example, if *Palette_Colors* represents an object, and *SetNumColors_Method* represents a method with a single-integer parameter, sending a message to the object would be accomplished by using the following statement:

```
Palette_Colors.SetNumColors_Method(16);
```

Friends

The concept of data hiding and data encapsulation implies a denied access to the inner structures that make up an object. The class' private section is normally totally off-limits to any function outside the class. C++ does allow other functions outside methods or classes to be declared to be a friend to a specified class. Friendship breaks down a normally impenetrable wall and permits access to the class' private data and methods.

Operator Overloading

With C++, the programmer can take the set of predefined operators and functions supplied with the compiler, or user-defined operators and functions, and give them multiple meanings. For example, different functions typically have different names, but for functions performing similar tasks on different types of objects, it is sometimes better to let these functions have the *same* name. When their argument types are different, the compiler can distinguish them and choose the right function to call. What follows is a coded example; you could have one function called total( ) that was overloaded for an array of integers, of floating points, and of double values.

```
int total(int isize, int iarray[]);
float total(int isize, float farray[]);
double total(int isize, double darray[]);
        .
        .
        .
```

Since you have declared the three different functions by the same name, the compiler can look at the invoking statement and automatically decide which function is appropriate for the formal parameter list's arguments:

```
    total(isize,iarray);
      total(isize,farray);
....total(isize,darray);
```

Derived Classes

A *derived class* can be seen as a subclass of a specified class, thereby forming a hierarchy of abstractions. Derived class objects typically inherit all or some of the methods of the parent class. It is also common for a derived class to then incorporate these inherited methods with new methods specific to the subclass. All subclass objects contain the fields of data from the parent class as well as any of their own private data.

Polymorphism Using Virtual Functions

Polymorphism involves a tree structure of parent classes and their subclasses. Each subclass within this tree can receive one or more messages with the same name. When an object of a class within this tree receives a message, the object determines the particular application of the message that is appropriate for an object of the specified subclass.

Stream Libraries

An additional library stream is included with the C++ language. The three classes cin, cout, and cerr are provided for terminal and file input and output. All of the operators within these three classes can be overloaded within a user-defined class. This capability allows the input and output operations to be easily tailored to an application's needs.

Fundamental Components for a C/C++ Program

You may have heard that C is a difficult language to master. However, while it is true that a brief encounter with C code may leave you scratching your head, this is only due to C's foreign syntax, structure, and indentation schemes. By the end of this chapter, you should have enough information to have developed a working knowledge of the C language that enables you to write short but meaningful code. In the next section, you will learn about the five fundamental components of a "good" program.

Five Elements of Good C Program Design

You may be familiar with a problem-solution format called an IPO diagram. *IPO diagrams* were a stylized approach to the age-old programming problem of input/process/output. The following list elaborates on these three fundamentals and encapsulates the entire application development cycle. All programs must address the following five components:

1. Programs must obtain information from some input source.

2. Programs must decide how this input is to be arranged and stored.

3. Programs use a set of instructions to manipulate the input. These instructions can be broken down into four major categories: single statements, conditional statements, loops, and subroutines.

4. Programs must report the results of the data manipulation.

5. A well-written application incorporates all of the fundamentals just listed, expressed by using good modular design, self-documenting code (meaningful variable names), and a good indentation scheme.

A Simple C Program

The following C program illustrates the basic components of a C application. It is suggested that you enter each example as you read about it to help you understand new concepts as you encounter them.

```
/*
 *   simple.c
 *   Your first example C program.
 *   Copyright (c) Chris H. Pappas and William H. Murray, 1998
 */

#include <stdio.h>

int main( )
{
  printf(" HELLO World! ");

  return(0);
}
```

There is a lot happening in this short piece of code. Let's begin with the comment block:

```
/*
 *   simple.c
 *   Your first example C program.
 *   Copyright (c) Chris H. Pappas and William H. Murray, 1998
 */
```

All well-written source code includes meaningful comments. A meaningful comment is one that neither insults the intelligence of the programmer nor assumes too much. In C, comments begin with /* and are terminated with */. Anything between these unique symbol pairs is ignored by the compiler.

The next statement represents one of C's unique features, known as a *preprocessor statement*.

```
#include <stdio.h>
```

A preprocessor statement is like a precompile instruction. In this case, the statement instructs the compiler to retrieve the code stored in the predefined STDIO.H file into the source code on the line requested. (The STDIO.H file is called a header file. *Header files* can include symbolic constants, identifiers, and function prototypes, and have these declarations pulled out of the main program for purposes of modularity.)

Following the **#include( )** statement is the main function declaration:

```
int main( )
{
```

```
    .
    .
    .
  return(0);   /*   or return 0;  */
}
```

All C programs are made up of function calls. Every C program must have one called main( ). The main( ) function is usually where program execution begins, and it ends with a return( ) from the main( ). The int to the left of main( ) defines the function's **return** type, in this case integer, and explains why the return( ) statement contains a number inside the parentheses. A value of 0 is interpreted as meaning a successful program termination. It is also legal to use return( ) statements without the parentheses.

Following the main( ) function header is the body of the function itself. Notice the { and } symbol pairs. These are called *braces*. You use braces to encapsulate multiple statements. These braces may define the body for a function, or they may bundle together statements that are dependent on the same logic control statement, as is the case when several statements are executed based on the validity of an **if** statement. In this example, the braces define the body of the main program.

The next line is the only statement in the body of the main( ) function and is the simplest example of an output statement:

```
printf(" HELLO World! ");
```

The printf( ) function was previously prototyped in STDIO.H. Because no other parameters are specified, the sentence will be printed to the display monitor.

A Simple C++ Program

The example that follows performs the same function as the one just discussed, but it takes advantage of those features unique to C++:

```
//
//  simple.cpp
//  Your first C++ example program.
//  Copyright (c) Chris H. Pappas and William H. Murray, 1998
//

#include <iostream.h>

int main( )
```

```
{
  cout << " HELLO World! ";

  return(0);
}
```

There are three major differences between this example and the last. First, the comment designator has been changed from the /* */ pair to //. Second, the #include filename has been changed to IOSTREAM.H. The third change involves a different output operator call, **cout**. Many of the examples in the book will highlight the sometimes subtle and sometimes dazzling differences between C and C++.

Adding a User Interface to a C Program

The following program is a slightly more meaningful example. It is a little more complete in that it not only outputs information but also prompts the user for input. Many of the components of this program will be elaborated on throughout the remainder of the book.

```
/*
 *   ui.c
 *   This C program prompts the user for a specified length,
 *   in feet, and then outputs the value converted to
 *   meters and centimeters
 *   Copyright (c) Chris H. Pappas and William H. Murray, 1998
 */

#include <stdio.h>

int main( )
{
  float feet, meters, centimeters;

  printf("Enter the number of feet to be converted: ");
  scanf("%f",&feet);

  while(feet > 0 ) {
    centimeters = feet * 12 * 2.54;
    meters = centimeters/100;
    printf("%8.2f feet equals\n", feet);
    printf("%8.2f meters \n",meters);
```

```
      printf("%8.2f centimeters \n",centimeters);
      printf("\nEnter another value to be \n");
      printf("converted (0 ends the program): ");
      scanf("%f",&feet);
   }
   printf(">>> Have a nice day! <<<");

   return(0);
}
```

Declaring Variables

The first thing you will notice that's new in the program is the declaration of three variables:

```
float feet, meters, centimeters;
```

All C variables must be declared before they are used. One of the standard data types supplied by the C language is **float**. The syntax for declaring variables in C requires the definition of the variable's type before the name of the variable. In this example, the float type is represented by the keyword float, and the three variables *feet*, *meters*, and *centimeters* are defined.

User Interaction

The next unconventional-looking statement is used to input information from the keyboard:

```
printf("Enter the number of feet to be converted: ");
scanf("%f",&feet);
```

The scanf( ) function has a requirement that is called a format string. *Format strings* define how the input data is to be interpreted and represented internally. The %f function parameter instructs the compiler to interpret the input as float data. In Microsoft C and C++, a **float** occupies 4 bytes. (Chapter 6 contains a detailed explanation of all of the C and C++ language data types.)

An Introduction to the Address Operator

In the previous statement, you may have noticed that the **float** variable *feet* was preceded by an ampersand symbol (**&**). The **&** is known as an *address operator*.

Whenever a variable is preceded by this symbol, the compiler uses the address of the specified variable instead of the value stored in the variable. The scanf( ) function has been written to expect the address of the variable to be filled.

A Simple while Loop

One of the simplest loop structures to code in C is the **while** loop:

```
while(feet > 0) {
  .
  .
  .
}
```

This pretest loop starts with the reserved word **while**, followed by a Boolean expression that returns either a TRUE or a FALSE. The opening brace ({) and closing brace (}) are optional; they are only needed when more than one executable statement is to be associated with the loop repetition. Braced statements are sometimes referred to as *compound statements*, *compound blocks*, or *code blocks*.

If you are using compound blocks, make certain you use the agreed-upon brace style. While it doesn't matter to the compiler where the braces are placed (in terms of skipped spaces or lines), programmers reading your code will certainly appreciate the style and effort. An opening loop brace is placed at the end of the test condition, and the closing brace is placed in the same column as the first character in the test condition.

Screen Output

In analyzing the second program, you will notice more complex printf( ) function calls:

```
printf("%8.2f feet equals\n", feet);
printf("%8.2f meters \n",meters);
printf("%8.2f centimeters \n",centimeters);
printf("\nEnter another value to be \n");
printf("converted (0 ends the program): ");
```

If you are familiar with the PL/I language developed by IBM, you will be right at home with the concept of a format or control string. Whenever a printf( ) function is invoked to print not only *literal strings* (any set of characters between double quote marks), but also values, a format string is required. The format string represents two things: a picture of how the output string is to look, combined with the format interpretation for each of the values printed. Format strings are always between double quote marks.

Let's break down the first printf( ) format string ("%8.2f feet equals\n", feet) into its separate components:

Control	Action
%8.2f	Take the value of feet, interpret it as a **float,** and print it in a field of eight spaces with two decimal places.
feet equals	After printing the **float** feet, skip one space and then print the literal string "feet equals".
\n	Once the line is complete, execute a new line feed.
,	The comma separates the format string from the variable name(s) used to satisfy all format descriptors. (In this case, there is only one %8.2f.)

The next two printf( ) statements are similar in execution. Each statement prints a formatted float value, followed by a literal string, and ending with a new line feed. If you were to run the program, your output would look similar to this:

```
Enter the number of feet to be converted: 10
   10.00 feet equals
    3.05 meters
  304.80 centimeters

Enter another value to be
converted (0 stops program): 0
```

The C *escape sequences,* or *output control characters,* allow you to use a sequence of characters to represent special characters. Table 5-2 lists all of the output control symbols and a description of how they can be used in format strings. All leading zeros are ignored by the compiler for characters notated in hexadecimal. The compiler determines the end of a hex-specified escape character when it encounters either a nonhex character or more than two hex characters, excluding leading zeros.

Also on the subject of format strings—though this is a bit advanced—are the scanf( ) formatting controls. Table 5-3 describes the scanf( ) formatting controls and their meanings. If you wish to input a string without automatically appending a terminating null character (\0), use %nc, where n is a decimal integer. In this case, the c format symbol indicates that the argument is a pointer to a character array. The next n characters are read from the input stream into the specified location, and no null character (\0) is appended. If n is not specified, the default character array length is 1.

As you learn more about the various C data types, you will be able to refer back to Tables 5-2 and 5-3 for a reminder of how the different controls affect input and output.

Sequence	Name	Sequence	Name
\a	Alert (bell)	\?	Literal quotation mark
\b	Backspace	\'	Single quotation mark
\f	Form feed	\"	Double quotation mark
\n	Newline	\\	Backslash
\r	Carriage return	\ddd	ASCII character in octal notation
\t	Horizontal tab	\xdd	ASCII character in hex notation
\v	Vertical tab		

Table 5-2.   *Output Control Symbols*

Character	Input Type Expected	Argument Type
d	Decimal integer	Pointer to **int**
o	Octal integer	Pointer to **int**
x, X	Hexadecimal integer	Pointer to **int**
I	Decimal, hexadecimal	Pointer to **int** or octal integer
u	Unsigned decimal integer	Pointer to **unsigned int**
e, E	Floating-point value	Pointer to **float**
f g, G	Consisting of an optional sign (+ or −), a series of one or more decimal digits possibly containing a decimal point, and an optional exponent ("e" or "E") followed by an optionally signed integer value	
c	Character. White-space characters that are ordinarily skipped are read when c is specified; to read the next nonwhite-space character, use %1s	Pointer to **char**
s	String	Pointer to character array autocreate NULL string

Table 5-3.   *Format Control Symbols*

Character	Input Type Expected	Argument Type
n	No input read from stream or buffer	Pointer to **int**, into which is stored the number of characters read from the stream or buffer up to that point in call to scanf( )
p	In the form xxxx:yyyy, where x digits and y digits are uppercase hexadecimal digits	Pointer to **far**; pointer to **void**

Table 5-3. *Format Control Symbols* (continued)

Using the Integrated Debugger

To examine the actual operation of the C code presented in this section, you can use the integrated debugger. When you compile your program, make certain you have turned on debug information. This is done in conjunction with the Project utility. Once your application is compiled and linked, use the debugger to keep an eye on the variables *yard, feet,* and *inch.*

Adding a User Interface to a C++ Program

The following C++ example is identical in function to the previous C example except for some minor variations in the syntax used:

```
//
//  ui.cpp
//  This C++ program prompts the user for a specified length,
//  in feet, and then outputs the value converted to
//  meters and centimeters.
//  Copyright (c) Chris H. Pappas and William H. Murray, 1998
//

#include <iostream.h>
#include <iomanip.h>

int main( )
{
  float feet,meters,centimeters;
```

```
cout << "Enter the number of feet to be converted: ";
cin  >> feet;

while(feet > 0 ) {
  centimeters = feet * 12 * 2.54;
  meters = centimeters/100;
  cout << setw(8) << setprecision \
       << setiosflags(ios::fixed) << feet << " feet equals \n";
  cout << setw(8) << setprecision \
       << meters << " meters \n";
  cout << setw(8) << setprecision \
       << centimeters << " centimeters \n";
  cout << "\nEnter another value to be \n";
  cout << "converted (0 ends the program): ";
  cin >>  feet;
}
cout << ">>> Have a nice day! <<<";

return(0);
}
```

There are six major differences between the C++ example and its C counterpart. The first two changes involve the use of **cin** and **cout** for I/O. These statements use the << ("put to," or insertion) and >> ("get from," or extraction) **iostream** operators. Both operators have been overloaded to handle the output/input of all the predefined types. They can also be overloaded to handle user-defined types such as rational numbers.

The last four changes are all related to formatting C++ output. To gain the same output precision easily afforded by C's "%8.2f" format string, the program requires four additional statements. The file IOMANIP.H is included in the program to give access to three specific class-member inline functions: setw( ), setprecision( ), and setiosflags( ). As you look at the code, you will notice that the calls to setw( ) and setprecision( ) are repeated. This is because their effect is only for the next output value, unlike setiosflags( ), which makes a global change to fixed output.

C++ programmers who like the power and flexibility of the C output function printf( ) can use printf( ) directly from library STDIO.H. The next two statements show the C and C++ equivalents:

```
printf("%8.2f feet equals\n", feet);
cout << setw(8) << setprecision \
     << setiosflags(ios::fixed) << feet << " feet equals \n";
```

Adding File I/O

Of course, there will be times when an application wants either its input or output, rather than the keyboard and display monitor, to deal directly with files. This brief introduction serves as an example of how to declare and use simple data files:

```
/*
 *    file1.cpp
 *    This C++ program demonstrates how to declare and use both
 *    input and output files. The example program
 *    takes the order_price from customer.dat and generates
 *    a billing_price that is printed to billing.dat.
 *    Copyright (c) Chris H. Pappas and William H. Murray, 1998
 */

#include <stdio.h>
#define MIN_DISCOUNT .97
#define MAX_DISCOUNT .95

int main( )
{
  float forder_price, fbilling_price;
  FILE *fin,*fout;

  fin=fopen("a:\\customer.dat","r");
  fout=fopen("a:\\billing.dat","w");

  while (fscanf(fin,"%f",&forder_price) != EOF) {
    fprintf(fout,"Your order of \t\t$%8.2f\n", forder_price);
    if (forder_price < 10000)
       fbilling_price = forder_price * MIN_DISCOUNT;
    else fbilling_price = forder_price * MAX_DISCOUNT;
    fprintf(fout,"is discounted to \t$%8.2f.\n\n",
            fbilling_price);
  }
  return(0);
}
```

Each file in a C program must be associated with a file pointer, which points to information that defines various things about a file, including the path to the file, its name, and its status. A file pointer is a pointer variable of type FILE and is defined in STDIO.H. The following statement from the example program declares two files, *fin and *fout:

```
, FILE *fin,*fout;
```

The next two statements in the program open two separate streams and associate each file with its respective stream:

```
fin=fopen("a:\\customer.dat","r");
fout=fopen("a:\\billing.dat","w");
```

The statements also return the file pointer for each file. Since these are pointers to files, your application should never alter their values.

The second parameter to the fopen( ) function is the file mode. Files may be opened in either Text or Binary mode. When in Text mode, most C compilers translate carriage return/linefeed sequences into newline characters on input. During output, the opposite occurs. However, binary files do not go through such translations. Table 5-4 lists all of the valid file modes.

The r+, w+, and a+ file modes select both reading and writing. (The file is open for update.) When switching between reading and writing, you must remember to reposition the file pointer, using either fsetpos( ), fseek( ), or rewind( ).

C does perform its own file closing automatically whenever the application closes. However, there may be times when you want direct control over when a file is closed.

Access Type	Description
a	Opens in Append mode. It creates the file if it does not already exist. All write operations occur at the end of the file.
a+	Same as above, but also allows reading.
r	Opens for reading. If the file does not exist or cannot be found, the open call will fail.
r+	Opens for both reading and writing. If the file does not exist or cannot be found, the open call will fail.
w	Opens an empty file for writing. If the file exists, all contents are destroyed.
w+	Opens an empty file for both reading and writing. If the file exists, all contents are destroyed.

Table 5-4. *Valid C File Modes*

The following listing shows the same program modified to include the necessary closing function calls:

```c
/*
 *   file1.c
 *   This C program demonstrates how to declare and use both
 *   input and output files. The example program
 *   takes the order_price from customer.dat and generates
 *   a billing_price that is printed to billing.dat
 *   Copyright (c) Chrisf H. Pappas and William H. Murray, 1998
 */

#include <stdio.h>
#define MIN_DISCOUNT .97
#define MAX_DISCOUNT .95

int main( )
{
  float forder_price, fbilling_price;
  FILE *fin,*fout;

  fin=fopen("a:\\customer.dat","r");
  fout=fopen("a:\\billing.dat","w");

  while (fscanf(fin,"%f",&forder_price) != EOF) {
    fprintf(fout,"Your order of \t\t$%8.2f\n", forder_price);
    if (forder_price < 10000)
        fbilling_price = forder_price * MIN_DISCOUNT;
    else fbilling_price = forder_price * MAX_DISCOUNT;
    fprintf(fout,"is discounted to \t$%8.2f.\n\n",
fbilling_price);
  }

  fclose(fin);
  fclose(fout);

  return(0);
}
```

The following program performs the same function as the one just examined, but is coded in C++:

```
//
//   file2.cpp
//   This C++ program demonstrates how to declare and use both
//   input and output files. The example program
//   takes the order_price from customer.dat and generates
//   a billing_price that is printed to billing.dat.
//   Copyright (c) Chris H. Pappas and William H. Murray, 1998
//

#include <fstream.h>
#include <iomanip.h>
#define MIN_DISCOUNT .97
#define MAX_DISCOUNT .95

int main( )
{
  float forder_price, fbilling_price;
  ifstream fin("a:\\customer.dat");
  ofstream fout("a:\\billing.dat");

  fin >> forder_price;
  while (!fin.eof( )) {
    fout << setiosflags(ios::fixed);
    fout << "Your order of \t\t$" << setprecision \
         << setw(8) << forder_price << "\n";
    if (forder_price < 10000)
       fbilling_price = forder_price * MIN_DISCOUNT;
    else fbilling_price = forder_price * MAX_DISCOUNT;
    fout << "is discounted to \t$" << setprecision \
         << setw(8) << fbilling_price << ".\n\n";
    fin >> forder_price;
  }

  fin.close( );
  fout.close( );

  return(0);
}
```

Disk file input and output are slightly different in C++ than in C. C++ has a two-part design to its stream library: a streambuf( ) object and a stream. This same model performs I/O for keyboard and terminal as well as disk I/O. The same operators and operations perform in precisely the same way. This greatly simplifies a programming task that has always been difficult and confusing. To facilitate disk file I/O, the stream library defines a filebuf( ) object, which is a derivative of the standard streambuf( ) type. Like its progenitor type, filebuf( ) manages a buffer, but in this case, the buffer is attached to a disk file. You will learn more about files in Chapter 11.

Chapter 6

Working With Data

H ere is a true statement: "You will never truly be a C/C++ programmer until you stop thinking in some other language and *translating* into C/C++!" You may have formally learned either COBOL, FORTRAN, Pascal, or PL/I, and then with brute force taught yourself one or more of the other languages listed, and been quite successful at it.

The same approach will *not* work with C and C++. The reason for this is that these new state-of-the-art languages have unique features, constructs, and ways of doing things that *have no equivalent* in the older, high-level languages. If you attempt to do a mental translation, you will end up not taking advantage of all that C and C++ have to offer. Even worse, in the presence of a truly experienced C/C++ programmer, you will look like an obvious novice. Technically and philosophically correct C/C++ source code design has many nuances that quickly expose fraudulent claims of expertise!

Fully appreciating all that C and C++ have to offer takes time and practice. In this chapter, you begin your exploration of their underlying structures. The great stability of these languages begins with the standard C and C++ data types and the modifiers and operators that can be used with them.

Identifiers

Identifiers are the names you use to represent variables, constants, types, functions, and labels in your program. You create an identifier by specifying it in the declaration of a variable, type, or function. You can then use the identifier in later program statements to refer to the associated item.

An identifier is a sequence of one or more letters, digits, or underscores that begins with a letter or underscore. Identifiers can contain any number of characters, but only the first 31 are significant to the compiler. (However, other programs that read the compiler output, such as the linker, may recognize even fewer characters.)

C and C++ are *case sensitive*. This means that the C compiler considers uppercase and lowercase letters to be distinct characters. For example, the compiler sees the variables *NAME_LENGTH* and *Name_Length* as two unique identifiers representing different memory cells. This feature enables you to create distinct identifiers that have the same spelling but different cases for one or more of the letters.

The selection of case can also help you understand your code. For example, identifiers declared in **#include** header files are often created using only uppercase letters. Because of this, whenever you encounter an uppercase identifier in the source file, you have a visual clue as to where that particular identifier's definition can be found.

While it is syntactically legal, you should not use leading underscores in identifiers you create. Identifiers beginning with an underscore can cause conflicts with the names of system routines or variables and produce errors. As a result, programs containing names beginning with leading underscores are not guaranteed to be portable. Use of two sequential underscore characters (__) in an identifier is reserved for C++ implementations and standard libraries.

One stylistic convention adopted by many C programmers is to precede all identifiers with an abbreviation of the identifier's data type. For example, all integer identifiers would begin with an "i," floats would begin with an "f," null-terminated strings would begin with "sz," pointer variables would begin with a "p," and so on. With this naming convention, you can easily look at a piece of code and see not only which identifiers are being used, but also their data type. This makes it easier to learn how a particular section of code operates and to do line-by-line source debugging. The programs throughout this book use both variable naming conventions since many of the programs you encounter in real life will use one format or another.

The following are examples of identifiers:

```
i
itotal
frange1
szfirst_name
lfrequency
imax
iMax
iMAX
NULL
EOF
```

See if you can determine why the following identifiers are illegal:

```
1st_year
#social_security
Not_Done!
```

The first identifier is illegal because it begins with a decimal number. The second begins with a # symbol, and the last ends with an illegal character.

Take a look at the following identifiers. Are they legal or not?

```
O
OO
OOO
_____
```

Actually, all four identifiers are legal. The first three use the uppercase letter "O." Since each has a different number of O's, they are all unique. The fourth identifier is composed of five underscore (_) characters. Is it meaningful? Definitely not. Is it legal? Yes. While these identifiers meet the letter of the law, they greatly miss its spirit. The point is that all identifiers, functions, constants, and variables should have meaningful names.

Since uppercase and lowercase letters are considered distinct characters, each of the following identifiers is unique:

```
MAX_RATIO
max_ratio
Max_Ratio
```

The C compiler's case sensitivity can create tremendous headaches for the novice C programmer. For example, trying to reference the printf( ) function when it was typed PRINTF( ) will invoke "unknown identifier" complaints from the compiler. In Pascal, however, a writeln is a WRITELN is a WriteLn.

With experience, you would probably detect the preceding printf( ) error, but can you see what's wrong with this next statement?

```
printf("%D",integer_value);
```

Assuming that *integer_value* was defined properly, you might think that nothing was wrong. Remember, however, that C is case sensitive—the **%D** print format has never been defined; only **%d** has.

For more advanced applications, some linkers may further restrict the number and type of characters for globally visible symbols. Also, the linker, unlike the compiler, may not distinguish between uppercase and lowercase letters. By default, the Visual C/C++ LINK sees all public and external symbols, such as *MYVARIABLE*, *MyVariable*, and *myvariable* as the same. You can, however, make LINK case sensitive by using the /NOI option. This would then force LINK to see the preceding three example variables as unique. Use your PWB help utility for additional information on how to use this switch.

One last word on identifiers: an identifier cannot have the same spelling and case as a keyword of the language. The next section lists C and C++ keywords.

Keywords

Keywords are predefined identifiers that have special meanings to the C/C++ compiler. You can use them only as defined. Remember, the name of a program identifier cannot have the same spelling and case as a C/C++ keyword. The C/C++ language keywords are listed in Table 6-1.

You cannot redefine keywords. However, you can specify text to be substituted for keywords before compilation by using C preprocessor directives.

__asm	enum	__multiple_ inheritance	template	auto
__except	__single_ inheritance	this	__based	explicit
__virtual_ inheritance	thread	bool	extern	mutable
throw	break	false	naked	true
case	__fastcall	namespace	try	catch
__finally	new	__try	__cdecl	float
operator	typedef	char	for	private
typeid	class	friend	protected	typename
const	goto	public	union	const_cast
if	register	unsigned	continue	inline
reinterpret_cast	using declaration	using directive	__declspec	__inline
return	uuid	default	int	short
__uuidof	delete	__int8	signed	virtual
dllexport	__int16	sizeof	void	dllimport
__int32	static	volatile	do	__int64
static_cast	wmain	double	__leave	__stdcall
while	dynamic_cast	long	struct	xalloc
else	main	switch		

Table 6-1. *C/C++ Keywords (Those with Leading Underscores are Microsoft-specific)*

PROGRAMMING FOUNDATIONS

Standard C and C++ Data Types

All programs deal with some kind of information that you can usually represent by using one of the eight basic C and C++ types: text or **char**, integer values or **int**, floating-point values or **float**, double floating-point values or **double** (**long double**), enumerated or enum, valueless or void, pointers, and bool. Following is an explanation of the types:

- *Text* (data type **char**) is made up of single characters, such as a, Z, ?, and 3; and strings, such as "There is more to life than increasing its speed". (Usually, 8 bits, or 1 byte per character, with the range of 0 to 255.)

- *Integer values* are those numbers you learned to count with (1, 2, 7, –45, and 1,345). (Usually, 16 bits wide, 2 bytes, or 1 word, with the range of –32,768 to 32,767. Under Windows 98 and Windows NT, integers are now 32 bits wide with a range from –2147483648 to 2147483647.)

- *Floating-point values* are numbers that have a fractional portion, such as pi (3.14159), and exponents (7.563^{1021}). These are also known as real numbers. (Usually, 32 bits, 4 bytes, or 2 words, with the range of +/– 3.4E-38 to 3.4E+38.)

- *Double floating-point values* have an extended range (usually, 64 bits, 8 bytes, or 4 words, with the range of 1.7E-308 to 1.7E+308). **Long double** floating-point values are even more precise (usually, 80 bytes, or 5 words, with the range of +/– 1.18E-4932 to 1.18E+4932).

- *Enumerated* data types allow for user-defined types.

- The type **void** is used to signify values that occupy zero bits and have no value. (This type can also be used for the creation of generic pointers, as discussed in Chapter 10.)

- The *pointer* data type doesn't hold information in the normal sense of the other data types; instead, each pointer contains the address of the memory location holding the actual data. (This is also discussed in Chapter 10.)

- The new **bool** data type, which can be assigned the two constants, **true** and **false**.

Characters

Every language uses a set of characters to construct meaningful statements. For instance, all books written in English use combinations of 26 letters of the alphabet, the ten digits, and the punctuation marks. Similarly, C and C++ programs are written using a set of characters consisting of the 26 lowercase letters of the alphabet:

abcdefghijklmnopqrstuvwxyz

the 26 uppercase letters of the alphabet:

ABCDEFGHIJKLMNOPQRSTUVWXYZ

the ten digits:

0 1 2 3 4 5 6 7 8 9

and the following symbols:

+ – * / =, . _ : ; ? \ " ' ~ | ! # % $ & ( ) [ ] { } ^ @

C and C++ also use the blank space, sometimes referred to as white space. Combinations of symbols, with no blank space between them, are also valid C and C++ characters. In fact, the following is a mixture of valid C and C++ symbols:

++ – – == && | | << >> >= <= += –= *= /= ?: :: /* */ //

The following C program illustrates how to declare and use **char** data types:

```c
/*
 *   char.c
 *   A C program demonstrating the char data type and showing
 *   how a char variable can be interpreted as an integer.
 *   Copyright (c) Chris H. Pappas and William H. Murray, 1997
 */

#include <stdio.h>
#include <ctype.h>

int main( )
{
  char csinglechar, cuppercase, clowercase;

  printf("\nPlease enter a single character: ");
  scanf("%c",&csinglechar);

  cuppercase = toupper(csinglechar);
  clowercase = tolower(csinglechar);

  printf("The UPPERcase character \'%c\' has a decimal ASCII"
         " value of %d\n",cuppercase,cuppercase);
  printf("The ASCII value represented in hexadecimal"
         " is %X\n",cuppercase);
```

```
printf("If you add sixteen you will get \'%c\'\n",
       (cuppercase+16));
printf("The calculated ASCII value in hexadecimal"
       " is %X\n",(cuppercase+16));
printf("The LOWERcase character \'%c\' has a decimal ASCII"
       " value of %d\n",clowercase,clowercase);

return(0);
}
```

The output from the program looks like this:

Please enter a single character: d
The UPPERcase character 'D' has a decimal ASCII value of 68
The ASCII value represented in hexadecimal is 44
If you add sixteen you will get 'T'
The calculated ASCII value in hexadecimal is 54
The LOWERcase character 'd' has a decimal ASCII value of 100

The **%X** format control instructs the compiler to interpret the value as an uppercase hexadecimal number.

Three Integers

Microsoft Visual C/C++ supports three types of integers. Along with the standard type **int**, the compiler supports **short int** and **long int**. These are most often abbreviated to just **short** and **long**. While the C language is not hardware dependent (syntax, etc.), data types used by the C language are. Thus, the actual sizes of **short**, **int**, and **long** depend upon the implementation. Across all C compilers, the only guarantee is that a variable of type **short** will not be larger than one of type **long**. Microsoft Visual C/C++ allocates 2 bytes for both **short** and **int**. (Under Windows 98 and Windows NT, integers are now 32 bits). The type **long** occupies 4 bytes of storage.

Unsigned Modifier

All C and C++ compilers allow you to declare certain types to be **unsigned**. Currently, you can apply the **unsigned** modifier to four types: **char**, **short int**, **int**, and **long int**. When one of these data types is modified to be **unsigned**, you can think of the range of values it holds as representing the numbers displayed on a car odometer. An automobile odometer starts at 000..., increases to a maximum of 999..., and then recycles back to 000.... It also displays only positive whole numbers. In a similar way, an **unsigned** data type can hold only positive values in the range of zero to the maximum number that can be represented.

For example, suppose you are designing a new data type called *my_octal* and have decided that *my_octal* variables can hold only 3 bits. You have also decided that the data type *my_octal* is signed by default. Since a variable of type *my_octal* can only contain the bit patterns 000 through 111 (or zero to 7 decimal), and you want to represent both positive and negative values, you have a problem. You can't have both positive and negative numbers in the range zero to 7 because you need one of the 3 bits to represent the sign of the number. Therefore, *my_octal*'s range is a subset. When the most significant bit is zero, the value is positive. When the most significant bit is 1, the value is negative. This gives a *my_octal* variable the range of –4 to +3.

However, applying the **unsigned** data type modifier to a *my_octal* variable would yield a range of zero to 7, since the most significant bit can be combined with the lower 2 bits to represent a broader range of positive values instead of identifying the sign of the number. This simple analogy holds true for any of the valid C data types defined to be of type **unsigned**. The storage and range for the fundamental C/C++ data types are summarized in Table 6-2.

The **long double** data type (80-bit, 10-byte precision) is mapped directly to **double** (64-bit, 8-byte precision) in Windows NT and Windows 98. **Signed** and **unsigned** are modifiers that can be used with any integral type. The **char** type is signed by default, but you can specify /J to make it **unsigned** by default. The **int** and **unsigned int** types have the size of the system word. This is 2 bytes (the same as **short** and **unsigned short**) in MS-DOS and 16-bit versions of Windows, and 4 bytes in 32-bit operating systems. However, portable code should not depend on the size of **int**. Microsoft C/C++ also features support for sized integer types. Table 6-3 lists the valid data type modifiers in all of the various legal and abbreviated combinations.

Floating Point

Visual C/C++ uses the three floating-point types: **float**, **double**, and **long double**. While the ANSI C standard does not specifically define the values and storage that are to be allocated for each of these types, the standard did require each type to hold a minimum of any value in the range 1E–37 to 1E+37. As you saw in Table 6-2, the Microsoft Visual C/C++ environment has greatly expanded upon this minimum requirement. Historically, most C compilers have always had the types **float** and **double**. The ANSI C committee added the third type, **long double**. Here are some examples of floating-point numbers:

```
float altitude = 47000;
double joules;
long double budget_deficit;
```

Type Name	Bytes	Other Names	Range of Values
int	*	signed, signed int	System dependent
unsigned int	*	unsigned	System dependent
__int8	1	char, signed char	–128 to 127
__int16	2	short, short int, signed short int	–32,768 to 32,767
__int32	4	signed, signed int	–2,147,483,648 to 2,147,483,647
__int64	8	none	–9,223,372,036,854,775,808 to 9,223,372,036,854,775,807
char	1	signed char	–128 to 127
unsigned char	1	none	0 to 255
short	2	short int, signed short int	–32,768 to 32,767
unsigned short	2	unsigned short int	0 to 65,535
long	4	long int, signed long int	–2,147,483,648 to 2,147,483,647
unsigned long	4	unsigned long int	0 to 4,294,967,295
enum	*	none	Same as int
float	4	none	3.4E +/− 38 (7 digits)
double	8	none	1.7E +/− 308 (15 digits)
long double	10	none	1.2E +/ − 4932 (19

Table 6-2.   *ANSI C/C++ Standard Data Types and Sizes*

You can use the third type, **long double**, on any computer, even those that have only two types of floating-point numbers. However, if the computer does not have a specific data type of **long double**, then the data item will have the same size and storage capacity as a **double**.

Type Specifier	Equivalent(s)
signed char	char
signed int	signed, int
signed short int	short, signed short
signed long int	long, signed long
unsigned char	none
unsigned int	unsigned
unsigned short int	unsigned short
unsigned long int	unsigned long
float	none
long double	none

Table 6-3.   *Valid Data Type Modifier Abbreviations*

The following C++ program illustrates how to declare and use floating-point variables:

```
//
//  float.cpp
//  A C++ program demonstrating using the float data type.
//  Copyright (c) Chris H. Pappas and William H. Murray, 1997
//

#include <iostream.h>
#include <iomanip.h>

int main( )
{
  long loriginal_flags=cin.flags( );
  float fvalue;

  cout << "Please enter a float value to be formatted: ";
  cin >> fvalue;
```

```
cout << "Standard Formatting:   " << fvalue << "\n";
cout.setf(ios::scientific);
cout << "Scientific Formatting: " << fvalue << "\n";

cout.setf(ios::fixed);
cout << "Fixed Formatting:      " << setprecision
      << fvalue;

cout.flags(loriginal_flags);

return(0);
}
```

The output looks like this:

```
Please enter a float value to be formatted: 1234.5678
Standard Formatting:   1234.57
Scientific Formatting: 1.234568e+003
Fixed Formatting:      0x004010191234.57
```

Notice the different value printed depending on the print format specification standard, scientific, or fixed.

Enumerated

When an enumerated variable is defined, it is associated with a set of named integer constants called the *enumeration set*. (These are discussed in Chapter 13.) The variable can contain any one of the constants at any time, and the constants can be referred to by name. For example, the following definition creates the enumerated type *air_supply*; the enumerated constants EMPTY, USEABLE, and FULL; and the enumerated variable *instructor_tank*:

```
enum air_supply { EMPTY,
                  USEABLE,
                  FULL=5 } instructor_tank;
```

All the constants and variables are type **int**, and each constant is automatically provided a **default** initial value unless another value is specified. In the preceding example, the constant name EMPTY has the integer value zero by default since it is the first in the list and was not specifically overridden. The value of USEABLE is 1 since it occurs immediately after a constant with the value of zero. The constant FULL was specifically initialized to the value 5, and if another constant were included in the list after FULL, the new constant would have the integer value of 6.

Having created *air_supply*, you can later define another variable, *student_tank*, as follows:

```
enum air_supply student_tank;
```

After this statement it is legal to say

```
instructor_tank = FULL;
student_tank    = EMPTY;
```

This places the value 5 into the variable *instructor_tank* and the value of zero into the variable *student_tank*.

Note *When defining additional enumerated variables in C++, it is not necessary to repeat the **enum** keyword. However, both syntaxes are accepted by the C++ compiler.*

One common mistake is to think that *air_supply* is a variable. It is a "type" of data that can be used later to create additional enumerated variables like *instructor_tank* or *student_tank*.

Since the name *instructor_tank* is an enumerated variable of type air_supply, *instructor_tank* can be used on the left of an assignment operator and can receive a value. This occurred when the enumerated constant FULL was explicitly assigned to it. EMPTY, USEABLE, and FULL are names of constants; they are not variables and their values cannot be changed.

Tests can be performed on the variables in conjunction with the constants. The following is a complete C program that uses the preceding definitions:

```
/*
 *   enum.c
 *   A C program demonstrating the use of enumeration variables
 *   Copyright (c) Chris H. Pappas and William H. Murray, 1997
 */

#include <stdio.h>
#include <stdlib.h>

int main( )
{
  enum air_supply { EMPTY,
```

```
                    USEABLE,
                    FULL=5 }  instructor_tank;
    enum air_supply student_tank;

    instructor_tank = FULL;
    student_tank = EMPTY;

    printf("The value of instructor_tank is %d\n",instructor_tank);

    if (student_tank < USEABLE) {
      printf("Refill this tank.\n");
      printf("Class is cancelled.\n");
      exit(1);
    }
    if (instructor_tank >= student_tank)
      printf("Proceed with lesson\n");
    else
      printf("Class is cancelled!\n");

    return(0);
}
```

In C, an **enum** type is equivalent to the type **int**. This technically allows a program to assign integer values directly to enumerated variables. C++ enforces a stronger type check and does not allow this mixed-mode operation. The output from the program looks like this:

```
The value of instructor_tank is 5
Refill this tank.
Class is cancelled.
```

And, the New C++ Type—bool

This keyword is an integral type. A variable of this type can have values true and false. All conditional expressions now return a value of type **bool**. For example, myvar! = 0 now returns **true** or **false** depending on the value of *myvar*.

The values true and false have the following relationship:

```
!false == true
!true == false
```

Look at the following statement:

```
if (myexpression)
  statement1;
```

If *myexpression* evaluates to true, statement1 is always executed; if *myexpression* evaluates to false, statement1 is never executed. An important fundamental to keep in mind when writing test expressions is this: Both C and C++ view *any* non-zero (!0) value as true, and *any* expression evaluating to zero (0) as false.

Note | *When a postfix or prefix ++ operator is applied to a variable of type **bool**, the variable is set to true. The postfix or prefix — operator cannot be applied to a variable of this type. Also, the **bool** type participates in integral promotions. An r-value of type **bool** can be converted to an r-value of type **int**, with false becoming zero and true becoming 1.*

Access Modifiers

The **const** and **volatile** modifiers are new to C and C++. They were added by the ANSI C standard to help identify which variables will never change (**const**) and which can change unexpectedly (**volatile**).

const Modifier

At certain times you will need to use a value that does not change throughout the program. Such a quantity is called a *constant*. For example, if a program deals with the area and circumference of a circle, the constant value pi=3.14159 would be used frequently. In a financial program, an interest rate might be a constant. In such cases, you can improve the readability of the program by giving the constant a descriptive name.

Using descriptive names can also help prevent errors. Suppose that a constant value (not a constant variable) is used at many points throughout the program. A typographical error might result in the wrong value being typed at one or more of these points. However, if the constant is given a name, a typographical error would then be detected by the compiler because the incorrectly spelled identifier would probably not have been declared.

Suppose you are writing a program that repeatedly uses the value pi. It might seem as though a *variable* called *pi* should be declared with an initial value of 3.14159. However, the program should not be able to change the value of a constant. For instance, if you inadvertently wrote "pi" to the left of an equal sign, the value of pi would be changed, causing all subsequent calculations to be in error. C and C++

provide mechanisms that prevent such an error from occurring: you can establish constants, the values of which cannot be changed.

In C and C++, you declare a constant by writing "**const**" before the keyword (such as **int**, **float**, or **double**) in the declaration. For example:

```
const int iMIN=1,iSALE_PERCENTAGE=25;
const float fbase_change=32.157;
int irow_index=1,itotal=100,iobject;
double ddistance=0,dvelocity;
```

Because a constant cannot be changed, it must be initialized in its declaration. The integer constants iMIN and iSALE_PERCENTAGE are declared with values 1 and 25, respectively; the constant *fbase_change* is of type **float** and has been initialized to 32.157. In addition, the integer (nonconstant) variables *irow_index*, *itotal*, and *iobject* have been declared. Initial values of 1 and 100 have been established for *irow_index* and *itotal*, respectively. Finally, *ddistance* and *dvelocity* have been declared to be (nonconstant) variables of type **double**. An initial value of zero has been set up for *ddistance*.

Constants and variables are used in the same way in a program. The only difference is that the initial values assigned to the constants cannot be changed. That is, the constants are not *lvalues*; they cannot appear to the left of an equal sign. (Expressions that refer to memory locations are called *lvalue expressions*. Expressions referring to modifiable locations are *modifiable lvalues*. One example of a modifiable *lvalue* expression is a variable name declared without the **const** specifier.)

Normally, the assignment operation assigns the value of the right-hand operand to the storage location named by the left-hand operand. Therefore, the left-hand operand of an assignment operation (or the single operand of a unary assignment expression) must be an expression that refers to a modifiable memory location.

#define Constants

C and C++ provide another method for establishing constants: the **#define** compiler directive. Let's look at an example. Suppose that at the beginning of a program you have the statement:

```
#define SALES_TEAM 10
```

The form of this statement is **#define** followed by two strings of characters separated by blanks. When the program is compiled, there are several passes made through it. The first step is accomplished by the *compiler preprocessor*, which does such things as carry out the **#include** and **#define** directives. When the preprocessor encounters the

#define directive, it replaces every occurrence of SALES_TEAM in the source file(s) with the number 10.

In general, when the preprocessor encounters a **#define** directive, it replaces every occurrence of the first string of characters, "SALES_TEAM," in the program with the second string of characters, "10." Additionally, no value can be assigned to SALES_TEAM because it has never been declared to be a variable. As a result of the syntax, SALES_TEAM has all the attributes of a constant. Note that the **#define** statement is *not* terminated by a semicolon. If a semicolon followed the value 10, then every occurrence of SALES_TEAM would be replaced with "10";. The directive's action is to replace the first string with *everything* in the second string.

All of the programs that have been discussed so far are short, and would usually be stored in a single file. If a statement such as the **#define** for SALES_TEAM appeared at the beginning of the file, the substitution of "10" for "SALES_TEAM" would take place throughout the program. (A later chapter of this book discusses breaking a program down into many subprograms, with each subprogram being broken down into separate files.) Under these circumstances, the compiler directive would be effective only for the single file in which it is written.

The preceding discussion explored two methods for defining constants—the keyword **const** and the **#define** compiler directive. In many programs, the action of each of these two methods is essentially the same. On the other hand, the use of the modifier keyword **const** results in a "variable" whose value cannot be changed. Later in this chapter, in "Storage Classes," you will see how variables can be declared in such a way that they exist only over certain regions of a program. The same can be said for constants declared with the keyword **const**. Thus, the **const** declaration is somewhat more versatile than the **#define** directive. Also, the **#define** directive is found in standard C and is therefore already familiar to C programmers.

volatile Modifier

The **volatile** keyword signifies that a variable can unexpectedly change because of events outside the control of the program. For example, the following definition indicates that the variable *event_time* can have its value changed without the knowledge of the program:

```
volatile int event_time;
```

A definition like this is needed, for example, if *event_time* is updated by hardware that maintains the current clock time. The program that contains the variable *event_time* could be interrupted by the timekeeping hardware and the variable *event_time* changed.

A data object should be declared **volatile** if it is a memory-mapped device register or a data object shared by separate processes, as would be the case in a multitasking operating environment.

const and volatile Used Together

You can use the **const** and **volatile** modifiers with any other data types (for example, **char** and **float**) and also with each other. The following definition specifies that the program does not intend to change the value in the variable *constant_event_time*:

```
const volatile constant_event_time;
```

However, the compiler is also instructed, because of the **volatile** modifier, to make no assumptions about the variable's value from one moment to the next. Therefore, two things happen. First, an error message will be issued by the compiler for any line of source code that attempts to change the value of the variable *constant_event_time*. Second, the compiler will not remove the variable *constant_event_time* from inside loops since an external process can also be updating the variable while the program is executing.

pascal, cdecl, near, far, and huge Modifiers

The first two modifiers, **pascal** and **cdecl**, are used most frequently in advanced applications. Microsoft Visual C/C++ allows you to write programs that can easily call other routines written in different languages. The opposite of this also holds true. For example, you can write a Pascal program that calls a C++ routine. When you mix languages this way, you have to take two very important issues into consideration: identifier names and the way parameters are passed.

When Microsoft Visual C/C++ compiles your program, it places all of the program's global identifiers (functions and variables) into the resulting object code file for linking purposes. By default, the compiler saves those identifiers using the same case in which they were defined (uppercase, lowercase, or mixed). Additionally, the compiler appends an underscore (_) to the front of the identifier. Since Microsoft Visual C/C++'s integrated linking (by default) is case sensitive, any external identifiers you declare in your program are also assumed to be in the same form with a prepended underscore and the same spelling and case as defined.

pascal

The Pascal language uses a different calling sequence than C and C++. Pascal (along with FORTRAN) passes function arguments from left to right and does not allow variable-length argument lists. In Pascal, it is also the called function's responsibility to remove the arguments from the stack, rather than having the invoking function do so when control returns from the invoked function.

A C and C++ program can generate this calling sequence in one of two ways. First, it can use the compile-time switch /Gc, which makes the Pascal calling sequence the **default** for all enclosed calls and function definitions. Second, the C program can override the **default** C calling sequence explicitly by using the **pascal** keyword in the function definition.

As mentioned earlier, when C generates a function call, by default it appends an underscore to the function name and declares the function as external. It also preserves the casing of the name. However, when the **pascal** keyword is used, the underscore is not prepended and the identifier (function or variable) is converted to all uppercase.

The following code segment demonstrates how to use the **pascal** keyword on a function. (The same keyword can be used to ensure FORTRAN code compatibility.)

```
float pascal pfcalculate(int iscore, int iweight)
{
    .
    .
    .
}
```

Of course, variables can also be given a Pascal convention, as seen in this next example:

```
#define TABLESIZE 30

float pascal pfcalculate(int iscore, int iweight)
{
    .
    .
    .
}

float pascal pfscore_table[TABLESIZE];

int main( )
{
    int iscore 95, iweight = 10;

    pfscore_table[0] = pfcalculate(iscore,iweight);

    return(0);
}
```

In this example, *pfscore_table* has been globally defined with the **pascal** modifier. Function main( ) also shows how to make an external reference to a **pascal** function type. Since both functions, main( ) and pfcalculate( ), are in the same source file, the function pfcalculate( ) is global to main( ).

cdecl

If the /Gz compile-time switch was used to compile your C or C++ program, all function and variable references were generated matching the Pascal calling convention. However, there may be occasions when you want to guarantee that certain identifiers you are using in your program remain case sensitive and keep the underscore at the front. This is most often the case for identifiers being used in another C file.

To maintain this C compatibility (preserving the case and having a leading underscore prepended), you can use the **cdecl** keyword. When the **cdecl** keyword is used in front of a function, it also affects how the parameters are passed.

Note that all C and C++ functions prototyped in the header files of Microsoft Visual C/C++—for example, STDIO.H—are of type **cdecl**. This ensures that you can link with the library routines, even when you are compiling using the /Gz option. The following example was compiled using the /Gz option and shows how you would rewrite the previous example to maintain C compatibility:

```
#define TABLESIZE 30

float cdecl cfcalculate(int iscore, int iweight)
{
   .

   .

   .

}

float cdecl cfscore_table[TABLESIZE];

int main( )
{
   int iscore 95, iweight = 10;

   cfscore_table[0] = cfcalculate(iscore,iweight);

   return(0);
}
```

near, far, and huge

Note | *These old-style C/C++ keywords are only mentioned here in case you run across them in an older text or program. They are 16-bit C/C++ compiler specific and are no longer needed by today's state-of-the-art 32-bit C/C++ compilers.*

However, this is an appropriate time to caution you. C and C++ are continuing to evolve, even as you read this text. Therefore, any time you peruse other C/C++

literature, beware: there are Historic C, C, ANSI C, Historic C++, C++, ANSI C++, and the flavor-of-the-month languages out there! Case in point: the old-style keywords **near**, **far**, and **huge**.

(You use the three modifiers—**near**, **far**, and **huge**--to affect the action of the indirection operator (*); in other words, they modify pointer sizes to data objects. A **near** pointer is only 2 bytes long, a **far** pointer is 4 bytes long, and a **huge** pointer is also 4 bytes long. The difference between the **far** pointer and the **huge** pointer is that the latter has to deal with the form of the address.)

Data Type Conversions

In the programs so far, the variables and numbers used in any particular statement were all of the same type—for example, **int** or **float**. You can write statements that perform operations involving variables of different types. These operations are called *mixed-mode operations*. In contrast to some other programming languages, C and C++ perform automatic conversions from one type to another. As you progress through the book, additional types will be introduced, and mixing of those types will be discussed.

Data of different types is stored differently in memory. Suppose that the number 10 is being stored. Its representation will depend upon its type. That is, the pattern of zeros and ones in memory will be different when 10 is stored as an integer than when it is stored as a floating-point number.

Suppose that the following operation is executed, where both *fresult* and *fvalue* are of type **float**, and the variable *ivalue* is of type **int**:

```
fresult = fvalue * ivalue;
```

The statement is therefore a mixed-mode operation. When the statement is executed, the value of *ivalue* will be converted into a floating-point number before the multiplication takes place. The compiler recognizes that a mixed-mode operation is occurring, and therefore generates code to perform the following operations. The integer value assigned to *ivalue* is read from memory. This value is then converted to the corresponding floating-point value, which is multiplied by the real value assigned to *fvalue*, and the resulting floating-point value is assigned to *fresult*. In other words, the compiler performs the conversion automatically. Note that the value assigned to *ivalue* is unchanged by this process and remains of type **int**.

You have seen that in mixed-mode operations involving a value of type **int** and another value of type **float**, the value of type **int** is converted into a value of type **float** for calculation. This is done without changing the stored integral value during the conversion process. Now let's consider mixed-mode operations between two different types of variables.

Actually, before doing this, you need to know that there is in fact a *hierarchy of conversions*, in that the object of lower priority is temporarily converted to the type of higher priority for the performance of the calculation. The hierarchy of conversions takes the following structure, from highest priority to lowest:

double
float
long
int
short

For example, the type **double** has a higher priority than the type **int**. When a type is converted to one that has more significant digits, the value of the number and its accuracy are unchanged.

Look at what happens when a conversion from type **float** to type **int** takes place. Suppose that the variables *ivalue1* and *ivalue2* have been defined to be of type **int**, while *fvalue* and *fresult* have been defined to be of type **float**. Consider the following sequence of statements:

```
ivalue1 = 3;
ivalue2 = 4;
fvalue = 7.0;
fresult = fvalue + ivalue1/ivalue2;
```

The statement *ivalue1/ivalue2* is *not* a mixed-mode operation; instead, it represents the division of two integers, and its result is zero since the fractional part (0.75, in this case) is *discarded* when integer division is performed. Therefore, the value stored in *fresult* is 7.0.

What if *ivalue2* had been defined to be of type **float**? In this case, *fresult* would have been assigned the floating-point value 7.75, since the statement *ivalue1/ivalue2* would be a mixed-mode operation. Under these circumstances, the value of *ivalue1* is temporarily converted to the floating-point value 3.0, and the result of the division is 0.75. When that is added to *fvalue*, the result is 7.75.

It is important to know that the type of the value to the left of the assignment statement determines the type of the result of the operation. For example, suppose that *fx* and *fy* have been declared to be of type **float** and *iresult* has been declared to be of type **int**. Consider the following statements:

```
fx = 7.0;
fy = 2.0;
iresult = 4.0 + fx/fy
```

The result of executing the statement *fx/fy* is 3.5; when this is added to 4.0, the floating-point value generated is 7.5. However, this value cannot be assigned to *iresult* because *iresult* is of type **int**. The number 7.5 is therefore converted into an integer. When this is done, the fraction part is truncated. The resulting whole number is converted from a floating-point representation to an integer representation, and the value assigned to *iresult* is the integer number 7.

Explicit Type Conversions Using the Cast Operator

You have seen that the C and C++ compiler automatically changes the format of a variable in mixed-mode operations using different data types. However, there are circumstances where, although automatic conversion is *not* performed, type conversion would be desirable. For those occasions, you must specifically designate that a change of type is to be made. These explicit specifications also clarify to other programmers the statements involved. The C language provides several procedures that allow you to designate that type conversion must occur.

One of these procedures is called the *cast operator*. Whenever you want to temporarily change the format of a variable, you simply precede the variable's identifier with the parenthesized type you want it converted to. For example, if *ivalue1* and *ivalue2* were defined to be of type **int** and *fvalue* and *fresult* have been defined to be of type **float**, the following three statements would perform the same operation:

```
fresult = fvalue + (float)ivalue1/ivalue2;
fresult = fvalue + ivalue1/(float)ivalue2;
fresult = fvalue + (float)ivalue1/(float)ivalue2;
```

All three statements perform a floating-point conversion and division of the variables *ivalue1* and *ivalue2*. Because of the usual rules of mixed-mode arithmetic discussed earlier, if either variable is cast to type **float**, a floating-point division occurs. The third statement explicitly highlights the operation to be performed.

Storage Classes

Visual C/C++ supports four storage-class specifiers. They are

> **auto**
> **register**
> **static**
> **extern**

The storage class precedes the variable's declaration and instructs the compiler how the variable should be stored. Items declared with the **auto** or **register** specifier have local lifetimes; items declared with the **static** or **extern** specifier have global lifetimes.

The four storage-class specifiers affect the visibility of a variable or function, as well as its storage class. *Visibility* (sometimes defined as *scope*) refers to that portion of the source program in which the variable or function can be referenced by name. An item with a global lifetime exists throughout the execution of the source program.

The placement of a variable or a function declaration within a source file also affects storage class and visibility. Declarations outside all function definitions are said to appear at the *external level*, while declarations within function definitions appear at the *internal level*.

The exact meaning of each storage-class specifier depends on two factors: whether the declaration appears at the external or internal level and whether the item being declared is a variable or a function.

Variable Declarations at the External Level

Variable declarations at the external level may only use the **static** or **extern** storage class, not **auto** or **register**. They are either definitions of variables or references to variables defined elsewhere. An external variable declaration that also initializes the variable (implicitly or explicitly) is a defining declaration:

```
static int ivalue1;       // implicit 0 by default
static int ivalue1 = 10   // explicit

int ivalue2 = 20;         // explicit
```

Once a variable is defined at the external level, it is visible throughout the rest of the source file in which it appears. The variable is not visible prior to its definition in the same source file. Also, it is not visible in other source files of the program unless a referencing declaration makes it visible, as described shortly.

You can define a variable at the external level only once within a source file. If you give the **static** storage-class specifier, you can define another variable with the same name and the **static** storage-class specifier in a different source file. Since each static definition is visible only within its own source file, no conflict occurs.

The **extern** storage-class specifier declares a reference to a variable defined elsewhere. You can use an external declaration to make a definition in another source file visible or to make a variable visible above its definition in the same source file. The variable is visible throughout the remainder of the source file in which the declared reference occurs.

For an external reference to be valid, the variable it refers to must be defined once, and only once, at the external level. The definition can be in any of the source files that form the program. The following C++ program demonstrates the use of the **extern** keyword:

```
//
//      Source File A - incomplete file do not compile.
//
#include <iostream.h>

extern int ivalue;                  // makes ivalue visible
                                    // above its declaration

int main( )
{
  ivalue++;                         // uses the above extern
                                    // reference
  cout << ivalue << "\n";           // prints 11
  function_a( );

  return(0);
}

int ivalue = 10;                    // actual definition of
                                    // ivalue

void function_a(void)
{
  ivalue++;                         // references ivalue
  cout << ivalue << "\n";           // prints 12
  function_b( );
}


----------------------------------------

//
//      Source File B
//

#include <iostream.h>

extern int ivalue;                  // references ivalue
                                    // declared in Source A

void function_b(void)
```

```
{
   ivalue++;
   cout <<("%d\n", ivalue);          // prints 13
}
```

Variable Declarations at the Internal Level

You can use any of the four storage-class specifiers for variable declarations at the internal level. (The **default** is **auto**.) The **auto** storage-class specifier declares a variable with a local lifetime. It is visible only in the block in which it is declared and can include initializers.

The **register** storage-class specifier tells the compiler to give the variable storage in a register, if possible. This specifier speeds access time and reduces code size. It has the same visibility as an **auto** variable. If no registers are available when the compiler encounters a **register** declaration, the variable is given the **auto** storage class and stored in memory.

ANSI C does not allow for taking the address of a **register** object. However, this restriction does not apply to C++. Applying the address operator (**&**) to a C++ register variable forces the compiler to store the object in memory, since the compiler must put the object in a location for which an address can be represented.

A variable declared at the internal level with the **static** storage-class specifier has a global lifetime but is visible only within the block in which it is declared. Unlike **auto** variables, **static** variables keep their values when the block is exited. You can initialize a **static** variable with a constant expression. It is initialized to zero by default.

A variable declared with the **extern** storage-class specifier is a reference to a variable with the same name defined at the external level in any of the source files of the program. The internal **extern** declaration is used to make the external-level variable definition visible within the block. The next program demonstrates these concepts:

```
int ivalue1=1; // incomplete file do not compile.

void main( )
{ // references the ivalue1 defined above
    extern int ivalue1;

  // default initialization of 0, ivalue2 only visible
  // in main( )
    static int ivalue2;

  // stored in a register (if available), initialized
  // to 0
    register int rvalue = 0;
```

```
    // default auto storage class, int_value3 initialized
    // to 0
        int int_value3 = 0;

    // values printed are 1, 0, 0, 0:
        cout << ivalue1 << rvalue \
            <<ivalue2 << int_value3;
        function_a( );
}

void function_a(void)
{
    // stores the address of the global variable ivalue1
        static int *pivalue1= &ivalue1;

    // creates a new local variable ivalue1 making the
    // global ivalue1 unreachable
        int ivalue1 = 32;

    // new local variable ivalue2
    // only visible within function_a
        static int ivalue2 = 2;

        ivalue2 += 2;

    // the values printed are 32, 4, and 1:
        cout << ivalue1 << ivalue2 \
        << *pivalue1);
}
```

Since *ivalue1* is redefined in function_a( ), access to the global *ivalue1* is denied. However, by using the data pointer *pivalue1* (discussed in Chapter 10), the address of the global *ivalue1* was used to print the value stored there.

Variable Scope Review

To review, there are four rules for variable visibility, also called *scope rules*. The four scopes for a variable are the block, function, file, and program. A variable declared within a block or function is known only within the block or function. A variable declared external to a function is known within the file in which it appears, from the point of its appearance to the end of the file. A variable declared as external in one source file and declared as external in other files has program scope.

Function Declarations at the External Level

When declaring a function at the external or internal level, you can use either the **static** or the **extern** storage-class specifier. Functions, unlike variables, always have a global lifetime. The visibility rules for functions vary slightly from the rules for variables.

Functions declared to be **static** are visible only within the source file in which they are defined. Functions in the same source file can call the **static** function, but functions in *other* source files cannot. Also, you can declare another **static** function with the same name in a different source file without conflict.

Functions declared as external are visible throughout *all* source files that make up the program (unless you later redeclare such a function as **static**). Any function can call an external function. Function declarations that omit the storage-class specifier are external by default.

Operators

C has many operators not found in other languages. These include bitwise operators, increment and decrement operators, conditional operators, the comma operator, and assignment and compound assignment operators.

Bitwise Operators

Bitwise operators treat variables as combinations of bits rather than as numbers. They are useful in accessing the individual bits in memory, such as the screen memory for a graphics display. Bitwise operators can operate only on integral data types, not on floating-point numbers. Three bitwise operators act just like the logical operators, but on each bit in an integer. These are AND (&), OR (|), and XOR (^). An additional operator is the one's complement (~), which simply inverts each bit.

AND

The bitwise AND operation compares two bits; if both bits are a 1, the result is a 1, as shown here:

Bit 0	Bit 1	Result
0	0	0
0	1	0
1	0	0
1	1	1

Note that this is different from binary addition, where the comparison of two 1 bits would result in a sum flag set to zero and the carry flag set to 1. Very often, the AND operation is used to select out, or *mask*, certain bit positions.

OR

The bitwise OR operation compares two bits and generates a 1 result if either or both bits are a 1, as shown here:

Bit 0	Bit 1	Result
0	0	0
0	1	1
1	0	1
1	1	1

The OR operation is useful for setting specified bit positions.

XOR

The EXCLUSIVE OR operation compares two bits and returns a result of 1 when and only when the two bits are complementary, as shown here:

Bit 0	Bit 1	Result
0	0	0
0	1	1
1	0	1
1	1	0

This logical operation can be very useful when it is necessary to complement specified bit positions, as in the case of computer graphics applications.

Following is an example of using these operators with the hexadecimal and octal representation of constants. The bit values are shown for comparison.

```
0xF1      &   0x35          yields 0x31 (hexadecimal)
0361      &   0065          yields 061 (octal)
11110011  &   00110101      yields 00110001 (bitwise)
```

```
0xF1        |   0x35              yields 0xF5 (hexadecimal)
0361        |   0065              yields 0365 (octal)
11110011    |   00110101         yields 11110111 (bitwise)

0xF1        ^   0x35              yields 0xC4 (hexadecimal)
0361        ^   0065              yields 0304 (octal)
11110011    ^   00110101         yields 00000000 11000110 (bitwise)

~0xF1                            yields 0xFF0E (hexadecimal)
~0361                            yields 0177416 (octal)
~11110011                       yields 11111111 00001100 (bitwise)
```

Left Shift and Right Shift

C incorporates two shift operators, the left shift (<<) and the right shift (>>). The left shift moves the bits to the left and sets the rightmost (least significant) bit to zero. The leftmost (most significant) bit shifted out is thrown away.

In terms of unsigned integers, shifting the number one position to the left and filling the LSB with a zero doubles the number's value. The following C++ code segment demonstrates how this would be coded:

```
unsigned int value1 = 65;
value1 <<= 1;
cout << value1;
```

If you were to examine *value1*'s lower byte, you would see the following bit changes performed.

```
<< 0100 0001 ( 65 decimal)
--------------------------
   1000 0010 (130 decimal)
```

The right shift operator moves bits to the right. The lower-order bits shifted out are thrown away. Halving an unsigned integer is as simple as shifting the bits one position to the right, filling the MSB position with a zero. A C-coded example would look very similar to the preceding example except for the compound operator assignment statement (discussed later in the chapter) and the output statement:

```
unsigned int value1 = 10;
value1 >>= 1;
printf("%d",value1);
```

Examining just the lower byte of the variable *value1* would reveal the following bit changes:

```
>> 0000 1010 (10 decimal)
-----------------------
   0000 0101 ( 5 decimal)
```

Increment and Decrement

Adding 1 to or subtracting 1 from a number is so common in programs that C has a special set of operators to do this. They are the *increment* (**++**) and *decrement* (**– –**) *operators*. The two characters must be placed next to each other without any white space. They can be applied only to variables, not to constants. Instead of coding as follows:

```
value1 + 1;
```

you can write

```
value1++;
```

or

```
++value1;
```

When these two operators are the sole operators in an expression, you will not have to worry about the difference between the different syntaxes. A **for** loop very often uses this type of increment for the loop control variable:

```
sum = 0;
for(i = 1; i <= 20; i++)
  sum = sum + i;
```

A decrement loop would be coded as

```
sum = 0;
for(i = 20; i >= 1; i--)
  sum = sum + i;
```

If you use these operators in complex expressions, you have to consider *when* the increment or decrement actually takes place.

The postfix increment, for example *i++*, uses the value of the variable in the expression first and then increments its value. However, the prefix increment—for example, *++I*—increments the value of the variable first and then uses the value in the expression. Assume the following data declarations:

```
int i=3,j,k=0;
```

See if you can figure out what happens in each of the following statements. For simplicity, for each statement assume the original initialized values of the variables:

```
k = ++i;              // i = 4, k = 4
k = i++;              // i = 4, k = 3
k = --i;              // i = 2, k = 2
k = i--;              // i = 2, k = 3
i = j = k--;          // i = 0, j = 0, k = -1
```

While the subtleties of these two different operations may currently elude you, they are included in the C language because of specific situations that cannot be eloquently handled in any other way. In Chapter 10, you will look at a program that uses array indexes that need to be manipulated by using the initially confusing prefix syntax.

Arithmetic Operators

The C language naturally incorporates the standard set of arithmetic operators for addition (+), subtraction (−), multiplication (*), division (/), and modulus (%). The first four are straightforward and need no amplification. However, an example of the modulus operator will help you understand its usage and syntax:

```
int a=3,b=8,c=0,d;

d = b % a;            // returns 2
d = a % b;            // returns 3

d = b % c;            // returns an error message
```

The modulus operator returns the remainder of integer division. The last assignment statement attempts to divide 8 by zero, resulting in an error message.

Assignment Operator

The assignment operator in C is different than the assignment statement in other languages. Assignment is performed by an assignment operator rather than an assignment statement. Like other C operators, the result of an assignment operator is a value that is assigned. An expression with an assignment operator can be used in a large expression such as this:

8 * (value2 = 5);

Here, *value2* is first assigned the value 5. This is multiplied by the 8, with *value1* receiving a final value of 40.

Overuse of the assignment operator can rapidly lead to unmanageable expressions. There are two places in which this feature is normally applied. First, it can be used to set several variables to a particular value, as in the following:

```
value1 = value2 = value3 = 0;
```

The second use is most often seen in the condition of a **while** loop, such as the following:

```
while ((c = getchar( )) != EOF) {
    .
    .
    .
}
```

This assigns the value that getchar( ) returned to *c* and then tests the value against EOF. If it is EOF, the loop is not executed. The parentheses are necessary because the assignment operator has a lower precedence than the **nonequality** operator. Otherwise, the line would be interpreted as

```
c = (getchar( ) != EOF)
```

The variable *c* would be assigned a value of 1 (TRUE) each time **getchar( )** returned EOF.

Compound Assignment Operators

The C language also incorporates an enhancement to the assignment statement used by other languages. This additional set of assignment operators allows for a more concise way of expressing certain computations. The following code segment shows the standard assignment syntax applicable in many high-level languages:

```
irow_index = irow_index + irow_increment;
ddepth = ddepth - d1_fathom;
```

```
fcalculate_tax = fcalculate_tax * 1.07;
fyards = fyards / ifeet_convert;
```

C's compound assignment statements would look like this:

```
irow_index += irow_increment;
ddepth -= d1_fathom;
fcalculate_tax *= 1.07;
fyards /= ifeet_convert;
```

If you look closely at these two code segments, you will quickly see the required syntax. Using a C compound assignment operator requires you to remove the redundant variable reference from the right-hand side of the assignment operator and place the operation to be performed immediately before the =. The bottom of Table 6-4 lists all of the compound assignment operators. Other parts of this table are discussed in the section "Understanding Operator Precedence Levels" later in this chapter.

Relational and Logical Operators

All relational operators are used to establish a relationship between the values of the operands. They always produce a value of !0 if the relationship evaluates to TRUE or a 0 value if the relationship evaluates to FALSE. Following is a list of the C and C++ relational operators:

Operator	Meaning
==	Equality (not assignment)
!=	Not equal
>	Greater than
<	Greater than or equal
<=	Less than or equal

The logical operators AND (&&), OR (| |), and NOT (!) produce a TRUE (!0) or FALSE (zero) based on the logical relationship of their arguments. The simplest way to remember how the logical AND && works is to say that an ANDed expression will only return a TRUE (!0) when both arguments are TRUE (!0). The logical OR | | operation in turn will only return a FALSE (zero) when both arguments are FALSE

Symbol	Name or Meaning	Associates from
++	Post-increment	Left to right
--	Post-decrement	
( )	Function call	
[ ]	Array element	
->	Pointer to structure member	
.	Structure or union member	
++	Pre-increment	Right to left
--	Pre-decrement	
!	Logical NOT	
~	Bitwise NOT	
-	Unary minus	
+	Unary plus	
&	Address	
*	Indirection	
sizeof	Size in bytes	
new	Allocate program memory	
delete	Deallocate program memory	
(type)	type cast [for example, (int) i]	
.*	Pointer to member (objects)	Left to right
->*	Pointer to member (pointers)	
*	Multiply	Left to right
/	Divide	
%	Remainder	
+	Add	Left to right

Table 6-4. *C/C++ Operator Precedence Levels (from Highest to Lowest)*

Symbol	Name or Meaning	Associates from
–	Subtract	
<<	Left shift	Left to right
>>	Right shift	
<	Less than	Left to right
<=	Less than or equal to	
>	Greater than	
>=	Greater than or equal to	
==	Equal	Left to right
!=	Not equal	
&	Bitwise AND	Left to right
^	Bitwise EXCLUSIVE OR	Left to right
|	Bitwise OR	Left to right
&&	Logical AND	Left to right
||	Logical OR	Left to right
? :	Conditional	Right to left
=	Assignment	Right to left
*=, /=, %=, +=, -=, <<=, >>=, &=, ^=, |=	Compound assignment	
,	Comma	Left to right

Table 6-4. *C/C++ Operator Precedence Levels (from Highest to Lowest)* (continued)

(zero). The logical NOT ! simply inverts the value. Following is a list of the C and C++ logical operators:

Operator	Meaning
!	NOT
&&	AND
||	OR

Have some fun with the following C program as you test the various combinations of relational and logical operators. See if you can predict the results ahead of time.

```c
/*
 *   oprs.c
 *   A C program demonstrating some of the subtleties of
 *   logical and relational operators.
 *   Copyright (c) William H. Murray and Chris H. Pappas, 1998
 */

#include <stdio.h>

int main( )
{
  float foperand1, foperand2;

  printf("\nEnter foperand1 and foperand2: " );
  scanf("%f%f",&foperand1,&foperand2);

  printf("\n  foperand1  > foperand2 is %d",
              (foperand1  > foperand2));
  printf("\n  foperand1  < foperand2 is %d",
              (foperand1  < foperand2));
  printf("\n  foperand1 >= foperand2 is %d",
              (foperand1 >= foperand2));
  printf("\n  foperand1 <= foperand2 is %d",
              (foperand1 <= foperand2));
  printf("\n  foperand1 == foperand2 is %d",
              (foperand1 == foperand2));
  printf("\n  foperand1 != foperand2 is %d",
              (foperand1 != foperand2));
  printf("\n  foperand1 && foperand1 is %d",
              (foperand1 && foperand2));
  printf("\n  foperand1 || foperand2 is %d",
              (foperand1 || foperand2));

  return(0);
}
```

You may be surprised at some of the results obtained for some of the logical comparisons. Remember, there is a very strict comparison that occurs for both data types **float** and **double** when values of these types are compared with zero—a number that is very slightly different from another number is still not equal. Also, a number that is just slightly above or below zero is still TRUE (!0).

The C++ equivalent of the program just examined follows:

```
//
//  oprs.cpp
//  A C++ program demonstrating some of the subtleties of
//  logical and relational operators.
//  Copyright (c) William H. Murray and Chris H. Pappas, 1998
//

#include <iostream.h>

int main( )
{
  float foperand1, foperand2;

  cout << "\nEnter foperand1 and foperand2: ";
  cin >> foperand1 >> foperand2;
  cout << "\n";
  cout << "  foperand1  > foperand2 is "
       <<   (foperand1  > foperand2) << "\n";
  cout << "  foperand1  < foperand2 is "
       <<   (foperand1  < foperand2) << "\n";
  cout << "  foperand1 >= foperand2 is "
       <<   (foperand1 >= foperand2) << "\n";
  cout << "  foperand1 <= foperand2 is "
       <<   (foperand1 <= foperand2) << "\n";
  cout << "  foperand1 == foperand2 is "
       <<   (foperand1 == foperand2) << "\n";
  cout << "  foperand1 != foperand2 is "
       <<   (foperand1 != foperand2) << "\n";
  cout << "  foperand1 && foperand1 is "
       <<   (foperand1 && foperand2) << "\n";
  cout << "  foperand1 || foperand2 is "
       <<   (foperand1 || foperand2) << "\n";

  return(0);
}
```

Conditional Operator

You can use the conditional operator (?:) in normal coding, but its main use is for creating macros. The operator has the syntax

```
condition ? true_expression : false-expression
```

If the condition is TRUE, the value of the conditional expression is *true-expression*. Otherwise, it is the value of *false-expression*. For example, look at the following statement:

```
if('A' <= c && c <= 'Z')
  printf("%c",'a' + c - 'A');
else
  printf("%c",c);
```

You could rewrite the statement using the conditional operator:

```
printf("%c",('A' <= c && c <= 'Z') ? ('a' + c - 'A') : c );
```

Both statements will make certain that the character printed, "c," is always lowercase.

Comma Operator

The comma operator (,) evaluates two expressions where the syntax allows only one. The value of the comma operator is the value of the right-hand expression. The format for the expression is

```
left-expression, right-expression
```

One place where the comma operator commonly appears is in a **for** loop, where more than one variable is being iterated. For example:

```
for(min=0,max=length-1; min < max; min++,max--) {
  .
  .
  .
}
```

Understanding Operator Precedence Levels

The order of evaluation of an expression in C is determined by the compiler. This normally does not alter the value of the expression, unless you have written one with side effects. Side effects are those operations that change the value of a variable while yielding a value that is used in the expression, as seen with the increment and decrement operators. The other operators that have side effects are the assignment and compound assignment operators.

Calls to functions that change values of external variables also are subject to side effects. For example:

```
inum1 = 3;
ianswer = (inum1 = 4) + inum1;
```

This could be evaluated in one of two ways: either *inum1* is assigned 4 and *ianswer* is assigned 8 (4+4); or the value of 3 is retrieved from *inum1* and 4 is then assigned to *inum1*, with the result being assigned a 7.

There are, however, four operators for which the order of evaluation is guaranteed to be left to right: logical AND (**&&**), logical OR (**| |**), the comma operator (**,**), and the conditional operator (**?:**). Because of this **default** order of evaluation, you can specify a typical test as follows:

```
while((c=getchar( )) != EOF) && (C!='\n'))
```

The second part of the logical AND (**&&**) is performed after the character value is assigned to *c*.

Table 6-4 lists all of the C and C++ operators from highest precedence to lowest and describes how each operator is associated (left to right or right to left). All operators between lines have the same precedence level. Throughout the book you will be introduced to the various operators and how their precedence level affects their performance.

Standard C and C++ Libraries

Certain calculations are routinely performed in many programs and are written by almost all programmers. Taking the square root of a number is an example of such a calculation. Mathematical procedures for calculating square roots make use of combinations of the basic arithmetic operations of addition, subtraction, multiplication, and division.

It would be a waste of effort if every programmer had to design and code a routine to calculate the square root and then to incorporate that routine into the program. C and C++ resolve difficulties like this by providing you with *libraries* of functions that perform particular common calculations. With the libraries, you need only a single statement to invoke such a function.

This section discusses functions that are commonly provided with the C and C++ compiler. These library functions are usually not provided in source form but in compiled form. When linking is performed, the code for the library functions is combined with the compiled programmer's code to form the complete program.

Library functions not only perform mathematical operations, they also deal with many other commonly encountered operations. For example, there are library functions that deal with reading and writing disk files, managing memory, input/output, and a variety of other operations. Library functions are not part of standard C or C++, but virtually every system provides certain library functions.

Most library functions are designed to use information contained in particular files that are supplied with the system. These files, therefore, must be included when the library functions are used, and are provided with the Visual C/C++ compiler. They usually have the extension .H and are called *header files*. To see the most up-to-date list of header files supplied with your Microsoft Visual C++ Development Studio, route your File Manager over to the \include subdirectory, found nested within the Development Studio subdirectory. Table 6-5 lists many of the more frequently used header files.

Header	Size	Header	Size
ACCCTRL.H	8,711	NDDESEC.H	3,146
ACLAPI.H	14,090	NEW.H	2,509
ACTIVSCP.H	45,596	NSPAPI.H	18,996
ALPHAOPS.H	43,059	NTSDEXTS.H	1,502
ASPTLB.H	17,564	OAIDL.H	197,254
ASSERT.H	1,469	OBJBASE.H	30,028
ATALKWSH.H	4,608	OBJERROR.H	301
BASETYPS.H	8,965	OBJIDL.H	330,903
CDERR.H	2,197	OBJSAFE.H	7,808
CGUID.H	3,497	OCIDL.H	244,528
COLORDLG.H	1,434	ODBCINST.H	15,315
COMCAT.H	32,382	OLE.H	25,650
COMDEF.H	39,062	OLE2.H	12,682
COMIP.H	22,023	OLE2VER.H	664
COMMCTRL.H	131,448	OLEAUTO.H	33,100
COMMDLG.H	28,166	OLECTL.H	20,424
COMPOBJ.H	435	OLECTLID.H	824

Table 6-5. *Header Files Shipped with Visual C++*

Header	Size	Header	Size
COMUTIL.H	43,037	OLEDLG.H	74,489
CONIO.H	3,183	OLEIDL.H	159,627
CPL.H	8,282	OLENLS.H	22,637
CPLEXT.H	2,158	OSTREAM.H	4,908
CRTDBG.H	13,860	PBT.H	1,409
CTL3D.H	2,673	PCRT32.H	1,534
CTYPE.H	12,848	PDH.H	16,235
CUSTCNTL.H	8,537	PDHMSG.H	8,303
CUSTOMAW.H	3,368	PENWIN.H	106,402
D3D.H	18,414	PLAN32.H	915
D3DCAPS.H	13,527	POPPACK.H	1,023
D3DRM.H	5,488	PROCESS.H	9,450
D3DRMDEF.H	14,133	PRSHT.H	12,580
D3DRMOBJ.H	32,372	PSHPACK1.H	911
D3DRMWIN.H	1,180	PSHPACK2.H	911
D3DTYPES.H	31,957	PSHPACK4.H	911
DAOGETRW.H	5,143	PSHPACK8.H	911
DBDAOERR.H	69,776	RAS.H	32,269
DBDAOID.H	11,933	RASDLG.H	6,445
DBDAOINT.H	43,043	RASERROR.H	18,219
DBT.H	10,633	RASSAPI.H	10,573
DDE.H	5,072	RASSHOST.H	4,620
DDEML.H	17,868	RECGUIDS.H	567
DDRAW.H	102,313	RECONCIL.H	5,560
DIGITALV.H	37,699	REGSTR.H	60,127
DIRECT.H	3,595	RICHEDIT.H	29,848

Table 6-5.   *Header Files Shipped with Visual C++ (continued)*

Header	Size	Header	Size
DISPATCH.H	437	RICHOLE.H	6,473
DISPDIB.H	11,161	RPC.H	1,983
DLCAPI.H	33,975	RPCDCE.H	42,018
DLGS.H	5,692	RPCDCEP.H	9,678
DOCOBJ.H	51,721	RPCNDR.H	75,799
DOS.H	4,605	RPCNSI.H	14,654
DPLAY.H	10,913	RPCNSIP.H	1,176
DRIVINIT.H	34	RPCNTERR.H	1,569
DSOUND.H	13,356	RPCPROXY.H	18,105
DVOBJ.H	424	SCODE.H	214
EH.H	2,144	SCRNSAVE.H	8,622
ERRNO.H	2,641	SEARCH.H	2,559
ERROR.H	14,337	SEHMAP.H	557
EXCHEXT.H	30,413	SERVPROV.H	5,953
EXCHFORM.H	1,796	SETJMP.H	8,092
EXCPT.H	3,960	SETJMPEX.H	956
EXDISP.H	10,024	SETUPAPI.H	102,225
EXDISPID.H	1,518	SHARE.H	828
FCNTL.H	2,292	SHELLAPI.H	16,824
FLOAT.H	11,052	SHLGUID.H	4,747
FPIEEE.H	5,260	SHLOBJ.H	94,740
FSTREAM.H	4,619	SIGNAL.H	2,833
FTSIFACE.H	6,789	SMPAB.H	1,233
HLIFACE.H	1,879	SMPMS.H	1,892
HLINK.H	69,266	SMPXP.H	3,778
HTTPEXT.H	7,775	SNMP.H	16,987

Table 6-5. *Header Files Shipped with Visual C++* (continued)

Header	Size	Header	Size
HTTPFILT.H	12,861	SPORDER.H	1,944
IDF.H	12,538	SQL.H	29,810
IDISPIDS.H	430	SQLEXT.H	76,694
IMAGEHLP.H	23,452	SQLTYPES.H	6,621
IME.H	6,939	SQLUCODE.H	22,825
IMESSAGE.H	8,229	STDARG.H	4,730
IMM.H	20,961	STDDEF.H	2,458
INETSDK.H	1,892	STDEXCPT.H	1,935
INITGUID.H	1,442	STDIO.H	13,087
INITOID.H	1,467	STDIOSTR.H	2,082
INTSHCUT.H	15,073	STDLIB.H	19,150
IO.H	7,986	STL.H	6,704
IOMANIP.H	4,408	STORAGE.H	435
IOS.H	9,101	STREAMB.H	5,419
IOSTREAM.H	2,373	STRING.H	9,170
ISGUIDS.H	747	STRSTREA.H	3,074
ISO646.H	419	SVCGUID.H	16,113
ISTREAM.H	6,626	SVRAPI.H	47,005
LARGEINT.H	5,279	TAPI.H	150,246
LIMITS.H	4,133	TCHAR.H	27,828
LM.H	1,284	TIME.H	7,494
LMACCESS.H	40,810	TLHELP32.H	6,068
LMALERT.H	3,738	TNEF.H	14,111
LMAPIBUF.H	1,321	TSPI.H	41,575
LMAT.H	3,576	TYPEINFO.H	2,074
LMAUDIT.H	10,910	UNKNWN.H	9,289

Table 6-5.   *Header Files Shipped with Visual C++* (continued)

Header	Size	Header	Size
LMBROWSR.H	5,967	URLHLINK.H	89
LMCHDEV.H	5,439	URLMON.H	83,404
LMCONFIG.H	1,698	USE_ANSI.H	812
LMCONS.H	7,239	USEOLDIO.H	1,028
LMERR.H	36,393	VARARGS.H	4,675
LMERRLOG.H	38,479	VARIANT.H	435
LMMSG.H	2,125	VCR.H	20,052
LMREMUTL.H	2,921	VDMDBG.H	13,476
LMREPL.H	6,726	VER.H	113
LMSERVER.H	47,741	VFW.H	139,508
LMSHARE.H	10,475	WCHAR.H	24,960
LMSNAME.H	3,065	WCTYPE.H	7,037
LMSTATS.H	5,134	WDBGEXTS.H	13,287
LMSVC.H	13,334	WFEXT.H	6,531
LMUSE.H	3,641	WINBASE.H	154,540
LMUSEFLG.H	676	WINCON.H	14,592
LMWKSTA.H	16,742	WINCRYPT.H	13,176
LOADPERF.H	1,407	WINDEF.H	6,760
LOCALE.H	3,308	WINDOWS.H	4,903
LSAPI.H	11,774	WINDOWSX.H	73,255
LZEXPAND.H	1,679	WINERROR.H	203,050
MALLOC.H	4,429	WINGDI.H	147,629
MAPI.H	11,857	WININET.H	78,807
MAPICODE.H	10,528	WINIOCTL.H	30,511
MAPIDBG.H	24,876	WINNETWK.H	22,739
MAPIDEFS.H	103,616	WINNLS.H	39,651

Table 6-5. *Header Files Shipped with Visual C++ (continued)*

PROGRAMMING
FOUNDATIONS

Header	Size	Header	Size
MAPIFORM.H	28,081	WINNLS32.H	2,125
MAPIGUID.H	11,650	WINNT.H	179,078
MAPIHOOK.H	2,649	WINPERF.H	28,279
MAPINLS.H	6,893	WINREG.H	14,324
MAPIOID.H	2,759	WINRESRC.H	53,424
MAPISPI.H	47,359	WINSOCK.H	33,611
MAPITAGS.H	68,440	WINSOCK2.H	93,959
MAPIUTIL.H	30,573	WINSPOOL.H	52,635
MAPIVAL.H	90,055	WINSVC.H	19,076
MAPIWIN.H	15,665	WINTRUST.H	11,053
MAPIWZ.H	1,977	WINUSER.H	192,575
MAPIX.H	28,494	WINVER.H	9,504
MATH.H	20,528	WINWLX.H	21,983
MBCTYPE.H	4,712	WOWNT16.H	4,380
MBSTRING.H	7,570	WOWNT32.H	9,744
MCIAVI.H	2,989	WPAPI.H	2,731
MCX.H	3,915	WPGUID.H	800
MEMORY.H	2,660	WPOBJ.H	2,038
MGMTAPI.H	5,210	WPSPI.H	8,411
MIDLES.H	5,962	WS2ATM.H	16,643
MINMAX.H	451	WS2SPI.H	18,485
MMREG.H	69,235	WS2TCPIP.H	2,611
MMSYSTEM.H	154,496	WSHISOTP.H	3,355
MONIKER.H	435	WSIPX.H	1,941
MSACM.H	58,508	WSNETBS.H	2,257
MSACMDLG.H	1,029	WSNWLINK.H	9,315

Table 6-5.   *Header Files Shipped with Visual C++* (continued)

Header	Size	Header	Size
MSCONF.H	13,545	WSVNS.H	1,250
MSFS.H	16,926	WSVV.H	1,590
MSPAB.H	2,143	WTYPES.H	29,754
MSPST.H	4,977	XCMC.H	14,014
MSSTKPPG.H	1,191	XCMCEXT.H	2,726
MSWSOCK.H	4,189	XCMCMSX2.H	1,039
MTX.H	19,513	XCMCMSXT.H	1,816
MTXATTR.H	1,522	XLOCINFO.H	3,052
MTXSPM.H	26,216	YMATH.H	1,616
NB30.H	12,693	YVALS.H	2,111
NDDEAPI.H	14,642	ZMOUSE.H	7,305

Table 6-5. *Header Files Shipped with Visual C++* (continued)

In general, different header files are required by different library functions. The header files a function needs will be listed in the description for that function. For example, the sqrt( ) function needs the declarations found in the MATH.H header file. Your *Microsoft Visual C/C++ Run-Time Library Reference* lists all of the library functions and their associated header files.

The following list briefly summarizes the library categories provided by the Visual C/C++ compiler:

Classification routines
Conversion routines
Directory control routines
Diagnostic routines
Graphics routines
Input/output routines
Interface routines (DOS, 8086, BIOS)
Manipulation routines
Math routines
Memory allocation routines
Process control routines

Standard routines
Text window display routines
Time and date routines

Check your reference manual for a detailed explanation of the individual functions provided by each library.

After reading this chapter, you should understand C's basic data types and operators, so it's time to move on to the topic of logic control. Chapter 7 introduces you to C's decision, selection, and iteration control statements.

Chapter 7

Program Control

few tools will need to be added to the toolkit in order to begin writing simple C/C++ programs. This chapter discusses C/C++'s control statements. Many of these control statements are similar to other high-level language controls, such as **if**, **if-else**, and **switch** statements and **for**, **while**, and **do-while** loops. However, there are several new control statements unique to C/C++, such as the **?** (conditional), **break**, and **continue** statements.

The *new* controls, introduced here, typically have no equivalent in the traditional, older high-level languages such as FORTRAN, COBOL, and Pascal. Therefore, beginner C/C++ programmers leave them out of their problem solutions. That is unfortunate for two reasons. First, it means they are not taking advantage of the coding efficiencies provided by these new controls. Second, it immediately flags them as beginners.

Conditional Controls

The C/C++ language supports four basic conditional statements: the **if**, the **if-else**, the conditional **?**, and the **switch**. Before a discussion of the individual conditional statements, however, one general rule needs to be highlighted.

Most of the conditional statements can be used to selectively execute either a single line of code or multiple lines of related code (called a *block*). Whenever a conditional statement is associated with only one line of executable code, braces ({}) are *not* required around the executable statement. However, if the conditional statement is associated with multiple executable statements, braces are required to relate the block of executable statements with the conditional test. For this reason, **switch** statements are required to have an opening and a closing brace.

if

The **if** statement can be used to conditionally execute a segment of code. The simplest form of the **if** statement is

```
if (expression)
    true_action;
```

You will notice that the expression must be enclosed in parentheses. To execute an **if** statement, the expression must evaluate to either TRUE or FALSE. If *expression* is TRUE, *true_action* will be performed and execution will continue on to the next statement following the action. However, if *expression* evaluates to FALSE, *true_action* will *not* be executed, and the statement following *action* will be executed. For example, the following code segment will print the message "Have a great day!" whenever the variable *ioutside_temp* is greater than or equal to 72:

```
if(ioutside_temp >= 72)
  printf("Have a great day!");
```

The syntax for an **if** statement associated with a block of executable statements looks like this:

```
if (expression) {
  true_action1;
true_action2;
true_action3;
true_action4;
}
```

The syntax requires that all of the associated statements be enclosed by a pair of braces ({}) and that each statement within the block must also end with a semicolon (;). Here is an example of a compound **if** statement:

```
/*
 *   if.c
 *   A C program demonstrating an if statement
 *   Copyright (c) Chris H. Pappas and William H. Murray, 1998
 *
 */

#include <stdio.h>

int main( )
{
  int inum_As, inum_Bs, inum_Cs;
  float fGPA;

  printf("\nEnter number of courses receiving a grade of A: ");
  scanf("%d",&inum_As);
  printf("\nEnter number of courses receiving a grade of B: ");
  scanf("%d",&inum_Bs);
  printf("\nEnter number of courses receiving a grade of C: ");
  scanf("%d",&inum_Cs);
  fGPA = (inum_As * 4 + inum_Bs * 3 + inum_Cs * 2)/
         (float) (inum_As + inum_Bs + inum_Cs);
  printf("\nYour overall GPA is: %5.2f\n",fGPA);
```

PROGRAMMING
FOUNDATIONS

```
if(fGPA >= 3.5) {
  printf("\nC O N G R A T U L A T I O N S !\n");
  printf("You are on the President's list.");
}
return(0);
}
```

If *fGPA* is greater than or equal to 3.5, in this example, a congratulatory message is added to the calculated *fGPA*. Regardless of whether the **if** block was entered, the calculated *fGPA* is printed.

if-else

The **if-else** statement allows a program to take two separate actions based on the validity of a particular expression. The simplest syntax for an **if-else** statement looks like this:

```
if (expression)
  true_action;

else
false_action;
```

In this case, if *expression* evaluates to TRUE, *true_action* will be taken; otherwise, when *expression* evaluates to FALSE, *false_action* will be executed. Here is a coded example:

```
if(ckeypressed == UP)
  iy_pixel_coord++;

else
  iy_pixel_coord--;
```

This example takes care of either incrementing or decrementing the current horizontal coordinate location based on the current value stored in the character variable *ckeypressed*.

Of course, either *true_action*, *false_action*, or both could be compound statements, or blocks, requiring braces. The syntax for these three combinations is straightforward:

```
if (expression) {
  true_action1;
  true_action2;
```

```
    true_action3;
  }
else
  false_action;


if (expression)
  true_action;
else {
  false_action1;
  false_action2;
  false_action3;
}


if (expression) {
true_action1;
  true_action2;
  true_action3;
}
else {
  false_action1;
  false_action2;
  false_action3;
}
```

Remember, whenever a block action is being taken, you do not follow the closing brace (}) with a semicolon.

The C program that follows uses an **if-else** statement, with the **if** part being a compound block:

```
/*
 *    cmpif.c
 *    A C program demonstrating the use of a compound
 *    if-else statement.
 *    Copyright (c) Chris H. Pappas and William H. Murray, 1998
 */

#include <stdio.h>

int main( )
```

```
{
  char c;
  int ihow_many,i,imore;

  imore=1;

  while(imore == 1) {
    printf("Please enter the product name: ");
    if(scanf("%c",&c) != EOF) {
      while(c != '\n') {
        printf("%c",c);
        scanf("%c",&c);
      }
      printf("s purchased? ");
      scanf("%d",&ihow_many);
      scanf("%c",&c);

      for(i = 1;i <= ihow_many; i++)
        printf("*");
      printf("\n");
    }
    else
      imore=0;
  }
  return(0);
}
```

This program prompts the user for a product name, and if the user does not enter a ^Z (EOF), the program inputs the product name character by character, echo printing the information to the next line. The "s purchased" string is appended to the product, requesting the number of items sold. Finally, a **for** loop prints out the appropriate number of asterisks (*). Had the user entered a ^Z, the **if** portion of the **if-else** statement would have been ignored and program execution would have picked up with the **else** setting the imore flag to zero, thereby terminating the program.

Nested if-elses

When **if** statements are nested, care must be taken to ensure that you know which **else** action will be matched up with which **if**. Look at the following example and see if you can figure out what will happen:

```
if(iout_side_temp < 50)
if(iout_side_temp < 30) printf("Wear the down jacket!");
else printf("Parka will do.");
```

The listing was purposely misaligned so as not to give you any visual clues as to which statement went with which **if**. The question becomes: What happens if *iout_side_temp* is 55? Does the "Parka will do." message get printed? The answer is no. In this example, the **else** action is associated with the second **if** expression. This is because C matches each **else** with the first unmatched **if**.

To make debugging as simple as possible under such circumstances, the C compiler has been written to associate each **else** with the closest **if** that does not already have an **else** associated with it.

Of course, proper indentation will always help clarify the situation:

```
if(iout_side_temp < 50)
  if(iout_side_temp < 30) printf("Wear the down jacket!");
  else printf("Parka will do.");
```

The same logic can also be represented by the alternate listing that follows:

```
if(iout_side_temp < 50)
  if(iout_side_temp < 30)
    printf("Wear the down jacket!");
  else
    printf("Parka will do.");
```

Each particular application you write will benefit most by one of the two styles, as long as you are consistent throughout the source code.

See if you can figure out this next example:

```
if(test1_expression)
  if(test2_expression)
    test2_true_action;
else
  test1_false_action;
```

You may be thinking this is just another example of what has already been discussed. That's true, but what if you really did want *test1_false_action* to be associated with *test1_expression* and not *test2_expression*? The examples so far have all associated the **else** action with the second, or closest, **if**. (By the way, many a programmer has spent needless time debugging programs of this nature. They're indented to work the way you are logically thinking, as was the preceding example, but unfortunately, the compiler doesn't care about your "pretty printing.")

Correcting this situation requires the use of braces:

```
if(test1_expression) {
   if(test2_expression)
      test2_true_action;
   }
else
   test1_false_action;
```

The problem is solved by making *test2_expression* and its associated *test2_true_action* a block associated with a TRUE evaluation of *test1_expression*. This makes it clear that *test1_false_action* will be associated with the **else** clause of *test1_expression*.

if-else-if

The **if-else-if** statement combination is often used to perform multiple successive comparisons. The general form of this statement looks like this:

```
if(expression1)
   test1_true_action;

else if(expression2)
   test2_true_action;

else if(expression3)
   test3_true_action;
```

Each action, of course, could be a compound block requiring its own set of braces (with the closing brace *not* followed by a semicolon). This type of logical control flow evaluates each expression until it finds one that is TRUE. When this occurs, all remaining test conditions are bypassed. In the preceding example, if none of the expressions evaluated to TRUE, no action would be taken.

Consider the next example and see if you can guess the result:

```
if(expression1)
   test1_true_action;
```

```
else if(expression2)
   test2_true_action;

else if(expression3)
   test3_true_action;

else
   default_action;
```

This differs from the previous example. This **if-else-if** statement combination will always perform some action. If none of the **if** expressions evaluate to TRUE, the **else** *default_action* will be executed. For example, the following program checks the value assigned to *econvert_to* to decide which type of conversion to perform. If the requested *econvert_to* is not one of the ones provided, the code segment prints an appropriate message.

```
if(econvert_to == YARDS)
   fconverted_value = length / 3;

else if(econvert_to == INCHES)
   fconverted_value = length * 12;

else if(econvert_to == CENTIMETERS)
   fconverted_value = length * 12 * 2.54;

else if(econvert_to == METERS)
   fconverted_value = (length * 12 * 2.54)/100;

else
   printf("No conversion required");
```

The ?: Conditional Operator

The conditional statement **?** provides a quick way to write a test condition. Associated actions are performed depending on whether *test_expression* evaluates to TRUE or FALSE. The operator can be used to replace an equivalent **if-else** statement. The syntax for a conditional statement is

```
test_expression ? true_action : false_action;
```

The **?** operator is also sometimes referred to as the ternary operator because it requires three operands. Examine this statement:

```
if(fvalue >= 0.0)
  fvalue = fvalue;
else
  fvalue = -fvalue;
```

You can rewrite the statement using the conditional operator:

```
fvalue=(fvalue >= 0.0) ? fvalue : -fvalue;
```

In this situation, both statements yield the absolute value of *fvalue*. The precedence of the conditional operator is less than that of any of the other operators used in the expression; therefore, no parentheses are required in the example. Nevertheless, parentheses are frequently used to enhance readability.

The following C++ program uses the **?** operator to cleverly format the program's output:

```
//
//  condit.cpp
//  A C++ program using the CONDITIONAL OPERATOR
//  Copyright (c) Chris H. Pappas and William H. Murray, 1998
//

#include <math.h>                          // for abs macro def.
#include <iostream.h>

int main( )
{
  float fbalance, fpayment;

  cout << "Enter your loan balance: ";
  cin  >> fbalance;

  cout << "\nEnter your loan payment amount: ";
  cin  >> fpayment;

  cout << "\n\nYou have ";
  cout << ((fpayment > fbalance) ? "overpaid by $" : "paid $");
  cout << ((fpayment > fbalance) ? abs(fbalance - fpayment)) :
```

```
                                      fpayment);
    cout << " on your loan of $" << fbalance << ".";

    return(0);
}
```

The program uses the first conditional statement inside a **cout** statement to decide which string—"overpaid by $" or "paid $"—is to be printed. The following conditional statement calculates and prints the appropriate dollar value.

```
cout << ((fpayment > fbalance) ? abs(fbalance - fpayment)) :
                                 fpayment);
```

switch-case

It is often the case that you will want to test a variable or an expression against several values. You could use nested **if-else-if** statements to do this, or you could use a **switch** statement. Be very careful, though, because the C **switch** statement has a few peculiarities. The syntax for a **switch** statement is

```
switch (integral_expression) {
 case constant1:
   statements1;
   break;
 case constant2:
   statements2;
   break;
   .
   .
   .
 case constantn:
   statementsn;
   break;
 default: statements;
}
```

The redundant statement you need to pay particular attention to is the **break** statement. In the preceding syntax, if the **break** statement had been removed from *constant1*'s section of code, a match similar to the one used in the preceding paragraph would have left *statements2* as the next statement to be executed. It is the **break** statement that causes the remaining portion of the **switch** statements to be skipped. Let's look at a few examples.

Examine the following **if-else-if** code segment:

```
if(emove == SMALL_CHANGE_UP)
  fycoord =   5;

else if(emove == SMALL_CHANGE_DOWN)
  fycoord =  -5;

else if(emove == LARGE_CHANGE_UP)
  fycoord =  10;

else
  fycoord = -10;
```

This code can be rewritten using a **switch** statement:

```
switch(emove) {
  case  SMALL_CHANGE_UP:
    fycoord =   5;
    break;
  case  SMALL_CHANGE_DOWN:
    fycoord =  -5;
    break;
  case  LARGE_CHANGE_UP:
    fycoord =  10;
    break;
  default:
    fycoord = -10;
}
```

The value of *emove*, in this example, is consecutively compared to each **case** value looking for a match. When one is found, *fycoord* is assigned the appropriate value. Then the break statement is executed, skipping over the remainder of the **switch** statements. However, if no match is found, the default assignment is performed (fycoord = –10). Since this is the last option in the **switch** statement, there is no need to include a **break**. A **switch** default is optional.

Proper placement of the **break** statement within a **switch** statement can be very useful. Look at the following example:

```
/*
 *    switch.c
 *    A C program demonstrating the
```

```
 *   drop-through capabilities of the switch statement.
 *   Copyright (c) Chris H. Pappas and William H. Murray, 1998
 */

int main( )
{
  char c='a';
  int ivowelct=0, iconstantct=0;

  switch(c) {
    case 'a':
    case 'A':
    case 'e':
    case 'E':
    case 'i':
    case 'I':
    case 'o':
    case 'O':
    case 'u':
    case 'U': ivowelct++;
              break;
    default : iconstantct++;
  }
  return(0);
}
```

This program actually illustrates two characteristics of the **switch** statement: the enumeration of several test values that all execute the same code section and the drop-through characteristic.

Other high-level languages have their own form of selection (the **case** statement in Pascal and the **select** statement in PL/I), which allows for several test values, all producing the same result, to be included on the same selection line. C and C++, however, require a separate **case** for each. But notice in this example how the same effect has been created by not inserting a break statement until all possible vowels have been checked. Should c contain a constant, all of the vowel case tests will be checked and skipped until the **default** statement is reached.

The next example shows a C program that uses a **switch** statement to invoke the appropriate function:

```
/*
 *   fnswth.c
 *   A C program demonstrating the switch statement
```

```
*     Copyright (c) Chris H. Pappas and William H. Murray, 1998
*/

#include <stdio.h>

#define QUIT 0
#define BLANK ' '

double fadd(float fx,float fy);
double fsub(float fx,float fy);
double fmul(float fx,float fy);
double fdiv(float fx,float fy);

int main( )
{
  float fx,fy;
  char cblank, coperator = BLANK;

  while (coperator != QUIT) {
    printf("\nPlease enter an expression (a (operator) b): ");
    scanf("%f%c%c%f", &fx, &cblank, &coperator, &fy);

    switch (coperator) {
      case '+': printf("answer = %8.2f\n", fadd(fx,fy));
                break;
      case '-': printf("answer = %8.2f\n", fsub(fx,fy));
                break;
      case '*': printf("answer = %8.2f\n", fmul(fx,fy));
                break;
      case '/': printf("answer = %8.2f\n", fdiv(fx,fy));
                break;
      case 'x': coperator = QUIT;
                break;
      default : printf("\nOperator not implemented");
    }
  }
  return(0);
}

double fadd(float fx,float fy)
  {return(fx + fy);}
```

```
double fsub(float fx,float fy)
  {return(fx - fy);}

double fmul(float fx,float fy)
  {return(fx * fy);}

double fdiv(float fx,float fy)
  {return(fx / fy);}
```

While the use of functions in this example is a bit advanced (functions are discussed in detail in Chapter 8), the use of the **switch** statement is very effective. After the user has entered an expression such as 10 + 10 or 23 * 15, the *coperator* is compared in the body of the **switch** statement to determine which function to invoke. Of particular interest is the last set of statements, where the *coperator* equals *x*, and the **default** statement.

When the user enters an expression with an *x* operator, the *coperator* variable is assigned a QUIT value, and the **break** statement is executed, skipping over the default printf( ) statement. However, if the user enters an unrecognized operator—for example, %—only the **default** statement is executed, printing the message that the *coperator* has not been implemented.

The following C++ program illustrates the similarity in syntax between a C **switch** statement and its C++ counterpart:

```
//
//   calndr.cpp
//   A C++ program using a switch statement
//   to print a yearly calendar.
//   Copyright (c) Chris H. Pappas and William H. Murray, 1998
//

#include <iostream.h>

int main( )
{
  int jan_1_start_day,num_days_per_month,
      month,date,leap_year_flag;

  cout << "Please enter January 1's starting day;\n";
  cout << "\nA 0 indicates January 1 is on a Monday,";
  cout << "\nA 1 indicates January 1 is on a Tuesday, etc: ";
  cin >> jan_1_start_day;
```

```
cout << "\nEnter the year you want the calendar generated: ";
cin >> leap_year_flag;
cout << "\n\n The calendar for the year " << leap_year_flag;

leap_year_flag=leap_year_flag % 4;
cout.width(20);

for (month = 1;month <= 12;month++) {
  switch(month) {
    case 1:
      cout << "\n\n\n" << " January" << "\n";
      num_days_per_month = 31;
      break;
    case 2:
      cout << "\n\n\n" << " February" << "\n";
      num_days_per_month = leap_year_flag ? 28 : 29;
      break;
    case 3:
      cout << "\n\n\n" << "  March " << "\n";
      num_days_per_month = 31;
      break;
    case 4:
      cout << "\n\n\n" << "  April " << "\n";
      num_days_per_month = 30;
      break;
    case 5:
      cout << "\n\n\n" << "   May  " << "\n";
      num_days_per_month = 31;
      break;
    case 6:
      cout << "\n\n\n" << "  June  " << "\n";
      num_days_per_month = 30;
      break;
    case 7:
      cout << "\n\n\n" << "  July  " << "\n";
      num_days_per_month = 31;
      break;
    case 8:
      cout << "\n\n\n" << " August " << "\n";
      num_days_per_month = 31;
      break;
    case 9:
```

```
      cout << "\n\n\n" << "September" << "\n";
      num_days_per_month = 30;
      break;
    case 10:
      cout << "\n\n\n" << " October " << "\n";
      num_days_per_month = 31;
      break;
    case 11:
      cout << "\n\n\n" << "November " << "\n";
      num_days_per_month = 30;
      break;
    case 12:
      cout << "\n\n\n" << "December " << "\n";
      num_days_per_month = 31;
      break;
  }

  cout.width(0);
  cout << "\nSun  Mon  Tue  Wed  Thu  Fri  Sat\n";
  cout << "---  ---  ---  ---  ---  ---  ---\n";

  for ( date = 1; date <= 1 + jan_1_start_day * 5; date++ )
    cout <<  " ";

  for ( date = 1; date <= num_days_per_month; date++ ) {
    cout.width;
    cout << date;
    if ( ( date + jan_1_start_day ) % 7 > 0 )
      cout <<  "   ";
    else
      cout <<  "\n ";
  }
  jan_1_start_day=(jan_1_start_day + num_days_per_month) % 7;
  }
  return(0);
}
```

This application starts by asking the user to enter an integer code representing the day of the week on which January 1st occurs (zero for Monday, 1 for Tuesday, and so on). The second prompt asks for the year for the calendar. The program can now print the calendar heading, and use the year entered to generate a *leap_year_flag*. Using the modulus operator (%) with a value of 4 generates a remainder of zero whenever it is leap year and a nonzero value whenever it is not leap year.

Next, a 12-iteration loop is entered, printing the current month's name and assigning *num_days_per_month* the correct number of days for that particular month. All of this is accomplished by using a **switch** statement to test the current *month* integer value.

Outside the **switch** statement, after the month's name has been printed, day-of-the-week headings are printed and an appropriate number of blank columns is skipped, depending on when the first day of the month was.

The last **for** loop actually generates and prints the dates for each month. The last statement in the program prepares the *day_code* for the next month to be printed.

Combining if-else-if and switch

The next example application uses an enumerated type (enum) to perform the requested length conversions:

```c
/*
*   ifelsw.c
*   A C program demonstrating the if-else-if statement
*   used in a meaningful way with several switch statements.
*   Copyright (c) Chris H. Pappas and William H. Murray, 1998
*/

typedef enum conversion_type {YARDS, INCHES, CENTIMETERS, \
                              METERS} C_TYPE;
#include <stdio.h>

int main( )
{
  int iuser_response;
  C_TYPE C_Tconversion;
  int ilength=30;
  float fmeasurement;

  printf("\nPlease enter the measurement to be converted : ");
  scanf("%f",&fmeasurement);

  printf("\nPlease enter :          \
          \n\t\t 0 for YARDS        \
          \n\t\t 1 for INCHES       \
          \n\t\t 2 for CENTIMETERS  \
```

```
        \n\t\t 3 for METERS          \
        \n\n\t\tYour response -->> ");

scanf("%d",&iuser_response);

switch(iuser_response) {
  case 0  :  C_Tconversion = YARDS;
             break;
  case 1  :  C_Tconversion = INCHES;
             break;
  case 2  :  C_Tconversion = CENTIMETERS;
             break;
  default :  C_Tconversion = METERS;
}


if(C_Tconversion == YARDS)
  fmeasurement = ilength / 3;

else if(C_Tconversion == INCHES)
  fmeasurement = ilength * 12;

else if(C_Tconversion == CENTIMETERS)
  fmeasurement = ilength * 12 * 2.54;

else if(C_Tconversion == METERS)
  fmeasurement = (ilength * 12 * 2.54)/100;

else
  printf("No conversion required");


switch(C_Tconversion) {
  case YARDS       : printf("\n\t\t  %4.2f yards",
                            fmeasurement);
                     break;
  case INCHES      : printf("\n\t\t  %4.2f inches",
                            fmeasurement);
                     break;
  case CENTIMETERS : printf("\n\t\t  %4.2f centimeters",
                            fmeasurement);
                     break;
```

```
   default          : printf("\n\t\t  %4.2f meters",
                               fmeasurement);
   }

   return(0);
}
```

This application uses an enumerated type to perform the specified length conversion. In standard C, enumerated types exist only within the code itself (for reasons of readability) and cannot be input or output directly. The program uses the first **switch** statement to convert the input code to its appropriate *C_Tconversion* type. The nested **if-else-if** statements perform the proper conversion. The last **switch** statement prints the converted value with its appropriate "literal" type. Of course, the nested **if-else-if** statements could have been implemented by using a **switch** statement. (A further discussion of enumerated types can be found in Chapter 12.)

Loop Controls

The C and C++ language include the standard set of repetition control statements: **for** loops, **while** loops, and **do-while** loops (called repeat-until loops in several other high-level languages). You may be surprised, however, by the ways a program can leave a repetition loop. C and C++ provide four methods for altering the repetitions in a loop. All repetition loops can naturally terminate based on the expressed test condition. In C and C++, however, a repetition loop can also terminate because of an anticipated error condition by using either a **break** or **exit** statement. Repetition loops can also have their logic control flow altered by a **break** statement or a **continue** statement.

The basic difference between a **for** loop and a **while** or **do-while** loop has to do with the "known" number of repetitions. Typically, **for** loops are used whenever there is a definite predefined required number of repetitions, and **while** and **do-while** loops are reserved for an "unknown" number of repetitions.

for

The syntax for a **for** loop is

```
for(initialization_exp; test_exp; increment_exp)
statement;
```

When the **for** loop statement is encountered, the *initialization_exp* is executed first. This is done at the start of the loop, and it is never executed again. Usually, this statement involves the initialization of the loop control variable. Following this, *test_exp*, which is called the *loop terminating condition*, is tested. Whenever *test_exp* evaluates to TRUE, the statement or statements within the loop are executed. If the loop was entered, then after all of the statements within the loop are executed, *increment_exp* is executed. However, if *test_exp* evaluates to FALSE, the statement or statements within the loop are ignored, along with *increment_exp*, and execution continues with the statement following the end of the loop. The indentation scheme applied to **for** loops with several statements to be repeated looks like this:

```
for(initialization_exp; test_exp; increment_exp) {
statement_a;
statement_b;
statement_c;
statement_n;
}
```

In the case where several statements need to be executed, a pair of braces is required to tie their execution to the loop control structure. Let's examine a few examples of **for** loops.

The following example sums up the first five integers. It assumes that *isum* and *ivalue* have been predefined as integers:

```
isum = 0;
for(ivalue=1; ivalue <= 5; ivalue++)
  isum += ivalue;
```

After *isum* has been initialized to zero, the **for** loop is encountered. First, *ivalue* is initialized to 1 (this is done only once); second, *ivalue*'s value is checked against the loop terminating condition, <= 5. Since this is TRUE, a 1 is added to *isum*. Once the statement is executed, the loop control variable (*ivalue*) is incremented by 1. This process continues four more times until *ivalue* is incremented to 6 and the loop terminates.

In C++, the same code segment could be written as follows. See if you can detect the subtle difference:

```
for(int ivalue=1; ivalue <= 5; ivalue++)
  isum += ivalue;
```

C++ allows the loop control variable to be declared and initialized within the **for** loop. This brings up a very sensitive issue among structured programmers, which is the proper placement of variable declarations. In C++, you can declare variables right before the statement that actually uses them. In the preceding example, since *ivalue* is

PROGRAMMING FOUNDATIONS

used only to generate an *isum*, with *isum* having a larger scope than *ivalue*, the local declaration for *ivalue* is harmless. However, look at the following code segment:

```
int isum = 0;
for(int ivalue=1; ivalue <= 5; ivalue++)
  isum += ivalue;
```

This would obscure the visual "desk check" of the variable *isum* because it was not declared below the function head. For the sake of structured design and debugging, it is best to localize all variable declarations. It is the rare code segment that can justify the usefulness of moving a variable declaration to a nonstandard place, in sacrifice of easily read, easily checked, and easily modified code.

The value used to increment **for** loop control variables does not always have to be 1 or ++. The following example sums all the odd numbers up to 9:

```
iodd_sum = 0;
for(iodd_value=1; iodd_value <= 9; iodd_value+=2);
  iodd_sum += iodd_value;
```

In this example, the loop control variable *iodd_value* is initialized to 1 and is incremented by 2.

Another unique feature is that **for** loops don't always have to go from a smaller value to a larger one. The following example uses a **for** loop to read into an array of characters and then print the character string backward:

```
//
// forlp.cpp
// A C++ program that uses a for loop to input a character array
// Copyright (c) Chris H. Pappas and William H. Murray, 1998
//

#include <stdio.h>

#define CARRAY_SIZE 10

int main( )
{
  int ioffset;
  char carray[CARRAY_SIZE];
```

```
for(ioffset = 0; ioffset < CARRAY_SIZE; ioffset++)
  carray[ioffset] = getchar( );
for(ioffset = CARRAY_SIZE - 1; ioffset >= 0; ioffset--)
  putchar(carray[ioffset]);

return(0);
}
```

In this application, the first **for** loop initialized *ioffset* to zero (necessary since all array indexes are offsets from the starting address of the first array element), and while there is room in *carray*, reads characters in one at a time. The second **for** loop initializes the loop control variable *ioffset* to the offset of the last element in the array and, while *ioffset* contains a valid offset, prints the characters in reverse order. This process could be used to parse an infix expression that was being converted to prefix notation.

When combining or nesting **for** loops, as in the next example, take care to include the appropriate braces to make certain the statements execute properly:

```
/*
 *    nslop1.c
 *    A C program demonstrating
 *    the need for caution when nesting for loops.
 *    Copyright (c) Chris H. Pappas and William H. Murray, 1998
 */

#include <stdio.h>

int main( )
{
  int iouter_val, iinner_val;

  for(iouter_val = 1; iouter_val <= 4; iouter_val++) {
    printf("\n%3d --",iouter_val);
    for(iinner_val = 1; iinner_val <= 5; iinner_val++ )
      printf("%3d",iouter_val * iinner_val);
  }

  return(0);
}
```

The output produced by this program looks like this:

```
1 --   1  2  3  4  5
2 --   2  4  6  8 10
3 --   3  6  9 12 15
4 --   4  8 12 16 20
```

However, suppose the outer **for** loop had been written without the braces, like this:

```
/*
 *    nslop2.c
 *    A C program demonstrating what happens when you nest
 *    for loops without the logically required braces {}.
 *    Copyright (c) Chris H. Pappas and William H. Murray, 1998
 */

#include <stdio.h>

int main( )
{
  int iouter_val, iinner_val;

 for(iouter_val = 1; iouter_val <= 4; iouter_val++)
   printf("\n%3d --",iouter_val);
   for(iinner_val = 1; iinner_val <= 5; iinner_val++ )
     printf("%3d",iouter_val * iinner_val);

  return(0);
}
```

The output now looks quite different:

```
1 --
2 --
3 --
4 --   5 10 15 20 25
```

Without the braces surrounding the first **for** loop, only the first **printf( )** statement is associated with the loop. Once the **printf( )** statement is executed four times, the second **for** loop is entered. The inner loop uses the last value stored in *iouter_val*, or 5, to generate the values printed by its **printf( )** statement.

The need to include or not include braces can be a tricky matter at best that needs to be approached with some thought to readability. Look at the next two examples and see if you can figure out if they would produce the same output.

Here is the first application:

```
/*
 *   lpdmo1.c
 *   Another C program demonstrating the need
 *   for caution when nesting for loops.
 *   Copyright (c) Chris H. Pappas and William H. Murray, 1998
 */

#include <stdio.h>

int main( )
{
  int iouter_val, iinner_val;

  for(iouter_val = 1; iouter_val <= 4; iouter_val++) {
    for(iinner_val = 1; iinner_val <= 5; iinner_val++ )
      printf("%d ",iouter_val * iinner_val);
  }

  return(0);
}
```

Compare the preceding program with the following example:

```
/*
 *   lpdmo2.c
 *   A comparison C program demonstrating the need
 *   for caution when nesting for loops.
 *   Copyright (c) Chris H. Pappas and William H. Murray, 1998
 */

#include <stdio.h>

int main( )
{
  int iouter_val, iinner_val;

  for(iouter_val = 1; iouter_val <= 4; iouter_val++)
```

```
    for(iinner_val = 1; iinner_val <= 5; iinner_val++ )
      printf("%d ",iouter_val * iinner_val);

  return(0);
}
```

Both programs produce the identical output:

```
1 2 3 4 5 2 4 6 8 10 3 6 9 12 15 4 8 12 16 20
```

In these last two examples, the only statement associated with the outer **for** loop is the inner **for** loop. The inner **for** loop is considered a single statement. This would still be the case even if the inner **for** loop had multiple statements to execute. Since braces are needed only around code blocks or multiple statements, the outer **for** loop does not need braces to execute the program properly.

while

The C and C++ **while** loop is a *pretest loop* just like the **for** loop. This means that the program evaluates *test_exp* before entering the statement or statements within the body of the loop. Because of this, pretest loops may be executed from zero to many times. The syntax for a C **while** loop is

```
while(test_exp)
  statement;
```

For **while** loops with several statements, braces are needed:

```
while(test_exp) {
  statement1;
  statement2;
  statement3;
  statementn;
}
```

Typically, **while** loop control structures are used whenever an indefinite number of repetitions is expected. The following C program uses a **while** loop to control the number of times *ivalue* is shifted to the right. The program prints the binary representation of a signed integer.

```c
/*
 *   while.c
 *   A C program using a pretest while loop with flag
 *   Copyright (c) Chris H. Pappas and William H. Murray, 1998
 */

#include <stdio.h>

#define WORD 16
#define ONE_BYTE 8

int main( )
{
  int ivalue = 256, ibit_position=1;
  unsigned int umask = 1;

  printf("The following value %d,\n",ivalue);
  printf("in binary form looks like: ");

  while(ibit_position <= WORD) {
    if((ivalue >> (WORD - ibit_position)) & umask) /*shift each*/
      printf("1");                                 /*bit to 0th*/
    else                                           /*position &*/
      printf("0");                                 /*compare to*/
    if(ibit_position == ONE_BYTE)                  /*umask     */
      printf(" ");
    ibit_position++;
  }

  return(0);
}
```

This application begins by defining two constants, *WORD* and *ONE_BYTE*, that can be easily modified for different architectures. *WORD* will be used as a flag to determine when the **while** loop will terminate. Within the **while** loop, *ivalue* is shifted, compared to *umask*, and printed from most significant bit to least. This allows the algorithm to use a simple **printf( )** statement to output the results.

In the next example, the application prompts the user for an input filename and an output filename. The program then uses a **while** loop to read in and echo print the input file of unknown size.

```c
/*
 *   dowhile.c
 *   A C program using a while loop to echo print a file
 *   The program demonstrates additional file I/O techniques
 *   Copyright (c) Chris H. Pappas and William H. Murray, 1998
 */

#include <stdio.h>
#include <process.h>

#define sz_TERMINATOR 1          /* sz, null-string designator */
#define MAX_CHARS 30

int main( )
{
  int c;
  FILE *ifile, *ofile;
  char sziDOS_file_name[MAX_CHARS + sz_TERMINATOR],
       szoDOS_file_name[MAX_CHARS + sz_TERMINATOR];

  fputs("Enter the input file's name: ",stdout);
  gets(sziDOS_file_name);

  if((ifile=fopen(sziDOS_file_name,"r")) == NULL) {
    printf("\nFile: %s cannot be opened",sziDOS_file_name);
    exit;
  }

  fputs("Enter the output file's name: ",stdout);
  gets(szoDOS_file_name);

  if((ofile=fopen(szoDOS_file_name,"w")) == NULL) {
    printf("\nFile: %s cannot be opened",szoDOS_file_name);
    exit;
  }
  while(!feof(ifile)) {
    c=fgetc(ifile);
    fputc(c,ofile);
```

```
    }

    return(0);
}
```

Here, the **while** loop contains two executable statements, so the brace pair is required. The program also illustrates the use of several file I/O statements like **fgetc( )** and **fputc( )**, along with **feof( )** (discussed in Chapter 11).

do-while

The **do-while** loop differs from the **for** and **while** loops. The **do-while** loop is a *post-test loop*. In other words, the loop is always entered at least once, with the loop condition being tested at the end of the first iteration. In contrast, **for** loops and **while** loops may execute from zero to many times, depending on the loop control variable. Since **do-while** loops always execute at least one time, they are best used whenever there is no doubt you want the particular loop entered. For example, if your program needs to present a menu to the user, even if all the user wants to do is immediately quit the program, he or she needs to see the menu to know which key terminates the application.

The syntax for a **do-while** loop is

```
do
  action;
while(test_condition);
```

Braces are required for **do-while** statements that have compound actions:

```
do {
  action1;
  action2;
  action3;
  actionn;
} while(test_condition);
```

The following application uses a **do-while** loop to calculate some statistics for a user-entered sentence:

```
//
//  dowhile.cpp
//  A C++ program demonstrating the usefulness of a
```

```
//  do-while loop to process user-defined sentence.
//  Copyright (c) Chris H. Pappas and William H. Murray, 1998
//

#include <iostream.h>

#define LENGTH 80
#define NULL_TERM 1


int main( )
{
  const int LENGTH 80;
  char cSentence[LENGTH + NULL_TERM];
  int iNumChars = 0, iNumWords = 1;

  do {
    cout << "Please enter your sentence : ";
    cin.getline(cSentence,LENGTH);
  } while (cSentence[0] == '\0';

  while (cSentence[iNumChars] != '\0') {
    if (cSentence[iNumChars] == ' ')
      iNumWords++;
    iNumChars++;
  }

  cout << "You entered " << iNumChars << " characters\n";
  cout << "You entered " << iNumWords << " words";

  return (0);
}
```

The **do-while** loop in this program repeats the prompt and input statements for the user-requested sentence until the user enters at least one character. Simply pressing the ENTER key causes the getline( ) function to store the null character in the first array element position, repeating the loop. Once the user enters the sentence, the program jumps out of the **do-while** loop printing the calculated statistics.

break

The **break** statement can be used to exit a loop before the test condition becomes FALSE. The **break** statement is similar in many ways to a **goto** statement, only the point jumped to is not known directly. When breaking out of a loop, program execution continues with the next statement following the loop itself. Look at this simple application:

```
/*
 *    break.c
 *    A C program demonstrating the use of the break statement.
 *    Copyright (c) Chris H. Pappas and William H. Murray, 1998
 */

int main( )
{
  int itimes = 1, isum = 0;

  while(itimes < 10){
    isum += isum + itimes;
    if(isum > 20)
      break;
    itimes++;
  }

  return(0);
}
```

Debugger Trace

Use the integrated debugger to trace through the preceding program. Trace the variables *isum* and *itimes*. Pay particular attention to which statements are executed after *isum* reaches the value 21. What you should have noticed is that when *isum* reached the value 21, the **break** statement was executed. This caused the increment of *itimes* to be jumped over, *itimes++*, with program execution continuing on the line of code below the loop. In this example, the next statement executed was the return.

continue

There is a subtle difference between the **break** statement and the **continue** statement. As you have already seen from the last example program, **break** causes the loop to terminate execution altogether. In contrast, the **continue** statement causes all of the statements following the **continue** statement to be ignored but does *not* circumvent incrementing the loop control variable or the loop control test condition. In other words, if the loop control variable still satisfies the loop test condition, the loop will continue to iterate.

The following program demonstrates this concept, using a number guessing game:

```c
/*
 *    contnu.c
 *    A C program demonstrating the use of the continue
 *    statement.
 *    Copyright (c) Chris H. Pappas and William H. Murray, 1998
 */

#include <stdio.h>

#define TRUE 1
#define FALSE 0

int main( )
{
  int ilucky_number=77,
      iinput_val,
      inumber_of_tries=0,
      iam_lucky=FALSE;

  while(!iam_lucky){
    printf("Please enter your lucky guess: ");
    scanf("%d",&iinput_val);
    inumber_of_tries++;
    if(iinput_val == ilucky_number)
      iam_lucky=TRUE;
    else
      continue;
    printf("It only took you %d tries to get lucky!",
      inumber_of_tries);
  }

  return(0);
}
```

Debugger Trace

As an exercise, enter the preceding program and trace the variables *iinput_val*, *inumber_of_tries*, and *iam_lucky*. Pay particular attention to which statements are executed after *iinput_val* is compared to *ilucky_number*.

The program uses a **while** loop to prompt the user for a value, increments the *inumber_of_tries* for each guess entered, and then determines the appropriate action to take based on the success of the match. If no match was found, the **else** statement is executed. This is the **continue** statement. Whenever the **continue** statement is executed, the **printf( )** statement is ignored. Note, however, that the loop continues to execute. When *iinput_val* matches *ilucky_number*, the *iam_lucky* flag is set to TRUE and the **continue** statement is ignored, allowing the **printf( )** statement to execute.

Combining break and continue

The **break** and **continue** statements can be combined to solve some interesting program problems. Look at the following C++ example:

```
//
// bracntg.cpp
// A C++ program demonstrating the usefulness of combining
// the break and continue statements.
// Copyright (c) Chris H. Pappas and William H. Murray, 1998
//

#include <iostream.h>
#include <ctype.h>

#define NEWLINE '\n'

int main( )
{
  int c;

  while((c=getchar( )) != EOF)
  {
    if(isascii(c) == 0) {
      cout << "Not an ASCII character; ";
      cout << "not going to continue/n";
      break;
    }
```

```
    if(ispunct(c) || isspace(c)) {
      putchar(NEWLINE);
      continue;
    }

    if(isprint(c) == 0) {
      c = getchar( );
      continue;
    }

    putchar(c);
  }

  return(0);
}
```

Before seeing how the program functions, take a look at the input to the program:

```
word control ^B exclamation! apostrophe' period.
^Z
```

Also examine the output produced:

```
word
control
B
exclamation

apostrophe

period
```

This application continues to read character input until the EOF character ^Z is typed. It then examines the input, removing any nonprintable characters, and places each "word" on its own line. It accomplishes all of this by using some very interesting functions defined in CTYPE.H, including isascii( ), ispunct( ), isspace( ), and isprint( ). Each of the functions is passed a character parameter and returns either a zero or some other value indicating the result of the comparison.

The function isascii( ) indicates whether the character passed falls into the acceptable ASCII value range, ispunct( ) indicates whether the character is a punctuation mark, isspace( ) indicates whether the character is a space, and function isprint( ) reports whether the character parameter is a printable character.

By using these functions, the application determines whether to continue the program at all and, if it is to continue, what it should do with each of the characters input.

The first test within the **while** loop evaluates whether the file is even in readable form. For example, the input data could have been saved in binary format, rendering the program useless. If this is the case, the associated **if** statements are executed, printing a warning message and breaking out of the **while** loop permanently.

If no errors are encountered, the second **if** statement is encountered; it checks whether the character input is either a punctuation mark or a blank space. If either of these conditions is TRUE, the associated **if** statements are executed. This causes a blank line to be skipped in the output and executes the **continue** statement. The **continue** statement efficiently jumps over the remaining test condition and output statement but does not terminate the loop. It merely indicates that the character's form has been diagnosed properly and that it is time to obtain a new character.

The third **if** statement asks whether the character is printable or not, but only if the file is in an acceptable format and the character input is not punctuation or a blank. This test takes care of any control codes. Notice that the example input to the program included a control ^B. Since ^B is not printable, this **if** statement immediately obtains a new character and then executes a **continue** statement. In like manner, this **continue** statement indicates that the character in question has been diagnosed, the proper action has been taken, and it is time to get another character. The **continue** statement also causes the **putchar( )** statement to be ignored while *not* terminating the **while** loop.

exit( )

Under some circumstances, it is possible for a program to terminate long before all of the statements in the program have been examined and/or executed. For these specific circumstances, C incorporates the exit( ) library function. The function exit( ) expects one integer argument, called a *status value*. The UNIX and MS-DOS operating systems interpret a status value of zero as signaling a normal program termination, while any nonzero status values signify different kinds of errors.

The particular status value passed to exit( ) can be used by the process that invoked the program to take some action. For example, if the program were invoked from the command line and the status value indicated some type of error, the operating system might display a message. In addition to terminating the program, exit( ) writes all output waiting to be written and closes all open files.

The following application averages a list of up to 30 grades. The program will exit if the user requests to average more than *SIZE* number of integers.

```
//
//  exit1.cpp
```

PROGRAMMING
FOUNDATIONS

```cpp
//  A C++ program demonstrating the use of the exit function
//  Copyright (c) Chris H. Pappas and William H. Murray, 1998
//

#include <iostream.h>
#include <process.h>

#define LIMIT 30

int main( )
{
  int irow,irequested_qty,iscores[LIMIT];
  float fsum=0,imax_score=0,imin_score=100,faverage;

  cout << "\nEnter the number of scores to be averaged: ";
  cin >>  irequested_qty;
  if(irequested_qty > LIMIT) {
    cout << "\nYou can only enter up to " << LIMIT << \
            " scores" << " to be averaged.\n";
    cout << "\n         >>> Program was exited. <<<\n";
    exit;
  }

  for(irow = 0; irow < irequested_qty; irow++) {
    cout << "\nPlease enter a grade " << irow+1 << ":   ";
    cin >> iscores[irow];
  }

  for(irow = 0; irow < irequested_qty; irow++)
    fsum = fsum + iscores[irow];

  faverage = fsum/(float)irequested_qty;

  for(irow = 0; irow < irequested_qty; irow++) {
    if(iscores[irow] > imax_score)
      imax_score = iscores[irow];
    if(iscores[irow] < imin_score)
      imin_score = iscores[irow];
  }

  cout << "\nThe maximum grade is " << imax_score;
  cout << "\nThe minimum grade is " << imin_score;
```

```
   cout << "\nThe average grade is " << faverage;

   return(0);
}
```

The application starts by including the PROCESS.H header file. Either PROCESS.H or STDLIB.H can be included to prototype the function exit( ). The constant *LIMIT* is declared to be 30 and is used to dimension the array of integers, *iscores*. After the remaining variables are declared, the program prompts the user for the number of *iscores* to be entered. For this program, the user's response is to be typed next to the prompt.

The application inputs the requested value into the variable *irequested_qty* and uses this for the **if** comparison. When the user wants to average more numbers than will fit in *iscores*, the two warning messages are printed and then the **exit( )** statement is executed. This terminates the program altogether.

Examine the following listing and see if you can detect the two subtle differences between the preceding program and this one:

```
//
//   exit2.cpp
//   A C++ program demonstrating the use of the exit function
//   in relation to the difference between the process.h
//   and stdlib.h header files.
//   Copyright (c) Chris H. Pappas and William H. Murray, 1998
//

#include <iostream.h>
#include <stdlib.h>

#define LIMIT 30

int main( )
{
  int irow,irequested_qty,iscores[LIMIT];
  float fsum=0,imax_score=0,imin_score=100,faverage;

  cout << "\nEnter the number of scores to be averaged: ";
  cin >> irequested_qty;
  if(irequested_qty > LIMIT) {
    cout << "\nYou can only enter up to " << LIMIT << \
            " scores" << " to be faveraged.\n";
    cout << "\n         >>> Program was exited. <<<\n";
```

```
      exit(EXIT_FAILURE);
  }

  for(irow = 0; irow < irequested_qty; irow++) {
    cout << "\nPlease enter a grade " << irow+1 << ":   ";
    cin >> iscores[irow];
  }

  for(irow = 0; irow < irequested_qty; irow++)
    fsum = fsum + iscores[irow];

  faverage = fsum/(float)irequested_qty;

  for(irow = 0; irow < irequested_qty; irow++) {
    if(iscores[irow] > imax_score)
      imax_score = iscores[irow];
    if(iscores[irow] < imin_score)
      imin_score = iscores[irow];
  }

  cout << "\nThe maximum grade is " << imax_score;
  cout << "\nThe minimum grade is " << imin_score;
  cout << "\nThe average grade is " << faverage;

  return(0);
}
```

Here, by the inclusion of the STDLIB.H header file instead of PROCESS.H, two additional definitions became visible: EXIT_SUCCESS (which returns a value of zero) and EXIT_FAILURE (which returns an unsuccessful value). This program used the EXIT_SUCCESS definition for a more readable parameter to the function exit( ).

atexit( )

Whenever a program invokes the exit( ) function or performs a normal program termination, it can also call any registered "exit functions" posted with atexit( ). The following C program demonstrates this capability:

```
/*
 *   atexit.c
 *   A C program demonstrating the relationship between the
```

```
 *    function atexit and the order in which the functions
 *    declared are executed.
 *    Copyright (c) Chris H. Pappas and William H. Murray, 1998
 */

#include <stdio.h>
#include <stdlib.h>

void atexit_fn1(void);
void atexit_fn2(void);
void atexit_fn3(void);

int main( )
{

  atexit(atexit_fn1);
  atexit(atexit_fn2);
  atexit(atexit_fn3);

  printf("Atexit program entered.\n");
  printf("Atexit program exited.\n\n");
  printf(">>>>>>>>>> <<<<<<<<<<\n\n");

  return(0);
}

void atexit_fn1(void)
{
  printf("atexit_fn1 entered.\n");
}

void atexit_fn2(void)
{
  printf("atexit_fn2 entered.\n");
}

void atexit_fn3(void)
{
  printf("atexit_fn3 entered.\n");
}
```

The output from the program looks like this:

```
Atexit program entered.
Atexit program exited.


>>>>>>>>>>> <<<<<<<<<<<

atexit_fn3 entered.
atexit_fn2 entered.
atexit_fn1 entered.
```

The atexit( ) function uses the name of a function as its only parameter and registers the specified function as an exit function. Whenever the program terminates normally, as in the preceding example, or invokes the exit( ) function, all atexit( ) declared functions are executed.

Technically, each time the **atexit( )** statement is encountered in the source code, the specified function is added to a list of functions to execute when the program terminates. When the program terminates, any functions that have been passed to atexit( ) are executed, with the *last* function added being the *first* one executed. This explains why the *atexit_fn3* output statement was printed before the similar statement in *atexit_fn1*. atexit( ) functions are normally used as cleanup routines for dynamically allocated objects. Since one object (B) can be built upon another (A), atexit( ) functions execute in reverse order. This would delete object B before deleting object A.

Chapter 8

Writing and Using Functions

T he cornerstone of C and C++ programming can be described in one word—
functions. This chapter introduces the concept of a function and how it is
prototyped under the latest ANSI C standard. Many example programs will
be used to examine the different types of functions and how arguments are passed.
You will also learn how to use the standard C/C++ variables *argc* and *argv* to pass
command-line arguments to the main( ) function. Additionally, this chapter explores
several unique features available in C++.

Functions form the main building blocks of most C and C++ programs.
Functions allow you to separate and code parts of your program in separate modules.
Thus, functions allow your program to take on a modular appearance. Modular
programming allows a program to be separated into workable parts that contribute to
a final program form. For example, one function might be used to capture input data,
another to print information, and yet another to write data to the disk. As a matter of
fact, all C and C++ programming is done within a function. The one function every C
or C++ program has is main( ).

You will find that C and C++ functions are similar to programming modules in
other languages. For example, Pascal uses functions and procedures, while FORTRAN
uses just functions. The proper development of functions determines, to a great extent,
the efficiency, readability, and portability of your program code.

This chapter contains many programming examples that will show you how to
create and implement a wide range of functions. Many of the example programs also
use built-in C and C++ library functions that give your program extended power.

What Is Function Prototyping?

When the ANSI C standard was implemented for C, it was the C functions that
underwent the greatest change. The ANSI C standard for functions is based upon the
function prototype that has already been extensively used in C++.

At this point, the world of C programming is still in transition. As you read
magazine articles and books that use C code, you will see many forms used to
describe C functions. These may or may not conform to the new ANSI C standard as
programmers attempt to bring themselves in line with this standard. The Visual
C/C++ compiler uses the ANSI C standard for functions, but will also compile the
earlier forms. The C programs in this book conform to the ANSI C standard. An
attempt has been made to pattern C++ programs after the ANSI C standard for C
since one has not yet been set for C++.

The Syntax for Prototypes

If you are not familiar with writing C functions, you probably have a few questions.
What does a function look like? Where do functions go in a program? How are
functions declared? What constitutes a function? Where is type checking performed?

With the new ANSI C standard, all functions must be prototyped. The prototyping can take place in the C or C++ program itself or in a header file. For the programs in this book, most function prototyping is contained within the program itself. Function declarations begin with the C and C++ function prototype. The function prototype is simple, and it is usually included at the start of program code to notify the compiler of the type and number of arguments that a function will use. Prototyping enforces stronger type checking than was previously possible when C standards were less strongly enforced.

Although other prototyping style variations are legal, this book recommends the function prototype form that is a replication of the function's declaration line, with the addition of a semicolon at the end, whenever possible. For example:

```
return_type function_name(argument_type optional_argument_name
        [,...]);
```

The function can be of type **void, int, float,** and so on. The *return_type* gives this specification. The *function_name( )* is any meaningful name you choose to describe the function. If any information is passed to the function, an *argument_type* followed by an *optional_argument_name* should also be given. Argument types can also be of type **void, int, float,** and so on. You can pass many values to a function by repeating the argument type and name separated by a comma. It is also correct to list just the argument type, but that prototype form is used specifically for library routine prototypes.

The function itself is actually an encapsulated piece of C or C++ program code that usually follows the main( ) function definition. A function can take the following form:

```
return_type function_name(argument_types and names)
{
   .
   .
   (data declarations and body of function)
   .
   .
   return();
}
```

Notice that the first line of the actual function is identical to the prototype that is listed at the beginning of a program, with one important exception: it does *not* end with a semicolon. A function prototype and function used in a program are shown in the following application:

```
/*
*   proto.c
```

```
    *    A C program to illustrate function prototyping.
    *    Function adds two integers
    *    and returns an integer result.
    *    Copyright (c) Chris H. Pappas and William H. Murray, 1998
    */

    #include <stdio.h>

    int iadder(int ix,int iy);              /* function prototype  */

    int main()
    {
      int ia=23;
      int ib=13;
      int ic;

      ic=iadder(ia,ib);
      printf("The sum is: %d\n", ic);

      return (0);
    }

    int iadder(int ix,int iy)               /* function declaration */
    {
      int iz;

      iz=ix+iy;
      return(iz);                           /* function return      */
    }
```

The function is called iadder( ). The prototype states that the function will accept two integer arguments and return an integer type. Actually, the ANSI C standard suggests that all functions be prototyped in a separate header file. This, as you might guess, is how header files are associated with their appropriate C libraries. For simple programs, as already mentioned, including the function prototype within the body of the program is acceptable.

The same function written for C++ takes on an almost identical appearance:

```
    //  proto.cpp
    //  C++ program to illustrate function prototyping.
    //  Function adds two integers
```

```
//   and returns an integer result.
//   Copyright (c) Chris H. Pappas and William H. Murray, 1998
//

#include <iostream.h>

int iadder(int ix,int iy);              // function prototype

int main()
{
  int ia=23;
  int ib=13;
  int ic;

  ic=iadder(ia,ib);
  cout << "The sum is: " << ic << endl;

  return (0);
}

int iadder(int ix,int iy)               // function declaration
{
  int iz;

  iz=ix+iy;
  return(iz);                           // function return
}
```

Ways to Pass Actual Arguments

In the previous two examples, arguments have been *passed by value* to the functions. When variables are passed by value, a copy of the variable's actual contents is passed to the function. Since a copy of the variable is passed, the variable in the calling function itself is not altered. Calling a function by value is the most popular means of passing information to a function, and it is the default method in C and C++. The major restriction to the call-by-value method is that the function typically returns only one value.

When you use a *call-by-reference*, the address of the argument, rather than the actual value, is passed to the function. This approach also requires less program memory than a call-by-value. When you use call-by-reference, the variables in the calling function can be altered. Another advantage to a call-by-reference is that more than one value can be returned by the function.

The next example uses the iadder( ) function from the previous section. The arguments are now passed by a call-by-reference. In C, you accomplish a call-by-reference by using a pointer as an argument, as shown next. This same method can be used with C++.

```c
/*
 *   cbref.c
 *   A C program to illustrate call by reference.
 *   Copyright (c) Chris H. Pappas and William H. Murray, 1998
 */

#include <stdio.h>

int iadder(int *pix,int *piy);

int main()
{
  int ia=23;
  int ib=13;
  int ic;

  ic=iadder(&ia,&ib);
  printf("The sum is: %d\n", ic);

  return (0);
}

int iadder(int *pix,int *piy)
{
  int iz;

  iz=*pix+*piy;
  return(iz);
}
```

You have learned in C that you can use variables and pointers as arguments in function declarations. C++ uses variables and pointers as arguments in function declarations and adds a third type. In C++, the third argument type is called a *reference type*. The reference type specifies a location but does not require a dereferencing operator. Many advanced C++ programs use this syntax to simplify the use of pointer variables within called subroutines. Examine the following syntax carefully and compare it with the previous example:

```
//
//   refrnc.cpp
//   C++ program to illustrate an equivalent
//   call-by-reference, using the C++ reference type.
//   Copyright (c) Chris H. Pappas and William H. Murray, 1998
//

#include <iostream.h>

int iadder(int &rix,int &riy);

int main()
{
  int ia=23;
  int ib=13;
  int ic;

  ic=iadder(ia,ib);
  cout << "The sum is: " << ic << endl;

  return (0);
}

int iadder(int &rix,int &riy)
{
  int iz;

  iz=rix+riy;
  return(iz);
}
```

Did you notice the lack of pointers in the previous C++ program code? The reference types in this example are *rix* and *riy*. In C++, references to references, references to bit-fields, arrays of references, and pointers to references are not allowed. Regardless of whether you use call-by-reference or a reference type, C++ always uses the address of the argument.

Storage Classes

Storage classes can be affixed to data type declarations, as you saw earlier in Chapter 6. A variable might, for example, be declared as

```
static float fyourvariable;
```

Functions can also use **extern** and **static** storage class types. A function is declared with an **extern** storage class when it has been defined in another file, external to the present program. A function can be declared **static** when external access, apart from the present program, is not permitted.

Identifier Visibility Rules

The *scope* of a variable, when used in a function, refers to the range of effect that the variable has. The scope rules are similar for C and C++ variables used with functions. Variables can have a local, file, or class scope. (Class scope is discussed in Chapter 16.)

It is possible to use a *local variable* completely within a function definition. Its scope is then limited to the function itself. The variable is said to be accessible, or visible, within the function only and has a local scope.

Variables with a *file scope* are declared outside of individual functions or classes. These variables have visibility or accessibility throughout the file in which they are declared and are global in range.

A variable may be used with a file scope and later within a function definition with a *local scope*. When this is done, the local scope takes precedence over the file scope. C++ offers a new programming feature called the scope resolution operator (::). When the C++ resolution operator is used, a variable with local scope is changed to one with file scope. In this situation, the variable would possess the value of the "global" variable. The syntax for referencing the global variable is

```
::yourvariable
```

The scope rules allow unique programming errors to occur. Various scope rule errors are discussed at the end of this chapter.

Recursion

Recursion takes place in a program when a function calls itself. Initially, this might seem like an endless loop, but it is not. Both C and C++ support recursion. Recursive algorithms allow for creative, readable, and terse problem solutions. For example, the next program uses recursion to generate the factorial of a number. The *factorial* of a number is defined as the number multiplied by all successively lower integers. For example:

```
8 * 7 * 6 * 5 * 4 * 3 * 2 * 1
= 40320
```

Care must be taken when choosing data types since the product increases very rapidly. The factorial of 15 is 1,307,674,368,000.

```c
/*
 *   factr.c
 *   A C program illustrating recursive function calls.
 *   Calculation of the factorial of a number.
 *   Example:   7! = 7 x 6 x 5 x 4 x 3 x 2 x 1 = 5040
 *   Copyright (c) Chris H. Pappas and William H. Murray, 1998
 */

#include <stdio.h>

double dfactorial(double danswer);

int main()
{
  double dnumber=15.0;
  double dresult;

  dresult=dfactorial(dnumber);

  printf("The factorial of %15.0lf is: %15.0lf\n",
         dnumber,dresult);

  return (0);
}

double dfactorial(double danswer)
{
  if (danswer <= 1.0)
    return(1.0);
  else
    return(danswer*dfactorial(danswer-1.0));
}
```

Recursion occurs because the function, dfactorial( ), has a call to itself within the function. Notice, too, that the printf( ) function uses a new format code for printing a double value: %...lf. Here, the "l" is a modifier to the "f" and specifies a **double** instead of a **float**.

Function Arguments

This section discusses how to pass function arguments to a function. These arguments go by many different names. Some programmers call them arguments, while others refer to them as parameters or dummy variables.

Function arguments are optional. Some functions you design may receive no arguments, while others may receive many. Function argument types can be mixed; that is, you can use any of the standard data types as a function argument. Many of the following examples illustrate passing various data types to functions. Furthermore, these programs employ functions from the various C and C++ libraries. Additional details on these library functions and their prototypes can be found in the Visual C/C++ reference manuals.

Actual vs. Formal Parameters

Each function definition contains an argument list, called the *formal argument list*. Items in the list are optional, so the actual list may be empty or it may contain any combination of data types, such as integer, float, and character.

When the function is called by the program, an argument list is also passed to the function. This list is called the actual argument list. In general, there is usually a 1:1 match, when writing ANSI C code, between the formal and actual argument lists, although in reality no strong enforcement is used.

Examine the following line of C code:

```
printf("This is hexadecimal %x and octal %o",ians);
```

In this situation, only one argument is being passed to printf( ), although two are expected. When fewer arguments are supplied, the missing arguments are initialized to meaningless values. C++ overcomes this problem, to a degree, by permitting a default value to be supplied with the formal argument list. When an argument is missing in the actual argument list, the default argument is automatically substituted. For example, in C++, the function prototype might appear as

```
int iyourfunction(int it,float fu=4.2,int iv=10)
```

Notice, if either *fu* or *iv* is not specified in the call to the function iyourfunction( ), the values shown (4.2 or 10) will be used. C++ requires that all formal arguments using default values be listed at the end of the formal argument list. In other words, iyourfunction(10) and iyourfunction(10,15.2) are valid. If *fu* is not supplied, *iv* cannot be supplied either.

void Parameters

In ANSI C, **void** should be used to explicitly state the absence of function arguments. In C++, the use of **void** is not yet required, but its use is considered wise. The following program has a simple function named voutput( ) that receives no arguments and does not return a value. The main( ) function calls the function voutput( ). When the voutput( ) function is finished, control is returned to the main( ) function. This is one of the simplest types of functions you can write.

```
/*
 *    fvoid.c
 *    A C program that will print a message with a function.
 *    Function uses a type void argument and sqrt function
 *    from the standard C library.
 *    Copyright (c) Chris H. Pappas and William H. Murray, 1998
 */

#include <stdio.h>
#include <math.h>

void voutput(void);

int main()
{
  printf("This program will find the square root. \n\n");
  voutput();

  return (0);
}

void voutput(void)
{
  double dt=12345.0;
  double du;

  du=sqrt(dt);
  printf("The square root of %lf is %lf  \n",dt,du);
}
```

PROGRAMMING
FOUNDATIONS

As you study the example, notice that the voutput( ) function calls a C library function named sqrt( ). The prototype for the sqrt( ) library function is contained in MATH.H. It accepts a double as an argument and returns the square root as a **double** value.

char Parameters

Character information can also be passed to a function. In the next example, a single character is intercepted from the keyboard, in the function main( ), and passed to the function voutput( ). The getch( ) function reads the character. There are other functions that are closely related to getch( ) in the standard C library: getc( ), getchar( ), and getche( ). These functions can also be used in C++, but in many cases a better choice will probably be **cin**. Additional details for using getch( ) are contained in your Visual C/C++ reference manuals and are available as online help. The getch( ) function intercepts a character from the standard input device (keyboard) and returns a character value, without echo to the screen, as shown here:

```
/*
 *    fchar.c
 *    C program will accept a character from keyboard,
 *    pass it to a function and print a message using
 *    the character.
 *    Copyright (c) Chris H. Pappas and William H. Murray, 1998
 */

#include <stdio.h>

void voutput(char c);

int main()
{
  char cyourchar;

  printf("Enter one character from the keyboard. \n");
  cyourchar=getch();
  output(cyourchar);

  return (0);
}

void voutput(char c)
{
  int j;
```

```
  for(j=0;j<16;j++)
    printf("The character typed is %c  \n",c);
}
```

Notice, in the previous listing, that a single character is passed to the function. The function then prints a message and the character 16 times. The %c in the printf( ) function specifies that a single character is to be printed.

int Parameters

In the following application, a single integer will be read from the keyboard with C's scanf( ) function. That integer will be passed to the function vside( ). The vside( ) function uses the supplied length to calculate and print the area of a square, the volume of a cube, and the surface area of a cube.

```
/*
 *   fint.c
 *   C program will calculate values given a length.
 *   Function uses a type int argument, accepts length
 *   from keyboard with scanf function.
 *   Copyright (c) Chris H. Pappas and William H. Murray, 1998
 */

#include <stdio.h>

void vside(int is);

int main()
{
  int iyourlength;

  printf("Enter the length, as an integer,\n");
  printf("from the keyboard. \n");
  scanf("%d",&iyourlength);
  vside(iyourlength);

  return (0);
}

void vside(int is)
{
```

```
    int iarea,ivolume,isarea;

    iarea=is*is;
    ivolume=is*is*is;
    isarea=6*area;

    printf("The length of a side is %d  \n\n",is);
    printf("A square would have an area of %d \n",iarea);
    printf("A cube would have a volume of %d \n",ivolume);
    printf("The surface area of the cube is %d \n",isarea);
}
```

Note that the variable *is* and all calculated values are integers. What would happen
if *is* represented the radius of a circle and sphere to the calculated types?

float Parameters

Floats can also be passed as arguments to a function. In the following example, two
floating-point values are passed to a function called vhypotenuse( ). The scanf( )
function is used to intercept both float values from the keyboard.

```
/*
 *   ffloat.c
 *   C program will find hypotenuse of a right triangle.
 *   Function uses a type float argument and accepts
 *   input from the keyboard with the scanf function.
 *   Copyright (c) Chris H. Pappas and William H. Murray, 1998
 */

#include <stdio.h>
#include <math.h>

void vhypotenuse(float fx,float fy);

int main()
{
  float fxlen,fylen;

  printf("Enter the base of the right triangle. \n");
  scanf("%f",&fxlen);
  printf("Enter the height of the right triangle. \n");
  scanf("%f",&fylen);
```

```
   vhypotenuse(fxlen,fylen);

   return (0);
}

void vhypotenuse(float ft,float fu)
{
   double dresult;
   dresult=hypot((double) ft,(double) fu);
   printf("The hypotenuse of the right triangle is %g \n",
          dresult);
}
```

Observe that both arguments received by vhypotenuse( ) are cast to doubles when used by the hypot( ) function from MATH.H. All MATH.H functions accept and return **double** types. Your programs can use the additional math functions listed in Table 8-1. You can also display the contents of your MATH.H header file for additional details.

double _hypot(double, double);	double _cabs(struct _complex);
double _j1(double);	double _j0(double);
double _y0(double);	double _jn(int, double);
double _yn(int, double);	double _y1(double);
double asin(double);	double acos(double);
double atan2(double, double);	double atan(double);
double cabs(struct _complex);	double atof(const char *);
double cos(double);	double ceil(double);
double exp(double);	double cosh(double);
double floor(double);	double fabs(double);
double frexp(double, int *);	double fmod(double, double);
double j0(double);	double hypot(double, double);
double jn(int, double);	double j1(double);
double log(double);	double ldexp(double, int);
double modf(double, double *);	double log10(double);
double sin(double);	double pow(double, double);
double sqrt(double);	double sinh(double);

Table 8-1.   *Macro and Function Prototypes Provided by MATH.H*

double tanh(double);   double tan(double);

double y1(double);   double y0(double);

double abs(double _X)   double yn(int, double);

double pow(int _X, int _Y)   double pow(double _X, int _Y)

float acosf(float);   float asinf(float);

float atan2f(float, float);   float atanf(float);

float ceilf(float);   float cosf(float);

float coshf(float);   float expf(float);

float fabsf(float);   float floorf(float);

float fmodf(float, float);   float hypotf(float, float);

float log10f(float);   float logf(float);

float modff(float, float*);   float powf(float, float);

float sinf(float);   float sinhf(float);

float sqrtf(float);   float tanf(float);

float tanhf(float);   float abs(float _X)

float acos(float _X)   float asin(float _X)

float atan(float _X)   float atan2(float _Y, float _X)

float ceil(float _X)   float cos(float _X)

float cosh(float _X)   float exp(float _X)

float fabs(float _X)   float floor(float _X)

float fmod(float _X, float _Y)   float frexp(float _X, int * _Y)

float ldexp(float _X, int _Y)   float log(float _X)

float log10(float _X)   float modf(float _X, float * _Y)

float pow(float _X, float _Y)   float pow(float _X, int _Y)

float sin(float _X)   float sinh(float _X)

float sqrt(float _X)   float tan(float _X)

float tanh(float _X)   float acosf(float _X)

float asinf(float _X)   float atan2f(float _X, float _Y)

float atanf(float _X)   float ceilf(float _X)

float cosf(float _X)   float coshf(float _X)

float expf(float _X)   float fabsf(float _X)

Table 8-1.   *Macro and Function Prototypes Provided by MATH.H* (continued)

float floorf(float _X)

float frexpf(float _X, int *_Y)

float log10f(float _X)

float modff(float _X, float *_Y)

float sinf(float _X)

float sqrtf(float _X)

float tanhf(float _X)

long abs(long _X)

long double _cabsl(struct _complexl);

long double _j0l(long double);

long double _jnl(int, long double);

long double _y1l(long double);

long double acosl(long double);

long double atan2l(long double, long double);

long double ceill(long double);

long double cosl(long double);

long double fabsl(long double);

long double fmodl(long double, long double);

long double ldexpl(long double, int);

long double logl(long double);

long double powl(long double, long double);

long double sinl(long double);

long double tanhl(long double);

long double abs(long double _X)

long double asin(long double _X)

long double atan2(long double _Y, long double _X)

long double cos(long double _X)

float fmodf(float _X, float _Y)

float ldexpf(float _X, int _Y)

float logf(float _X)

float powf(float _X, float _Y)

float sinhf(float _X)

float tanf(float _X)

long double _atold(const char *);

long double _hypotl(long double, long double);

long double _j1l(long double);

long double _y0l(long double);

long double _ynl(int, long double);

long double asinl(long double);

long double atanl(long double);

long double coshl(long double);

long double expl(long double);

long double floorl(long double);

long double frexpl(long double, int *);

long double log10l(long double);

long double modfl(long double, long double *);

long double sinhl(long double);

long double sqrtl(long double);

long double tanl(long double);

long double acos(long double _X)

long double atan(long double _X)

long double ceil(long double _X)

long double cosh(long double _X)

Table 8-1.   *Macro and Function Prototypes Provided by MATH.H (continued)*

long double exp(long double _X)	long double fabs(long double _X)
long double floor(long double _X)	long double fmod(long double _X, long double _Y)
long double frexp(long double _X, int * _Y)	long double ldexp(long double _X, int _Y)
long double log(long double _X)	long double log10(long double _X)
long double modf(long double _X, long double * _Y)	long double pow(long double _X, int _Y)
long double pow(long double _X, long double _Y)	long double sin(long double _X)
long double sinh(long double _X)	long double sqrt(long double _X)
long double tan(long double _X)	long double tanh(long double _X)
long double acosl(long double _X)	long double asinl(long double _X)
long double atan2l(long double _X, long double _Y)	long double atanl(long double _X)
long double ceill(long double _X)	long double coshl(long double _X)
long double cosl(long double _X)	long double expl(long double _X)
long double fabsl(long double _X)	long double floorl(long double _X)
long double fmodl(long double _X, long double _Y)	long double frexpl(long double _X, int *_Y)
long double ldexpl(long double _X, int _Y)	long double log10l(long double _X)
long double logl(long double _X)	long double modfl(long double _X, long double *_Y)
long double powl(long double _X, long double _Y)	long double sinhl(long double _X)
long double sinl(long double _X)	long double sqrtl(long double _X)
long double tanhl(long double _X)	long double tanl(long double _X)

Table 8-1. *Macro and Function Prototypes Provided by MATH.H (continued)*

double Parameters

The **double** type is a very precise float value. All MATH.H functions accept and return **double** types. The next program accepts two double values from the keyboard. The function named vpower( ) will raise the first number to the power specified by the second number. Since both values are of type **double**, you can calculate 45.7 and find that it equals 428,118,741.757.

```
/*
 *    fdoubl.c
 *    C program will raise a number to a power.
 *    Function uses a type double argument and the pow function.
 *    Copyright (c) Chris H. Pappas and William H. Murray, 1998
 */

#include <stdio.h>
#include <math.h>

void vpower(double dt,double du);

int main()
{
  double dtnum,dunum;

  printf("Enter the base number. \n");
  scanf("%lf",&dtnum);
  printf("Enter the power. \n");
  scanf("%lf",&dunum);
  vpower(dtnum,dunum);

  return (0);
}

void vpower(double dt,double du)
{
  double danswer;

  danswer=pow(dt,du);
  printf("The result is %lf \n",answer);
}
```

This function uses the library function pow( ) to raise one number to a power, prototyped in MATH.H.

Array Parameters

The next application shows how the contents of an array are passed to a function as a call-by-reference. In this example, the address of the first array element is passed via a pointer.

```
/*
 *    fpntr.c
 *    C program will call a function with an array.
```

```
*       Function uses a pointer to pass array information.
*       Copyright (c) Chris H. Pappas and William H. Murray, 1998
*/

#include <stdio.h>

void voutput(int *pinums);

int main()
{
  int iyourarray[7]={2,7,15,32,45,3,1};

  printf("Send array information to function. \n");
  voutput(iyourarray);

  return (0);
}

void voutput(int *pinums)
{
  int t;

  for(t=0;t<7;t++)
    printf("The result is %d \n",pinums[t]);
}
```

When the function is called, only the name *iyourarray* is specified. In Chapter 9, you will learn more details concerning arrays. In this example, by specifying the name of the array, you are providing the address of the first element in the array. Since *iyourarray* is an array of integers, it is possible to pass the array by specifying a pointer of the element type.

It is also permissible to pass the address information by using an unsized array. The next example shows how you can do this in C++. (The same approach can be used in C.) The information in *iyourarray* is transferred by passing the address of the first element.

```
//
// farray.cpp
// C++ program will call a function with an array.
// Function passes array information, and calculates
// the average of the numbers.
// Copyright (c) Chris H. Pappas and William H. Murray, 1998
//
```

```
#include <iostream.h>

void avg(float fnums[]);

int main()
{
  float iyourarray[8]={12.3,25.7,82.1,6.0,7.01,
                       0.25,4.2,6.28};

  cout << "Send information to averaging function. \n";
  avg(iyourarray);

  return (0);
}

void avg(float fnums[])
{
  int iv;
  float fsum=0.0;
  float faverage;

  for(iv=0;iv<8;iv++) {
    fsum+=fnums[iv];
    cout << "number " << iv+1 << " is " << fnums[iv] << endl;
  }
  faverage=fsum/iv;
  cout << "\nThe average is " << faverage << endl;
}
```

The average is determined by summing each of the terms together and dividing by the total number of terms. The **cout** stream is used to format the output to the screen.

Function Return Types

In this section, you will find an example for each of the important return types for functions possible in C and C++ programming. Function types specify the type of value returned by the function. None of the examples in the last section returned information from the function and thus were of type **void**.

void Return Type

Since **void** was used in all of the previous examples, the example for this section is a little more involved. You have learned that both C and C++ permit numeric information to be formatted in hexadecimal, decimal, and octal—but not binary.

Specifying data in a binary format is useful for doing binary arithmetic or developing bit masks. The function vbinary( ) will convert a decimal number entered from the keyboard to a binary representation on the screen. The binary digits are not packed together as a single binary number, but are stored individually in an array. Thus, to examine the binary number, the contents of the array must be printed out.

```c
/*
 *   voidf.c
 *   C program illustrates the void function type.
 *   Program will print the binary equivalent of a number.
 *   Copyright (c) Chris H. Pappas and William H. Murray, 1998
 */

#include <stdio.h>

void vbinary(int ivalue);

int main()
{
  int ivalue;

  printf("Enter a number (base 10) for conversion to
binary.\n");
  scanf("%d",&ivalue);
  vbinary(ivalue);

  return (0);
}

void vbinary(int idata)
{
  int t=0;
  int iyourarray[50];

  while (idata !=0) {
    iyourarray[t]=(idata % 2);
    idata/=2;
    t++;
  }

  t--;
  for(;t>=0;t--)
    printf("%1d",iyourarray[t]);
  printf("\n");
}
```

The conversion process from higher-order to lower-order bases is a rather simple mathematical algorithm. For example, base 10 numbers can be converted to another base by dividing the number by the new base a successive number of times. If conversion is from base 10 to base 2, a 2 is repeatedly divided into the base 10 number. This produces a quotient and a remainder. The quotient becomes the dividend for each subsequent division. The remainder becomes a digit in the converted number. In the case of binary conversion, the remainder is either a 1 or a zero.

In the function vbinary( ), a **while** loop is used to perform the arithmetic as long as *idata* has not reached zero. The modulus operator determines the remainder and saves the bit in the array. Division is then performed on *idata*, saving only the integer result. This process is repeated until the quotient (also *data* in this case) is reduced to zero.

The individual array bits, which form the binary result, must be unloaded from the array in reverse order. You can observe this in the program listing. Examine the **for** loop used in the function. Can you think of a way to perform this conversion and save the binary representation in a variable instead of an array?

char Return Type

Let's examine an example that is a minor variation of an earlier application. The C function clowercase( ) accepts a character argument and returns the same character type. For this example, an uppercase letter received from the keyboard is passed to the function. The function uses the library function tolower( ) (from the standard library and prototyped in CTYPE.H) to convert the character to a lowercase letter. Related functions to tolower( ) include toascii( ) and toupper( ).

```c
/*
 *    charf.c
 *    C program illustrates the character function type.
 *    Function receives uppercase character and
 *    converts it to lowercase.
 *    Copyright (c) Chris H. Pappas and William H. Murray, 1998
 */

#include <stdio.h>
#include <ctype.h>

char clowercase(char c);

int main()
{
  char clowchar,chichar;

  printf("Enter an uppercase character.\n");
  chichar=getchar();
  clowchar=clowercase(chichar);
```

```
    printf("%c\n",clowchar);

    return (0);
}

char clowercase(char c)
{
    return(tolower(c));
}
```

bool Return Type

The use of the new **bool** data type is illustrated in the following application by defining two functions, is_upper( ) and is_lower( ), that return this new ANSI C type:

```
/*
 *   bool.c
 *   C program illustrating the use
 *   of the new ANSI C/C++ type bool
 *   Copyright (c) Chris H. Pappas and William H. Murray, 1998
 */

#include <stdio.h>

bool is_upper(void);
bool is_lower(void);

int main()
{
    char cTestChar = 'T';
    bool bIsUppercase, bIsLowercase;

    bIsUppercase = is_upper(cTestChar);
    bIsLowercase = is_lower(cTestChar);

    printf("The letter %s upper case.", bIsUppercase ? "is" :
            "isn't");
    printf("the letter %s lower case.", bIsLowercase ? "is" :
            "isn't");

    return(0);
}
```

```
bool is_upper(int ch)
{
  return ( ch >= 'A' && ch <= 'Z' );
}

bool is_lower(int ch)
{
  return ( ch >= 'a' && ch <= 'z' );
}
```

Here the use of the conditional operator **?:** is used to reduce each **printf( )** statement to a single line each, instead of the more verbose **if-else** alternative.

int Return Type

The following function accepts and returns integers. The function icube( ) accepts a number generated in main( ) (0, 2, 4, 6, 8, 10, and so on), cubes the number, and returns the integer value to main( ). The original number and its cube are printed to the screen.

```
/*
 *    intf.c
 *    C program illustrates the integer function type.
 *    Function receives integers, one at a time, and
 *    returns the cube of each, one at a time.
 *    Copyright (c) Chris H. Pappas and William H. Murray, 1998
 */

#include <stdio.h>

int icube(int ivalue);

int main()
{
  int k,inumbercube;

  for (k=0;k<20;k+=2) {
    inumbercube=icube(k);
    printf("The cube of the number %d is %d \n",
           k,inumbercube);
  }

  return (0);
}
```

```
int icube(int ivalue)
{
  return (ivalue*ivalue*ivalue);
}
```

long Return Type

In the following C++ application, you'll see how a program accepts an integer value as an argument and returns a type **long**. The **long** type, used by Visual C/C++ and other popular compilers, is not recognized as a standard ANSI C type. The function will raise the number 2 to an integer power.

```cpp
//
//  longf.cpp
//  C++ program illustrates the long integer function type.
//  Function receives integers, one at a time, and
//  returns 2 raised to that integer power.
//  Copyright (c) Chris H. Pappas and William H. Murray, 1998
//

#include <iostream.h>

long lpower(int ivalue);

int main()
{
  int k;
  long lanswer;

  for (k=0;k<31;k++) {
    lanswer=lpower(k);
    cout << "2 raised to the " << k << " power is "
         << lanswer << endl;
  }

  return (0);
}

long lpower(int ivalue)
{
  int t;
  long lseed=1;

  for (t=0;t<ivalue;t++)
```

```
    lseed*=2;
  return (lseed);
}
```

In this application, the function simply multiplies the original number by the number of times it is to be raised to the specified power. For example, if you wanted to raise 2 to the 6th power, the program will perform the following multiplication:

```
2 * 2 * 2 * 2 * 2 * 2  = 64
```

Can you think of a function described in MATH.H that could achieve the same results? See Table 8-1 for some ideas.

float Return Type

The following application illustrates how a float array argument will be passed to a function and a **float** will be returned. This C++ example will find the product of all the elements in an array.

```
//
//  floatf.cpp
//  C++ program illustrates the float function type.
//  Function receives an array of floats and returns
//  their product as a float.
//  Copyright (c) Chris H. Pappas and William H. Murray, 1998
//

#include <iostream.h>

float fproduct(float farray[]);

int main()
{
  float fmyarray[7]={4.3,1.8,6.12,3.19,0.01234,0.1,9876.2};
  float fmultiplied;

  fmultiplied=fproduct(fmyarray);
  cout << "The product of all array entries is: "
       << fmultiplied << endl;

  return (0);
}
```

```
float fproduct(float farray[])
{
  int i;
  float fpartial;

  fpartial=farray[0];
  for (i=1;i<7;i++)
    fpartial*=farray[i];
  return (fpartial);
}
```

Since the elements are multiplied together, the first element of the array must be loaded into *fpartial* before the **for** loop is entered. Observe that the loop in the function fproduct( ) starts at 1 instead of the normal zero value.

double Return Type

The next application shows how a program accepts and returns a **double** type. The function dtrigcosine( ) will convert an angle, expressed in degrees, to its cosine value.

```
/*
 *    double.c
 *    C program illustrates the double function type.
 *    Function receives integers from 0 to 90, one at a
 *    time, and returns the cosine of each, one at a time.
 *    Copyright (c) Chris H. Pappas and William H. Murray, 1998
 */

#include <stdio.h>
#include <math.h>

const double dPi=3.14159265359;

double dtrigcosine(double dangle);

int main()
{
  int j;
  double dcosine;

  for (j=0;j<91;j++) {
    dcosine=dtrigcosine((double) j);
    printf("The cosine of %d degrees is %19.18lf \n",
           j,dcosine);
```

```
  }

  return (0);
}

double dtrigcosine(double dangle)
{
  double dpartial;
  dpartial=cos((dPi/180.0)*dangle);
  return (dpartial);
}
```

Note that the cos( ) function found in MATH.H is used by dtrigcosine( ) for obtaining the results. Angles must be converted from degrees to radians for all trigonometric functions. Recall that pi radians equals 180 degrees.

Command Line Arguments

Both C and C++ share the ability to accept command-line arguments. *Command-line arguments* are those arguments entered along with the program name when called from the operating system's command line. This gives you the ability to pass arguments directly to your program without additional program prompts. For example, a program might pass four arguments from the command line:

```
YOURPROGRAM  Tia, ThinkingDog, Tango, BigDog
```

In this example, four values are passed from the command line to YOURPROGRAM. Actually, it is main( ) that is given specific information. One argument received by main( ), *argc,* is an integer giving the number of command-line terms plus 1. The program title is counted as the first term passed from the command line. The second argument is a pointer to an array of string pointers called *argv.* All arguments are strings of characters, so *argv* is of type **char** **[argc]*. Since all programs have a name, *argc* is always 1 greater than the number of command-line arguments. In the following examples, you will learn different techniques for retrieving various data types from the command line. The argument names *argc* and *argv* are the commonly agreed upon variable names used in all C/C++ programs.

Alphanumeric

Arguments are passed from the command line as strings of characters, and thus they are the easiest to work with. In the next example, the C program expects that the user will enter several names on the command line. To ensure that the user enters several names, if *argc* isn't greater than 2, the user will be returned to the command line with a reminder to try again.

```c
/*
 *   sargv.c
 *   C program illustrates how to read string data
 *   into the program with a command-line argument.
 *   Copyright (c) Chris H. Pappas and William H. Murray, 1998
 */

#include <stdio.h>
#include <process.h>

int main(int argc,char *argv[])
{
  int t;

  if(argc<2) {
    printf("Enter several names on the command line\n");
    printf("when executing this program!\n");
    printf("Please try again.\n");
    exit(0);
  }

  for (t=1; t<argc; t++)
    printf("Entry #%d is %s\n",t,argv[t]);

  return (0);
}
```

You might have noticed that this program is completely contained in main( ) and does not use additional functions. The names entered on the command line are printed to the screen in the same order. If numeric values are entered on the command line, they will be interpreted as an ASCII string of individual characters and must be printed as such.

Integral

It is often desirable to be able to enter integer numbers on the command line, perhaps in a program that would find the average of a student's test scores. In such a case, the ASCII character information must be converted to an integer value. The C++ example in this section will accept a single integer number on the command line. Since the number is actually a character string, it will be converted to an integer with the atoi( ) library function. The command-line value *ivalue* is passed to a function used earlier, called vbinary( ). The function will convert the number in *ivalue* to a string of binary digits and print them to the screen. When control is returned to main( ), the *ivalue* will be printed in octal and hexadecimal formats.

```cpp
//
//  iargv.cpp
//  C++ program illustrates how to read an integer
//  into the program with a command-line argument.
//  Copyright (c) Chris H. Pappas and William H. Murray, 1998
//

#include <iostream.h>
#include <stdlib.h>
#include <process.h>

void vbinary(int idigits);

int main(int argc, char *argv[])
{
  int ivalue;

  if(argc!=2) {
    cout << "Enter a decimal number on the command line.\n";
    cout << "It will be converted to binary, octal and\n";
    cout << "hexadecimal.\n";
    exit(1);
  }

  ivalue=atoi(argv[1]);
  vbinary(ivalue);
  cout << "The octal value is: " << oct
       << ivalue << endl;
  cout << "The hexadecimal value is: "
       << hex << ivalue << endl;

  return (0);
}

void vbinary(int idigits)
{
  int t=0;
  int iyourarray[50];

  while (idigits != 0) {
    iyourarray[t]=(idigits % 2);
```

```
    idigits/=2;
    t++;
  }

  t--;
  cout << "The binary value is: ";
  for(;t>=0;t--)
    cout << dec << iyourarray[t];
    cout << endl;
}
```

You might be interested in the formatting of the various numbers. You learned earlier that the binary number is saved in the array and printed one digit at a time, using decimal formatting, by unloading the array *iyourarray* in reverse order:

```
cout << dec << myarray[i];
```

To print the number in octal format, the statement is

```
cout << "The octal value is: "
     << oct << ivalue << endl;
```

It is also possible to print the hexadecimal equivalent by substituting hex for oct, as shown here:

```
cout << "The hexadecimal value is: "
     << hex << ivalue << endl;
```

Without additional formatting, the hexadecimal values a, b, c, d, e, and f are printed in lowercase. You'll learn many formatting techniques for C++ in Chapters 11 and 12, including how to print those characters in uppercase.

Float

You will find that floats are just as easy as integers to intercept from the command-line. The following C example will allow several angles to be entered on the command line. The cosine of the angles will be extracted and printed to the screen. Since the angles are of type **float**, they can take on values such as 12.0, 45.78, 0.12345, or 15.

```
/*
 *   fargv.c
 *   C program illustrates how to read float data types
```

```
*    into the program with a command-line argument.
*    Copyright (c) Chris H. Pappas and William H. Murray, 1998
*/

#include <stdio.h>
#include <math.h>
#include <process.h>

const double dPi=3.14159265359;

int main(int argc, char *argv[])
{
  int t;
  double ddegree;

  if(argc<2) {
    printf("Type several angles on the command line.\n");
    printf("Program will calculate and print\n");
    printf("the cosine of the angles entered.\n");
    exit(1);
  }

  for (t=1; t<argc; t++) {
    ddegree=(double) atof(argv[t]);
    printf("The cosine of %f is %15.14lf\n",
           ddegree,cos((dPi/180.0)*ddegree));
  }

  return (0);
}
```

The atof( ) function converts the command-line string argument to a **float** type. The program uses the cos( ) function within the printf( ) function to retrieve the cosine information.

Functions in C vs. C++

C++ allows the use of several special features when writing functions. The ability to write inline functions is one such advantage. The code for an inline function is reproduced at the spot where the function is called in the main program. Since the compiler places the code at the point of the function call, execution time is saved when using short, frequently called functions.

C++ also allows function overloading. *Overloading* permits several function prototypes to be given the same function name. The numerous prototypes are then recognized by their type and argument list, not just by their name. Overloading is very useful when a function is required to work with different data types.

When Is a Function a Macro?

Think of the **inline** keyword as a directive or, better yet, a suggestion to the C++ compiler to insert the function inline. The compiler may ignore this suggestion for any of several reasons. For example, the function might be too long. Inline functions are used primarily to save time when short functions are called many times within a program.

```
//
//  inline.cpp
//  C++ program illustrates the use of an inline function.
//  Inline functions work best on short functions that are
//  used repeatedly. This example calculates the square
//  of an integer.
//  Copyright (c) Chris H. Pappas and William H. Murray, 1998
//

#include <iostream.h>

inline long squareit(int iValue) {return iValue * iValue;}

int main()
{
  int iValue = 5;

  cout << squareit(iValue)
       << endl;

  return (0);
}
```

The function squareit( ) is declared **inline**, which returns the square of the formal integer argument *iValue*. When the function main( ) calls function squareit( ), the compiler substitutes the function call with the expression *iValue * iValue*. In other words, the compiler replaces the function call with the function's statement and also replaces the function's parameters with the function's arguments.

One advantage of inline functions versus macros is error checking. Invoking a macro with the wrong data type goes unchecked by the compiler. However, since an inline function has a prototype, the compiler performs type matching between the formal argument type(s) in the prototype and the actual argument(s) in the function call.

Prototyping Multiple Functions with the Same Name

The next example illustrates function overloading. Notice that two functions with the same name are prototyped within the same scope. The correct function will be selected based on the arguments provided. A function call to adder( ) will process integer or float data correctly.

```
//
//  ovrlod.cpp
//  C++ program illustrates function overloading.
//  Overloaded function receives an array of integers or
//  floats and returns either an integer or float product.
//  Copyright (c) Chris H. Pappas and William H. Murray, 1998
//

#include <iostream.h>

int adder(int iarray[]);
float adder(float farray[]);

int main()
{
  int iarray[7]={5,1,6,20,15,0,12};
  float farray[7]={3.3,5.2,0.05,1.49,3.12345,31.0,2.007};
  int isum;
  float fsum;

  isum=adder(iarray);
  fsum=adder(farray);
  cout << "The sum of the integer numbers is: "
       << isum << endl;
  cout << "The sum of the float numbers is: "
       << fsum << endl;

  return (0);
}

int adder(int iarray[])
{
```

```
    int i;
    int ipartial;

    ipartial=iarray[0];
    for (i=1;i<7;i++)
      ipartial+=iarray[i];
    return (ipartial);
}

float adder(float farray[])
{
    int i;
    float fpartial;

    fpartial=farray[0];
    for (i=1;i<7;i++)
      fpartial+=farray[i];
    return (fpartial);
}
```

There are a few programming snags to function overloading that must be avoided. For example, if a function differs only in the function type and not in the arguments, the function cannot be overloaded. Also, the following attempt at overloading is not permitted:

```
int yourfunction(int number)
int yourfunction(int &value)    //not allowed
```

This syntax is not allowed because each prototype would accept the same type of arguments. Despite these limitations, overloading is a very important topic in C++ and is fully explored starting with Chapter 14.

Functions with Varying-length Formal Argument Lists

For functions with varying-length formal argument lists, you'll use the ellipsis. The ellipsis is used when the number of arguments is not known. As such, they can be specified within the function's formal argument statement. For example:

```
void yourfunction(int t,float u,...);
```

This syntax tells the C compiler that other arguments may or may not follow *t* and *u*, which are required. Naturally, type checking is suspended with the ellipsis.

The following C program demonstrates how to use the ellipsis. You may want to delay an in-depth study of the algorithm, however, until you have a thorough understanding of C string pointer types (see Chapters 9 and 10).

```c
/*
 *   elip.c
 *   A C program demonstrating the use of ... and its support
 *   macros va_arg, va_start, and va_end
 *   Copyright (c) Chris H. Pappas and William H. Murray, 1998
 */

#include <stdio.h>
#include <stdarg.h>
#include <string.h>

void vsmallest(char *szmessage, ...);

int main()
{
  vsmallest("Print %d integers, %d %d %d",10,4,1);

  return(0);
}

void vsmallest(char *szmessage, ...)
{
  int inumber_of_percent_ds=0;
  va_list type_for_ellipsis;
  int ipercent_d_format = 'd';
  char *pchar;
  pchar=strchr(szmessage,ipercent_d_format);

  while(*++pchar != '\0') {
    pchar++;
    pchar=strchr(pchar,ipercent_d_format);
    inumber_of_percent_ds++;
  }
  printf("print %d integers,",inumber_of_percent_ds);
```

```
va_start(type_for_ellipsis,szmessage);

while(inumber_of_percent_ds--)
  printf(" %d",va_arg(type_for_ellipsis,int));

va_end(type_for_ellipsis);
}
```

The function vsmallest( ) has been prototyped to expect two arguments, a string pointer, and an argument of type ..., or a varying length argument list. Naturally, functions using a varying-length argument list are not omniscient. Something within the argument list must give the function enough information to process the varying part. In ELIP.C, this information comes from the string argument.

In a very crude approach, vsmallest( ) attempts to mimic the printf( ) function. The subroutine scans the *szmessage* format string to see how many %ds it finds. It then uses this information to make a calculated fetching and printing of the information in the variable argument. While this sounds straightforward, the algorithm requires a sophisticated sequence of events.

The strchr( ) function returns the address of the location containing the "d" in %d. The first %d can be ignored since this is required by the output message. The **while** loop continues processing the remainder of the *szmessage* string looking for the variable number of %ds and counting them (*inumber_of_percent_ds*). With this accomplished, the beginning of the output message is printed.

The va_start( ) macro sets the *type_for_ellipsis* pointer to the beginning of the variable argument list. The va_arg( ) support macro retrieves the next argument in the variable list. The macro uses its second parameter to know what data type to retrieve; for the example program, this is type **int**. The function vsmallest( ) terminates with a call to va_end( ). The last of the three standard C ellipsis support macros; va_end( ) resets the pointer to null.

Things Not to Do with Functions

When variables are used with different scope levels, it is possible to run into completely unexpected programming results, called *side effects*. For example, it is possible to use a variable of the same name with both file and local scopes. The scope rules state that the variable with a local scope (called a *local variable*) will take precedence over the variable with a file scope (called a *global variable*). That all seems easy enough, but let's now consider some problem areas you might encounter in programming that are not so obvious.

Attempting to Access Out-of-Scope Identifiers

In the following example, four variables are given a local scope within the function main( ). Copies of the variables *il* and *im* are passed to the function iproduct( ). This does not violate scope rules. However, when the iproduct( ) function attempts to use the variable *in*, it cannot find the variable. Why? Because the scope of the variable was local to main( ) only.

```c
/*
 *   scopep.c
 *   C program to illustrate problems with scope rules.
 *   Function is supposed to form a product of three numbers.
 *   Compiler signals problems since variable n isn't known
 *   to the function multiplier.
 *   Copyright (c) Chris H. Pappas and William H. Murray, 1998
 */

#include <stdio.h>

int iproduct(int iw,int ix);

int main()
{
  int il=3;
  int im=7;
  int in=10;
  int io;

  io=iproduct(il,im);
  printf("The product of the numbers is: %d\n", io);

  return (0);
}

int iproduct(int iw,int ix)
{
  int iy;

  iy=iw*ix*in;
  return(iy);
}
```

The C compiler issues a warning and an error message. It first reports a warning that the *in* variable is never used within the function and then the error message that *in* has never been declared in the function iproduct( ). One way around this problem is to give the variable, *in*, a file scope.

External vs. Internal Identifier Access

In the following application, the variable *in* is given a file scope. Making *in* global to the whole file allows both main( ) and iproduct( ) to use it. Also note that both main( ) and iproduct( ) can change the value of the variable. It is good programming practice not to allow functions to change global program variables if they are created to be truly portable.

```c
/*
 *   fscope.c
 *   C program to illustrate problems with scope rules.
 *   Function is supposed to form a product of three numbers.
 *   Previous problem is solved, c variable is given file
 *   scope.
 *   Copyright (c) Chris H. Pappas and William H. Murray, 1998
 */

#include <stdio.h>

int iproduct(int iw,int ix);

int in=10;

int main()
{
  int il=3;
  int im=7;
  int io;

  io=iproduct(il,im);
  printf("The product is: %d\n", io);

  return (0);
}

int iproduct(int iw,int ix)
{
```

```
    int iy;

    iy=iw*ix*in;
    return(iy);
}
```

This program will compile correctly and print the product 210 to the screen.

Internal vs. External Identifier Access

The scope rules state that a variable with both file and local scope will use the local variable value over the global value. Here is a small program that illustrates this point:

```
/*
 *    lscope.c
 *    C program to illustrate problems with scope rules.
 *    Function forms a product of three numbers, but which
 *    three?  Two are passed as function arguments. The
 *    variable c has both a file and local scope.
 *    Copyright (c) Chris H. Pappas and William H. Murray, 1998
 */

#include <stdio.h>

int iproduct(int iw,int ix);

int in=10;

int main()
{
  int il=3;
  int im=7;
  int io;

  io=iproduct(il,im);
  printf("The product of the numbers is: %d\n", io);

  return (0);
}

int iproduct(int iw,int ix)
```

```
{
  int iy;
  int in=2;

  iy=iw*ix*in;
  return(iy);
}
```

In this example, the variable *in* has both file and local scope. When *in* is used within the function iproduct( ), the local scope takes precedence and the product of 3 * 7 * 2 = 42 is returned.

It's Legal, But Don't Ever Do It!

In the next C++ example, everything works fine up to the point of printing the information to the screen. The **cout** statement prints the values for *il* and *im* correctly. When selecting the *in* value, it chooses the global variable with file scope. The program reports that the product of 3 * 7 * 10 = 42 is clearly a mistake. You know that in this case the iproduct( ) function used the local value of *in*.

```
//
//  scopep.cpp
//  C++ program to illustrate problems with scope rules.
//  Function forms a product of three numbers. The n
//  variable is of local scope and used by function
//  product. However, main function reports that
//  the n value used is 10. What is wrong here?
//  Copyright (c) Chris H. Pappas and William H. Murray, 1998
//

#include <iostream.h>

int iproduct(int iw,int ix);

int in=10;

int main()
{
  int il=3;
  int im=7;
  int io;
```

```
    io=iproduct(il,im);
    cout << "The product of " << il <<" * " << im
         << " * " << in << " is: " << io << endl;

    return (0);
}

int iproduct(int iw,int ix)
{
  int iy;
  int in=2;

  iy=iw*ix*in;
  return(iy);
}
```

If you actually wanted to form the product with the global value of *in*, how could this conflict be resolved? C++ would permit you to use the scope resolution operator mentioned earlier in the chapter, as shown here:

```
    iy=iw*ix*::in;
```

Overriding Internal Precedence

In this example, the scope resolution operator (::) is used to avoid conflicts between a variable with both file and local scope. The last program reported an incorrect product since the local value was used in the calculation. Notice in the following listing that the iproduct( ) function uses the scope resolution operator.

```
//
//  gscope.cpp
//  C++ program to illustrate problems with scope rules,
//  and how to use the scope resolution operator.
//  Function product uses resolution operator to "override"
//  local scope and utilize variable with file scope.
//  Copyright (c) Chris H. Pappas and William H. Murray, 1998
//

#include <iostream.h>

int iproduct(int iw,int ix);
```

```
int in=10;

int main()
{
  int il=3;
  int im=7;
  int io;

  io=iproduct(il,im);
  cout << "The product of " << il <<" * " << im
       << " * " << in << " is: " << io;

  return (0);
}

int iproduct(int iw,int ix)
{
  int iy;
  int in=2;

  iy=iw*ix*(::in);
  return(iy);
}
```

The scope resolution operators need not be enclosed in parentheses—they were used for emphasis in this example. Now, the value of the global variable, with file scope, will be used in the calculation. When the results are printed to the screen, you will see that 3 * 7 * 10 = 210.

The scope resolution operator is very important in C++. Additional examples illustrating the resolution operator are given starting with Chapter 16.

Chapter 9

Arrays

In C and C++, the topics of arrays, pointers, and strings are all related. In this chapter, you learn how to define and use arrays. Many C/C++ books combine the topics of arrays and pointers in one discussion. This is unfortunate because there are many uses for arrays in C and C++ that are not dependent on a detailed understanding of pointers. Also, since there is a great deal of material to cover about arrays in general, it is best not to confuse the topic with a discussion of pointers. Pointers, however, allow you to fully comprehend just how an array is processed. Chapter 10 examines the topic of pointers and completes this chapter's discussion of arrays.

What Are Arrays?

Think of *arrays* as variables containing several homogeneous data types. Each individual data item can be accessed by using a subscript, or index, into the variable. In the C and C++ language, an array is not a standard data type; instead, it is an aggregate type made up of any other types of data. It is possible to have an array of anything: characters, integers, floats, doubles, arrays, pointers, structures, and so on. The concept of arrays and their use is basically the same in both C and C++.

Array Properties

There are four basic properties to an array:

- The individual data items in the array are called elements.
- All elements must be of the same data type.
- All elements are stored contiguously in the computer's memory, and the subscript (or index) of the first element is zero.
- The name of the array is a constant value that represents the address of the first element in the array.

Since all elements of an array are assumed to be the same size, arrays cannot be defined by using mixed data types. Without this assumption, it would be very difficult to determine where any given element was stored. Since the elements are all the same size, and since that fact is used to help determine how to locate a given element, it follows that the elements are stored contiguously in the computer's memory (with the lowest address corresponding to the first element, the highest address to the last element). This means that there is no filler space between elements and that they are physically adjacent in the computer.

It is possible to have arrays within arrays, that is, multidimensional arrays. Actually, if an array element is a structure (which will be covered in Chapter 13), then mixed data types can exist in the array by existing inside the structure member.

The name of an array represents a constant value that cannot change during the execution of the program. For this reason, arrays can never be used as *lvalues*. *lvalues* represent storage locations that can have their contents altered by the program; they frequently appear to the left of assignment statements. If array names were legal *lvalues*, your program could change their contents. The effect would be to change the starting address of the array itself. This may seem like a small thing, but some forms of expressions that might appear valid on the surface are not allowed. All programmers eventually learn these subtleties, but it helps if you understand why these differences exist.

Array Declarations

The following are examples of array declarations:

```
int  iarray[12];   /* an array of twelve integers    */
char carray[20];   /* an array of twenty characters  */
```

As is true with all data declarations, an array's declaration begins with its data type, followed by a valid array name and a pair of matching square brackets enclosing a constant expression. The constant expression defines the size of the array. It is illegal to use a variable name inside the square brackets. For this reason, it is not possible to avoid specifying the array size until the program executes. The expression must reduce to a constant value so that the compiler knows exactly how much storage space to reserve for the array.

It is best to use defined constants to specify the size of the array:

```
#define iARRAY_MAX 20
#define fARRAY_MAX 15

int iarray[iARRAY_MAX];
float farray[fARRAY_MAX];
```

Use of defined constants guarantees that subsequent references to the array will not exceed the defined array size. For example, it is very common to use a **for** loop to access array elements:

```
#include <stdio.h>

#define iARRAY_MAX 20

int iarray[iARRAY_MAX];
```

```
main( )
{
  int i;
  for(i = 0; i < iARRAY_MAX; i++) {
  .

  .

  .
  }
  return(0);
}
```

Initializing Arrays

There are three techniques for initializing arrays:

- By default when they are created. This applies only to global and static arrays.
- Explicitly when they are created, by supplying constant initializing data.
- During program execution, when you assign or copy data into the array.

You can only use constant data to initialize an array when it is created. If the array elements must receive their values from variables, you must initialize the array by writing explicit statements as part of the program code.

Default Initialization

The ANSI C standard specifies that arrays are either global (defined outside of main( ) and any other function) or static automatic (static, but defined after any opening brace) and will always be initialized to binary zero if no other initialization data is supplied. C initializes numeric arrays to zero. Pointer arrays are initialized to NULL. You can run the following program to make certain that a compiler meets this standard:

```
/*
 *   initar.c
 *   A C program verifying array initialization
 *   Copyright (c) Chris H. Pappas and William H. Murray, 1998
 */

#include <stdio.h>

#define iGLOBAL_ARRAY_SIZE 10
#define iSTATIC_ARRAY_SIZE 20
```

```
int iglobal_array[iGLOBAL_ARRAY_SIZE];           /*a global array*/

main( )
{
  static int istatic_array[iSTATIC_ARRAY_SIZE]; /*a static array*/
  printf("iglobal_array[0]: %d\n",iglobal_array[0]);
  printf("istatic_array[0]: %d\n",istatic_array[0]);

  return(0);
}
```

When the program is run, you should see zeroes printed verifying that both array types are automatically initialized. This program also highlights another very important point: that the first subscript for all arrays in C is zero. Unlike other languages, there is no way to make a C program think that the first subscript is 1. If you are wondering why, remember that one of C's strengths is its close link to assembly language. In assembly language, the first element in a table is always at the zeroth offset.

Explicit Initialization

Just as you can define and initialize variables of type **int**, **char**, **float**, **double**, and so on, you can also initialize arrays. The ANSI C standard lets you supply initialization values for any array, global or otherwise, defined anywhere in a program. The following code segment illustrates how to define and initialize four arrays:

```
int iarray[3] = {-1,0,1};
static float fpercent[4] = {1.141579,0.75,55E0,-.33E1};
static int idecimal[3] = {0,1,2,3,4,5,6,7,8,9};
char cvowels[] = {'A','a','E','e','I','i','O','o','U','u'};
```

The first line of code declares the *iarray* array to be three integers and provides the values of the elements in curly braces, separated by commas. As usual, a semicolon ends the statement. The effect of this is that after the compiled program loads into the memory of the computer, the reserved space for the *iarray* array will already contain the initial values, so they won't need assignments when the program executes. It is important to realize that this is more than just a convenience—it happens at a different time. If the program goes on to change the values of the *iarray* array, they stay changed. Many compilers permit you to initialize arrays only if they are global or static, as in the second line of code. This statement initializes the array *fpercent* when the entire program loads.

The third line of code illustrates putting the wrong count in the array declaration. Many compilers consider this an error, while others reserve enough space to hold whichever is greater—the number of values you ask for or the number of values you provide. This example will draw complaints from the Visual C/C++ compiler by way of an error message indicating too many initializers. In the opposite case, when you ask for more space than you provide values for, the values go into the beginning of the array and the extra elements become zeros. This also means that you do not need to count the values when you provide all of them. If the count is empty, as in the fourth line of code, the number of values determines the size of the array.

Unsized Initialization

You can provide the size of the array or the list of actual array values. It usually doesn't matter for most compilers, as long as you provide at least one of them. For example, a program will frequently want to define its own set of error messages. This can be done two ways. Here is the first method:

```
char szInput_Error[37] = "Please enter a value between 0 - 9:\n";
char szDevice_Error[16] = "Disk not ready\n";
char szMonitor_Error[32] = "Program needs a color monitor.\n";
char szWarning[44]="This operation will erase the active file!\n";
```

This method requires you to count the number of characters in the string, remembering to add 1 to the count for the unseen null-string terminator \0. This can become a very tedious approach at best, straining the eyes as you count the number of characters, and very error prone. The second method allows C to automatically dimension the arrays through the use of unsized arrays, as shown here:

```
char szInput_Error[] = "Please enter a value between 0 - 9:\n";
char szDevice_Error[] = "Disk not ready\n";
char szMonitor_Error[] = "Program needs a color monitor.\n";
char szWarning[] = "This operation will erase the active file!\n";
```

When an array initialization statement is encountered and the array size is not specified, the compiler automatically creates an array big enough to hold all of the specified data.

There are a few major pitfalls that await the inexperienced programmer when initializing arrays. For example, an array with an empty size declaration and no list of values has a null length. If there are any data declarations after the array, then the name of the null array refers to the same address, and storing values in the null array puts them in addresses allocated to other variables.

Unsized array initializations are not restricted to one-dimensional arrays. For multidimensional arrays, you must specify all but the leftmost dimension for C to properly index the array. With this approach you can build tables of varying lengths, with the compiler automatically allocating enough storage.

Accessing Array Elements

A variable declaration usually reserves one or more cells in internal memory and, through a lookup table, associates a name with the cell or cells that you can use to access the cells. For example, the following definition reserves only one integer-sized cell in internal memory and associates the name *ivideo_tapes* with that cell. See the top of Figure 9-1.

```
int ivideo_tapes;
```

On the other hand, the next definition reserves seven contiguous cells in internal memory and associates the name *ivideo_library* with the seven cells. See the bottom of Figure 9-1.

```
int ivideo_library[7];
```

Since all array elements must be of the same data type, each of the seven cells in the array *ivideo_library* can hold one integer.

Consider the difference between accessing the single cell associated with the variable *ivideo_tapes* and the seven cells associated with the array *ivideo_library*. To access the cell associated with the variable *ivideo_tapes*, you simply use the name *ivideo_tapes*. For the array *ivideo_library*, you must specify an *index* to indicate exactly

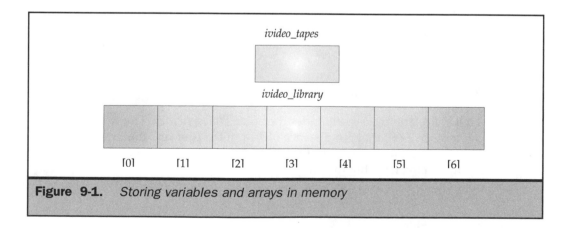

Figure 9-1.   *Storing variables and arrays in memory*

PROGRAMMING
FOUNDATIONS

which cell among the seven you wish to access. The following statements designate the first cell, the second cell, the third cell, and so on, up to the last cell of the array:

```
ivideo_library[0];
ivideo_library[1];
ivideo_library[2];
ivideo_library[3];
       .
       .
       .
ivideo_library[6];
```

When accessing an array element, the integer enclosed in the square brackets is the index, which indicates the *offset*, or the distance between the cell to be accessed and the first cell.

One of the principal mistake novice programmers make has to do with the index value used to reference an array's first element. The first element is not at index position [1]; instead, it is [0] since there is zero distance between the first element and itself. The third cell has an index value of 2 because its distance from the first cell is 2.

When working with arrays, you can use the square brackets in two quite different ways. When you are defining an array, the number of cells is specified in square brackets:

```
int ivideo_library[7];
```

However, when you are accessing a specific array element, you use the array's name together with an index enclosed in square brackets:

```
ivideo_library[3];
```

Assuming the previous declaration for the array *ivideo_library*, the following statement is logically incorrect:

```
ivideo_library[7] = 53219;
```

It is not a legal reference to a cell under the name *ivideo_library*. The statement attempts to reference a cell that is a distance of 7 from the first cell, that is, the eighth cell. Because there are only seven cells, this is an error. It is up to you to ensure that index expressions remain within the array's bounds.

Examine the following declarations:

```
#define iDAYS_OF_WEEK 7

int ivideo_library[iDAYS_OF_WEEK];
int iweekend = 1;
int iweekday = 2;
```

Take a look at what happens with this set of executable statements:

```
ivideo_library[2];
ivideo_library[iweekday];
ivideo_library[iweekend + iweekday];
ivideo_library[iweekday - iweekend];
ivideo_library[iweekend - iweekday];
```

The first two statements both reference the third element of the array. The first statement accomplishes this with a constant value expression, while the second statement uses a variable. The last three statements demonstrate that you can use expressions as subscripts, as long as they evaluate to a valid integer index. Statement three has an index value of 3 and references the fourth element of the array. The fourth statement, with an index value of 1, accesses the second element of the array. The last statement is illegal because the index value –1 is invalid.

It is also possible to access any element in an array without knowing how big each element is. For example, suppose you want to access the third element in *ivideo_library*, an array of integers. Remember from Chapter 6 that different systems allocate different size cells to the same data type. On one computer system, an integer might occupy 2 bytes of storage, whereas on another system, an integer might occupy 8 bytes of storage. On either system, you can access the third element as *ivideo_library[2]*. The index value indicates the number of elements to move, regardless of the number of bits allocated.

This offset addressing holds true for other array types. On one system, integer variables might require twice as many bits of storage as does a char type; on another system, integer variables might require four times as many bits as do character variables. Yet to access the fourth element in either an array of integers or an array of characters, you would use an index value of 3.

Calculating Array Dimensions

You have already learned that the sizeof( ) operator returns the physical size, in bytes, of the data object to which it is applied. You can use it with any type of data object except bit-fields. A frequent use of sizeof( ) is to determine the physical size of a variable when the size of the variable's data type can vary from machine to machine. You have already seen how an integer can be either 2 or 4 bytes, depending on the machine being used. If an additional amount of memory to hold seven integers will be requested from the operating system, some way is needed to determine whether 14 bytes (7×2 bytes/integer) or 28 bytes (7×4 bytes/integer) are needed. The following program automatically takes this into consideration (and prints a value of 28 for systems allocating 4 bytes per integer cell):

```
/*
 *    sizeof.c
 *    A C program applying sizeof( ) to determine an array's size
 *    Copyright (c) Chris H. Pappas and William H. Murray, 1998
 */

#include <stdio.h>

#define iDAYS_OF_WEEK 7

main( )
{
  int ivideo_library[iDAYS_OF_WEEK]={1,2,3,4,5,6,7};

  printf("There are %d number of bytes in the array"
    " ivideo_library.\n",(int)sizeof(ivideo_library));

  return(0);
}
```

This concept becomes essential when the program must be portable and independent of any particular hardware. If you are wondering why there is an int type cast on the result returned by sizeof( ), in the ANSI C standard sizeof( ) does not return an int type. Instead, sizeof( ) returns a data type, size_t, that is large enough to hold the return value. The ANSI C standard added this to C because on certain computers an integer is not big enough to represent the size of all data items. In the example, casting the return value to an integer allows it to match the %d conversion character of the printf( ) function. Otherwise, if the returned value had been larger than an integer, the printf( ) function would not have worked properly.

By changing *iarray*'s data type in the following program, you can explore how various data types are stored internally:

```
/*
 *    array.c
 *    A C program illustrating contiguous array storage
```

```
*     Copyright (c) Chris H. Pappas and William H. Murray, 1998
*/

#include <stdio.h>

#define iDAYS 7

main( )
{
  int index, iarray[iDAYS];

  printf("sizeof(int) is %d\n\n", (int)sizeof(int));

  for(index = 0; index < iDAYS; index++)
    printf("&iarray[%d] = %X\n", index,
             &iarray[index]);

  return(0);
}
```

If the program is run on a machine with a word length of 2 bytes, the output will
look similar to the following:

```
sizeof(int) is 4

&iarray[0] = 64FDDC
&iarray[1] = 64FDE0
&iarray[2] = 64FDE4
&iarray[3] = 64FDE8
&iarray[4] = 64FDEC
&iarray[5] = 64FDF0
&iarray[6] = 64FDF4
```

Notice how the & (address) operator can be applied to any variable, including an
array element. An array element can be treated like any other variable; its value can
form an expression, it can be assigned a value, and it can be passed as an argument (or
parameter) to a function. In this example you can see how the array elements'
addresses are exactly 2 bytes apart. You will see the importance of this contiguous
storage when you use arrays in conjunction with pointer variables.

The following C++ listing is similar in structure to the program just discussed:

```
//
//  array.cpp
//  A C++ program illustrating contiguous array storage
//  Copyright (c) Chris H. Pappas and William H. Murray, 1998
//

#include <iostream.h>

#define iMAX 10

main( )
{
  int index, iarray[iMAX];

  cout << "sizeof(int) is " << (int)sizeof(int) << "\n\n";

  for(index = 0; index < iMAX; index++)
    cout << "&iarray[" << index << "] = " << index
         << &iarray[index] << endl;

  return(0);
}
```

Array Index Out of Bounds

There is a popular saying that states, "You don't get something for nothing." This holds true with array types. The "something" you get is faster executing code at the expense of the "nothing," which is zero boundary checking. Remember, since C and C++ were designed to replace assembly language code, error checking was left out of the compiler to keep the code lean. Without any compiler error checking, you must be very careful when dealing with array boundaries. For example, the following program elicits no complaints from the compiler, yet it can change the contents of other variables or even crash the program by writing beyond the array's boundary:

```
/*
 *  norun.c
 *  Do NOT run this C program
 *  Copyright (c) Chris H. Pappas and William H. Murray, 1998
 */

#include <stdio.h>
```

```
#define iMAX 10
#define iOUT_OF_RANGE 50

main( )
{
  int inot_enough_room[iMAX], index;

  for(index=0; index < iOUT_OF_RANGE; index++)
    inot_enough_room[index]=index;

  return(0);
}
```

Output and Input of Strings

While C and C++ do supply the data type char, they do not have a data type for character strings. Instead, the programmer must represent a string as an array of characters. The array uses one cell for each character in the string, with the final cell holding the null character \0.

The next example shows how you can represent the three major types of transportation as a character string. The array *szmode1* is initialized character by character by use of the assignment operator, the array *szmode2* is initialized by use of the function scanf( ), and the array *szmode3* is initialized in the following definition.

```
/*
 *    string.c
 *    This C program demonstrates the use of strings
 *    Copyright (c) Chris H. Pappas and William H. Murray, 1998
 */

#include <stdio.h>

main( )
{
  char        szmode1[4],          /* car   */
              szmode2[6];          /* plane */
  static char szmode3[5] = "ship"; /* ship  */

  szmode1[0] = 'c';
  szmode1[1] = 'a';
  szmode1[2] = 'r';
```

PROGRAMMING FOUNDATIONS

```
    szmode1[3] = '\0';

    printf("\n\n\tPlease enter the mode --> plane ");
    scanf("%s",szmode2);

    printf("%s\n",szmode1);
    printf("%s\n",szmode2);
    printf("%s\n",szmode3);

    return(0);
}
```

The next definitions show how C treats character strings as arrays of characters:

```
char    szmode1[4],                     /* car   */
        szmode2[6];                     /* plane */
static char szmode3[5] = "ship";        /* ship  */
```

Even though the *szmode1* "car" has three characters, the array *szmode1* has four cells—one cell for each letter in the mode "car" and one for the null character. Remember, \0 counts as one character. Similarly, the mode "plane" has five characters ("ship" has four) but requires six storage cells (five for *szmode3*), including the null character. Remember, you could also have initialized the *szmode3[5]* array of characters by using braces:

```
static char szmode3[5] = {'s','h','i','p','\0'};
```

When you use double quotes to list the initial values of the character array, the system will automatically add the null terminator \0. Also, remember that the same line could have been written like this:

```
static char szmode3[] = "ship";
```

This uses an unsized array. Of course, you could have chosen the tedious approach to initializing an array of characters that was done with *szmode1*. A more common approach is to use the scanf( ) function to read the string directly into the array as was done with *szmode2*. The scanf( ) function uses a %s conversion specification. This causes the function to skip white space (blanks, tabs, and carriage returns) and then to read into the character array *szmode2* all characters up to the next white space. The system will then automatically add a null terminator. Remember, the array's dimension must be large enough to hold the string along with a null terminator. Look at this statement one more time:

```
scanf("%s",szmode2);
```

Are you bothered by the fact that *szmode2* was not preceded by the address operator &? While it is true that scanf( ) was written to expect the address of a variable, as it turns out, an array's name, unlike simple variable names, is an address expression—the address of the first element in the array.

When you use the printf( ) function in conjunction with a %s, the function is expecting the corresponding argument to be the address of some character string. The string is printed up to but not including the null character.

The following listing illustrates these principles by using an equivalent C++ algorithm:

```cpp
//
//   string.cpp
//   This C++ program demonstrates the use of strings
//   Copyright (c) Chris H. Pappas and William H. Murray, 1998
//

#include <iostream.h>

main( )
{
  char          szmode1[4],              // car
                szmode2[6];              // plane
  static char szmode3[5] = "ship";       // ship

  szmode1[0] = 'c';
  szmode1[1] = 'a';
  szmode1[2] = 'r';
  szmode1[3] = '\0';

  cout << "\n\n\tPlease enter the mode --> plane ";
  cin >> szmode2;

  cout << szmode1 << "\n";
  cout << szmode2 << "\n";
  cout << szmode3 << "\n";
```

```
    return(0);
}
```

The output from the program looks like this:

```
car
plane
ship
```

Multidimensional Arrays

The term *dimension* represents the number of indexes used to reference a particular element in an array. All of the arrays discussed so far have been one-dimensional and require only one index to access an element. By looking at an array's declaration, you can tell how many dimensions it has. If there is only one set of brackets ([ ]), the array is one-dimensional, two sets of brackets ([ ][ ]) indicate a two-dimensional array, and so on. Arrays of more than one dimension are called *multidimensional arrays*. For real-world modeling, the working maximum number of dimensions is usually three.

The following declarations set up a two-dimensional array that is initialized while the program executes:

```
/*
 *    2daray.c
 *    A C program demonstrating the use of a two-dimensional array
 *    Copyright (c) Chris H. Pappas and William H. Murray, 1998
 */

#include <stdio.h>

#define iROWS 4
#define iCOLUMNS 5

main( )
{
    int irow;
    int icolumn;
    int istatus[iROWS][iCOLUMNS];
    int iadd;
    int imultiple;

    for(irow=0; irow < iROWS; irow++)
```

```
    for(icolumn=0; icolumn < iCOLUMNS; icolumn++) {
      iadd = iCOLUMNS - icolumn;
      imultiple = irow;
      istatus[irow][icolumn] = (irow+1) *
        icolumn + iadd * imultiple;
    }

  for(irow=0; irow<iROWS; irow++) {
    printf("CURRENT ROW: %d\n",irow);
    printf("RELATIVE DISTANCE FROM BASE:\n");
    for(icolumn=0; icolumn<iCOLUMNS; icolumn++)
      printf(" %d ",istatus[irow][icolumn]);
    printf("\n\n");
  }

  return(0);
}
```

PROGRAMMING
FOUNDATIONS

The program uses two for loops to calculate and initialize each of the array elements to its respective "offset from the first element." The created array has 4 rows (*iROWS*) and 5 columns (*iCOLUMNS*) per row, for a total of 20 integer elements. Multidimensional arrays are stored in linear fashion in the computer's memory. Elements in multidimensional arrays are grouped from the rightmost index inward. In the preceding example, row 1, column 1 would be element three of the storage array. Although the calculation of the offset appears a little tricky, note how easily each array element itself is referenced:

```
istatus[irow][icolumn] = . . .
```

The output from the program looks like this:

```
CURRENT ROW: 0
RELATIVE DISTANCE FROM BASE:
 0  1  2  3  4

CURRENT ROW: 1
RELATIVE DISTANCE FROM BASE:
 5  6  7  8  9

CURRENT ROW: 2
RELATIVE DISTANCE FROM BASE:
```

```
10   11   12   13   14

CURRENT ROW: 3
RELATIVE DISTANCE FROM BASE:
 15   16   17   18   19
```

Multidimensional arrays can also be initialized in the same way as one-dimensional arrays. For example, the following program defines a two-dimensional array *dpowers* and initializes the array when it is defined. The function pow( ) returns the value of *x* raised to the *y* power:

```c
/*
 *    2dadbl.c
 *    A C program using a 2-dimensional array of doubles
 *    Copyright (c) Chris H. Pappas and William H. Murray, 1998
 */

#include <stdio.h>
#include <math.h>

#define iBASES 6
#define iEXPONENTS 3
#define iBASE 0
#define iRAISED_TO 1
#define iRESULT 2

main( )
{
  double dpowers[iBASES][iEXPONENTS]={
    1.1,  1,  0,
    2.2,  2,  0,
    3.3,  3,  0,
    4.4,  4,  0,
    5.5,  5,  0,
    6.6,  6,  0
  };

  int irow_index;

  for(irow_index=0; irow_index < iBASES; irow_index++)
    dpowers[irow_index][iRESULT] =
```

```
        pow(dpowers[irow_index][iBASE],
        dpowers[irow_index][iRAISED_TO]);

    for(irow_index=0; irow_index < iBASES; irow_index++) {
      printf("     %d\n",(int)dpowers[irow_index][iRAISED_TO]);
      printf(" %2.1f = %.2f\n\n",dpowers[irow_index][iBASE],
                              dpowers[irow_index][iRESULT]);
    }

    return(0);
}
```

The array *dpowers* was declared to be of type double because the function pow( ) expects two double variables and returns a double. Of course, you must take care when initializing two-dimensional arrays; you must make certain you know which dimension is increasing the fastest. Remember, this is always the rightmost dimension.

The output from the program looks like this:

```
    1
1.1 = 1.10

    2
2.2 = 4.84

    3
3.3 = 35.94

    4
4.4 = 374.81

    5
5.5 = 5032.84

    6
6.6 = 82653.95
```

Arrays as Function Arguments

Just like other variables, arrays can be passed from one function to another. Because arrays as function arguments can be discussed in full only after an introduction to pointers, this chapter begins the topic and Chapter 10 expands upon this base.

Passing Arrays to C Functions

Consider a function isum( ) that computes the sum of the array elements *inumeric_values[0], inumeric_values[1],..., numeric_values[n].* Two parameters are required—an array parameter called *iarray_address_received* to hold a copy of the array's address and a parameter called *imax_size* to hold the index of the last item in the array to be summed. Assuming that the array is an array of integers and that the index is also of type **int**, the parameters in isum( ) can be described as

```
int isum(int iarray_address_received[], int imax_size)
```

The parameter declaration for the array includes square brackets to signal the function isum( ) that *iarray_address_received* is an array name and not the name of an ordinary parameter. Note that the number of cells is not enclosed in the square brackets. Of course, the simple parameter *imax_size* is declared as previously described. Invoking the function is as simple as this:

```
isum(inumeric_values,iactual_index);
```

Passing the array *inumeric_values* is a simple process of entering its name as the argument. When passing an array's name to a function, you are actually passing the *address* of the array's first element. Look at the following expression:

```
inumeric_values
is really shorthand for
&inumeric_values[0]
```

Technically, you can invoke the function isum( ) with either of the following two valid statements:

```
isum(inumeric_values,iactual_index);
itotal = isum(&inumeric_values[0],iactual_index);
```

In either case, within the function isum( ) you can access every cell in the array.

When a function is going to process an array, the calling function includes the name of the array in the function's argument list. This means that the function receives and carries out its processing on the actual elements of the array, not on a local copy as in single-value variables where functions pass only their values.

By default all arrays are passed call-by-variable or call-by-reference. This prevents the frequent "stack overruns heap" error message many Pascal programmers encounter if they have forgotten to include the **var** modifier for formal array argument declarations. In contrast, the Pascal language passes all array arguments call-by-value. A call-by-value forces the compiler to duplicate the array's contents. For large arrays, this is time consuming and wastes memory.

When a function is to receive an array name as an argument, there are two ways to declare the argument locally: as an array or as a pointer. Which one you use depends on how the function processes the set of values. If the function steps through the elements with an index, the declaration should be an array with square brackets following the name. The size can be empty since the declaration does not reserve space for the entire array, just for the address where it begins. Having seen the array declaration at the beginning of the function, the compiler then permits brackets with an index to appear after the array name anywhere in the function.

The following example declares an array of five elements, and after printing its values, calls in a function to determine what the smallest value in the array is. To do this, it passes the array name and its size to the function iminimum( ), which declares them as an array called *iarray[]* and an integer called *isize*. The function then passes through the array, comparing each element against the smallest value it has seen so far, and every time it encounters a smaller value, it stores that new value in the variable *icurrent_minimum*. At the end, it returns the smallest value it has seen for the main( ) to print.

```c
/*
 *   pasary.c
 *   A C program using arrays as parameters
 *   Copyright (c) Chris H. Pappas and William H. Murray, 1998
 */

#include <stdio.h>

#define iMAX 10
#define iUPPER_LIMIT 100

main( )
{
  int iarray[iMAX] = {3,7,2,1,5,6,8,9,0,4};
  int i, ismallest;
  int iminimum(int iarray[],int imax);

  printf("The original list looks like: ");
  for(i = 0; i < iMAX; i++)
    printf("%d ",iarray[i]);
  ismallest = iminimum(iarray,iMAX);
  printf("\nThe smallest value is: %d: \n",ismallest);
```

```
  return(0);
}

int iminimum(int iarray[], int imax)
{
  int i, icurrent_minimum;

  icurrent_minimum = iUPPER_LIMIT;
  for(i = 0; i < imax; i++)
    if (iarray[i] < icurrent_minimum)
      icurrent_minimum = iarray[i];
  return(icurrent_minimum);
}
```

Passing Arrays to C++ Functions

The following C++ program format is very similar to the C programs examined so far.
The program demonstrates how to declare and pass an array argument.

```
//
//  fncary.cpp
//  A C++ program demonstrating how to use arrays with
//  functions
//  Copyright (c) Chris H. Pappas and William H. Murray, 1998
//

#include <iostream.h>

#define iSIZE 5
void vadd_1(int iarray[]);

main( )
{
  int iarray[iSIZE]={0,1,2,3,4};
  int i;

  cout << "iarray before calling add_1:\n\n";
  for(i=0; i < iSIZE; i++)
    cout << "   " << iarray[i];

  vadd_1(iarray);
```

```
   cout << "\n\niarray after calling vadd_1:\n\n";
   for(i=0; i < iSIZE; i++)
     cout << "   " << iarray[i];

   return(0);
}

void vadd_1(int iarray[])
{
   int i;

   for(i=0; i < iSIZE; i++)
     iarray[i]++;
}
```

The output from the program looks like this:

```
iarray before calling vadd_1:

  0   1   2   3   4

iarray after calling vadd_1:

  1   2   3   4   5
```

Here is a question you should be able to answer. What do the values in the output tell you about the array argument? Is the array passed call-by-value or call-by-reference? The function vadd_1( ) simply adds 1 to each array element. Since this incremented change is reflected back in main( ) *iarray*, it would appear that the parameter was passed call-by-reference. Previous discussions about what an array name really is indicate that this is true. Remember, array names are addresses to the first array cell.

The following C++ program incorporates many of the array features discussed so far, including multidimensional array initialization, referencing, and arguments:

```
//
//  2daray.cpp
//  A C++ program that demonstrates how to define, pass,
//  and walk through the different dimensions of an array
//  Copyright (c) Chris H. Pappas and William H. Murray, 1998
//
```

```cpp
#include <iostream.h>

void vdisplay_results(char carray[][3][4]);

char cglobal_cube[5][4][5]= {
                {
                  {'P','L','A','N','E'},
                  {'Z','E','R','O',' '},
                  {' ',' ',' ',' ',' '},
                  {'R','O','W',' ','3'},
                },
                {
                  {'P','L','A','N','E'},
                  {'O','N','E',' ',' '},
                  {'R','O','W',' ','2'}
                },
                {
                  {'P','L','A','N','E'},
                  {'T','W','O',' ',' '}
                },
                {
                  {'P','L','A','N','E'},
                  {'T','H','R','E','E'},
                  {'R','O','W',' ','2'},
                  {'R','O','W',' ','3'}
                },
                {
                  {'P','L','A','N','E'},
                  {'F','O','U','R',' '},
                  {'r','o','w',' ','2'},
                  {'a','b','c','d','e'}
                }
};


int imatrix[4][3]={ {1},{2},{3},{4} };

main( )
{
  int irow_index, icolumn_index;
  char clocal_cube[2][3][4];

  cout << "sizeof clocal_cube         = "<< sizeof(clocal_cube)
                                       << "\n";
```

```
    cout << "sizeof clocal_cube[0]        = "<< sizeof(clocal_cube[0])
                                              << "\n";
    cout << "sizeof clocal_cube[0][0]   = "<<
             sizeof(clocal_cube[0][0])       << "\n";
    cout << "sizeof clocal_cube[0][0][0]= "<<
             sizeof(clocal_cube[0][0][0])  << "\n";

    vdisplay_results(clocal_cube);

    cout << "cglobal_cube[0][1][2] is     = "
         << cglobal_cube[0][1][2] << "\n";
    cout << "cglobal_cube[1][0][2] is     = "
         << cglobal_cube[1][0][2] << "\n";

    cout << "\nprint part of the cglobal_cube's plane 0\n";
    for(irow_index=0; irow_index < 4; irow_index++) {
      for(icolumn_index=0; icolumn_index < 5; icolumn_index++)
        cout << cglobal_cube[0][irow_index][icolumn_index];
      cout << "\n";
    }

    cout << "\nprint part of the cglobal_cube's plane 4\n";
    for(irow_index=0; irow_index < 4; irow_index++) {
      for(icolumn_index=0; icolumn_index < 5; icolumn_index++)
        cout << cglobal_cube[4][irow_index][icolumn_index];
      cout << "\n";
    }

    cout << "\nprint all of imatrix\n";
    for(irow_index=0; irow_index < 4; irow_index++) {
      for(icolumn_index=0; icolumn_index < 3; icolumn_index++)
        cout << imatrix[irow_index][icolumn_index];
      cout << "\n";
    }

    return (0);
}

void vdisplay_results(char carray[][3][4])
{
cout << "sizeof carray         =" << sizeof(carray) << "\n";
cout << " sizeof  carray[0]      =" << sizeof(carray[0]) << "\n";
```

```
cout << " sizeof  cglobal_cube =" << sizeof(cglobal_cube) << "\n";
cout << " sizeof cglobal_cube[0]=" << sizeof(cglobal_cube[0])
                                   << "\n";
}
```

Notice, first, how *cglobal_cube* is defined and initialized. Braces are used to group the characters together so that they have a form similar to the dimensions of the array. This helps in visualizing the form of the array. The braces are not required in this case since you are not leaving any gaps in the array with the initializing data. If you were initializing only a portion of any dimension, various sets of the inner braces would be required to designate which initializing values should apply to which part of the array. The easiest way to visualize the three-dimensional array is to imagine five layers, each having a two-dimensional, four-row by five-column array (see Figure 9-2).

The first four lines of the program output show the size of the *clocal_cube* array, various dimensions, and an individual element. The output illustrates how the total size of the multidimensional array is the product of all the dimensions times the size of the array data type, that is, 2 * 3 * 4 * *sizeof(char)*, or 24.

Observe how the array element *clocal_cube[0]* is in itself an array that contains a two-dimensional array of [3][4], thereby giving *clocal_cube[0]* the size of 12. The size of *clocal_cube[0][0]* is 4, which is the number of elements in the final dimension since each element has a size of 1, as the *sizeof(clocal_cube[0][0][0])* shows.

To fully understand multidimensional arrays, it is very important to realize that *clocal_cube[0]* is both an array name and a pointer constant. Because the program did not subscript the last dimension, the expression does not have the same type as the data type of each fundamental array element. Because *clocal_cube[0]* does not refer to an individual element, but rather to another array, it does not have the type of char. Since *clocal_cube[0]* has the type of pointer constant, it is not a legal *lvalue* and cannot appear to the left of an assignment operator in an assignment expression.

Something very interesting happens when you use an array name in a function argument list, as was done when the function vdisplay_results( ) was invoked with *clocal_cube*. While inside the function, if you perform a sizeof( ) operation against the formal parameter that represents the array name, you do not correctly compute the actual size of *carray*. What the function sees is only a copy of the address of the first element in the array. Therefore, the function sizeof( ) will return the size of the address, not the item to which it refers.

The sizeof( ) *carray[0]* in function vdisplay_results( ) is 12 because it was declared in the function that the formal parameter was an array whose last two dimensions were [3] and [4]. You could not have used any values when you declared the size of these last two dimensions because the function prototype defined them to be [3] and [4]. Without a prototype, the compiler would not be able to detect the difference in the way the array was dimensioned. This would let you redefine the way in which you viewed the array's organization. The function vdisplay_results( ) also outputs the size of the

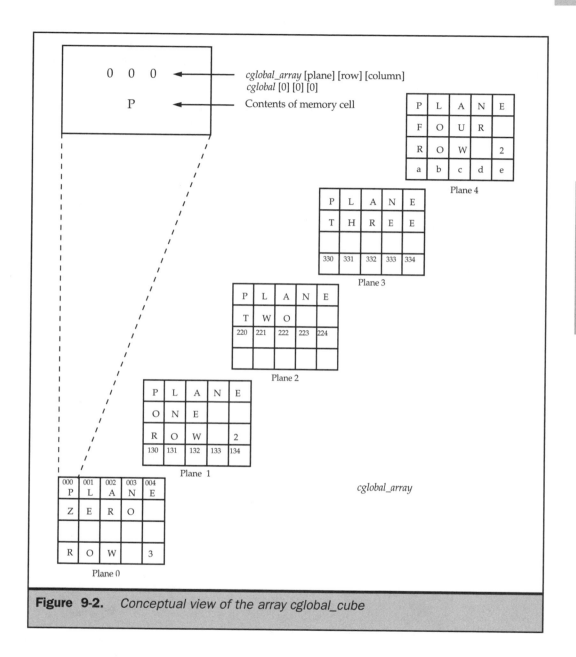

Figure 9-2. *Conceptual view of the array cglobal_cube*

global *cglobal_cube.* This points out that while a function may have access to global data directly, it has access only to the address of an array that is passed to a function as an argument.

With regard to the main( ) function, the next two statements demonstrate how to reference specific elements in *cglobal_cube* when they are executed. *cglobal_cube[0][1][2]* references the zeroth layer, second row, third column, or "R." *cglobal_cube[1][0][2]* references the second layer, row zero, third column, or "A."

The next block of code in main( ) contains two nested for loops demonstrating that the arrays are stored in plane-row-column order. As already seen, the rightmost subscript (column) of the array varies the fastest when you view the array in a linear fashion. The first for loop pair hardwires the output to the zeroth layer and selects a row, with the inner loop traversing each column in *cglobal_cube*. The program continues by duplicating the same loop structures but printing only the fifth layer (plane [4]), of the *cglobal_cube*.

The last for loop pair displays the elements of *imatrix* in the form of a rectangle, similar to the way many people visualize a two-dimensional array.

The output from the program looks like this:

```
sizeof clocal_cube            = 24
sizeof clocal_cube[0]         = 12
sizeof clocal_cube[0][0]      = 4
sizeof clocal_cube[0][0][0]   = 1
sizeof carray                 = 4
sizeof carray[0]              = 12
sizeof cglobal_cube           = 100
sizeof cglobal_cube[0]        = 20
cglobal_cube[0][1][2] is      = R
cglobal_cube[1][0][2] is      = A

print part of the cglobal_cube's plane 0
PLANE
ZERO

ROW 3

print part of the cglobal_cube's plane 4
PLANE
FOUR
row 2
abcde

print all of imatrix
100
200
300
400
```

Does the output catch your attention? Look at the initialization of *imatrix*. Because each inner set of braces corresponds to one row of the array and enough values were not supplied inside the inner braces, the system padded the remaining elements with zeroes. Remember, C and C++ automatically initialize all undefined static automatic numeric array elements to zero.

String Functions and Character Arrays

Because of the way string data types are handled, many of the functions that use character arrays as function arguments were not discussed. Specifically, these functions are gets( ), puts( ), fgets( ), fputs( ), sprintf( ), stpcpy( ), strcat( ), strncmp( ), and strlen( ). Understanding how these functions operate will be much easier now that you are familiar with the concepts of character arrays and null-terminated strings. One of the easiest ways to explain these functions is to show a few program examples.

gets( ), puts( ), fgets( ), fputs( ), and sprintf( )

The following example program demonstrates how you can use gets( ), puts( ), fgets( ), fputs( ), and sprintf( ) to format I/O:

```
/*
 *   strio.c
 *   A C program using several string I/O functions
 *   Copyright (c) Chris H. Pappas and William H. Murray, 1998
 */

#include <stdio.h>

#define iSIZE 20

main( )
{
  char sztest_array[iSIZE];

  fputs("Please enter the first string  : ",stdout);
  gets(sztest_array);
  fputs("The first string entered is    : ",stdout);
  puts(sztest_array);

  fputs("Please enter the second string : ",stdout);
  fgets(sztest_array,iSIZE,stdin);
  fputs("The second string entered is   : ",stdout);
```

```
    fputs(sztest_array,stdout);

    sprintf(sztest_array,"This was %s a test","just");
    fputs("sprintf( ) created            : ",stdout);
    fputs(sztest_array,stdout);

    return(0);
}
```

Here is the output from the first run of the program:

```
Please enter the first string  : string one
The first string entered is     : string one
Please enter the second string : string two
The second string entered is    : string two
sprintf( ) created              : This was just a test
```

Since the strings that were entered were less than the size of *sztest_array*, the program works fine. However, when you enter a string longer than *sztest_array*, something similar to the following can occur when the program is run:

```
Please enter the first string  : one two three four five
The first string entered is     : one two three four five
Please enter the second string : six seven eight nine ten
The second string entered is    : six seven eight ninsprintf( ) created
    : This was just a testPlease enter the first string  : The first
         string entered is    :e ten
The second string entered is    :
```

Take care when running the program. The gets( ) function receives characters from standard input (stdin, the keyboard by default for most computers) and places them into the array whose name is passed to the function. When you press the ENTER key to terminate the string, a newline character is transmitted. When the gets( ) function receives this newline character, it changes it into a null character, thereby ensuring that the character array contains a string. No checking occurs to ensure that the array is big enough to hold all the characters entered.

The puts( ) function echoes to the terminal just what was entered with gets( ). It also adds a newline character on the end of the string in the place where the null character appeared. The null character, remember, was automatically inserted into the string by the gets( ) function. Therefore, strings that are properly entered with gets( ) can be displayed with puts( ).

When you use the fgets( ) function, you can guarantee a maximum number of input characters. This function stops reading the designated file stream when *one fewer* character is read than the second argument specifies. Since *sztest_array size* is 20, only 19 characters will be read by fgets( ) from stdin. A null character is automatically placed into the string in the last position; and if a newline were entered from the keyboard, it would be retained in the string. (It would appear before the null debug example.) The fgets( ) function does not eliminate the newline character like gets( ) did; it merely adds the null character at the end so that a valid string is stored. In much the same way as gets( ) and puts( ) are symmetrical, so too are fgets( ) and fputs( ). fgets( ) does not eliminate the newline, nor does fputs( ) add one.

To understand how important the newline character is to these functions, look closely at the second run output given. Notice the phrase "sprintf( ) created..."; it follows immediately after the numbers six, seven, eight, and nine that had just been entered. The second input string actually had five more characters than the fgets( ) function read in (one fewer than *iSIZE* of 19 characters). The others were left in the input buffer. Also dropped was the newline that terminated the input from the keyboard. (It is left in the input stream because it occurs after the 19th character.) Therefore, no newline character was stored in the string. Since fputs( ) does not add 1 back, the next fputs( ) output begins on the line where the previous output ended. Reliance was on the newline character read by fgets( ) and printed by fputs( ) to help control the display formatting.

The function sprintf( ) stands for "string printf( )." It uses a control string with conversion characters in exactly the same way as does printf( ). The additional feature is that sprintf( ) places the resulting formatted data in a string rather than immediately sending the result to standard output. This can be beneficial if the exact same output must be created twice—for example, when the same string must be output to both the display monitor and the printer.

To review:

- gets( ) converts newline to a null.
- puts( ) converts null to a newline.
- fgets( ) retains newline and appends a null.
- fputs( ) drops the null and does not add a newline; instead, it uses the retained newline (if one was entered).

strcpy( ), strcat( ), strncmp( ), and strlen( )

All of the functions discussed in this section are predefined in the STRING.H header file. When using these functions, make certain to include the header file in your program. Remember, all of the string functions prototyped in STRING.H expect null-terminated string parameters. The following program demonstrates how to use the strcpy( ) function:

```
/*
 *   strcpy.c
 *   A C program using the strcpy function
 *   Copyright (c) Chris H. Pappas and William H. Murray, 1998
 */

#include <stdio.h>
#include <string.h>

#define iSIZE 20

main( )
{
  char szsource_string[iSIZE]="Initialized String!",
       szdestination_string[iSIZE];

  strcpy(szdestination_string,"String Constant");
  printf("%s\n",szdestination_string);

  strcpy(szdestination_string,szsource_string);
  printf("%s\n",szdestination_string);

  return(0);
}
```

The function strcpy( ) copies the contents of one string, *szsource_string*, into a second string, *szdestination_string*. The preceding program initializes *szsource_string* with the message, "Initialized String!" The first strcpy( ) function call actually copies "String Constant" into the *szdestination_string*, while the second call to the strcpy( ) function copies *szsource_string* into *szdestination_string* variable. The program outputs this message:

```
String Constant
Initialized String!
```

The following example is an equivalent C++ program.

```
//
//   strcpy.cpp
//   A C++ program using the strcpy function
//   Copyright (c) Chris H. Pappas and William H. Murray, 1998
//
```

```
#include <iostream.h>
#include <string.h>

#define iSIZE 20

main( )
{
  char szsource_string[iSIZE]="Initialized String!",
       szdestination_string[iSIZE];

  strcpy(szdestination_string,"String Constant");
  cout << "\n" << szdestination_string;

  strcpy(szdestination_string,szsource_string);
  cout << "\n" << szdestination_string;

  return(0);
}
```

The strcat( ) function appends two separate strings. Both strings must be null-terminated and the result itself is null terminated. The following program builds on your understanding of the strcpy( ) function and introduces strcat( ):

```
/*
 *    strcat.c
 *    A C program demonstrating how to use the strcat function
 *    Copyright (c) Chris H. Pappas and William H. Murray, 1998
 */

#include <stdio.h>
#include <string.h>

#define iSTRING_SIZE 35

main( )
{
  char szgreeting[] = "Good morning",
       szname[] =" Carolyn, ",
       szmessage[iSTRING_SIZE];

  strcpy(szmessage,szgreeting);
```

```
strcat(szmessage,szname);
strcat(szmessage,"how are you?");
printf("%s\n",szmessage);

return(0);
}
```

In this example, both *szgreeting* and *szname* are initialized, while *szmessage* is not.
The first thing the program does is to use the function strcpy( ) to copy the *szgreeting*
into *szmessage*. Next, the strcat( ) function is used to concatenate *szname* (" Carolyn, ") to
"*Good morning,*" which is stored in *szmessage*. The last strcat( ) function call
demonstrates how a string constant can be concatenated to a string. Here, "how are
you?" is concatenated to the now current contents of *szmessage* ("Good morning
Carolyn, "). The program outputs the following:

```
Good morning Carolyn, how are you?
```

The next program demonstrates how to use strncmp( ) to decide if two strings
are identical:

```
/*
 *    srncmp.c
 *    A C program that uses strncmp to compare two strings with
 *    the aid of the strlen function
 *    Copyright (c) Chris H. Pappas and William H. Murray, 1998
 */

#include <stdio.h>
#include <string.h>

main( )
{
  char szstringA[]="Adam", szstringB[]="Abel";
  int istringA_length,iresult=0;

  istringA_length=strlen(szstringA);
  if (strlen(szstringB) >= strlen(szstringA))
    iresult = strncmp(szstringA,szstringB,istringA_length);
  printf("The string %s found", iresult == 0 ? "was" : "wasn't");

  return(0);
}
```

The strlen( ) function is very useful; it returns the number of characters, not including the null-terminator, in the string pointed to. In the preceding program it is used in two different forms just to give you additional exposure to its use. The first call to the function assigns the length of *szstringA* to the variable *istringA_length*. The second invocation of the function is actually encountered within the if condition. Remember, all test conditions must evaluate to a TRUE (not 0 or !0) or FALSE (0). The if test takes the results returned from the two calls to strlen( ) and then asks the relational question >=. If the length of *szstringB* is >= to that of *szstringA*, the strncmp( ) function is invoked.

Why is the program using a >= test instead of an = =? To know the answer you need a further explanation of how strncmp( ) works. The function strncmp( ) compares two strings, starting with the first character in each string. If both strings are identical, the function returns a value of zero. However, if the two strings aren't identical, strncmp( ) will return a value less than zero if *szstringA* is less than *szstringB*, or a value greater than zero when *szstringA* is greater than *szstringB*. The relational test >= was used in case you wanted to modify the code to include a report of equality, greater than, or less than for the compared strings.

The program terminates by using the value returned by *iresult*, along with the conditional operator (?:), to determine which string message is printed. For this example, the program output is

```
The string wasn't found
```

Before moving on to the next chapter, remind yourself that two of the most frequent causes for irregular program behavior deal with exceeding array boundaries and forgetting that character arrays, used as strings, must end with \0, a null-string terminator. Both errors can sit dormant for months until that one user enters a response one character too long.

Chapter 10

Using Pointers

U nless you have taken a formal course in data structures, you have probably
never encountered pointer variables. Pointer variables take the normally
invisible memory address of a variable and bring it into the foreground. This
can make for extremely efficient algorithms and definitely adds some complexity to
your coding. It's similar to the difference between an automobile with an automatic
transmission (or static variables—see definition below) versus a manual transmission
(or dynamic variables—see definition below). So, while with a manual transmission
you have the ability to select just the right gear at the right time, you also need to know
how to clutch! And if you remember back to the first time you attempted to drive a
stick shift, you know there were a few bumps and grinds until you perfected your skill.

In C/C++, the topics of pointers, arrays, and strings are closely related.
Consequently, you can consider this chapter to be an extension of Chapter 9. Learning
about pointers—what they are and how to use them—can be a challenging experience
to the novice programmer. However, by mastering the concept of pointers, you will be
able to author extremely efficient, powerful, and flexible C/C++ applications.

It is very common practice for most introductory-level programs to use only the
class of variables known as static. Static variables, in this sense, are variables declared
in the variable declaration block of the source code. While the program is executing,
the application can neither obtain more of these variables nor deallocate storage for a
variable. In addition, you have no way of knowing the address in memory for each
variable or constant. Accessing an actual cell is a straightforward process—you simply
use the variable's name. For example, in C/C++, if you want to increment the **int**
variable *idecade* by 10, you access *idecade* by name:

```
idecade += 10;
```

Pointer Variables

Another (and often more convenient and efficient) way to access a variable is through a
second variable that holds the address of the variable you want to access. Chapter 8
introduced the concept of pointer variables, which are covered in more detail in this
chapter. For example, suppose you have an **int** variable called *imemorycell_contents* and
another variable called *pimemorycell_address* (admittedly verbose, but highly symbolic)
that can hold the address of a variable of type **int**. In C/C++, you have already seen
that preceding a variable with the **&** address operator returns the address of the
variable instead of its contents. Therefore, the syntax for assigning the address of a
variable to another variable of the type that holds addresses should not surprise you:

```
pimemorycell_address = &imemorycell_contents;
```

A variable that holds an address, such as *pimemorycell_address*, is called a pointer
variable, or simply a pointer. Figure 10-1 illustrates this relationship. The variable

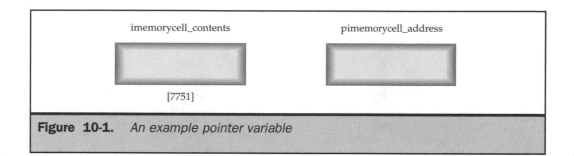

imemorycell_contents   pimemorycell_address

[7751]

Figure 10-1.   *An example pointer variable*

imemorycell_contents has been placed in memory at address 7751. After the preceding
statement is executed, the address of *imemorycell_contents* will be assigned to the
pointer variable *pimemorycell_address.* This relationship is expressed in English by
saying that *pimemorycell_address* points to *imemorycell_contents.* Figure 10-2 illustrates
this relationship. The arrow is drawn from the cell that stores the address to the cell
whose address is stored.

   Accessing the contents of the cell whose address is stored in *pimemorycell_address* is
as simple as preceding the pointer variable with an asterisk: **pimemorycell_address.*
What you have done is dereference the pointer *pimemorycell_address.* For example, if
you execute the following two statements, the value of the cell named
imemorycell_contents will be 20 (see Figure 10-3).

```
pimemorycell_address = &imemorycell_contents;
*pimemorycell_address = 20;
```

   You can think of the * as a directive to follow the arrow (see Figure 10-3) to find the
cell referenced. Notice that if *pimemorycell_address* holds the address of
imemorycell_contents, then both of the following statements will have the same effect;
that is, both will store the value of 20 in *imemorycell_contents*:

```
imemorycell_contents = 20;
*pimemorycell_address = 20;
```

Declaring Pointers

C/C++, like any other language, requires a definition for each variable. To define a
pointer variable *pimemorycell_address* that can hold the address of an **int** variable,
you write

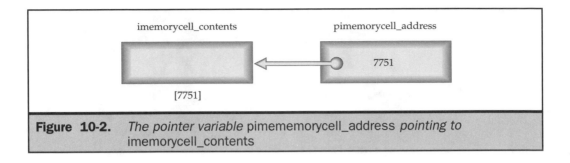

Figure 10-2.   *The pointer variable* pimememorycell_address *pointing to* imemorycell_contents

```
int *pimemorycell_address;
```

Actually, there are two separate parts to this declaration. The data type of *pimemorycell_address* is

```
int *
```

and the identifier for the variable is

```
pimemorycell_address
```

The asterisk following **int** means "pointer to." That is, the following data type is a pointer variable that can hold an address to an **int**:

```
int *
```

This is a very important concept to remember. In C/C++, unlike many other languages, a pointer variable holds the address of a particular data type.

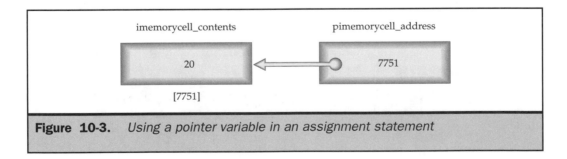

Figure 10-3.   *Using a pointer variable in an assignment statement*

Let's look at an example:

```
char *pcaddress;
int *piaddress;
```

The data type of *pcaddress* is distinctly different from the data type of the pointer variable *piaddress*. Run-time errors and compile-time warnings may occur in a program that defines a pointer to one data type and then uses it to point to some other data type. It would be poor programming practice to define a pointer in one way and then use it in some other way. For example, look at the following code segment:

```
int *pi;
float real_value = 98.26;
pi = &real_value;
```

Here *pi* is defined to be of type **int ***, meaning it can hold the address of a memory cell of type **int**. The third statement attempts to assign *pi* the address, *&real_value*, of a declared **float** variable.

Using Pointer Variables

The following code segment exchanges the contents of the variables *iresult_a* and *iresult_b* but uses the address and dereferencing operators to do so:

```
int iresult_a = 15, iresult_b = 37, itemporary;
int *piresult;

piresult = &iresult_a;
itemporary = *piresult;
*piresult = iresult_b;
iresult_b = itemporary;
```

The first line of the program contains standard definitions and initializations. The statement allocates three cells to hold a single **integer**, gives each cell a name, and initializes two of them (see Figure 10-4). For discussion purposes, assume that the cell named *iresult_a* is located at address 5328, the cell named *iresult_b* is located at address 7916, and the cell named *itemporary* is located at address 2385.

The second statement in the program defines *piresult* to be a pointer to an **int** data type. The statement allocates the cell and gives it a name (placed at address 1920). Remember, when the * is combined with the data type (in this case, **int**), the variable contains the *address* of a cell of the same data type. Because *piresult* has not been initialized, it does not point to any particular **int** variable. If your program were to try

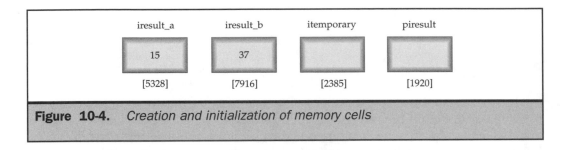

Figure 10-4.   *Creation and initialization of memory cells*

to use *piresult*, the compiler would not give you any warning and would try to use the variable's garbage contents to point with. The fourth statement assigns *piresult* the address of *iresult_a* (see Figure 10-5).

The next statement in the program uses the expression **piresult* to access the contents of the cell to which *piresult* points—*iresult_a*:

```
itemporary = *piresult;
```

Therefore, the **integer** value 15 is stored in the variable *itemporary* (see Figure 10-6). If you left off the * in front of *piresult*, the assignment statement would illegally store the contents of *piresult*—the address 5328—in the cell named *itemporary*, but *itemporary* is supposed to hold an **integer**, not an address. This can be a very annoying bug to locate since many compilers will not issue any warnings/errors. (The Visual C/C++ compiler issues the warning "different levels of indirection.")

To make matters worse, most pointers are **near**, meaning they occupy 2 bytes, the same data size as a PC-based **integer**. The fifth statement in the program copies the

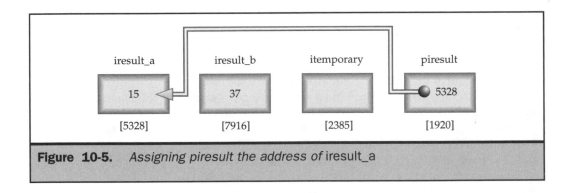

Figure 10-5.   *Assigning piresult the address of iresult_a*

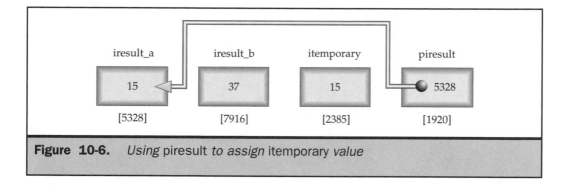

Figure 10-6. *Using* piresult *to assign* itemporary *value*

contents of the variable *iresult_b* into the cell pointed to by the address stored in *piresult* (see Figure 10-7):

```
*piresult = iresult_b;
```

The last statement in the program simply copies the contents of one **integer** variable, *itemporary*, into another integer variable, *iresult_a* (see Figure 10-8). Make certain you understand the difference between what is being referenced when a pointer variable is preceded (*piresult) and when it is not preceded (*piresult*) by the dereference operator *. For this example, the first syntax is a pointer to a cell that can contain an **integer** value. The second syntax references the cell that holds the address to another cell that can hold an integer.

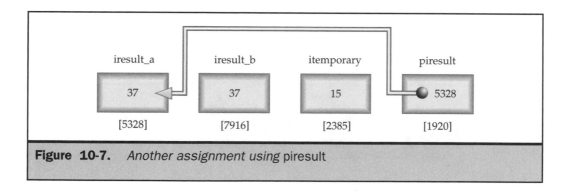

Figure 10-7. *Another assignment using* piresult

PROGRAMMING FOUNDATIONS

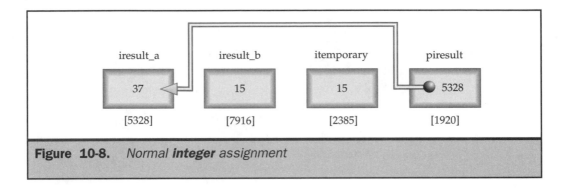

Figure 10-8.   *Normal **integer** assignment*

The following short program illustrates how to manipulate the addresses in pointer variables. Unlike the previous example, which swapped the program's data within the variables, this program swaps the addresses to where the data resides:

```
char cswitch1 = 'S', cswitch2 = 'T';
char *pcswitch1, *pcswitch2, *pctemporary;

pcswitch1   = &cswitch1;
pcswitch2   = &cswitch2;
pctemporary = pcswitch1;
pcswitch1   = pcswitch2;
pcswitch2   = pctemporary;
printf( "%c%c", *pcswitch1, *pcswitch2);
```

Figure 10-9 shows the cell configuration and values after the execution of the first four statements of the program. When the fifth statement is executed, the contents of *pcswitch1* are copied into *pctemporary* so that both *pcswitch1* and *pctemporary* point to *cswitch1* (see Figure 10-10).

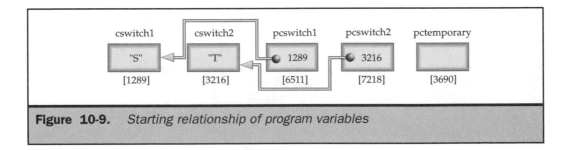

Figure 10-9.   *Starting relationship of program variables*

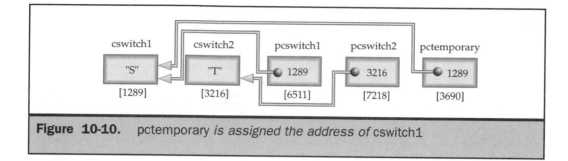

Figure 10-10.   pctemporary *is assigned the address of* cswitch1

Executing the following statement copies the contents of *pcswitch2* into *pcswitch1* so that both pointers point to *cswitch2* (see Figure 10-11):

```
pcswitch1 = pcswitch2;
```

Notice that if the code had not preserved the address to *cswitch1* in a temporary location, *pctemporary*, there would be no pointer access to *cswitch1*. The next-to-last statement copies the address stored in *pctemporary* into *pcswitch2* (see Figure 10-12). When the printf( ) statement is executed, since the value of **pcswitch1* is "*T*" and the value of **pcswitch2* is "*S*," you will see

```
TS
```

Notice how the actual values stored in the variables *cswitch1* and *cswitch2* haven't changed from their original initializations. However, since you have swapped the contents of their respective pointers, **pcswitch1* and **pcswitch2*, it appears that their order has been reversed. This is an important concept to grasp. Depending on the size of a data object, moving a pointer to the object can be much more efficient than copying the entire contents of the object.

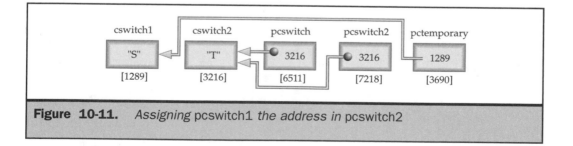

Figure 10-11.   *Assigning* pcswitch1 *the address in* pcswitch2

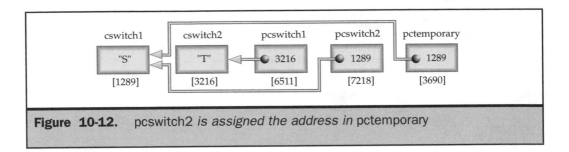

Figure 10-12. pcswitch2 *is assigned the address in* pctemporary

Initializing Pointers

Pointer variables can be initialized in their definitions, just like many other variables in C/C++. For example, the following two statements allocate storage for the two cells *iresult* and *piresult*:

```
int iresult;
int *piresult = &iresult;
```

The variable *iresult* is an ordinary **integer** variable, and *piresult* is a pointer to an **integer**. Additionally, the code initializes the pointer variable *piresult* to the address of *iresult*. Be careful: the syntax is somewhat misleading; you are *not* initializing *piresult* (which would have to be an **integer** value) but *piresult* (which must be an address to an **integer**). The second statement in the preceding listing can be translated into the following two equivalent statements:

```
int *piresult;
piresult = &iresult;
```

The following code segment shows how to declare a string pointer and then initialize it:

```
/*
 *   psz.c
 *   A C program that initializes a string pointer and
 *   then prints the palindrome backwards then forwards
 *   Copyright (c) Chris H. Pappas and William H. Murray, 1998
 */

#include <stdio.h>
#include <string.h>
```

```
void main( )
{
  char *pszpalindrome="MADAM I'M ADAM";
  int i;

  for (i=strlen(pszpalindrome)-1; i >= 0; i--)
    printf("%c",pszpalindrome[i]);
    printf("%s",pszpalindrome);
}
```

Technically, the C/C++ compiler stores the address of the first character of the string "MADAM I'M ADAM" in the variable *pszpalindrome*. While the program is running, it can use *pszpalindrome* like any other string. This is because all C/C++ compilers create a string table, which is used internally by the compiler to store the string constants a program is using.

The strlen( ) function prototyped in STRING.H calculates the length of a string. The function expects a pointer to a null-terminated string and counts all of the characters up to, but not including, the null character itself. The index variable *i* is initialized to one less than the value returned by strlen( ) since the **for** loop treats the string *psz* like an array of characters. The palindrome has 14 letters. If *psz* is treated as an array of characters, each element is indexed from 0 to 13. This example program highlights the somewhat confusing relationship between pointers to character strings and arrays of characters. However, if you remember that an array's name is actually the address of the first element, you should understand why the compiler issues no complaints.

What Not to Do with the Address Operator

You cannot use the address operator on every C/C++ expression. The following examples demonstrate those situations where the & address operator cannot be applied:

```
/*
   not with CONSTANTS
*/

pivariable = &48;


/*
   not with expressions involving operators such as + and /
```

```
   given the definition int iresult = 5;
*/


pivariable = &(iresult + 15);


/*
   not preceding register variables
   given the definition register register1;
*/


pivariable = &register1;
```

The first statement tries to illegally obtain the address of a hardwired constant value. Since the 48 has no memory cell associated with it, the statement is meaningless.

The second assignment statement attempts to return the address of the expression *iresult* + 15. Since the expression itself is actually a stack manipulation process, there is no address associated with the expression.

Normally, the last example honors the programmer's request to define *register1* as a register rather than as a storage cell in internal memory. Therefore, no memory cell address could be returned and stored. Microsoft Visual C/C++ gives the variable memory, not register storage.

Pointers to Arrays

As mentioned, pointers and arrays are closely related topics. Recall from Chapter 9 that an array's name is a constant whose value represents the address of the array's first element. For this reason, the value of an array's name cannot be changed by an assignment statement or by any other statement. Given the following data declarations, the array's name, *ftemperatures*, is a constant whose value is the address of the first element of the array of 20 **float**s:

```
#define IMAXREADINGS 20

float ftemperatures[IMAXREADINGS];
float *pftemp;
```

The following statement assigns the address of the first element of the array to the pointer variable *pftemp*:

```
pftemp = ftemperatures;
```

An equivalent statement looks like this:

```
pftemp = &ftemperatures[0];
```

However, if *pftemp* holds the address of a **float**, the following statements are illegal:

```
ftemperatures = pftemp;
&ftemperatures[0] = pftemp;
```

These statements attempt to assign a value to the constant *ftemperatures* or its equivalent *&ftemperatures[0]*, which makes about as much sense as

```
10 = pftemp;
```

Pointers to Pointers

In C/C++, it is possible to define pointer variables that point to other pointer variables, which in turn point to the data, such as an **integer**. Figure 10-13 illustrates this relationship; *ppi* is a pointer variable that points to another pointer variable whose contents can be used to point to 10.

You may be wondering why this is necessary. The arrival of Windows and the Windows NT programming environment signals the development of multitasking operating environments designed to maximize the use of memory. To minimize the use of memory, the operating system has to be able to move objects in memory. If your program points directly to the physical memory cell where the object is stored and the operating system moves it, disaster will strike. Instead of pointing directly to a data object, your application points to a memory cell address that will not change while your program is running (for example, let's call this a *virtual_address*), and the *virtual_address* memory cell holds the *current_physical_address* of the data object. Now, whenever the operating environment wants to move the data object, all the operating system has to do is update the *current_physical_address* pointed to by the *virtual_address*. As far as your application is concerned, it still uses the unchanged address of the *virtual_address* to point to the updated address of the *current_physical_address*.

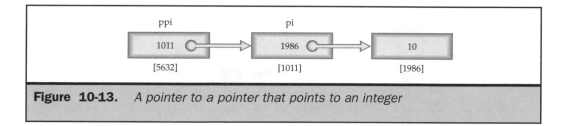

Figure 10-13. *A pointer to a pointer that points to an integer*

To define a pointer to a pointer in C/C++, you simply increase the number of asterisks preceding the identifier:

```
int **ppi;
```

In this example, the variable *ppi* is defined to be a pointer to a pointer that points to an **int** data type. *ppi*'s data type is

```
int **
```

Each asterisk is read "pointer to." The number of pointers that must be followed to access the data item or, equivalently, the number of asterisks that must be attached to the variable to reference the value to which it points, is called the "level of indirection" of the pointer variable. A pointer's level of indirection determines how much dereferencing must be done to access the data type given in the definition. Figure 10-14 illustrates several variables with different levels of indirection.

The first four lines of code in Figure 10-14 define four variables: the **integer** variable *ivalue*, the *pi* pointer variable that points to an **integer** (one level of indirection), the *ppi* variable that points to a pointer that points to an **integer** (two levels of indirection), and *pppi*, illustrating that this process can be extended beyond two levels of indirection. The fifth line of code is

```
pi = &ivalue;
```

This is an assignment statement that uses the address operator. The expression assigns the address of *&ivalue* to *pi*. Therefore, *pi*'s contents contain 1111. Notice that

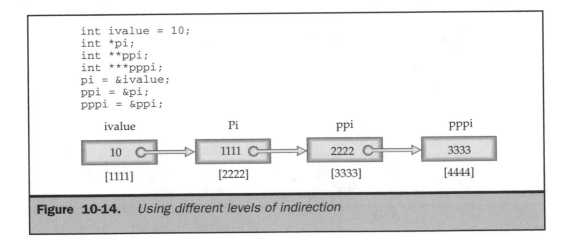

Figure 10-14.   *Using different levels of indirection*

there is only one arrow from *pi* to *ivalue*. This indicates that *ivalue*, or 10, can be accessed by dereferencing *pi* just once. The next statement, along with its accompanying picture, illustrates double indirection:

```
ppi = &pi;
```

Because *ppi*'s data type is **int ****, to access an **integer** you need to dereference the variable twice. After the preceding assignment statement, *ppi* holds the address (not the contents) of *pi*, so *ppi* points to *pi*, which in turn points to *ivalue*. Notice that you must follow two arrows to get from *ppi* to *ivalue*.

The last statement demonstrates three levels of indirection:

```
pppi = &ppi;
```

It also assigns the address (not the contents) of *ppi* to *pppi*. Notice that the accompanying illustration shows that three arrows are now necessary to reference *ivalue*.

To review, *pppi* is assigned the address of a pointer variable that indirectly points to an **integer**, as in the preceding statement. However, ***pppi (the cell pointed to) can only be assigned an **integer** value, not an address, since ***pppi is an **integer**:

```
***pppi = 10;
```

C/C++ allows pointers to be initialized like any other variable. For example, *pppi* could have been defined and initialized using the following single statement:

```
int ***pppi = &ppi;
```

Pointers to Strings

A string constant such as "File not ready" is actually stored as an array of characters with a null terminator added as the last character (see Figure 10-15). Because a **char**

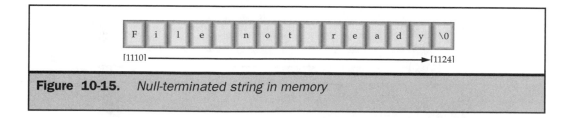

Figure 10-15.   *Null-terminated string in memory*

pointer can hold the address of a character, it is possible to define and initialize it. For example:

```
char *psz = "File not ready";
```

This statement defines the **char** pointer *psz* and initializes it to the address of the first character in the string (see Figure 10-16). Additionally, the storage is allocated for the string itself. The same statement could have been written as follows:

```
char *psz;
psz = "File not ready";
```

Again, care must be taken to realize that *psz* was assigned the address, not **psz*, which points to the "F." The second example given helps to clarify this by using two separate statements to define and initialize the pointer variable.

The following example highlights a common misconception when dealing with pointers to strings and pointers to arrays of characters:

```
char *psz = "File not ready";
char pszarray[] = "Drive not ready";
```

The main difference between these two statements is that the value of *psz* can be changed (since it is a pointer variable), but the value of *pszarray* cannot be changed (since it is a pointer constant). Along the same line of thinking, the following assignment statement is illegal:

```
/* NOT LEGAL */
char pszarray[16];
pszarray = "Drive not ready";
```

While the syntax looks similar to the correct code in the preceding example, the assignment statement attempts to copy the *address* of the first cell of the storage for the

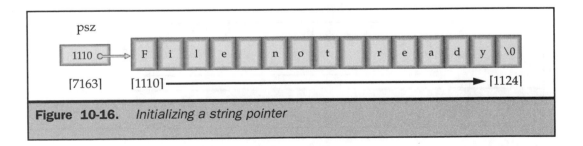

Figure 10-16.   *Initializing a string pointer*

string "Drive not ready" into *pszarray*. Because *pszarray* is a pointer constant, not a pointer variable, an error results.

The following input statement is incorrect because the pointer *psz* has not been initialized:

```
/* NOT LEGAL */
char *psz;
cin >> psz;
```

Correcting the problem is as simple as reserving storage for and initializing the pointer variable *psz*:

```
char sztring[10];
char *psz = sztring;
cin.get(psz,10);
```

Since the value of *sztring* is the address of the first cell of the array, the second statement in the code not only allocates storage for the pointer variable, but it also initializes it to the address of the first cell of the array *sztring*. At this point, the cin.get( ) statement is satisfied since it is passed the valid address of the character array storage.

Pointer Arithmetic

If you are familiar with assembly language programming, then you are already comfortable with using actual physical addresses to reference information stored in tables. For those of you who are only used to using subscript indexing into arrays, believe it or not, you have been effectively using the same assembly language equivalent. The only difference is that in the latter case you were allowing the compiler to manipulate the addresses for you.

Remember that one of C/C++'s strengths is their closeness to the hardware. In C/C++, you can actually manipulate pointer variables. Many of the example programs seen so far have demonstrated how one pointer variable's address, or address contents, can be assigned to another pointer variable of the same data type. C/C++ allows you to perform only two arithmetic operations on a pointer address—namely, addition and subtraction. Let's look at two different pointer variable types and perform some simple pointer arithmetic:

```
//
//   ptarth.cpp
//   A C++ program demonstrating pointer arithmetic
//   Copyright (c) Chris H. Pappas and William H. Murray, 1998
//
```

```
#include <iostream.h>

void main( )
{
  int *pi;
  float *pf;

  int an_integer;
  float a_real;

  pi = &an_integer;
  pf = &a_real;

  pi++;
  pf++;

}
```

Let's also assume that an **integer** is 2 bytes and a **float** is 4 bytes (for 16-bit C/C++ environments). Also, *an_integer* is stored at memory cell address 2000, and *a_real* is stored at memory cell address 4000. When the last two lines of the program are executed, *pi* will contain the address 2002 and *pf* will contain the address 4004. But wait a minute—didn't you think that the increment operator **++** incremented by 1? This is true for character variables, but not always for pointer variables.

In Chapter 6, you were introduced to the concept of operator overloading. Increment (**++**) and decrement (**– –**) are examples of this C/C++ construct. For the immediate example, since *pi* was defined to point to **integer**s (which, for the system in this example, are 2 bytes), when the increment operation is invoked, it checks the variable's type and then chooses an appropriate increment value. For **integer**s, this value is 2; for **float**s, the value is 4 (on the example system). This same principle holds true for whatever data type the pointer is pointing to. Should the pointer variable point to a structure of 20 bytes, the increment or decrement operator would add or subtract 20 from the current pointer's address.

You can also modify a pointer's address by using **integer** addition and subtraction, not just the **++** and **– –** operators. For example, moving four **float** values over from the one currently pointed to can be accomplished with the following statement:

```
pf = pf + 4;
```

Look at the following program carefully and see if you can predict the results. Does the program move the **float** pointer *pf* one number over?

```
//
//   sizept.cpp
//   A C++ program using sizeof and pointer arithmetic
//   Copyright (c) Chris H. Pappas and William H. Murray, 1998
//

#include <iostream.h>
#include <stddef.h>

void main( )
{
  float fvalues[] = {15.38,12.34,91.88,11.11,22.22};
  float *pf;
  size_t fwidth;

  pf = &fvalues[0];

  fwidth = sizeof(float);

  pf = pf + fwidth;

}
```

Try using the integrated debugger to single-step through the program. Use the Variables window to keep an eye on the variables *pf* and *fwidth*.

Assume that the debugger has assigned *pf* the address of *fvalues* and that *pf* contains an FFCA. The variable *fwidth* is assigned the *sizeof(float)* that returns a 4. When you executed the final statement in the program, what happened? The variable *pf* changed to FFDA, not FFDE. Why? You forgot that pointer arithmetic takes into consideration the size of the object pointed to (4 x (4-byte **float**s) = 16). The program actually moves the *pf* pointer over four **float** values to 22.22.

Actually, you were intentionally misled by the naming of the variable *fwidth*. To make logical sense, the program should have been written as

```
//
//   ptsize.cpp
//   The same C++ program using meaningful variable names
//   Copyright (c) Chris H. Pappas and William H. Murray, 1998
//

#include <iostream.h>
```

```
void main( )
{
  float fvalues[] = {15.38,12.34,91.88,11.11,22.22};
  float *pf;
  int inumber_of_elements_to_skip;

  pf = fvalues;

  inumber_of_elements_to_skip = 1;

  pf = pf + inumber_of_elements_to_skip;

}
```

Pointer Arithmetic and Arrays

The following two programs index into a ten-character array. Both programs read in ten characters and then print out the same ten characters in reverse order. The first program uses the more conventional high-level-language approach of indexing with subscripts. The second program is identical except that the array elements are referenced by address, using pointer arithmetic. Here is the first program:

```
/*
 *   arysub.c
 *   A C program using normal array subscripting
 *   Copyright (c) Chris H. Pappas and William H. Murray, 1998
 */

#include <stdio.h>

#define ISIZE 10

void main( )
{
  char string10[ISIZE];
  int i;

  for(i = 0; i < ISIZE; i++)
    string10[i]=getchar( );

  for(i = ISIZE-1; i >= 0; i--)
```

```
      putchar(string10[i]);
  }
```

Here is the second example:

```
/*
 *    aryptr.c
 *    A C program using pointer arithmetic to access elements
 *    Copyright (c) Chris H. Pappas and William H. Murray, 1998
 */

#include <stdio.h>

#define ISIZE 10

void main( )
{
  char string10[ISIZE];
  char *pc;
  int icount;

  pc=string10;

  for(icount = 0; icount < ISIZE; icount++) {
    *pc=getchar( );
    pc++;
  }

  pc=string10 + (ISIZE - 1);

  for(icount = 0; icount < ISIZE; icount++) {
    putchar(*pc);
    pc--;
  }
}
```

Since the first example is straightforward, the discussion will center on the second program, which uses pointer arithmetic. *pc* has been defined to be of type **char ***, which means it is a pointer to a character. Because each cell in the array *string10* holds a character, *pc* is suitable for pointing to each. The following statement stores the address of the first cell of *string10* in the variable *pc*:

```
pc=string10;
```

The **for** loop reads *ISIZE* characters and stores them in the array *string10*. The following statement uses the dereference operator * to ensure that the target—the left-hand side of this assignment (another example of an lvalue)—will be the cell to which *pc* points, not *pc* (which itself contains just an address).

```
*pc=getchar( );
```

The idea is to store a character in each cell of *string10*, not to store it in *pc*.

To start printing the array backward, the program first initializes the *pc* to the last element in the array:

```
pc=string10 + (ISIZE - 1);
```

By adding 9 (*ISIZE - 1*) to the initial address of *string10*, *pc* points to the *tenth* element. Remember, these are offsets. The first element in the array is at offset zero. Within the **for** loop, *pc* is decremented to move backward through the array elements. Make certain you use the integrated debugger to trace through this example if you are unsure of how *pc* is modified.

Problems with the Operators ++ and − −

Just as a reminder, the following two statements do *not* perform the same cell reference:

```
*pc++=getchar( );
*++pc=getchar( );
```

The first statement assigns the character returned by getchar( ) to the current cell pointed to by *pc* and then increments *pc*. The second statement increments the address in *pc* first and then assigns the character returned by the function to the cell pointed to by the updated address. Later in this chapter you will use these two different types of pointer assignments to reference the elements of *argv*.

Using const with Pointers

Just when you think you are getting the hang of it, C/C++ throws you a subtle potential curveball. Look at the following two pointer variable declarations and see if you can detect the subtle differences:

```
const MYTYPE *pmytype_1;
MYTYPE * const pmytype_2 = &mytype;
```

The first pointer declaration defines *pmytype_1* as a pointer variable that may be assigned any address to a memory location of type *MYTYPE*. The second declaration defines *pmytype_2*, as a pointer constant to *mytype*. Was that enough of a hint?

OK, let's try that one more time. The identifier *pmytype_1* is a pointer variable. Variables can be assigned any value appropriate to their defined type—in this case, *pmytype_1* can be assigned any address to a previously defined location of type *MYTYPE*. Well then, you might ask, what does the **const** keyword do in the declaration? What that **const** tells the compiler is this: While *pmytype_1* may be assigned any address to a memory cell of type *MYTYPE*, when you use *pmytype_1* to actually point to a memory location, what you point to cannot be changed. The following sample statements highlight these subtleties:

```
pmytype_1 = &mytype1; // legal
pmytype_1 = &mytype2; // legal
*pmytype_1 = (MYTYPE)some_legal_value; // illegal attempting to
              change contents
```

Now, compare *pmytype_1* with *pmytype_2*, which is declared as a pointer constant. In other words, *pmytype_2* can hold the address to a memory location of type *MYTYPE*. However, it is a locked address. Therefore, *pmytype_2* must be initialized to hold a valid address when the pointer constant is declared (= &*mytype*;). On the other hand, the contents of the memory location pointed to by *pmytype_2* are not locked. Look at the following statements, which highlight these subtleties:

```
pmytype_2 = &mytype_n; // illegal, attempting to change locked
              pointer address
*pmytype_2 = (MYTYPE) some_legal_value_1; // legal to change memory
              contents
*pmytype_2 = (MYTYPE) some_legal_value_n; // legal to change memory
              contents
```

Now, of the two uses for the **const** keyword with pointer declarations, which do you think is closest to an array declaration? Answer: the second use of **const**, as in *pmytype_2*'s declaration. Remember, the name of an array is a locked address to the array's first element:

```
int iarray[ SIZE ];
```

For this reason, the compiler views the identifier *iarray* as if you had actually declared it as

```
int * const iarray = &array[0];
```

Comparing Pointers

You have already seen examples demonstrating the effect of incrementing and decrementing pointers using the **++** and **– –** operators and the effect of adding an **integer** to a pointer. There are other operations that may be performed on pointers. These include

- Subtracting an **integer** from a pointer
- Subtracting two pointers (usually pointing to the same object)
- Comparing pointers using a relational operator such as **<=**, **=**, or **>=**

Since (pointer – **integer**) subtraction is so similar to (pointer + **integer**) addition (these have already been discussed by example), it should be no surprise that the resultant pointer value points to a storage location for **integer** elements before the original pointer.

Subtracting two pointers yields a constant value that is the number of array elements between the two pointers. This assumes that both pointers are of the same type and initially point into the same array. Subtracting pointers that are not of the same type or that initially point to different arrays will yield unpredictable results.

> **Note** *No matter which pointer arithmetic operation you choose, there is no check to see if the pointer value calculated is outside the defined boundaries of the array.*

Pointers of like type (that is, pointers that reference the same kind of data, like **int** and **float**) can also be compared to each other. The resulting TRUE (!0) or FALSE (0) can either be tested or assigned to an **integer**, just like the result of any logical expression. Comparing two pointers tests whether they are equal, not equal, greater than, or less than each other. One pointer is less than another pointer if the first pointer refers to an array element with a lower number subscript. (Remember that pointers and subscripts are virtually identical.) This operation also assumes that the pointers reference the same array.

Finally, pointers can be compared to zero, the null value. In this case, only the test for equal or not equal is valid since testing for negative pointers makes no sense. The null value in a pointer means that the pointer has no value, or does not point to anything. Null, or zero, is the only numeric value that can be directly assigned into a pointer without a type cast.

It should be noted that pointer conversions are performed on pointer operands. This means that any pointer may be compared to a constant expression evaluating to zero and any pointer may be compared to a pointer of type **void ***. (In this last case, the pointer is first converted to **void ***.)

Pointer Portability

The examples in this section have represented addresses as **integer**s. This may suggest to you that a C/C++ pointer is of type **int**. It is not. A pointer holds the address of a particular type of variable, but a pointer itself is not one of the primitive data types **int**, **float**, and the like. A particular C/C++ system may allow a pointer to be copied into an **int** variable and an **int** variable to be copied into a pointer; however, C/C++ does not guarantee that pointers can be stored in **int** variables. To guarantee code portability, the practice should be avoided.

Also, not all arithmetic operations on pointers are allowed. For example, it is illegal to add two pointers, to multiply two pointers, or to divide one pointer by another.

Using sizeof with Pointers Under 16-bit DOS Environments

Note   *The following section describes old, outdated keywords. These pointer size modifiers are no longer needed under the newer 32-bit C/C++ compilers and operating systems. Under a 32-bit operating system and C/C++ compiler, all addresses are a full 32 bits (equivalent to the _ _far and _ _huge modifiers described below). However, as many readers already know, you often encounter code, for purposes of reference or modification, that is written in historic C/C++, ANSI C/C++, and so forth. For this reason, the discussion of these old-style keywords is presented here.*

The actual size of a pointer variable depends on one of two things: the size of the memory model you have chosen for the application or the use of the nonportable, implementation-specific _ _**near**, _ _**far**, and _ _**huge** keywords.

The 80486 to 8088 microprocessors use a segmented addressing scheme that breaks an address into two pieces: a segment and an offset. Many local post offices have several walls of post office boxes, with each box having its own unique number. Segment:offset addressing is similar to this design. To get to your post office box, you first need to know which bank of boxes, or wall, yours is on (the segment), and then the actual box number (the offset).

When you know that all of your application's code and data will fit within a single 64K of memory, you choose the small memory model. Applying this to the post office box metaphor, this means that all of your code and data will be in the same location, or wall (segment), with the application's code and data having a unique box number (offset) on the wall.

For those applications where this compactness is not feasible, possibly because of the size and the amount of data that must be stored and referenced, you would choose a large memory model. Using the analogy, this could mean that all of your application's code would be located on one wall, while all the data would be on a completely separate wall.

When an application shares the same memory segment for code and data, calculating an object's memory location merely involves finding out the object's offset within the segment. This is a very simple calculation.

When an application has separate segments for code and data, calculating an object's location is a bit more complicated. First, the code or data's segment must be calculated, and then its offset within the respective segment. Naturally, this requires more processor time.

C++ also allows you to override the default pointer size for a specific variable by using the keywords _ _**near**, _ _**far**, and _ _**huge**. Note, however, that by including these in your application, you make your code less portable since the keywords produce different results on different compilers. The _ _**near** keyword forces an offset-only pointer when the pointers would normally default to segment:offset. The _ _**far** keyword forces a segment:offset pointer when the pointers would normally default to offset-only. The _ _**huge** keyword also forces a segment:offset pointer that has been normalized. The _ _**near** keyword is generally used to increase execution speed, while the _ _**far** keyword forces a pointer to do the right thing regardless of the memory model chosen.

For many applications, you can simply ignore this problem and allow the compiler to choose a default memory model. But eventually you will run into problems with this approach—for example, when you try to address an absolute location (some piece of hardware, perhaps, or a special area in memory) outside your program's segment area.

On the other hand, you may be wondering why you can't just use the largest memory model available for your application. You can, but you pay a price in efficiency. If all of your data is in one segment, the pointer is the size of the offset. However, if your data and code range all over memory, your pointer is the size of the segment *and* the offset, and both must be calculated every time you change the pointer. The following program uses the function sizeof( ) to print out the smallest pointer size and largest pointer size available.

This C++ program prints the default pointer sizes, their _ _**far** sizes, and their _ _**near** sizes. The program also uses the *stringize* preprocessor directive (#) with the *A_POINTER* argument, so the name as well as the size of the pointer will be printed.

```
//
//   strize.cpp
//   A C++ program illustrating the sizeof(pointers) and
//   program is only valid under 16-bit C/C++ environments.
//   Copyright (c) Chris H. Pappas and William H. Murray, 1998
//
```

```
#include <stdio.h>

#define PRINT_SIZEOF(A_POINTER) \
  printf("sizeof\t("#A_POINTER")\t= %d\n", \
  sizeof(A_POINTER))

void main( )
{
  char *reg_pc;
  long double *reg_pldbl;
  char _ _far *far_pc;
  long double _ _far *far_pldbl;
  char _ _near *near_pc;
  long double _ _near *near_pldbl;

  PRINT_SIZEOF(reg_pc);
  PRINT_SIZEOF(reg_pldbl);
  PRINT_SIZEOF(far_pc);
  PRINT_SIZEOF(far_pldbl);
  PRINT_SIZEOF(near_pc);
  PRINT_SIZEOF(near_pldbl);
}
```

The output from the program looks like this:

```
sizeof    (reg_pc)      = 2
sizeof    (reg_pldbl)   = 2
sizeof    (far_pc)      = 4
sizeof    (far_pldbl)   = 4
sizeof    (near_pc)     = 2
sizeof    (near_pldbl)  = 2
```

Pointers to Functions

All the examples so far have shown you how various items of data can be referenced by a pointer. As it turns out, you can also access portions of code by using a pointer to a function. Pointers to functions serve the same purpose as do pointers to data; that is, they allow the function to be referenced indirectly, just as a pointer to a data item allows the data item to be referenced indirectly.

A pointer to a function can have a number of important uses. For example, consider the qsort( ) function. The qsort( ) function has as one of its parameters a pointer to a function. The referenced function contains the necessary comparison that is to be performed between the array elements being sorted. qsort( ) has been written to require a function pointer because the comparison process between two elements can be a complex process beyond the scope of a single control flag. It is not possible to pass a function by value—that is, pass the code itself. C/C++, however, does support passing a pointer to the code, or a pointer to the function.

The concept of function pointers is frequently illustrated by using the qsort( ) function supplied with the compiler. Unfortunately, in many cases, the function pointer is declared to be of a type that points to other built-in functions. The following C and C++ programs demonstrate how to define a pointer to a function and how to "roll your own" function to be passed to the STDLIB.H function qsort( ). Here is the C program:

```
/*
 *    fncptr.c
 *    A C program illustrating how to declare your own
 *    function and function pointer to be used with qsort( )
 *    Copyright (c) Chris H. Pappas and William H. Murray, 1998
 */

#include <stdio.h>
#include <stdlib.h>

#define IMAXVALUES 10

int icompare_funct(const void *iresult_a, const void *iresult_b);
int (*ifunct_ptr)(const void *, const void *);

void main( )
{
  int i;
  int iarray[IMAXVALUES]={0,5,3,2,8,7,9,1,4,6};

  ifunct_ptr=icompare_funct;
  qsort(iarray,IMAXVALUES,sizeof(int),ifunct_ptr);
  for(i = 0; i < IMAXVALUES; i++)
    printf("%d ",iarray[i]);
}

int icompare_funct(const void *iresult_a, const void *iresult_b)
{
  return((*(int *)iresult_a) - (*(int *) iresult_b));
}
```

The function icompare_funct( ) (which will be called the reference function) was prototyped to match the requirements for the fourth parameter to the function qsort( ) (which will be called the invoking function).

To digress slightly, the fourth parameter to the function qsort( ) must be a function pointer. This reference function must be passed two **const void** * parameters and it must return a type **int**. Remember that the position of the **const** keyword, in the formal parameter list, locks the data pointed to, not the address used to point. This means that even if you write your compare routine so that it does not sort properly, it can in no way destroy the contents of your array! This is because qsort( ) uses the reference function for the sort comparison algorithm. Now that you understand the prototype of the reference function icompare_funct( ), take a minute to study the body of the reference function.

If the reference function returns a value < 0, then the reference function's first parameter value is less than the second parameter's value. A return value of zero indicates parameter value equality, with a return value > 0 indicating that the second parameter's value was greater than the first's. All of this is accomplished by the single statement in icompare_funct( ):

```
return((*(int *)iresult_a) - (*(int *) iresult_b));
```

Since both of the pointers were passed as type **void** *, they were cast to their appropriate pointer type **int** * and then dereferenced (*). The result of the subtraction of the two values pointed to returns an appropriate value to satisfy qsort( )'s comparison criterion.

While the prototype requirements for icompare_funct( ) are interesting, the meat of the program begins with the pointer function declaration below the icompare_funct( ) function prototype:

```
int icompare_funct(const void *iresult_a, const void *iresult_b);
int (*ifunct_ptr)(const void *, const void *);
```

A function's type is determined by its return value and argument list signature. A pointer to icompare_funct( ) must specify the same signature and return type. You might therefore think the following statement would accomplish this:

```
int *ifunct_ptr(const void *, const void *);
```

That is almost correct. The problem is that the compiler interprets the statement as the definition of a function ifunct_ptr( ) taking two arguments and returning a pointer of type **int** *. The dereference operator unfortunately is associated with the type specifier, not ifunct_ptr( ). Parentheses are necessary to associate the dereference operator with ifunct_ptr( ).

The corrected statement declares ifunct_ptr( ) to be a pointer to a function taking two arguments and with a return type **int**—that is, a pointer of the same type required by the fourth parameter to qsort( ).

In the body of main( ), the only thing left to do is to initialize ifunct_ptr( ) to the address of the function icompare_funct( ). The parameters to qsort( ) are the address to the base or zeroth element of the table to be sorted (*iarray*), the number of entries in the table (*IMAXVALUES*), the size of each table element (*sizeof(int)*), and a function pointer to the comparison function (*ifunct_ptr( )*).

The C++ equivalent follows:

```
//
//  qsort.cpp
//  A C program illustrating how to declare your own
//  function and function pointer to be used with qsort( )
//  Copyright (c) Chris H. Pappas and William H. Murray, 1998
//

#include <iostream.h>
#include <stdlib.h>

#define IMAXVALUES 10

int icompare_funct(const void *iresult_a, const void *iresult_b);
int (*ifunct_ptr)(const void *,const void *);

void main( )
{
  int i;
  int iarray[IMAXVALUES]={0,5,3,2,8,7,9,1,4,6};

  ifunct_ptr=icompare_funct;
  qsort(iarray,IMAXVALUES,sizeof(int),ifunct_ptr);
  for(i = 0; i < IMAXVALUES; i++)
    cout <<"[{||}]" << iarray[i];
}

int icompare_funct(const void *iresult_a, const void *iresult_b)
{
  return((*(int *)iresult_a) - (*(int *)iresult_b));
}
```

Learning to understand the syntax of a function pointer can be challenging. Let's look at just a few examples. Here is the first one:

```
int *(*(*ifunct_ptr)(int))[5];
float (*(*ffunct_ptr)(int,int))(float);
typedef double (*(*(*dfunct_ptr)( ))[5])( );
  dfunct_ptr A_dfunct_ptr;
(*(*function_ary_ptrs( ))[5])( );
```

The first statement defines ifunct_ptr( ) to be a function pointer to a function that is passed an integer argument and returns a pointer to an array of five **int** pointers.

The second statement defines ffunct_ptr( ) to be a function pointer to a function that takes two **integer** arguments and returns a pointer to a function taking a **float** argument and returning a **float**.

By using the **typedef** declaration, you can avoid the unnecessary repetition of complicated declarations. The **typedef** declaration (discussed in greater detail in Chapter 13) is read as follows: dfunct_ptr( ) is defined as a pointer to a function that is passed nothing and returns a pointer to an array of five pointers that point to functions that are passed nothing and return a **doubles**.

The last statement is a function declaration, not a variable declaration. The statement defines function_ary_ptrs( ) to be a function taking no arguments and returning a pointer to an array of five pointers that point to functions taking no arguments and returning **integer**s. The outer functions return the default C and C++ type **int**.

The good news is that you will rarely encounter complicated declarations and definitions like these. However, by making certain you understand these declarations, you will be able to confidently parse the everyday variety.

Dynamic Memory

When a C/C++ program is compiled, the computer's memory is broken down into four zones that contain the program's code, all global data, the stack, and the heap. The heap is an area of free memory (sometimes referred to as the "free store") that is manipulated by using the dynamic allocation functions malloc( ) and free( ).

When malloc( ) is invoked, it allocates a contiguous block of storage for the object specified and then returns a pointer to the start of the block. The function free( ) returns previously allocated memory to the heap, permitting that portion of memory to be reallocated.

The argument passed to malloc( ) is an **integer** that represents the number of bytes of storage that is needed. If the storage is available, malloc( ) will return a **void ***, which can be cast into whatever type pointer is desired. The concept of **void** pointers was introduced in the ANSI C standard and means a pointer of unknown type, or a generic pointer. A **void** pointer cannot itself be used to reference anything (since it doesn't point to any specific type of data), but it can contain a pointer of any other type. Therefore, any pointer can be converted into a **void** pointer and back without any loss of information.

The following code segment allocates enough storage for 300 **float** values:

```
float *pf;
int inum_floats = 300;

pf = (float *) malloc(inum_floats * sizeof(float));
```

The malloc( ) function has been instructed to obtain enough storage for 300 *, the current size of a **float**. The cast operator (**float ***) is used to return a **float** pointer type. Each block of storage requested is entirely separate and distinct from all other blocks of storage. Absolutely no assumption can be made about where the blocks are located. Blocks are typically "tagged" with some sort of information that allows the operating system to manage the location and size of the block. When the block is no longer needed, it can be returned to the operating system by using the following statement:

```
free((void *) pf);
```

Just as in C, C++ allocates available memory in two ways. When variables are declared, they are created on the stack by pushing the stack pointer down. When these variables go out of scope (for instance, when a local variable is no longer needed), the space for that variable is freed automatically by moving the stack pointer up. The size of stack-allocated memory must always be known at compilation.

Your application may also have to use variables with an unknown size at compilation. Under these circumstances, you must allocate the memory yourself on the free store. The free store can be thought of as occupying the bottom of the program's memory space and growing upward, while the stack occupies the top and grows downward.

Your C and C++ programs can allocate and release free store memory at any point. It is important to realize that free-store-allocated memory variables are not subject to scoping rules, as other variables are. These variables never go out of scope, so once you allocate memory on the heap, you are responsible for freeing it. If you continue to allocate free store space without freeing it, your program could eventually crash.

Most C compilers use the library functions malloc( ) and free( ), just discussed, to provide dynamic memory allocation, but in C++ these capabilities were considered so important they were made a part of the core language. C++ uses **new** and **delete** to allocate and free free store memory. The argument to **new** is an expression that returns the number of bytes to be allocated; the value returned is a pointer to the beginning of this memory block. The argument to **delete** is the starting address of the memory block to be freed. The following two programs illustrate the similarities and differences between a C and C++ application using dynamic memory allocation. Here is the C example:

```
/*
 *   malloc.c
 *   A simple C program using malloc( ), free( )
 *   Copyright (c) Chris H. Pappas and William H. Murray, 1998
 */

#include <stdio.h>
#include <stdlib.h>

#define ISIZE 512

void main( )
{
  int * pimemory_buffer;
  pimemory_buffer=malloc(ISIZE * sizeof(int));
  if(pimemory_buffer == NULL)
    printf("Insufficient memory\n");
  else
    printf("Memory allocated\n");
  free(pimemory_buffer);
}
```

The first point of interest in the program begins with the second **#include** statement that brings in the STDLIB.H header file, containing the definitions for both functions, malloc( ) and free( ). After the program defines the **int** * pointer variable *pimemory_buffer*, the malloc( ) function is invoked to return the address to a memory block that is *ISIZE * sizeof(int)* big. A robust algorithm will always check for the success or failure of the memory allocation, and it explains the purpose behind the **if-else** statement. The function malloc( ) returns a null whenever not enough memory is available to allocate the block. This simple program ends by returning the allocated memory to the free store by using the function free( ) and passing it the beginning address of the allocated block.

The C++ program does not look significantly different:

```
//
// newdel.cpp
```

```
//  A simple C++ program using new and delete
//  Copyright (c) Chris H. Pappas and William H. Murray, 1998
//

#include <iostream.h>
// #include <stdlib.h> not needed for malloc( ), free( )

#define NULL 0
#define ISIZE 512

void main( )
{
  int *pimemory_buffer;

  pimemory_buffer=new int[ISIZE];
  if(pimemory_buffer == NULL)
    cout << "Insufficient memory\n";
  else
    cout << "Memory allocated\n";
  delete(pimemory_buffer);
}
```

The only major difference between the two programs is the syntax used with the function free( ) and the operator **new**. Whereas the function malloc( ) requires the **sizeof** operator to ensure proper memory allocation, the operator **new** has been written to automatically perform the sizeof( ) function on the declared data type it is passed. Both programs will allocate 512 2-byte blocks of consecutive memory (on systems that allocate 2 bytes per **integer**).

Using void Pointers

Now that you have a detailed understanding of the nature of pointer variables, you can begin to appreciate the need for the pointer type **void**. To review, the concept of a pointer is that it is a variable that contains the address of another variable. If you always knew how big a pointer was, you wouldn't have to determine the pointer type at compile time. You would therefore also be able to pass an address of any type to a function. The function could then cast the address to a pointer of the proper type (based on some other piece of information) and perform operations on the result. This process would enable you to create functions that operate on a number of different data types.

That is precisely the reason C++ introduced the **void** pointer type. When **void** is applied to a pointer, its meaning is different from its use to describe function argument lists and return values (which mean "nothing"). A **void** pointer means a pointer to any type of data. The following C++ program demonstrates this use of **void** pointers:

```
//
//  voidpt.cpp
//  A C++ program using void pointers
//  Copyright (c) Chris H. Pappas and William H. Murray, 1998
//

#include <iostream.h>
#define ISTRING_MAX 50

void voutput(void *pobject, char cflag);

void main( )
{
  int *pi;
  char *psz;
  float *pf;
  char cresponse,cnewline;

  cout << "Please enter the dynamic data type\n";
  cout << "    you would like to create.\n\n";
  cout << "Use (s)tring, (i)nt, or (f)loat ";
  cin >> cresponse;
    cin.get(cnewline);
      switch(cresponse) {
        case 's':
          psz=new char[ISTRING_MAX];
          cout << "\nPlease enter a string: ";
          cin.get(psz,ISTRING_MAX);
          voutput(psz,cresponse);
          break;
        case 'i':
          pi=new int;
          cout << "\nPlease enter an integer: ";
          cin >> *pi;
          voutput(pi,cresponse);
          break;
        case 'f':
          pf=new float;
          cout << "\nPlease enter a float: ";
```

```
                         cin >> *pf; voutput(pf,cresponse);
                         break;
                     default:
                         cout << "\n\n  Object type not implemented!";
                 }
       }
       void voutput(void *pobject, char cflag)
       {
         switch(cflag) {
           case 's':
             cout << "\nThe string read in:  " << (char *) pobject;
             delete pobject;
             break;
           case 'i':
             cout << "\nThe integer read in: "
                  << *((int *) pobject);
             delete pobject;
             break;
           case 'f':
             cout << "\nThe float value read in: "
                  << *((float *) pobject);
             delete pobject;
             break;
           }

       }
```

The first statement of interest in the program is the voutput( ) function prototype. Notice that the function's first formal parameter, pobject, is of type **void ***, or a generic pointer. Moving down to the data declarations, you will find three pointer variable types: **int ***, **char ***, and **float ***. These will eventually be assigned valid pointer addresses to their respective memory cell types.

The action in the program begins with a prompt asking the user to enter the data type he or she would like to dynamically create. You may be wondering why the two separate input statements are used to handle the user's response. The first **cin** statement reads in the single-character response but leaves the \n linefeed hanging around. The second input statement, **cin.get(cnewline)**, remedies this situation.

The **switch** statement takes the user's response and invokes the appropriate prompt and pointer initialization. The pointer initialization takes one of three forms:

```
psz=new char;
pi=new int;
pf=new float;
```

The following statement is used to input the character string, and in this example it limits the length of the string to ISTRING_MAX (50) characters.

```
cin.get(psz,ISTRING_MAX);
```

Since the **cin.get( )** input statement expects a string pointer as its first parameter, there is no need to dereference the variable when the voutput( ) function is invoked:

```
voutput(psz,cresponse);
```

Things get a little quieter if the user wants to input an **integer** or a **float**. The last two case options are the same except for the prompt and the reference variable's type.

Notice how the three invocations of the function voutput( ) have different pointer types:

```
voutput(psz,cresponse);
voutput(pi,cresponse);
voutput(pf,cresponse);
```

Function voutput( ) accepts these parameters only because the matching formal parameter's type is **void ***. Remember, in order to use these pointers, you must first cast them to their appropriate pointer type. When using a string pointer with **cout**, you must first cast the pointer to type **char ***.

Just as creating **integer** and **float** dynamic variables was similar, printing their values is also similar. The only difference between the last two **case** statements is the string and the cast operator used.

While it is true that all dynamic variables pass into bit oblivion whenever a program terminates, each of the **case** options takes care of explicitly deleting the pointer variable. When and where your program creates and deletes dynamic storage is application dependent.

Pointers and Arrays—A Closer Look

The following sections include many example programs that deal with the topic of arrays and how they relate to pointers.

Strings (Arrays of Type char)

Many string operations in C/C++ are generally performed by using pointers and pointer arithmetic to reference character array elements. This is because character arrays or strings tend to be accessed in a strictly sequential manner. Remember, all strings in C/C++ are terminated by a null (\0). The following C++ program is a modification of a program used earlier in this chapter to print palindromes and illustrates the use of pointers with character arrays:

```
//
//   chrary.cpp
//   A C++ program that prints a character array backwards
//   using a character pointer and the decrement operator
//   Copyright (c) Chris H. Pappas and William H. Murray, 1998
//

#include <iostream.h>
#include <string.h>

void main( )
{
   char pszpalindrome[]="POOR DAN IN A DROOP";
   char *pc;

   pc=pszpalindrome+(strlen(pszpalindrome)-1);
   do {
      cout << *pc ;
      pc--;
   } while (pc >= pszpalindrome);
}
```

After the program declares and initializes the *pszpalindrome* palindrome, it creates a *pc* of type **char ***. Remember that the name of an array is in itself an address variable. The body of the program begins by setting the *pc* to the address of the last character in the array. This requires a call to the function strlen( ), which calculates the length of the character array.

Note   *The strlen( ) function counts just the number of characters, excluding the null terminator \0.*

You were probably thinking that was the reason for subtracting the 1 from the function's returned value. This is not exactly true; the program has to take into consideration the fact that the first array character's address is at offset zero. Therefore, you want to increment the pointer variable's offset address to one less than the number of valid characters.

Once the pointer for the last valid array character has been calculated, the **do-while** loop is entered. The loop simply uses the pointer variable to point to the memory location of the character to be printed and prints it. It then calculates the next character's memory location and compares this value with the starting address of *pszpalindrome*. As long as the calculated value is >=, the loop iterates.

Arrays of Pointers

In C and C++, you are not restricted to making simple arrays and simple pointers. You can combine the two into a very useful construct—arrays of pointers. An array of pointers is an array whose elements are pointers to other objects. Those objects can themselves be pointers. This means you can have an array of pointers that point to other pointers.

The concept of an array of pointers to pointers is used extensively in the *argc* and *argv* command-line arguments for main( ) you were introduced to in Chapter 8. The following program finds the largest or smallest value entered on the command line. Command-line arguments can include numbers only, or they may be prefaced by a command selecting a choice for the smallest value entered (–s,–S) or the largest (–l,–L).

```cpp
//
//  argcgv.cpp
//  A C++ program using an array of pointers to process
//  the command-line arguments argc, argv
//  Copyright (c) Chris H. Pappas and William H. Murray, 1998
//

#include <iostream.h>
#include <process.h>      // exit( )
#include <stdlib.h>       // atoi( )

#define IFIND_LARGEST 1
#define IFIND_SMALLEST 0

int main(int argc,char *argv[])
{
  char *psz;
  int ihow_many;
  int iwhich_extreme=0;
  int irange_boundary=32767;

  if(argc < 2) {
    cout << "\nYou need to enter an -S,-s,-L,-l"
         << " and at least one integer value";
    exit(1);
  }
```

```cpp
while(--argc > 0 && (*++argv)[0] == '-') {
  for(psz=argv[0]+1; *psz != '\0'; psz++) {
    switch(*psz) {
      case 's':
      case 'S':
        iwhich_extreme=IFIND_SMALLEST;
        irange_boundary=32767;
        break;
      case 'l':
      case 'L':
        iwhich_extreme=IFIND_LARGEST;
        irange_boundary=0;
        break;
      default:
        cout << "unknown argument "<< *psz << endl;
        exit(1);
    }
  }
}

if(argc==0) {
  cout << "Please enter at least one number\n";
  exit(1);
}

ihow_many=argc;

while(argc--) {
  int present_value;
  present_value=atoi(*(argv++));
  if(iwhich_extreme==IFIND_LARGEST && present_value >
     irange_boundary)
    irange_boundary=present_value;
  if(iwhich_extreme==IFIND_SMALLEST && present_value <
     irange_boundary)
    irange_boundary=present_value;
}

cout << "The ";
cout << ((iwhich_extreme) ? "largest" : "smallest");
cout << " of the " << ihow_many << " value(s) input is " <<
```

```
        irange_boundary << endl;

   return(0);
}
```

Before looking at the source code, take a moment to familiarize yourself with the possible command combinations that can be used to invoke the program. The following list illustrates the possible command combinations:

```
argcgv
argcgv 98
argcgv 98 21
argcgv -s 98
argcgv -S 98 21
argcgv -l 14
argcgv -L 14 67
```

Looking at the main( ) program, you will see the formal parameters *argc* and *argv* that you were introduced to in Chapter 8. To review, *argc* is an **integer** value containing the number of separate items, or arguments, that appeared on the command line. The variable *argv* refers to an array of pointers to character strings.

Note
argv is not a constant. It is a variable whose value can be altered, a key point to remember when viewing how argv is used below. The first element of the array, argv[0], is a pointer to a string of characters that contains the program name.

Moving down the code to the first **if** statement, you find a test to determine if the value of *argc* is less than 2. If this test evaluates to TRUE, it means that the user has typed just the name of the program *argcgv* without any switches. Since this action would indicate that the user does not know the switch and value options, the program will prompt the user at this point with the valid options and then exit( ).

The **while** loop test condition evaluates from left to right, beginning with the decrement of *argc*. If *argc* is still greater than zero, the right side of the logical expression will be examined.

The right side of the logical expression first increments the array pointer *argv* past the first pointer entry (++argv), skipping the program's name, so that it now points to the second array entry. Once the pointer has been incremented, it is then used to point (*++argv) to the zeroth offset ((*++argv)[0]) of the first character of the string pointed to. Obtaining this character, if it is a – symbol, the program diagnoses that the second program command was a possible switch—for example, –s or –L.

The **for** loop initialization begins by taking the current pointer address of *argv*, which was just incremented in the line above to point to the second pointer in the array. Since *argv*'s second element is a pointer to a character string, the pointer can be subscripted (argv[0]). The complete expression, argv[0]+1, points to the second character of the second string pointed to by the current address stored in *argv*. This second character is the one past the command switch symbol –. Once the program calculates this character's address, it stores it in the variable *psz*. The **for** loop repeats while the character pointed to by **psz* is not the null terminator \0.

The program continues by analyzing the switch to see if the user wants to obtain the smallest or largest of the values entered. Based on the switch, the appropriate constant is assigned to the *iwhich_extreme*. Each **case** statement also takes care of initializing the variable *irange_boundary* to an appropriate value for the comparisons that follow. Should the user enter an unrecognized switch—for example, -d—the default case will take care of printing an appropriate message.

The second **if** statement now checks to see if *argc* has been decremented to zero. An appropriate message is printed if the switches have been examined on the command line and there are no values left to process. If so, the program terminates with an exit code of decimal 1.

A successful skipping of this **if** test means there are now values from the command line that need to be examined. Since the program will now decrement *argc*, the variable *ihow_many* is assigned *argc*'s current value.

The **while** loop continues while there are at least two values to compare. The **while** loop needs to be entered only if there is more than one value to be compared, since the **cout** statement following the **while** loop is capable of handling a command line with a single value.

The function atoi( ) converts each of the remaining arguments into an **integer** and stores the result in the variable *present_value*. Remember, *argv++* needed to be incremented first so that it points to the first value to be compared. Also, the **while** loop test condition had already decremented the pointer to make certain the loop wasn't entered with only a single command value.

The last two **if** statements take care of updating the variable *irange_boundary* based on the user's desire to find either the smallest or largest of all values entered. Finally, the results of the program are printed by using an interesting combination of string literals and the conditional operator.

More on Pointers to Pointers

The next program demonstrates the use of pointer variables that point to other pointers. It is included at this point in the chapter instead of in the section describing pointers to pointers because the program uses dynamic memory allocation. You may want to refer back to the general discussion of pointers to pointers before looking at the program.

```
/*
 *   dblptr.c
```

```
*    A C program using pointer variables with double
*    indirection
*    Copyright (c) Chris H. Pappas and William H. Murray, 1998
*/

#include <stdio.h>
#include <stdlib.h>

#define IMAXELEMENTS 3

void voutput(int **ppiresult_a, int **ppiresult_b,
             int **ppiresult_c);
void vassign(int *pivirtual_array[],int *pinewblock);

void main( )
{
  int **ppiresult_a, **ppiresult_b, **ppiresult_c;
  int *pivirtual_array[IMAXELEMENTS];
  int *pinewblock, *pioldblock;

  ppiresult_a=&pivirtual_array[0];
  ppiresult_b=&pivirtual_array[1];
  ppiresult_c=&pivirtual_array[2];

  pinewblock=(int *)malloc(IMAXELEMENTS * sizeof(int));
  pioldblock=pinewblock;

  vassign(pivirtual_array,pinewblock);

  **ppiresult_a=7;
  **ppiresult_b=10;
  **ppiresult_c=15;

  voutput(ppiresult_a,ppiresult_b,ppiresult_c);

  pinewblock=(int *)malloc(IMAXELEMENTS * sizeof(int));

  *pinewblock=**ppiresult_a;
  *(pinewblock+1)=**ppiresult_b;
  *(pinewblock+2)=**ppiresult_c;

  free(pioldblock);
```

```
    vassign(pivirtual_array,pinewblock);

    voutput(ppiresult_a,ppiresult_b,ppiresult_c);
}

void vassign(int *pivirtual_array[],int *pinewblock)
{
  pivirtual_array[0]=pinewblock;
  pivirtual_array[1]=pinewblock+1;
  pivirtual_array[2]=pinewblock+2;
}

void voutput(int **ppiresult_a, int **ppiresult_b, int
              **ppiresult_c)
{
  printf("%d\n",**ppiresult_a);
  printf("%d\n",**ppiresult_b);
  printf("%d\n",**ppiresult_c);
}
```

The program is designed so that it highlights the concept of a pointer variable (*ppiresult_a*, *ppiresult_b*, and *ppiresult_c*), pointing to a constant address (&*pivirtual_array[0]*, &*pivirtual_array[1]*, and &*pivirtual_array[2]*), whose pointer address contents can dynamically change.

Look at the data declarations in main( ). *ppiresult_a*, *ppiresult_b*, and *ppiresult_c* have been defined as pointers to pointers that point to **integer**s. Let's take this slowly, looking at the various syntax combinations:

```
ppiresult_a
*ppiresult_a
**ppiresult_a
```

The first syntax references the address stored in the pointer variable *ppiresult_a*. The second syntax references the pointer address pointed to by the address in *ppiresult_a*. The last syntax references the **integer** that is pointed to by the pointer address pointed to by *ppiresult_a*. Make certain you do not proceed any further until you understand these three different references.

The three variables *ppiresult_a*, *ppiresult_b*, and *ppiresult_c* have all been defined as pointers to pointers that point to **integer**s int **. The variable *pivirtual_array* has been defined to be an array of **integer** pointers int *, of size IMAXELEMENTS. The last two variables, *pinewblock* and *pioldblock*, are similar to the variable *pivirtual_array*, except they are single variables that point to **integers int ***. Figure 10-17 shows what these seven variables look like after their storage has been allocated and, in particular, after *ppiresult_a*, *ppiresult_b*, and *ppiresult_c* have been assigned the address of their respective elements in the *pivirtual_array*.

It is this array that is going to hold the addresses of the dynamically changing memory cell addresses. Something similar actually happens in a true multitasking environment. Your program thinks it has the actual physical address of a variable stored in memory, when what it really has is a fixed address to an array of pointers that in turn point to the current physical address of the data item in memory. When the multitasking environment needs to conserve memory by moving your data objects, it simply moves their storage locations and updates the array of pointers. The variables in your program, however, are still pointing to the same physical address, albeit not the physical address of the data but of the array of pointers.

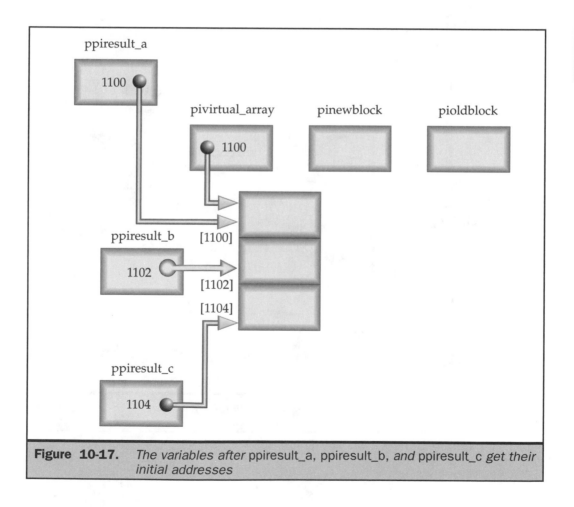

Figure 10-17. *The variables after* ppiresult_a, ppiresult_b, *and* ppiresult_c *get their initial addresses*

To understand how this operates, pay particular attention to the fact that the physical addresses stored in the pointer variables *ppiresult_a*, *ppiresult_b*, and *ppiresult_c* never change once they are assigned.

Figure 10-18 illustrates what has happened to the variables after the dynamic array *pinewblock* has been allocated and *pioldblock* has been initialized to the same address of the new array. Most important, notice how the physical addresses of *pinewblock*'s individual elements have been assigned to their respective counterparts in *pivirtual_array*.

The pointer assignments were all accomplished by the vassign( ) function. vassign( ) was passed the *pivirtual_array* (call-by-value) and the address of the recently allocated

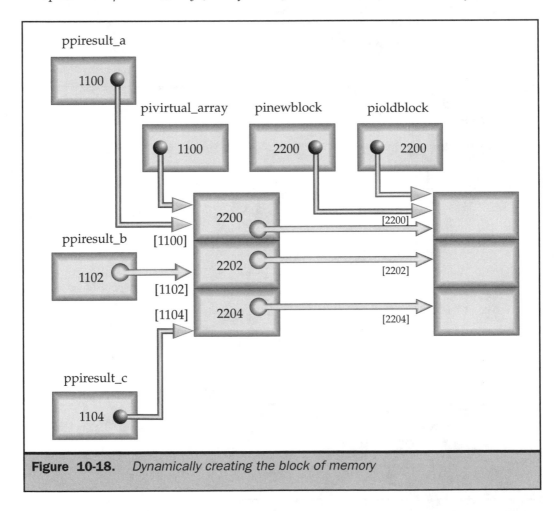

Figure 10-18. *Dynamically creating the block of memory*

dynamic memory block in the variable *pinewblock*. The function takes care of assigning the addresses of the dynamically allocated memory cells to each element of the *pivirtual_array*. Since the array was passed call-by-value, the changes are effective in the main( ).

At this point, if you were to use the debugger to print out *ppiresult_a*, you would see ACC8 (the address of *pivirtual_array*'s first element), and **ppiresult_a* would print 1630 (or the contents of the address pointed to). You would encounter a similar dump for the other two pointer variables, *ppiresult_b* and *ppiresult_c*.

Figure 10-19 shows the assignment of three **integer** values to the physical memory locations. Notice the syntax to accomplish this:

PROGRAMMING
FOUNDATIONS

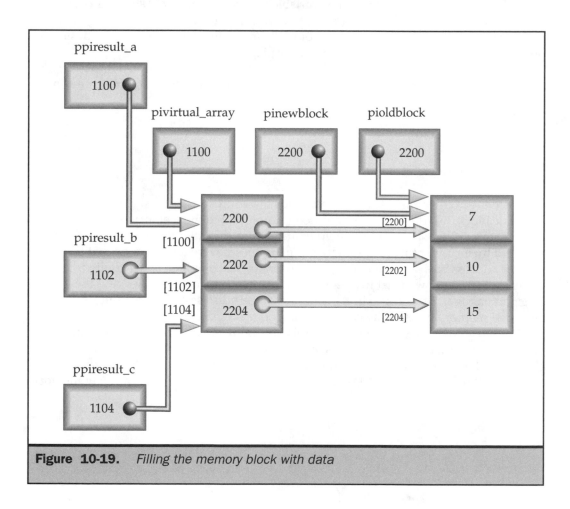

Figure 10-19. *Filling the memory block with data*

```
**ppiresult_a=7;
**ppiresult_b=10;
**ppiresult_c=15;
```

At this point, the program prints out the values 7, 10, and 15 by calling the function voutput( ). Notice that the function has been defined as receiving three **int **** variables. Notice that the actual parameter list does *not* need to precede the variables with the double indirection operator ****** since that is their type by declaration.

As shown in Figure 10-20, the situation has become very interesting. A new block of dynamic memory has been allocated with the malloc( ) function, with its new physical memory address stored in the pointer variable *pinewblock*. *pioldblock* still points to the previously allocated block of dynamic memory. Using the incomplete analogy to a multitasking environment, the figure would illustrate the operating system's desire to physically move the data objects' memory locations.

Figure 10-20 also shows that the data objects themselves were copied into the new memory locations. The program accomplished this with the following three lines of code:

```
*pinewblock=**ppiresult_a;
*(pinewblock+1)=**ppiresult_b;
*(pinewblock+2)=**ppiresult_c;
```

Since the pointer variable *pinewblock* holds the address to the first element of the dynamic block, its address is dereferenced (*), pointing to the memory cell itself, and the 7 is stored there. Using a little pointer arithmetic, the other two memory cells are accessed by incrementing the pointer. The parentheses were necessary so that the pointer address was incremented *before* the dereference operator * was applied.

Figure 10-21 shows what happens when the function free( ) is called and the function vassign( ) is called to link the new physical address of the dynamically allocated memory block to the *pivirtual_array* pointer address elements.

The most important fact to notice in this last figure is that the actual physical address of the three pointer variables *ppiresult_a*, *ppiresult_b*, and *ppiresult_c* has not changed. Therefore, when the program prints the values pointed to ***ppiresult_a* and so on, you still see the values 7, 10, and 15, even though their physical location in memory has changed.

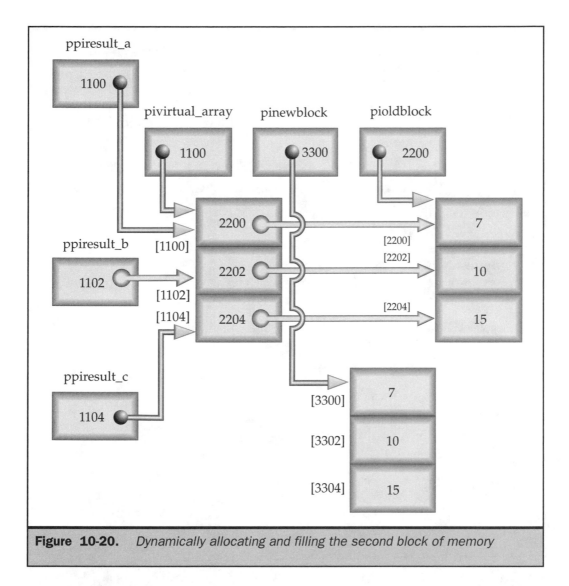

Figure 10-20. *Dynamically allocating and filling the second block of memory*

Arrays of String Pointers

One of the easiest ways to keep track of an array of strings is to define an array of pointers to strings. This is much simpler than defining a two-dimensional array of

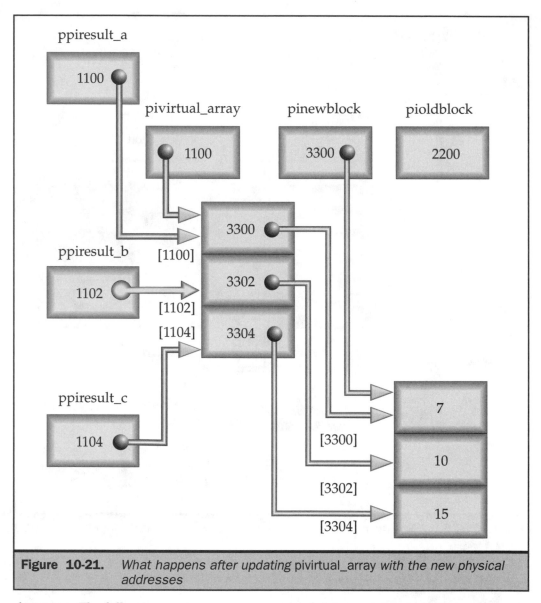

Figure 10-21. *What happens after updating* pivirtual_array *with the new physical addresses*

characters. The following program uses an array of string pointers to keep track of three function error messages.

```
/*
 *   aofptr.c
 *   A C program that demonstrates how to define and use
 *   arrays of pointers.
```

```c
*    Copyright Chris H. Pappas and William H. Murray, 1998
*/

#include <ctype.h>
#include <stdio.h>

#define INUMBER_OF_ERRORS 3

char *pszarray[INUMBER_OF_ERRORS] =
        {
          "\nFile not available.\n",
          "\nNot an alpha character.\n",
          "\nValue not between 1 and 10.\n"
        };

FILE *fopen_a_file(char *psz);
char cget_a_char(void);
int iget_an_integer(void);

FILE *pfa_file;

void main( )
{
  char cvalue;
  int ivalue;

  fopen_a_file("input.dat");
  cvalue = cget_a_char( );
  ivalue = iget_an_integer( );

}

FILE *fopen_a_file(char *psz)
{
  const ifopen_a_file_error = 0;

  pfa_file = fopen(psz,"r");
  if(!pfa_file)
    printf("%s",pszarray[ifopen_a_file_error]);
  return(pfa_file);
}

char cget_a_char(void)
{
```

```
    char cvalue;
    const icget_a_char_error = 1;

    printf("\nEnter a character: ");
    scanf("%c",&cvalue);
    if(!isalpha(cvalue))
      printf("%s",pszarray[icget_a_char_error]);
    return(cvalue);
}

int iget_an_integer(void)
{
  int ivalue;
  const iiget_an_integer = 2;
  printf("\nEnter an integer between 1 and 10: ");
  scanf("%d",&ivalue);
  if( (ivalue < 1) || (ivalue > 10) )
    printf("%s",pszarray[iiget_an_integer]);
  return(ivalue);
}
```

The *pszarray* is initialized outside all function declarations. This gives it a global lifetime. For large programs, an array of this nature could be saved in a separate source file dedicated to maintaining all error message control. Notice that each function, fopen_a_file( ), cget_a_char( ), and iget_an_integer( ), takes care of defining its own constant index into the array. This combination of an error message array and unique function index makes for a very modular solution to error exception handling. If a project requires the creation of a new function, the new piece of code selects a vacant index value and adds one error condition to *pszarray*. The efficiency of this approach allows each code segment to quickly update the entire application to its peculiar I/O requirements without having to worry about an elaborate error detection/alert mechanism.

The C++ Reference Type

C++ provides a form of call-by-reference that is even easier to use than pointers. First, let's examine the use of reference variables in C++. As with C, C++ enables you to declare regular variables or pointer variables. In the first case, memory is actually allocated for the data object; in the second case, a memory location is set aside to hold an address for an object that will be allocated at another time. C++ has a third kind of declaration, the reference type. Like a pointer variable, a reference variable refers to another variable location, but like a regular variable, it requires no special dereferencing operators. The syntax for a reference variable is straightforward:

```
int iresult_a=5;
int& riresult_a=iresult_a; // valid
int& riresult_b;           // invalid: uninitialized
```

This example sets up the reference variable *riresult_a* and assigns it to the existing variable *iresult_a*. At this point, the referenced location has two names associated with it—*iresult_a* and *riresult_a*. Because both variables point to the same location in memory, they are, in fact, the same variable. Any assignment made to *riresult_a* is reflected through *iresult_a*; the inverse is also true, and changes to *iresult_a* occur through any access to *riresult_a*. Therefore, with the reference data type, you can create what is sometimes referred to as an alias for a variable.

The reference type has a restriction that serves to distinguish it from pointer variables, which, after all, do something very similar. The value of the reference type must be set at declaration, and it cannot be changed during the run of the program. After you initialize this type in the declaration, it always refers to the same memory location. Therefore, any assignments you make to a reference variable change only the data in memory, not the address of the variable itself. In other words, you can think of a reference variable as a pointer to a constant location.

For example, using the preceding declarations, the following statement doubles the contents of *iresult_a* by multiplying 5 * 2:

```
riresult_a *= 2;
```

The next statement assigns *icopy_value* (assuming it is of type **int**) a copy of the value associated with *riresult_a*:

```
icopy_value = riresult_a;
```

The next statement is also legal when using reference types:

```
int *piresult_a = &riresult_a;
```

This statement assigns the address of *riresult_a* to the **int** * variable *piresult_a*.

The primary use of a reference type is as an argument or a return type of a function, especially when applied to user-defined class types (see Chapter 15).

Functions Returning Addresses

When you return an address from a function using either a pointer variable or a reference type, you are giving the user a memory address. The user can read the value at the address, and if you haven't declared the pointer type to be **const**, the user can always write the value. By returning an address, you are giving the user permission to read and, for non-**const** pointer types, write to private data. This is a significant design decision. See if you can anticipate what will happen in this next program:

```
//
//  refvar.cpp
//  A C++ program showing what NOT to do with address
//  variables
//  Copyright (c) Chris H. Pappas and William H. Murray, 1998
//

#include <iostream.h>

int *ifirst_function(void);
int *isecond_function(void);

void main( )
{
  int *pi=ifirst_function( );
  isecond_function( );
  cout << "Correct value? " << *pi;
}

int *ifirst_function(void)
{
  int ilocal_to_first=11;
  return &ilocal_to_first;
}

int *isecond_function(void)
{
  int ilocal_to_second=44;
```

```
    return &ilocal_to_second;
}
```

Using the Integrated Debugger

To examine the operation of this C++ code while it is actually working, you can use the integrated debugger. Use the Variables window to keep an eye on the variable *pi*.

What has happened? When the ifirst_function( ) is called, local space is allocated on the stack for the variable *ilocal_to_first*, and the value 11 is stored in it. At this point the ifirst_function( ) returns the address of this local variable (very bad news). The second statement in the main program invokes the isecond_function( ). isecond_function( ) in turn allocates local space for *ilocal_to_second* and assigns it a value of 44. So how does the **printf** statement print a value of 44 when it was passed the address of *ilocal_to_first* when ifirst_function( ) was invoked?

What happened was this. When the address of the *itemporary* local variable *ilocal_to_first* was assigned to *pi* by ifirst_function( ), the address to the *itemporary* location was retained even after *ilocal_to_first* went out of scope. When isecond_function() was invoked, it also needed local storage. Since *ilocal_to_first* was gone, *ilocal_to_second* was given the same storage location as its predecessor. With *pi* hanging onto this same busy memory cell, you can see why printing the value it now points to yields a 44. Extreme care must be taken not to return the addresses of local variables.

When Should You Use Reference Types?

To review, there are four main reasons for using C++ reference types:

■ They lend themselves to more readable code by allowing you to ignore details of how a parameter is passed.

■ They put the responsibility for argument passing on the programmer who writes the functions, not on the individual who uses them.

■ They are a necessary counterpart to operator overloading.

■ They are also used with passing classes to functions so constructors and destructors are not called.

These concepts are described in greater detail in Chapter 16.

Chapter 11

Complete I/O In C

M any commonly used high-level languages have restrictive input and output mechanisms. As a result, programmers generate convoluted algorithms to perform sophisticated data retrieval and display. This is not the case with C, which has a very complete I/O (input/output) function library, although historically I/O was not even part of the C language itself. However, if you have used only simple I/O statements like Pascal's **readln** and **writeln** statements, you're in for a surprise. This chapter discusses the more than 20 different ways to perform I/O in C.

The standard C library I/O routines allow you to read and write data to files and devices. However, the C language itself does not include any predefined file structures. C treats all data as a sequence of bytes. There are three basic types of I/O functions: stream, console and port, and low-level.

All of the stream I/O functions treat a data file or data items as a stream of individual characters. By selecting the appropriate stream function, your application can process data in any size or format required, from single characters to large, complicated data structures.

Technically, when a program opens a file for I/O using the stream functions, the opened file is associated with a structure of type FILE (predefined in STDIO.H) that contains basic information about the file. Once the stream is opened, a pointer to the file structure is returned. The file pointer, sometimes called the *stream pointer* or the *stream*, is used to refer to the file for all subsequent I/O.

All stream I/O functions provide buffered, formatted, or unformatted input and output. A *buffered stream* provides an intermediate storage location for all information that is input from the stream and output that is being sent to the stream.

Since disk I/O is such a time-consuming operation, stream buffering streamlines the application. Instead of inputting stream data one character at a time or one structure's worth at a time, stream I/O functions access data a block at a time. As the application needs to process the input, it merely accesses the buffer, a much less time-consuming process. When the buffer is empty, another disk block access is made.

The reverse situation holds true for *stream output*. Instead of all data being physically output at the time the output statement is executed, all output data is put into the buffer. When the buffer is full, the data is written to the disk.

Most high-level languages have a problem with buffered I/O that you need to take into consideration. For example, if your program has executed several output statements that do not fill the output buffer, causing it to dump to the disk, that information is lost when your program terminates.

The solution usually involves making a call to an appropriate function to flush the buffer. Unlike other high-level languages, C solves this problem with buffered I/O by automatically flushing the buffer's contents whenever the program terminates. Of course, a well-written application should not rely on these automatic features, but should always explicitly detail every action the program is to take. One additional note: when you use stream I/O, if the application terminates abnormally, the output buffers may not be flushed, resulting in loss of data.

Similar in function are the *console and port I/O routines*, which can be seen as an extension of the stream routines. They allow you to read or write to a terminal (console) or an input/output port (such as a printer port). The port I/O functions simply read and write data in bytes. Console I/O functions provide several additional options. For example, you can detect whether a character has been typed at the console and whether or not the characters entered are echoed to the screen as they are read.

The last type of input and output is called *low-level I/O*. None of the low-level I/O functions perform any buffering and formatting; instead, they invoke the operating system's input and output capabilities directly. These routines let you access files and peripheral devices at a more basic level than the stream functions. Files opened in this mode return a *file handle*. This handle is an integer value that is used to refer to the file in subsequent operations.

In general, it is very bad practice to mix stream I/O functions with low-level routines. Since stream functions are buffered and low-level functions are not, attempting to access the same file or device by two different methods leads to confusion and eventual loss of data in the buffers. Therefore, either stream or low-level functions should be used exclusively on a given file.

Stream Functions

To use the stream functions, your application must include the file STDIO.H. This file contains definitions for constants, types, and structures used in the stream functions and contains function prototypes and macro definitions for the stream routines.

Many of the constants predefined in STDIO.H can be useful in your application. For example, *EOF* is defined to be the value returned by input functions at end-of-file, and *NULL* is the null pointer. Also, *FILE* defines the structure used to maintain information about a stream, and *BUFSIZ* defines the default size, in bytes, of the stream buffers.

Opening Streams

You can use one of three functions to open a stream before input and output can be performed on the stream: fopen( ), fdopen( ), or freopen( ). The file mode and form are set at the time the stream is opened. The stream file can be opened for reading, writing, or both, and can be opened in either text or binary mode.

All three functions return a file pointer, which is used to refer to the stream. For example, if your program contains the following line, you can use the file pointer variable *pfinfile* to refer to the stream:

```
pfinfile = fopen("input.dat","r");
```

When your application begins execution, five streams are automatically opened. These streams are the standard input (**stdin**), standard output (**stdout**), standard error (**stderr**), standard printer (**stdprn**), and standard auxiliary (**stdaux**).

By default, the standard input, standard output, and standard error refer to the user's console. This means that whenever a program expects input from the standard input, it receives that input from the console. Likewise, a program that writes to the standard output prints its data to the console. Any error messages that are generated by the library routines are sent to the standard error stream, meaning that error messages appear on the user's console. The standard auxiliary and standard print streams usually refer to an auxiliary port and a printer, respectively.

You can use the five file pointers in any function that requires a stream pointer as an argument. Some functions, such as getchar( ) and putchar( ), are designed to use stdin or stdout automatically. Since the pointers **stdin**, **stdout**, **stderr**, **stdprn**, and **stdaux** are constants, not variables, do not try to reassign them to a new stream pointer value.

Input and Output Redirection

Modern operating systems consider the keyboard and video display as files. This is reasonable since the system can read from the keyboard just as it can read from a disk or tape file. Similarly, the system can write to the video display just as it can write to a disk or tape file.

Suppose your application reads from the keyboard and outputs to the video display. Now suppose you want the input to come from a file called SAMPLE.DAT. You can use the same application if you tell the system to replace input from the keyboard, considered now as a file, with input from another file, namely the file SAMPLE.DAT. The process of changing the standard input or standard output is called *input redirection* or *output redirection*.

Input and output redirection in MS-DOS are effortless. You use < to redirect the input and > to redirect the output. Suppose the executable version of your application is called REDIRECT. The following system-level command will run the program REDIRECT and use the file SAMPLE.DAT as input instead of the keyboard:

```
redirect < sample.dat
```

The next statement will redirect both the input (SAMPLE.DAT) and the output (SAMPLE.BAK):

```
redirect < sample.dat > sample.bak
```

This last example will redirect the output (SAMPLE.BAK) only:

```
redirect > sample.bak
```

Note *The standard error file **stderr** cannot be redirected.*

There are two techniques for managing the association between a standard filename and a physical file or device: redirection and piping. *Piping* is the technique of directly connecting the standard output of one program to the standard input of another. The control and invocation of redirection and piping normally occur outside the program, which is exactly the intent since the program itself need not care where the data is really coming from or going to.

The way to connect the standard output from one program to the standard input of another program is to pipe them together by using the vertical bar symbol, |. Therefore, to connect the standard output of the program PROCESS1 to the standard input of the program PROCESS2, you would type

```
process1 | process2
```

The operating system handles all the details of physically getting the output from PROCESS1 to the input of PROCESS2.

Altering the Stream Buffer

All files opened using the stream functions (stdin( ), stdout( ), and stdprn( )) are buffered by default except for the preopened streams **stderr** and **stdaux**. The two streams **stderr** and **stdaux** are unbuffered by default unless they are used in either the printf( ) or scanf( ) family of functions. In this case, they are assigned a temporary buffer. You can buffer **stderr** and **stdaux** with setbuf( ) or setvbuf( ). The **stdin**, **stdout**, and **stdprn** streams are flushed automatically whenever they are full.

You can use the two functions setbuf( ) and setvbuf( ) to make a buffered stream unbuffered, or you can use them to associate a buffer with an unbuffered stream. Note that buffers allocated by the system are not accessible to the user, but buffers allocated with the functions setbuf( ) and setvbuf( ) are named by the user and can be manipulated as if they were variables. These user-defined stream buffers are very useful for checking input and output before any system-generated error conditions.

You can define a buffer to be of any size; if you use the function setbuf( ), the size is set by the constant *BUFSIZ* defined in STDIO.H. The syntax for setbuf( ) looks like this:

```
void setbuf(FILE *stream, char *buffer);
```

The following example program uses setbuf( ) and *BUFSIZ* to define and attach a buffer to **stderr**. A buffered **stderr** gives an application greater control over error exception handling. Using the integrated debugger, single-step the application exactly as you see it.

```
/*
 *   setbf.c
```

```
 *    A C program demonstrating how to define and attach
 *    a buffer to the unbuffered stderr.
 *    Copyright (c) Bill/Chris H. Pappas and William H. Murray, 1998
 */

#include <stdio.h>
char cmyoutputbuffer[BUFSIZ];

void main(void)
{
   /* associate a buffer with the unbuffered output stream */
   setbuf(stderr, cmyoutputbuffer); /* line to comment out */

   /* insert into the output stream buffer */
   fputs("Sample output inserted into the\n",stderr);
   fputs("output stream buffer.\n",stderr);

   /* dump the output stream buffer */
   fflush(stderr);
}
```

Try running the program a second time with the setbuf( ) statement commented out. This will prevent the program from associating a buffer with **stderr**. When you ran the program, did you see the difference? Without a buffered **stderr**, the integrated debugger outputs each fputs( ) statement as soon as the line is executed.

The next application uses the function setvbuf( ). The syntax for setvbuf( ) looks like this:

```
int setvbuf(FILE *stream, char *buffer, int buftype, size_t bufsize);
```

Here, the program determines the size of the buffer instead of using *BUFSIZ* defined in STDIO.H:

```
/*
 *    setvbuf.c
 *    A C program demonstrating how to use setvbuf( )
 *    Copyright (c) Bill/Chris H. Pappas and William H. Murray, 1998
 */

#include <stdio.h>
#define MYBUFSIZ 512
```

```
void main(void)
{
   char ichar, cmybuffer[MYBUFSIZ];
   FILE *pfinfile, *pfoutfile;

   pfinfile = fopen("sample.in", "r");
   pfoutfile = fopen("sample.out", "w");

   if (setvbuf(pfinfile, cmybuffer, _IOFBF, MYBUFSIZ) != 0)
      printf("pfinfile buffer allocation error\n");
   else
      printf("pfinfile buffer created\n");

   if (setvbuf(pfoutfile, NULL, _IOLBF, 132) != 0)
      printf("pfoutfile buffer allocation error\n");
   else
      printf("pfoutfile buffer created\n");

   while(fscanf(pfinfile,"%c",&ichar) != EOF)
      fprintf(pfoutfile,"%c",ichar);

   fclose(pfinfile);
   fclose(pfoutfile);
}
```

The program creates a user-accessible buffer pointed to by *pfinfile* and a malloc( )-allocated buffer pointed to by *pfoutfile*. This last buffer is defined as *buftype*, _IOLBF, or line buffered. Other options defined in STDIO.H include _IOFBF, for fully buffered, and _IONBF, for no buffer.

Remember, both setbuf( ) and setvbuf( ) cause the user-defined *buffer* to be used for I/O buffering, instead of an automatically allocated buffer. With setbuf( ), if the *buffer* argument is set to null, I/O will be unbuffered. Otherwise, it will be fully buffered.

With setvbuf( ), if the *buffer* argument is null, a buffer will be allocated using malloc( ). The setvbuf( ) *buffer* will use the *bufsize* argument as the amount allocated and automatically free the memory on close.

Closing Streams

The two functions fclose( ) and fcloseall( ) close a stream or streams, respectively. The fclose( ) function closes a single file, while fcloseall( ) closes all open streams except **stdin**, **stdout**, **stderr**, **stdprn**, and **stdaux**. However, if your program does not explicitly close a stream, the stream is automatically closed when the application terminates. Since the number of streams that can be open at a given time is limited, it is a good practice to close a stream when you are finished with it.

Low-level Input and Output in C

Table 11-1 lists the most commonly used low-level input and output functions used by an application.

Low-level input and output calls do not buffer or format data. Files opened by low-level calls are referenced by a file handle (an **integer** value used by the operating system to refer to the file). You use the open( ) function to open files. You can use the sopen( ) macro to open a file with file-sharing attributes.

Low-level functions are different from their stream counterparts because they do not require the inclusion of the STDIO.H header file. However, some common constants that are predefined in STDIO.H, such as *EOF* and *NULL*, may be useful. Declarations for the low-level functions are given in the IO.H header file.

This second disk-file I/O system was originally created under the UNIX operating system. Because the ANSI C standard committee has elected not to standardize this low-level, UNIX-like, unbuffered I/O system, it cannot be recommended for future use. Instead, the standardized buffered I/O system described throughout this chapter is recommended for all new projects.

Function	Definition
close( )	Closes a disk file
lseek( )	Seeks to the specified byte in a file
open( )	Opens a disk file
read( )	Reads a buffer of data
unlink( )	Removes a file from the directory
write( )	Writes a buffer of data

Table 11-1. *Commonly Used Low-level Input and Output Functions*

Character Input and Output

There are certain character input and output functions defined in the ANSI C standard that are supplied with all C compilers. These functions provide standard input and output and are considered to be high-level routines (as opposed to low-level routines, which access the machine hardware more directly). I/O in C is implemented through vendor-supplied functions rather than keywords defined as part of the language.

Using getc( ), putc( ), fgetc( ), and fputc( )

The most basic of all I/O functions are those that input and output one character. The getc( ) function inputs one character from a specified file stream, like this:

```
int ic;
ic = getc(stdin);
```

The input character is passed back in the name of the function getc( ) and then assigns the returned value to *ic*. By the way, if you are wondering why *ic* isn't of type **char**, it is because the function getc( ) has been prototyped to return an **int** type. This is necessary because of the possible system-dependent size of the end-of-file marker, which might not fit in a single **char** byte size.

Function getc( ) converts the **integer** into an unsigned character. This use of an unsigned character preserved as an **integer** guarantees that the ASCII values above 127 are not represented as negative values. Therefore, negative values can be used to represent unusual situations like errors and the end of the input file. For example, the end-of-file has traditionally been represented by –1, although the ANSI C standard states only that the constant *EOF* represents some negative value.

Because an **integer** value is returned by getc( ), the data item that inputs the value from getc( ) must also be defined as an **integer**. While it may seem odd to be using an **integer** in a character function, the C language actually makes very little distinction between characters and integers. If a character is provided when an **integer** is needed, the character will be converted to an **integer**.

The complement to the getc( ) function is putc( ). The putc( ) function outputs one character to the file stream represented by the specified file pointer. To send the same character that was just input to the standard output, use the following statement:

```
putc(ic,stdout);
```

The getc( ) function is normally buffered, which means that when a request for a character is made by the application, control is not returned to the program until a carriage return is entered into the standard input file stream. All the characters entered before the carriage return are held in a buffer and delivered to the program one at a time. The application invokes the getc( ) function repeatedly until the buffer has been exhausted. After the carriage return has been sent to the program by getc( ), the next request for a character results in more characters accumulating in the buffer until a carriage return is again entered. This means that you cannot use the getc( ) function for one-key input techniques that do not require pressing the carriage return.

One final note: getc( ) and putc( ) are actually implemented as macros rather than as true functions. The functions fgetc( ) and fputc( ) are identical to their macro getc( ) and putc( ) counterparts.

Using getchar( ), putchar( ), fgetchar( ), and fputchar( )

The two macros getchar( ) and putchar( ) are actually specific implementations of the getc( ) and putc( ) macros, respectively. They are always associated with standard input (**stdin**) and standard output (**stdout**). The only way to use them on other file streams is to redirect either standard input or standard output from within the program.

The same two coded examples used earlier could be rewritten by using these two functions:

```
int ic;
ic = getchar( );
```

and

```
putchar(ic);
```

Like getc( ) and putc( ), getchar( ) and putchar( ) are implemented as macros. The function putchar( ) has been written to return an *EOF* value whenever an error condition occurs. The following code can be used to check for an *output* error condition. Because of the check for *EOF* on output, it tends to be a bit confusing, although it is technically correct.

```
if(putchar(ic) == EOF)
  printf("An error has occurred writing to stdout");
```

Both fgetchar( ) and fputchar( ) are the function equivalents of their macro getchar( ) and putchar( ) counterparts.

Using getch( ) and putch( )

Both getch( ) and putch( ) are true functions, but they do not fall under the ANSI C standard because they are low-level functions that interface closely with the hardware. For PCs, these functions do not use buffering, which means that they immediately input a character typed at the keyboard. They can be redirected, however, so they are not associated exclusively with the keyboard.

You can use the functions getch( ) and putch( ) exactly like getchar( ) and putchar( ). Usually, a program running on a PC will use getch( ) to trap keystrokes ignored by getchar( )—for example, PGUP, PGDN, HOME, and END. The function getchar( ) sees a character entered from the keyboard as soon as the key is pressed; a carriage return is not needed to send the character to the program. This ability allows the function getch( ) to provide a one-key technique that is not available with getc( ) or getchar( ).

On a PC, the function getch( ) operates very differently from getc( ) and getchar( ). This is partly due to the fact that the PC can easily determine when an individual key on the keyboard has been pressed. Other systems, such as the DEC and VAX C, do not allow the hardware to trap individual keystrokes. These systems typically echo the input character and require the pressing of a carriage return, with the carriage return character not seen by the program unless no other characters have been entered. Under such circumstances, the carriage return returns a null character or a decimal zero. Additionally, the function keys are not available, and if they are pressed, they produce unreliable results.

String Input and Output

In many applications, it is more natural to handle input and output in larger pieces than characters. For example, a file of boat salesmen may contain one record per line, with each record consisting of four fields: salesperson's name, base pay, commission, and number of boats sold, with white space separating the fields. It would be very tedious to use character I/O.

Using gets( ), puts( ), fgets( ), and fputs( )

Because of the organization of the file, it would be better to treat each record as a single character string and read or write it as a unit. The function fgets( ), which reads whole strings rather than single characters, is suited to this task. In addition to the function fgets( ) and its inverse fputs( ), there are also the macro counterparts gets( ) and puts( ).

The function fgets( ) expects three arguments: the address of an array in which to store the character string, the maximum number of characters to store, and a pointer to a file to read. The function will read characters into the array until the number of characters read in is one less than the size specified, all of the characters up to and including the next newline character have been read, or the end-of-file is reached, whichever comes first.

If fgets( ) reads in a newline, the newline will be stored in the array. If at least one character was read, the function will automatically append the null string terminator \0. Suppose the file SALESMAN.DAT looks like this:

```
Pat Pharr 32767 0.15 30
Beth Mollen 35000 0.12 23
Gary Kohut 40000 0.15 40
```

Assuming a maximum record length of 40 characters including the newline, the following program will read the records from the file and write them to the standard output:

```
/*
 *   fgets.c
 *   A C program that demonstrates how to read
 *   in whole records using fgets and prints
 *   them out to stdout using fputs.
 *   Copyright (c) Bill/Chris H. Pappas and William H. Murray, 1998
 */

#include <stdio.h>

#define INULL_CHAR 1
#define IMAX_REC_SIZE 40

void main( )
{
  FILE *pfinfile;
  char crecord[IMAX_REC_SIZE + INULL_CHAR];

  pfinfile=fopen("a:\\salesman.dat", "r");
  while(fgets(crecord,IMAX_REC_SIZE +INULL_CHAR,pfinfile) != NULL)
    fputs(crecord,stdout);
  fclose(pfinfile);
}
```

Because the maximum record size is 40, you must reserve 41 cells in the array; the extra cell is to hold the null terminator \0. The program does not generate its own newline when it prints each record to the terminal, but relies instead on the newline read into the character array by fgets( ). The function fputs( ) writes the contents of the character array, *crecord*, to the file specified by the file pointer, **stdout**.

If your program happens to be accessing a file on a disk drive other than the one where the compiler is residing, it may be necessary to include a path in your filename. Notice this description in the preceding program; the double backslashes (\\) are necessary syntactically to indicate a subdirectory. Remember that a single \ usually signals that an escape or line continuation follows.

While the functions gets( ) and fgets( ) are very similar in usage, the functions puts( ) and fputs( ) operate differently. The function fputs( ) writes to a file and expects two arguments: the address of a null-terminated character string and a pointer to a file; fputs( ) simply copies the string to the specified file. It does not add a newline to the end of the string.

The macro puts( ), however, does not require a pointer to a file since the output automatically goes to **stdout**, and it automatically adds a newline character to the end of the output string. An excellent example of how these functions differ can be found in Chapter 9 in the section "String Functions and Character Arrays."

Integer Input and Output

For certain types of applications, it may be necessary to read and write stream (or buffered) integer information. The C language incorporates two functions for this purpose: getw( ) and putw( ).

Using getw( ) and putw( )

The complementary functions getw( ) and putw( ) are very similar to the functions getc( ) and putc( ) except that they input and output **integer** data instead of character data to a file. You should use both getw( ) and putw( ) only on files that are opened in binary mode. The following program opens a binary file, writes ten integers to it, closes the file, and then reopens the file for input and echo print:

```
/*
 *   badfil.c
 *   A C program that uses the functions getw and putw on
 *   a file created in binary mode.
 *   Copyright (c) Bill/Chris H. Pappas and William H. Murray, 1998
 */

#include <stdio.h>
#include <stdlib.h>
```

```
#define ISIZE 10

void main( )
{
  FILE *pfi;
  int ivalue,ivalues[ISIZE],i;

  pfi = fopen("a:\\integer.dat", "wb");
  if(pfi == NULL) {
    printf("File could not be opened");
    exit(1);
  }

  for(i = 0; i < ISIZE; i++) {
    ivalues[i]=i+1;
    putw(ivalues[i],pfi);
  }

  fclose(pfi);

  pfi=fopen("a:\\integer.dat", "r+b");
  if(pfi == NULL) {
    printf("File could not be reopened");
    exit(1);
  }

    while(!feof(pfi)) {
      ivalue = getw(pfi);
      printf("%3d",ivalue);
    }
}
```

Look at the output from this program and see if you can figure out what went wrong:

```
 1  2  3  4  5  6  7  8  9 10 -1
```

Because the **integer** value read in by the last loop may have a value equal to *EOF*, the program uses the function feof( ) to check for the end-of-file marker. However, the function does not perform a look-ahead operation as do some other high-level language end-of-file functions. In C, an actual read of the end-of-file value must be performed in order to flag the condition.

To correct this situation, the program needs to be rewritten using what is called a *priming read statement*:

```c
/*
 *   geputw.c
 *   A C program that uses the functions getw and putw on
 *   a file created in binary mode.
 *   Copyright (c) Bill/Chris H. Pappas and William H. Murray, 1998
 */

#include <stdio.h>

#define ISIZE 10

void main( )
{
  FILE *pfi;
  int ivalue,ivalues[ISIZE],i;
  pfi = fopen("a:\\integer.dat", "w+b");
  if(pfi == NULL) {
    printf("File could not be opened");
    exit(1);
  }

  for(i = 0; i < ISIZE; i++) {
    ivalues[i]=i+1;
    putw(ivalues[i],pfi);
  }

  fclose(pfi);

  pfi=fopen("a:\\integer.dat", "rb");
  if(pfi == NULL) {
    printf("File could not be reopened");
    exit(1);
  }

  ivalue = getw(pfi);
  while(!feof(pfi)) {
    printf("%3d",ivalue);
    ivalue=getw(pfi);
  }
}
```

PROGRAMMING
FOUNDATIONS

Before the program enters the final **while** loop, the priming read is performed to check to see if the file is empty. If it is not, a valid **integer** value is stored in *ivalue*. If the file is empty, however, the function feof( ) will acknowledge this, preventing the **while** loop from executing.

Also notice that the priming read necessitated a rearrangement of the statements within the **while** loop. If the loop is entered, then *ivalue* contains a valid **integer**. Had the statements within the loop remained the same as the original program, an immediate second getw( ) function call would be performed. This would overwrite the first **integer** value. Because of the priming read, the first statement within the **while** loop must be an output statement. This is next followed by a call to getw( ) to get another value.

Suppose the **while** loop has been entered nine times. At the end of the ninth iteration, the **integer** numbers 1 through 8 have been echo printed and *ivalue* has been assigned a 9. The next iteration of the loop prints the 9 and inputs the 10. Since 10 is not *EOF*, the loop iterates, causing the 10 to be echo printed and *EOF* to be read. At this point, the **while** loop terminates because the function feof( ) sees the end-of-file condition.

These two simple example programs should highlight the need to take care when writing code that is based on the function feof( ). This is a peculiarly frustrating programming task since each high-level language tends to treat the end-of-file condition in a different way. Some languages read a piece of data and at the same time look ahead to see the end-of-file; others, like C, do not.

Formatting Output

C's rich assortment of output formatting controls makes it easy to create a neatly printed graph, report, or table. The two main functions that accomplish this formatted output are printf( ) and the file equivalent form, fprintf( ). These functions can use any of the format specifiers shown in Table 11-2. The format specification uses the following form:

```
%[flags] [width] [.precision] [{h | l | L}]type
```

The field of the specification is a character or a number that gives a format option. The simplest form can be just a percent sign and a type. For example, %f. *type* is used to determine if the argument is to be interpreted as a character, a string, or a number. *flags* are used to control the printing of signs, blanks, decimal points, radix of output, and so on. *width* refers to the minimum number of characters to print. *precision* refers to the maximum number of characters that are printed for the output. *h | l | L* are optional prefixes for giving the argument size.

TYPE FIELD:

Character	Type	Format of Output
c	int or wint_t	printf( )—means a single-byte character.
		wprintf( )—means a wide character.
C	int or wint_t	printf( )—means a wide character.
		wprintf( )—means a single-byte character.
d	int	Signed decimal integer.
e	double	Signed number of the form [–]d.ddd e [sign]dddd.
		Here, d is a single decimal digit, ddd is one or more decimal digits, dddd is exactly four decimal digits, and the sign is a + or –.
E	double	Same as e, except "E" is in front of exponent.
f	double	Signed number of the form [–]ddd.ddd. Here, ddd is one or more decimal digits. The number of digits after the decimal point depends upon the precision.
g	double	Signed number in f or e format. The most compact format is used. No trailing zeroes. No decimal point if no digits follow it.
G	double	Same as g format, except "E" is in front of exponent.

Table 11-2. *Format Specifiers for printf( ) and fprintf( ) Functions*

TYPE FIELD: Character	Type	Format of Output
i	int	Signed decimal integer.
n	Pointer to integer	The # of characters written to the stream or buffer.
		Address of buffer given as integer argument.
o	int	Unsigned octal integer.
p	Pointer to void	Address (given by argument) is printed.
s	String	printf( )—gives a single-byte-character string.
		wprintf( )—gives a wide-character string.
		(print to NULL or max precision)
S	String	printf( )—gives a wide-character string.
		wprintf( )—gives a single-byte-character string.
		(print to NULL or max precision)
u	int	Unsigned decimal integer.
x	int	Unsigned hexadecimal integer (lowercase letters used).
X	int	Unsigned hexadecimal integer (uppercase letters used).

Table 11-2. *Format Specifiers for printf( ) and fprintf( ) Functions (continued)*

FLAG FIELD: Flag	Meaning
–	Left-align the result (right alignment is the default).
+	Use a leading sign (+ or –) if number is a signed type (sign used with negative number only is the default).
0	When width has 0 prefix, zeroes will be added until the minimum width is reached (no padding is the default).
blank (' ')	Output is prefixed with a blank. If positive and signed, the blank will be ignored (no appearing blanks is the default).
#	Prefixes nonzero output value with 0, 0x, or 0X (no appearing blank is the default).
.	For e, E, or f formats, a # makes the output value contain a decimal point in all cases (point appears only if digits follow is the default).

Table 11-2.   *Format Specifiers for printf( ) and fprintf( ) Functions* (continued)

Using printf( ) and fprintf( )

The following example program defines four variable types: character, array-of-characters, **integer**, and real. It then demonstrates how to use the appropriate format controls on each variable. The source code has been heavily commented and output line numbering has been included to make associating the output generated with the statement that created it as simple as possible:

```c
/*
 *   printf.c
 *   A C program demonstrating advanced conversions and
 *   formatting
 *   Copyright (c) Bill/Chris H. Pappas and William H. Murray, 1998
 */

#include <stdio.h>

void main( )
{
  char    c         =    'A',
          psz1[]    =    "In making a living today many no ",
          psz2[]    =    "longer leave any room for life.";
  int     iln       =    0,
          ivalue    =    1234;
  double dPi         =    3.14159265;

  /*            conversions           */

  /* print the c                      */
  printf("\n[%2d] %c",++iln,c);

  /* print the ASCII code for c       */
  printf("\n[%2d] %d",++iln,c);

  /* print character with ASCII 90    */
  printf("\n[%2d] %c",++iln,90);

  /* print ivalue as octal value      */
  printf("\n[%2d] %o",++iln,ivalue);

  /* print lower-case hexadecimal      */
  printf("\n[%2d] %x",++iln,ivalue);

  /* print upper-case hexadecimal      */
  printf("\n[%2d] %X",++iln,ivalue);
```

```
/* conversions and format options   */

/* minimum width 1                   */
printf("\n[%2d] %c",++iln,c);

/* minimum width 5, right-justify    */
printf("\n[%2d] %5c",++iln,c);

/* minimum width 5, left-justify     */
printf("\n[%2d] %-5c",++iln,c);

/* 33 non-null, automatically        */
printf("\n[%d] %s",++iln,psz1);

/* 31 non-null, automatically        */
printf("\n[%d] %s",++iln,psz2);

/* minimum 5 overridden, auto 33     */
printf("\n[%d] %5s",++iln,psz1);

/* minimum width 38, right-justify   */
printf("\n[%d] %38s",++iln,psz1);

/* minimum width 38, left-justify    */
printf("\n[%d] %-38s",++iln,psz2);

/* default ivalue width, 4           */
printf("\n[%d] %d",++iln,ivalue);

/* printf ivalue with + sign         */
printf("\n[%d] %+d",++iln,ivalue);

/* minimum 3 overridden, auto 4      */
printf("\n[%d] %3d",++iln,ivalue);

/* minimum width 10, right-justify   */
printf("\n[%d] %10d",++iln,ivalue);

/* minimum width 10, left-justify    */
printf("\n[%d] %-d",++iln,ivalue);

/* right justify with leading 0's    */
printf("\n[%d] %010d",++iln,ivalue);
```

PROGRAMMING
FOUNDATIONS

```
/* using default number of digits  */
printf("\n[%d] %f",++iln,dPi);

/* minimum width 20, right-justify */
printf("\n[%d] %20f",++iln,dPi);

/* right-justify with leading 0's  */
printf("\n[%d] %020f",++iln,dPi);

/* minimum width 20, left-justify  */
printf("\n[%d] %-20f",++iln,dPi);

/* no longer available since R1.2   */
/* left-justify with trailing 0's   */


/* additional formatting precision */

/* minimum width 19, print all 17  */
printf("\n[%d] %19.19s",++iln,psz1);

/* prints first 2 chars            */
printf("\n[%d] %.2s",++iln,psz1);

/* prints 2 chars, right-justify   */
printf("\n[%d] %19.2s",++iln,psz1);

/* prints 2 chars, left-justify    */
printf("\n[%d] %-19.2s",++iln,psz1);

/* using printf arguments          */
printf("\n[%d] %*.*s",++iln,19,6,psz1);

/* width 10, 8 to right of '.'     */
printf("\n[%d] %10.8f",++iln,dPi);

/* width 20, 2 to right-justify    */
printf("\n[%d] %20.2f",++iln,dPi);

/* 4 decimal places, left-justify  */
```

```
    printf("\n[%d] %-20.4f",++iln,dPi);

    /* 4 decimal places, right-justify */
    printf("\n[%d] %20.4f",++iln,dPi);

    /* width 20, scientific notation   */
    printf("\n[%d] %20.2e",++iln,dPi);
}
```

The output generated by the program looks like this:

```
[ 1] A
[ 2] 65
[ 3] Z
[ 4] 2322
[ 5] 4d2
[ 6] 4D2
[ 7] A
[ 8]         A
[ 9] A
[10] In making a living today many no
[11] longer leave any room for life.
[12] In making a living today many no
[13]         In making a living today many no
[14] longer leave any room for life.
[15] 1234
[16] +1234
[17] 1234
[18]         1234
[19] 1234
[20] 0000001234
[21] 3.141593
[22]                 3.141593
[23] 0000000000003.141593
[24] 3.141593
[25] In making a living
[26] In
[27]                 In
[28] In
[29]             In mak
[30] 3.14159265
[31]                 3.14
```

```
[32] 3.1416
[33]                    3.1416
[34]           3.14e+000
```

You can neatly format your application's output by studying the preceding example and selecting those combinations that apply to your program's data types.

Using fseek( ), ftell( ), and rewind( )

You can use the functions fseek( ), ftell( ), and rewind( ) to determine or change the location of the file position marker. The function fseek( ) resets the file position marker, in the file pointed to by *pf*, to the number of *ibytes* from the beginning of the file (*ifrom* = 0), from the current location of the file position marker (*ifrom* = 1), or from the end of the file (*ifrom* = 2). C has predefined three constants that can also be used in place of the variable *ifrom*: *SEEK_SET* (offset from beginning-of-file), *SEEK_CUR* (current file marker position), and *SEEK_END* (offset from the end-of-file). The function fseek( ) will return zero if the seek is successful and *EOF* otherwise. The general syntax for the function fseek( ) looks like this:

```
fseek(pf,ibytes,ifrom);
```

The function ftell( ) returns the current location of the file position marker in the file pointed to by *pf*. This location is indicated by an offset, measured in bytes, from the beginning of the file. The syntax for the function ftell( ) looks like this:

```
long_variable=ftell(pf);
```

The value returned by ftell( ) can be used in a subsequent call to fseek( ).
The function rewind( ) simply resets the file position marker in the file pointed to by *pf* to the beginning of the file. The syntax for the function rewind( ) looks like this:

```
rewind(pf);
```

The following C program illustrates the functions fseek( ), ftell( ), and rewind( ):

```
/*
 *   fseek.c
 *   A C program demonstrating the use of fseek,
 *   ftell, and rewind.
 *   Copyright (c) Bill/Chris H. Pappas and William H. Murray, 1998
```

```
*/

#include <stdio.h>

void main( )
{
  FILE *pf;
  char c;
  long llocation;

  pf=fopen("test.dat","r+t");

  c=fgetc(pf);
  putchar(c);

  c=fgetc(pf);
  putchar(c);

  llocation=ftell(pf);

  c=fgetc(pf);
  putchar(c);

  fseek(pf,llocation,0);

  c=fgetc(pf);
  putchar(c);

  fseek(pf,llocation,0);
  fputc('E',pf);

  fseek(pf,llocation,0);

  c=fgetc(pf);
  putchar(c);

  rewind(pf);

  c=fgetc(pf);
  putchar(c);
}
```

The variable *llocation* has been defined to be of type **long**. This is because C supports files larger than 64K. The input file TEST.DAT contains the string "ABCD". After the program opens the file, the first call to fgetc( ) gets the letter "A" and then prints it to the video display. The next statement pair inputs the letter "B" and prints it.

When the function ftell( ) is invoked, *llocation* is set equal to the file position marker's current location. This is measured as an offset, in bytes, from the beginning of the file. Since the letter "B" has already been processed, *llocation* contains a 2. This means that the file position marker is pointing to the third character, which is 2 bytes over from the first letter, "A".

Another I/O pair of statements now reads the letter "C" and prints it to the video display. After the program executes this last statement pair, the file position marker is 3 offset bytes from the beginning of the file, pointing to the fourth character, "D".

At this point in the program, the function fseek( ) is invoked. It is instructed to move *location* offset bytes (or 2 offset bytes) from the beginning of the file (since the third parameter to the function fseek( ) is a zero, as defined earlier). This repositions the file position marker to the third character in the file. The variable *c* is again assigned the letter "C", and it is printed a second time.

The second time the function fseek( ) is invoked, it uses parameters identical to the first invocation. The function fseek( ) moves the pointer to the third character, "C" (2 offset bytes into the file). However, the statement that follows doesn't input the "C" a third time, but instead writes over it with a new letter, "E." Since the file position marker has now moved past this new "E," to verify that the letter was indeed placed in the file, the function fseek( ) is invoked still another time.

The nest statement pair inputs the new "E" and prints it to the video display. With this accomplished, the program invokes the function rewind( ), which moves the *pf* back to the beginning of the file. When the function fgetc( ) is then invoked, it returns the letter "A" and prints it to the file. The output from the program looks like this:

```
ABCCEA
```

You can use the same principles illustrated in this simple character example to create a random-access file of records. Suppose you have the following information recorded for a file of individuals: social security number, name, and address. Suppose also that you are allowing 11 characters for the social security number, in the form ddd-dd-dddd, with the name and address being given an additional 60 characters (or bytes). So far, each record would be 11 + 60 bytes long, or 71 bytes.

All of the possible contiguous record locations on a random-access disk file may not be full; the personnel record needs to contain a flag indicating whether or not that disk record location has been used. This requires adding one more byte to the personnel record, bringing the total for one person's record to 72 bytes, plus 2 additional bytes to represent the record number, for a grand total record byte count of 74 bytes. One record could look like the following:

Chapter 11: Complete I/O In C

> 1 U111-22-3333Linda Lossannie, 521 Alan Street, Anywhere, USA

Record 1 in the file would occupy bytes zero through 73; record 2 would occupy bytes 74 through 147; record 3, 148 through 221; and so on. If you use the record number in conjunction with the fseek( ) function, any record location can be located on the disk. For example, to find the beginning of record 2, use the following statements:

```
loffset=(iwhich_record - 1) * sizeof(stA_PERSON);
fseek(pfi,loffset,0);
```

Once the file position marker has been moved to the beginning of the selected record, the information at that location can either be read or written by using various I/O functions such as fread( ) and fwrite( ).

With the exception of the comment block delimiter symbols /* and */ and the header STDIO.H, the program just discussed would work the same in C++. Just substitute the symbol // for both /* and */ and change STDIO.H to IOSTREAM.H.

Using the Integrated Debugger

Try entering this next program and printing out the value stored in the variable *stcurrent_person.irecordnum* after you have asked to search for the 25th record:

```c
/*
 *   rndacs.c
 *   A C random access file program using fseek, fread,
 *   and fwrite.
 *   Copyright (c) Bill/Chris H. Pappas and William H. Murray, 1998
 */

#include <stdio.h>
#include <string.h>

#define iFIRST 1
#define iLAST 50
#define iSS_SIZE 11
#define iDATA_SIZE 60
#define cVACANT 'V'
#define cUSED 'U'

typedef struct strecord {
  int  irecordnum;
  char cavailable;                /* V free, U used */
```

```
    char csoc_sec_num[iSS_SIZE];
    char cdata[iDATA_SIZE];
} stA_PERSON;

void main( )
{
  FILE *pfi;
  stA_PERSON stcurrent_person;
  int i,iwhich_record;
  long int loffset;

  pfi=fopen("A:\\sample.fil","r+");

  for(i = iFIRST; i <= iLAST; i++) {
    stcurrent_person.cavailable=cVACANT;
    stcurrent_person.irecordnum=i;
    fwrite(&stcurrent_person,sizeof(stA_PERSON),1,pfi);
  }

  printf("Please enter the record you would like to find.");
  printf("\nYour response must be between 1 and 50: ");
  scanf("%d",&iwhich_record);

  loffset=(iwhich_record - 1) * sizeof(stA_PERSON);
  fseek(pfi,loffset,0);
  fread(&stcurrent_person,sizeof(stA_PERSON),1,pfi);

  fclose(pfi);
}
```

The **typedef** has defined *stA_PERSON* as a structure that has a 2-byte *irecordnum*, a 1-byte *cavailable* character code, an 11-byte character array to hold a *csoc_sec_num* number, and a 60-byte *cdata* field. This brings the total structure's size to 2 + 1 + 11 + 60, or 74 bytes.

Once the program has opened the file in read-and-update text mode, it creates and stores 50 records, each with its own unique *irecordnum* and all initialized to *cVACANT*. The fwrite( ) statement wants the address of the structure to output, the size in bytes of what it is outputting, how many to output, and which file to send it to. With this accomplished, the program next asks the user which record he or she would like to search for.

Finding the record is accomplished in two steps. First, an offset address from the beginning of the file must be calculated. For example, record 1 is stored in bytes zero to 73, record 2 is stored in bytes 74 to 148, and so on. By subtracting 1 from the record number entered by the user, the program multiplies this value by the number of bytes occupied by each structure and calculates the *loffset*. For example, finding record 2 is accomplished with the following calculation: $(2 - 1) \times 74$. This gives the second record a starting byte offset of 74. Using this calculated value, the fseek( ) function is then invoked and moves the file position marker *loffset* bytes into the file.

As you are tracing through the program asking to view records 1 through 10, all seems fine. However, when you ask to view the 11th record, what happens? You get garbage. The reason for this is that the program opened the file in text mode. Records 1 through 9 are all exactly 74 bytes, but records 10 and up take 75 bytes. Therefore, the 10th record starts at the appropriate *loffset* calculation, but it goes 1 byte further into the file. Therefore, the 11th record is at the address arrived at by using the following modified calculation:

```
loffset=((iwhich_record - 1) * sizeof(stA_PERSON)) + 1;
```

However, this calculation won't work with the first nine records. The solution is to open the file in binary mode:

```
pfi=fopen("A:\\sample.fil","r+b");
```

In character mode, the program tries to interpret any two-digit number as two single characters, increasing records with two-digit *record_number*s by 1 byte. In binary mode, the integer *record_number* is interpreted properly. Exercise care when deciding how to open a file for I/O.

Formatting Input

Formatted input can be obtained for a C program by using the very versatile functions scanf( ) and fscanf( ). The main difference between the two functions is that the latter requires that you specifically designate the input file from which the data is to be obtained.

Using scanf( ), fscanf( ), and sscanf( )

You can use all three input functions, scanf( ), fscanf( ), and sscanf( ), for extremely sophisticated data input. For example, look at the following statement:

```
scanf("%2d%5s%4f",&ivalue,psz,&fvalue);
```

The statement inputs only a two-digit **integer**, a five-character string, and a real number that occupies a maximum of four spaces (2.97, 12.5, and so on). See if you can even begin to imagine what this next statement does:

```
scanf("%*[ \t\n]\"%[^A-Za-z]%[^\"]\"",ps1,ps2);
```

The statement begins by reading and *not* storing any white space. This is accomplished with the following format specification: "%*[\t\n]". The * symbol instructs the function to obtain the specified data but not to save it in any variable. As long as only a space, tab, or newline is on the input line, scanf( ) will keep reading until it encounters a double quote ("). This is accomplished by the \" format specification, which says the input must match the designated symbol. However, the double quote is not input.

Once scanf( ) has found the double quote, it is instructed to input all characters that are digits into *ps1*. The %[^A-Za-z] format specification accomplishes this with the caret (^) modifier, which says to input anything not an uppercase letter "A" through "Z" or lowercase letter "a" through "z". Had the caret been omitted, the string would have contained only alphabetic characters. It is the hyphens between the two symbols "A" and "Z" and "a" and "z" that indicate the entire range is to be considered.

The next format specification, %[^\"], instructs the input function to read all remaining characters up to but not including a double quote into *ps2*. The last format specification, \", indicates that the string must match and end with a double quote. You can use the same types of input conversion control with the functions fscanf( ) and sscanf( ). The only difference between the two functions scanf( ) and fscanf( ) is that the latter requires that an input file be specified. The function sscanf( ) is identical to scanf( ) except that the data is read from an array rather than a file.

The next example shows how you can use sscanf( ) to convert a string (of digits) to an **integer**. If *ivalue* is of type **int** and *psz* is an array of type **char** that holds a string of digits, then the following statement will convert the string *psz* into type **int** and store it in the variable *ivalue*:

```
sscanf(psz,"%d",&ivalue);
```

Very often, the functions gets( ) and sscanf( ) are used in combination, since the function gets( ) reads in an entire line of input and the function sscanf( ) goes into a string and interprets it according to the format specifications.

One problem often encountered with scanf( ) occurs when programmers try to use it in conjunction with various other character input functions such as getc( ), getch( ), getchar( ), gets( ), and so on. The typical scenario goes like this: scanf( ) is used to input various data types that would otherwise require conversion from characters to something else. Then the programmer tries to use a character input function such as getch( ) and finds that getch( ) does not work as expected. The problem occurs because scanf( ) sometimes does not read all the data that is waiting to be read, and the waiting data can fool other functions (including scanf( )) into thinking that input has already been entered. To be safe, if you use scanf() in a program, don't also use other input functions in the same program.

Chapter 12 introduces you to the basics of C++ I/O. Chapters 13 through 16 explain the concepts necessary to do advanced C++ I/O, and Chapter 17 completes the subject of I/O in C++.

Chapter 12

An Introduction to I/O in C++

While it is technically true that C++ is a superset of the C language, this does not mean that by simply taking a C statement and translating it into a C++ equivalent form, you have written a C++ program! In many cases C++ has a better way of solving a programming problem. Often, the C++ equivalent of a C program streamlines the way your program inputs and outputs data. However, this is not always true. This chapter introduces you to C++ I/O.

The topic of advanced C++ input and output is continued in Chapter 17. The division of the topic is necessary because of the diverse I/O capabilities available to C++ programmers. Chapters 16 to 19 teach the fundamentals of object-oriented programming. Once you understand how objects are created, it will be much easier to understand advanced object-oriented C++ I/O. Chapter 17 picks up with C++'s ability to effortlessly manipulate objects.

Streamlining I/O with C++

The software supplied with the Microsoft Visual C++ compiler includes a standard library that contains functions commonly used by the C++ community. The standard I/O library for C, described by the header file STDIO.H, is still available in C++. However, C++ introduces its own header file, called IOSTREAM.H, which implements its own collection of I/O functions.

The C++ stream I/O is described as a set of classes in IOSTREAM.H. These classes overload the "put to" and "get from" operators, << and >>. To better understand why the stream library in C++ is more convenient than its C counterpart, let's first review how C handles input and output.

First, recall that C has no built-in input or output statements; functions such as printf( ) are part of the standard library but not part of the language itself. Similarly, C++ has no built-in I/O facilities. The absence of built-in I/O gives you greater flexibility to produce the most efficient user interface for the data pattern of the application at hand.

The problem with the C solution to input and output lies with its implementation of these I/O functions. There is little consistency among them in terms of return values and parameter sequences. Because of this, programmers tend to rely on the formatted I/O functions printf( ), scanf( ), and so on—especially when the objects being manipulated are numbers or other noncharacter values. These formatted I/O functions are convenient and, for the most part, share a consistent interface, but they are also big and unwieldy because they must manipulate many kinds of values.

In C++, the class provides modular solutions to your data manipulation needs. The standard C++ library provides three I/O classes as an alternative to C's general-purpose I/O functions. These classes contain definitions for the same pair of operators—>> and <<--that are optimized for all kinds of data. (See Chapter 16 for a discussion of classes.)

cin, cout, and cerr

The C++ stream counterparts to **stdin**, **stdout**, and **stderr**, prototyped in STDIO.H, are **cin**, **cout**, and **cerr**, which are prototyped in IOSTREAM.H. These three streams are opened automatically when your program begins execution and become the interface between the program and the user. The **cin** stream is associated with the terminal keyboard. The **cout** and **cerr** streams are associated with the video display.

The >> Extraction and << Insertion Operators

Input and output in C++ have been significantly enhanced and streamlined by the stream library operators >> ("get from" or extraction) and << ("put to" or insertion). One of the major enhancements that C++ added to C was operator overloading. Operator overloading allows the compiler to determine which like-named function or operator is to be executed based on the associated variables' data types. The extraction and insertion operators are good examples of this new C++ capability. Each operator has been overloaded so it can handle all of the standard C++ data types, including classes. The following two code segments illustrate the greater ease of use for basic I/O operations in C++. First, take a quick look at a C output statement using printf( ):

```
printf("Integer value: %d, Float value: %f",ivalue,fvalue);
```

Here is the C++ equivalent:

```
cout << "Integer value: " << ivalue << ", Float value: "
    << fvalue;
```

A careful examination of the C++ equivalent will reveal how the insertion operator has been overloaded to handle the three separate data types: **string**, **integer**, and **float**. If you are like many C programmers, you are not going to miss having to hunt down the % symbol needed for your printf( ) and scanf( ) format specifications. As a result of operator overloading, the insertion operator will examine the data type you have passed to it and determine an appropriate format.

An identical situation exists with the extraction operator, which performs data input. Look at the following C example and its equivalent C++ counterpart:

```
/* C code */
scanf("%d%f%c",&ivalue,&fvalue,&c);

// C++ code
cin >> ivalue >> fvalue >> c;
```

No longer is it necessary to precede your input variables with the & address operator. In C++, the extraction operator takes care of calculating the storage variable's address, storage requirements, and formatting.

Having looked at two examples of the C++ operators **<<** and **>>**, you might be slightly confused as to why they are named the way they are. The simplest way to remember which operator performs output and which performs input is to think of these two operators as they relate to the stream I/O files. When you want to input information, you extract it (**>>**) from the input stream, **cin**, and put the information into a variable—for example, *ivalue*. To output information, you take a copy of the information from the variable *fvalue* and insert it (**<<**) into the output stream, **cout**.

As a direct result of operator overloading, C++ will allow a program to expand upon the insertion and extraction operators. The following code segment illustrates how the insertion operator can be overloaded to print the new type **stclient**:

```
ostream& operator << (ostream& osout, stclient staclient)
{
  osout << " " << staclient.pszname;
  osout << " " << staclient.pszaddress;
  osout << " " << staclient.pszphone;
}
```

Assuming the structure variable *staclient* has been initialized, printing the information becomes a simple one-line statement:

```
cout << staclient;
```

Last but not least, the insertion and extraction operators have an additional advantage—their final code size. The general-purpose I/O functions printf( ) and scanf( ) carry along code segments into the final executable version of a program that are often unused. In C, even if you are dealing only with **integer** data, you still pull along all of the conversion code for the additional standard data types. In contrast, the C++ compiler incorporates only those routines actually needed.

The following program demonstrates how to use the input, or extraction, operator **>>** to read different types of data:

```
//
//  insrt1.cpp
//  A C++ program demonstrating how to use the
//  extraction >> operator to input a char,
//  integer, float, double, and string.
//  Copyright (c) Chris H. Pappas and William H. Murray, 1998
//
```

```
#include <iostream.h>

#define INUMCHARS 45
#define INULL_CHAR 1

void main(void)
{
  char canswer;
  int ivalue;
  float fvalue;
  double dvalue;
  char pszname[INUMCHARS + INULL_CHAR];

  cout << "This program allows you to enter various data types.";
  cout << "Would you like to try it? "<< "\n\n";
  cout << "Please type a Y for yes and an N for no: ";

  cin  >> canswer;

  if(canswer == 'Y') {

    cout << "\n" << "Enter an integer value: ";
    cin >> ivalue;
    cout << "\n\n";

    cout << "Enter a float value: ";
    cin >> fvalue;
    cout << "\n\n";

    cout << "Enter a double value: ";
    cin >> dvalue;
    cout << "\n\n";

    cout << "Enter your first name: ";
    cin >> pszname;
    cout << "\n\n";
  }

}
```

In this example, the insertion operator << is used in its simplest form to output literal string prompts. Notice that the program uses four different data types and yet each input statement, **cin >>**, looks identical except for the variable's name. For those of you who are fast typists but are tired of trying to find the infrequently used %, ", and & symbols (required by scanf( )), you can give your fingers and eyes a rest. The C++ extraction operator makes code entry much simpler and less error prone.

Because of the rapid evolutionary development of C++, you have to be careful when using C or C++ code found in older manuscripts. For example, if you had run the previous program under a C++ compiler, Release 1.2, the program execution would look like the following example:

```
This program allows you to enter various data types
Would you like to try it?

Please type a Y for yes and an N for no: Y

Enter an integer value:
                    10
```

This is because the C++ Release 1.2 input stream is processing the newline character you entered after typing the letter "Y." The extraction operator >> reads up to, but does not get rid of, the newline. The following program solves this problem by adding an additional input statement:

```
//
//   insrt2.cpp
//   A C++ program demonstrating how to use the
//   extraction >> operator to input a char,
//   integer, float, double, and string.
//   Copyright (c) Chris H. Pappas and William H. Murray, 1998
//

#include <iostream.h>

#define INUMCHARS 45
#define INULL_CHAR 1

void main(void)
{
  char canswer,cAnewline;
  int ivalue;
  float fvalue;
  double dvalue;
  char pszname[INUMCHARS + INULL_CHAR];
```

```
cout << "This program allows you to enter various data types.";
cout << "Would you like to try it?" << "\n\n";
cout << "Please type a Y for yes and an N for no: ";

cin  >> canswer;
cin.get(cAnewline);

if(canswer == 'Y') {

  cout << "\n" << "Enter an integer value: ";
  cin >> ivalue;
  cout << "\n\n";

  cout << "Enter a float value: ";
  cin >> fvalue;
  cout << "\n\n";

  cout << "Enter a double value: ";
  cin >> dvalue;
  cout << "\n\n";

  cout << "Enter your first name: ";
  cin >> pszname;
  cout << "\n\n";
 }

}
```

Did you notice the change? After *canswer* is read in, the program executes

```
cin.get(cAnewline);
```

This processes the newline character so that when the program runs, it then looks like this:

```
This program allows you to enter various data types
Would you like to try it?

Please type a Y for yes and an N for no:

Enter an integer value: 10
```

Both algorithms work properly since the introduction of C++ Release 2.0. However, it is worth mentioning that you must take care when modeling your code from older texts. Mixing what is known as historic C and C++ with current compilers can cause you to spend many hours trying to figure out why your I/O doesn't perform as expected.

This next example demonstrates how to use the output, or insertion, operator << in its various forms:

```
//
//   extrct.cpp
//   A C++ program demonstrating how to use the
//   insertion << operator to input a char,
//   integer, float, double, and string.
//   Copyright (c) Chris H. Pappas and William H. Murray, 1998
//

#include <iostream.h>

void main(void)
{
  char c='A';
  int ivalue=10;
  float fvalue=45.67;
  double dvalue=2.3e32;
  char fact[]="For all have...";

  cout << "Once upon a time there were ";
  cout << ivalue << " people."<< endl;
  cout << "Some of them earned " << fvalue;
  cout << " dollars per hour." << "\n";
  cout << "While others earned " << dvalue << " per year!";
  cout << "\n\n" << "But you know what they say: ";
  cout << fact << "\n\n";
  cout << "So, none of them get an ";
  cout << c;
  cout << "!";

}
```

The output from the program looks like this:

```
Once upon a time there were 10 people.
Some of them earned 45.67 dollars per hour.
While others earned 2.3e+32 per year!

But you know what they say: "For all have..."
```

```
So, none of them get an A!
```

When comparing the C++ source code with the output from the program, one thing you should immediately notice is that the insertion operator << does not automatically generate a newline. You still have complete control over when this occurs by including the newline symbol \n or **endl** when necessary.

endl is very useful for outputting data in an interactive program because it not only inserts a newline into the stream but also flushes the output buffer. You can also use **flush**; however, this does not insert a newline. Notice too that the placement of the newline symbol can be included after its own << insertion operator or as part of a literal string, as is contrasted in the second and fourth << statements in the program.

Also notice that while the insertion operator very nicely handles the formatting of **integer**s and **float**s, it isn't very helpful with **double**s. Another interesting facet of the insertion operator has to do with C++ Release 1.2 character information. Look at the following line of code:

```
cout << c;
```

This would have given you the following output in Release 1.2:

```
So, none of them get an 65!
```

This is because the character is translated into its ASCII equivalent. The Release 1.2 solution is to use the put( ) function for outputting character data. This would require you to rewrite the statement in the following form:

```
cout.put(c);
```

Try running this next example:

```
//
//   string.cpp
//   A C++ program demonstrating what happens when you use
//   the extraction operator >> with string data.
//   Copyright (c) Chris H. Pappas and William H. Murray, 1998
//

#include <iostream.h>

#define INUMCHARS 45
#define INULL_CHARACTER 1

void main(void)
```

```
{
  char pszname[INUMCHARS + INULL_CHARACTER];

  cout << "Please enter your first and last name: ";
  cin >> pszname;
  cout << "\n\nThank you, " << pszname;

}
```

A sample execution of the program looks like this:

```
Please enter your first and last name: Kirsten Tuttle

Thank you, Kirsten
```

There is one more fact you need to know when inputting string information. The extraction operator **>>** is written to stop reading in information as soon as it encounters white space. White space can be a blank, tab, or newline. Therefore, when *pszname* is printed, only the first name entered is output. You can solve this problem by rewriting the program and using the cin.get( ) function:

```
//
//  cinget.cpp
//  A C++ program demonstrating what happens when you use
//  the extraction operator >> with cin.get( ) to process an
//  entire string.
//  Copyright (c) Chris H. Pappas and William H. Murray, 1998
//

#include <iostream.h>

#define INUMCHARS 45
#define INULL_CHARACTER 1

void main(void)
{
  char pszname[INUMCHARS + INULL_CHARACTER];

  cout << "Please enter your first and last name: ";
  cin.get(pszname,INUMCHARS);
  cout << "\n\nThank you, " << pszname;
}
```

The output from the program now looks like this:

```
Please enter your first and last name: Kirsten Tuttle

Thank you, Kirsten Tuttle
```

The cin.get( ) function has two additional parameters. Only one of these, the number of characters to input, was used in the previous example. The function cin.get( ) will read everything, including white space, until the maximum number of characters specified has been read in or up to the next newline, whichever comes first. The optional third parameter, not shown, identifies a terminating symbol. For example, the following line would read into *pszname INUMCHARS* characters all of the characters up to but not including a * symbol, or a newline, whichever comes first:

```
cin.get(pszname,INUMCHARS,'*');
```

From STREAM.H to IOSTREAM.H

One of the most exciting enhancements to the compiler is the new C++ I/O library, referred to as the iostream library. By not including input/output facilities within the C++ language itself, but rather implementing them in C++ and providing them as a component of a C++ standard library, I/O can evolve as needed. This new iostream library replaces the earlier version of the I/O library referred to as the Release 1.2 stream library.

At its lowest level, C++ interprets a file as a sequence, or stream, of bytes. At this level, the concept of a data type is missing. One component of the I/O library is involved in the transfer of these bytes. From the user's perspective, however, a file is composed of a series of intermixed alphanumerics, numeric values, or (possibly) class objects. A second component of the I/O library takes care of the interface between these two viewpoints. The iostream library predefines a set of operations for handling reading and writing of the built-in data types. The library also provides for user-definable extensions to handle class types.

Basic input operations are supported by the **istream** class and basic output via the **ostream** class. Bidirectional I/O is supported via the **iostream** class, which is derived from both **istream** and **ostream**. There are four stream objects predefined for the user:

cin	An **istream** class object linked to standard input
cout	An **ostream** class object linked to standard output
cerr	An unbuffered output **ostream** class object linked to standard error
clog	A buffered output **ostream** class object linked to standard error

Any program using the iostream library must include the header file IOSTREAM.H. Since IOSTREAM.H treats STREAM.H as an alias, programs written using STREAM.H may or may not need alterations, depending on the particular structures used.

You can also use the new I/O library to perform input and output operations on files. You can tie a file to your program by defining an instance of one of the following three class types:

fstream	Derived from **iostream** and links a file to your application for both input and output
ifstream	Derived from **istream** and links a file to your application for input only
ofstream	Derived from **ostream** and links a file to your application for output only

Operators and Member Functions

The extraction operator and the << insertion operator have been modified to accept arguments of any of the built-in data types, including **char** *. They can also be extended to accept class argument types.

Probably the first upgrade incompatibility you will experience when converting a C++ program using the older I/O library will be the demised **cout << form** extension. Under the new release, each iostream library class object maintains a format state that controls the details of formatting operations, such as the conversion base for integral numeric notation or the precision of a floating-point value.

You can manipulate the format state flags by using the setf( ) and unsetf( ) functions. The setf( ) member function sets a specified format state flag. There are two overloaded instances:

```
setf(long);
setf(long,long);
```

The first argument can be either a format bit flag or a format bit field. Table 12-1 lists the format flags you can use with the **setf(long)** instance (using just the format flag).

The following table lists some of the format bit fields you can use with the **setf(long,long)** instance (using a format flag and format bit field).

Bit Field	Meaning	Flags
ios::basefield	Integral base	ios::hex, ios::oct, ios::dec
ios::floatfield	Floating point	ios::fixed, ios::scientific

Table 12-1.   *Format Flags*

There are certain predefined defaults. For example, **integers** are written and read in decimal notation. You can change the base to octal, hexadecimal, or back to decimal. By default, a floating-point value is output with six digits of precision. You can modify this by using the precision member function. The following C++ program uses these new member functions:

```
//
//   advio.cpp
//   A C++ program demonstrating advanced conversions and
//   formatting member functions since Release 2.0. The program
//   will also demonstrate how to convert each of the older
//   Release 1.2 form statements.
//   Copyright (c) Chris H. Pappas and William H. Murray, 1998
//

#include <string.h>
#include <strstrea.h>

#define INULL_TERMINATOR 1

void row (void);
main( )
{
  char    c        =    'A',
          psz1[]   =    "In making a living today many no ",
          psz2[]   =    "longer leave any room for life.";
  int     iln      =    0,
          ivalue   =    1234;
  double dPi        =    3.14159265;

  // new declarations needed for Release 2.0
  char psz_padstring5[5+INULL_TERMINATOR],
  psz_padstring38[38+INULL_TERMINATOR];

  // conversions

  // print the c
  // R1.2 cout << form("\n[%2d] %c",++ln,c);
  // Notice that << has been overloaded to output char
  row( ); // [ 1]
  cout << c;
```

```
// print the ASCII code for c
// R1.2  form("\n[%2d] %d",++ln,c);
row( ); // [ 2]
cout << (int)c;

// print character with ASCII 90
// R1.2  form("\n[%2d] %c",++ln,90);
row( ); // [ 3]
cout << (char)90;

// print ivalue as octal value
// R1.2  form("\n[%2d] %o",++ln,ivalue);
row( ); // [ 4]
cout << oct << ivalue;

// print lowercase hexadecimal
// R1.2  form("\n[%2d] %x",++ln,ivalue);
row( ); // [ 5]
cout << hex << ivalue;

// print uppercase hexadecimal
// R1.2  form("\n[%2d] %X",++ln,ivalue);
row( ); // [ 6] cout.setf(ios::uppercase);
cout << hex << ivalue;
cout.unsetf(ios::uppercase);    // turn uppercase off
cout << dec;                    // return to decimal base

// conversions and format options

// minimum width 1
// R1.2  form("\n[%2d] %c",++ln,c);
row( ); // [ 7]
cout << c;

// minimum width 5, right-justify
// R1.2  form("\n[%2d] %5c",++ln,c);
row( ); // [ 8]
ostrstream(psz_padstring5,sizeof(psz_padstring5))
<< "    " << c << ends;
cout << psz_padstring5;

// minimum width 5, left-justify
```

```
// R1.2   form("\n[%2d] %-5c",++ln,c);
row( ); // [ 9]
ostrstream(psz_padstring5,sizeof(psz_padstring5))
<< c << "    " << ends;
cout << psz_padstring5;

// 33 automatically
// R1.2   form("\n[%d] %s",++ln,psz1);
row( ); // [10]
cout << psz1;

// 31 automatically
// R1.2   form("\n[%d] %s",++ln,psz2);
row( ); // [11]
cout << psz2;

// minimum 5 overridden, auto
// R1.2   form("\n[%d] %5s",++ln,psz1);
// notice that the width of 5 cannot be overridden!
row( ); // [12]
cout.write(psz1,5);

// minimum width 38, right-justify
// R1.2   form("\n[%d] %38s",++ln,psz1);
// notice how the width of 38 ends with garbage data
row( ); // [13]
cout.write(psz1,38);

// the following is the correct approach
cout << "\n\nCorrected approach:\n";
ostrstream(psz_padstring38,sizeof(psz_padstring38)) << "    "
  << psz1 << ends;
row( ); // [14]
cout << psz_padstring38;

// minimum width 38, left-justify
// R1.2   form("\n[%d] %-38s",++ln,psz2);
ostrstream(psz_padstring38,sizeof(psz_padstring38))
  << psz2 << "      " << ends;
row( ); // [15]
cout << psz_padstring38;
```

```
// default ivalue width
// R1.2  form("\n[%d] %d",++ln,ivalue);
row( ); // [16]
cout << ivalue;

// printf ivalue with + sign
// R1.2  form("\n[%d] %+d",++ln,ivalue);
row( ); // [17]
cout.setf(ios::showpos);        // don't want row number with +
cout << ivalue;
cout.unsetf(ios::showpos);

// minimum 3 overridden, auto
// R1.2  form("\n[%d] %3d",++ln,ivalue);
row( ); // [18]
cout.width(3); // don't want row number padded to width of 3
cout << ivalue;

// minimum width 10, right-justify
// R1.2  form("\n[%d] %10d",++ln,ivalue);
row( ); // [19]
cout.width(10);     // only in effect for first value printed
cout << ivalue;

// minimum width 10, left-justify
// R1.2  form("\n[%d] %-d",++ln,ivalue);
row( ); // [20]
cout.width(10);
cout.setf(ios::left);
cout << ivalue;
cout.unsetf(ios::left);

// right-justify with leading 0's
// R1.2  form("\n[%d] %010d",++ln,ivalue);
row( ); // [21]
cout.width(10);
cout.fill('0');
cout << ivalue;
cout.fill(' ');

// using default number of digits
// R1.2  form("\n[%d] %f",++ln,dPi);
```

```
row( ); // [22]
cout << dPi;

// minimum width 20, right-justify
// R1.2  form("\n[%d] %20f",++ln,dPi);
row( ); // [23]
cout.width(20);
cout << dPi;

// right-justify with leading 0's
// R1.2  form("\n[%d] %020f",++ln,dPi);
row( ); // [24]
cout.width(20);
cout.fill('0');
cout << dPi;
cout.fill(' ');

// minimum width 20, left-justify
// R1.2  form("\n[%d] %-20f",++ln,dPi);
row( ); // [25]
cout.width(20);
cout.setf(ios::left);
cout << dPi;

// left-justify with trailing 0's
// R1.2  form("\n[%d] %-020f",++ln,dPi);
row( ); // [26]
cout.width(20);
cout.fill('0');
cout << dPi;
cout.unsetf(ios::left);
cout.fill(' ');

// additional formatting precision

// minimum width 19, print all 17
// R1.2  form("\n[%d] %19.19s",++ln,psz1);
row( ); // [27]
cout << psz1;

// prints first 2 chars
// R1.2  form("\n[%d] %.2s",++ln,psz1);
```

```
row( ); // [28]
cout.write(psz1,2);

// prints 2 chars, right-justify
// R1.2  form("\n[%d] %19.2s",++ln,psz1);
row( ); // [29]
cout << "                   "; cout.write(psz1,2);

// prints 2 chars, left-justify
// R1.2  form("\n[%d] %-19.2s",++ln,psz1);
row( ); // [30]
cout.write(psz1,2);

// using printf arguments
// R1.2  form("\n[%d] %*.*s",++ln,19,6,psz1);
row( ); // [31]
cout << "               "; cout.write(psz1,6);

// width 10, 8 to right of '.'
// R1.2  form("\n[%d] %10.8f",++ln,dPi);
row( ); // [32]
cout.precision(9);
cout << dPi;

// width 20, 2 to right-justify
// R1.2  form("\n[%d] %20.2f",++ln,dPi);
row( ); // [33]
cout.width(20);
cout.precision(2);
cout << dPi;

// 4 decimal places, left-justify
// R1.2  form("\n[%d] %-20.4f",++ln,dPi);
row( ); // [34]
cout.precision(4);
cout << dPi;

// 4 decimal places, right-justify
// R1.2  form("\n[%d] %20.4f",++ln,dPi);
row( ); // [35]
cout.width(20);
cout << dPi;
```

```
   // width 20, scientific notation
   // R1.2  form("\n[%d] %20.2e",++ln,dPi);
   row( ); // [36] cout.setf(ios::scientific); cout.width(20);
   cout << dPi; cout.unsetf(ios::scientific);

   return(0);
}

void row (void)
{
  static int ln=0;
  cout << "\n[";
  cout.width(2);
  cout << ++ln << "] ";
}
```

You can use the output from the program to help write advanced output
statements of your own:

```
[ 1] A
[ 2] 65
[ 3] Z
[ 4] 2322
[ 5] 4d2
[ 6] 4d2
[ 7] A
[ 8]        A
[ 9] A
[10] In making a living today many no
[11] longer leave any room for life.
[12] In ma
[13] In making a living today many no _U_°_

Corrected approach:

[14]        In making a living today many no
[15] longer leave any room for life.
[16] 1234
[17] +1234
[18] 1234
```

```
[19]          1234
[20] 1234
[21] 0000001234
[22] 3.14159
[23]                    3.14159
[24] 00000000000003.14159
[25] 3.14159
[26] 3.141590000000000000
[27] In making a living today many no
[28] In
[29]                         In
[30] In
[31]               In mak
[32] 3.14159265
[33]                    3.1
[34] 3.142
[35]                    3.142
[36] 3.142
```

The following section highlights those output statements used in the preceding program that need special clarification. One point needs to be made: IOSTREAM.H is automatically included by STRSTREAM.H. The latter file is needed to perform string output formatting. If your application needs to output numeric data or simple character and string output, you will need to include only IOSTREAM.H.

C++ Character Output

In the new I/O library (since Release 2.0), the insertion operator << has been overloaded to handle character data. With the earlier release, the following statement would have output the ASCII value of *c*:

```
cout << c;
```

In the current I/O library, the letter itself is output. For those programs needing the ASCII value, a cast is required:

```
cout << (int)C;
```

C++ Base Conversions

There are two approaches to outputting a value using a different base:

```
cout << hex << ivalue;
```

and

```
cout.setf(ios::hex,ios::basefield);
cout << ivalue;
```

Both approaches cause the base to be permanently changed from the statement forward (not always the effect you want). Each value output will now be formatted as a hexadecimal value. Returning to some other base is accomplished with the unsetf( ) function:

```
cout.unsetf(ios::hex,ios::basefield);
```

If you are interested in uppercase hexadecimal output, use the following statement:

```
cout.setf(ios::uppercase);
```

When it is no longer needed, you will have to turn this option off:

```
cout.unsetf(ios::uppercase);
```

C++ String Formatting

Printing an entire string is easy in C++. However, string formatting has changed because the Release 1.2 **cout << form** is no longer available. One approach to string formatting is to declare an array of characters and then select the desired output format, printing the string buffer:

```
pszpadstring38[38+INULL_TERMINATOR];
    .
    .
    .
ostrstream(pszpadstring38,sizeof(pszpadstring38))
    << "      "   << psz1;
```

The ostrstream( ) member function is part of STRSTREAM.H and has three parameters: a pointer to an array of characters, the size of the array, and the information to be inserted. This statement appends leading blanks to right-justify *psz1*. Portions of the string can be output using the **write** form of **cout**:

```
cout.write(psz1,5);
```

This statement will output the first five characters of *psz1*.

C++ Numeric Formatting

You can easily format numeric data with right or left justification, varying precisions, varying formats (floating-point or scientific), leading or trailing fill patterns, and signs. There are certain defaults. For example, the default for justification is right, and for floating-point precision it is six. The following code segment outputs *dPi* left-justified in a field width of 20, with trailing zeroes:

```
cout.width(20);
cout.setf(ios::left);
cout.fill('0');
cout << dPi;
```

Had the following statement been included, *dPi* would have been printed with a precision of two:

```
cout.precision(2);
```

With many of the output flags such as left justification, selecting uppercase hexadecimal output, base changes, and many others, it is necessary to unset these flags when they are no longer needed. The following statement turns left justification off:

```
cout.unsetf(ios::left);
```

Selecting scientific format is a matter of flipping the correct bit flag:

```
cout.setf(ios::scientific);
```

You can print values with a leading + sign by setting the *showpos* flag:

```
cout.setf(ios::showpos);
```

There are many minor details of the current I/O library functions that will initially cause some confusion. This has to do with the fact that certain operations, once executed, make a permanent change until turned off, while others take effect only for the next output statement. For example, an output width change, as in **cout.width(20);**, affects only the next value printed. That is why the function row( ) has to repeatedly change the width to get the output row numbers formatted within two spaces, as in [1]. However, other formatting operations like base changes, uppercase, precision, and floating-point/scientific remain active until specifically turned off.

C++ File Input and Output

All of the examples so far have used the predefined streams **cin** and **cout**. It is possible that your program will need to create its own streams for I/O. If an application needs to create a file for input or output, it must include the FSTREAM.H header file (FSTREAM.H includes IOSTREAM.H). The classes **ifstream** and **ofstream** are derived from **istream** and **ostream** and inherit the extraction and insertion operations, respectively. The following C++ program demonstrates how to declare a file for reading and writing using **ifstream** and **ofstream**, respectively:

```cpp
//
//  fstrm.cpp
//  A C++ program demonstrating how to declare an
//  ifstream and ofstream for file input and output.
//  Copyright (c) Chris H. Pappas and William H. Murray, 1998
//

#include <fstream.h>

int main(void)
{
  char c;

  ifstream ifsin("a:\\text.in",ios::in);
  if( !ifsin )
    cerr << "\nUnable to open 'text.in' for input.";

  ofstream ofsout("a:\\text.out",ios::out);
  if( !ofsout )
    cerr << "\nUnable to open 'text.out' for output.";

  while( ofsout && ifsin.get(c) )
    ofsout.put(c);

  ifsin.close( );
  ofsout.close( );

  return(0);
}
```

The program declares *ifsin* to be of class **ifstream** and is associated with the file TEXT.IN stored in the A drive. It is always a good idea for any program dealing with files to verify the existence or creation of the specified file in the designated mode. By using the handle to the file *ifsin*, a simple **if** test can be generated to check the condition of the file. A similar process is applied to *ofsout*, with the exception that the file is derived from the **ostream** class.

The **while** loop continues inputting and outputting single characters while the *ifsin* exists and the character read in is not *EOF*. The program terminates by closing the two files. Closing an output file can be essential to dumping all internally buffered data.

There may be circumstances when a program will want to delay a file specification or when an application may want to associate several file streams with the same file descriptor. The following code segment demonstrates this concept:

```
ifstream ifsin;
.
.
.
ifsin.open("week1.in");
.
.
.
ifsin.close( );
ifsin.open("week2.in");
.
.
.
ifsin.close( );
```

Whenever an application wishes to modify the way in which a file is opened or used, it can apply a second argument to the file stream constructors. For example:

```
ofstream ofsout("week1.out",ios::app|ios::noreplace);
```

This statement declares *ofsout* and attempts to append it to the file named WEEK1.OUT. Because ios::noreplace is specified, the file will not be created if WEEK1.OUT doesn't already exist. The ios::app parameter appends all writes to an existing file. The following table lists the second argument flags to the file stream constructors that can be logically ORed together:

Mode Bit	Action
ios::in	Opens for reading
ios::out	Opens for writing

Mode Bit	Action
ios::ate	Seeks to EOF after file is created
ios::app	All writes added to end of file
ios::trunc	If file already exists, truncates
ios::nocreate	Unsuccessful open if file does not exist
ios::noreplace	Unsuccessful open if file does exist
ios::binary	Opens file in binary mode (default text)

An **fstream** class object can also be used to open a file for both input and output. For example, the following definition opens the file UPDATE.DAT in both **input** and **append** mode:

```
fstream io("update.dat",ios::in|ios::app);
```

You can reposition all **iostream** class types by using either the seekg( ) or seekp( ) member function, either of which can move to an absolute address within the file or move a byte offset from a particular position. Both seekg( ) (sets or reads the **get** pointer's position) and seekp( ) (sets or reads the **put** pointer's position) can take one or two arguments. When used with one parameter, the **iostream** is repositioned to the specified pointer position. When it is used with two parameters, a relative position is calculated. The following listing highlights these differences, assuming the preceding declaration for *io*:

```
streampos current_position = io.tellp( );
io << obj1 << obj2 << obj3;
io.seekp(current_position);
io.seekp(sizeof(MY_OBJ),ios::cur);
io << objnewobj2;
```

The pointer *current_position* is first derived from **streampos** and initialized to the current position of the **put_file** pointer by the function tellp( ). With this information stored, three objects are written to *io*. Using seekp( ), the **put_file** pointer is repositioned to the beginning of the file. The second seekp( ) statement uses the sizeof( ) operator to calculate the number of bytes necessary to move one object's width into the file. This effectively skips over *obj1*'s position, permitting an *objnewobj2* to be written.

If a second argument is passed to seekg( ) or seekp( ), it defines the direction to move: ios::beg (from the beginning), ios::cur (from the current position), and ios::end (from the end of the file). For example, this line will move into the **get_file** pointer file 5 bytes from the current position:

```
io.seekg(5,ios::cur);
```

The next line will move the **get_file** pointer 7 bytes backward from the end of the file:

```
io.seekg(-7,ios::end);
```

C++ File Condition States

Associated with every stream is an error state. When an error occurs, bits are set in the state according to the general category of the error. By convention, inserters ignore attempts to insert things into an **ostream** with error bits set, and such attempts do not change the stream's state. The iostream library object contains a set of predefined condition flags, which monitor the ongoing state of the stream. The following table lists the six member functions that can be invoked:

Member Function	Action
eof( )	Returns a nonzero value on end-of-file
fail( )	Returns a nonzero value if an operation failed
bad( )	Returns a nonzero value if an error occurred
good( )	Returns a nonzero value if no state bits are set
rdstate( )	Returns the current stream state
clear( )	Sets the stream state (int=0)

You can use these member functions in various algorithms to solve unique I/O conditions and to make the code more readable:

```
ifstream pfsinfile("sample.dat",ios::in);
if(pfsinfile.eof( ))
  pfsinfile.clear( ); // sets the state of pfsinfile to 0

if(pfsinfile.fail( ))
  cerr << ">>> sample.dat creation error <<<";
```

```
if(pfsinfile.good( ))
  cin >> my_object;

if(!pfsinfile) // shortcut
  cout << ">>> sample.dat creation error <<<";
```

This chapter has served as an introduction to C++ I/O concepts. To really understand various formatting capabilities, you'll need to learn about C++ classes and various overloading techniques. Chapters 16 and 17 teach object-oriented programming concepts. With this information, you'll be introduced to additional C++ I/O techniques in Chapter 18.

Visual
C++ 6

Chapter 13

Structures, Unions, and
Miscellaneous Items

413

This 	chapter investigates several advanced C and C++ types, such as structures, unions, and bit-fields, along with other miscellaneous topics. You will learn how to create and use structures in programs. The chapter also covers how to pass structure information to functions, use pointers with structures, create and use unions in programs, and use other important features, such as **typedef** and enumerated types (**enum**).

The bulk of the chapter concentrates on two important features common to C and C++: the structure and the union. The C or C++ structure is conceptually an array or vector of closely related items. Unlike an array or vector, however, a structure permits the contained items to be of assorted data types.

The structure is very important to C and C++. Structures serve as the flagship of a more advanced C++ type, called the *class*. If you become comfortable with structures, it will be much easier for you to understand C++ classes. This is because C++ classes share, and expand upon, many of the features of a structure. Chapters 16 and 18 are devoted to the C++ class.

Unions are another advanced type. Unions allow you to store different data types at the same place in your system's memory. These advanced data types serve as the foundation of most spreadsheet and database programs.

In the section that follows, you will learn how to build simple structures, create arrays of structures, pass structures and arrays of structures to functions, and access structure elements with pointers.

Structures

The notion of a data structure is a very familiar idea in everyday life. A card file containing friends' addresses, telephone numbers, and so on, is a structure of related items. A file of favorite CDs or LP records is a structure. A computer's directory listing is a structure. These are examples that use a structure, but what is a structure? Literally, a *structure* can be thought of as a group of variables, which can be of different types, held together in a single unit. The single unit is the structure.

Structures: Syntax and Rules

A structure is formed in C or C++ by using the keyword **struct**, followed by an optional tag field, and then a list of members within the structure. The optional tag field is used to create other variables of the particular structure's type. The syntax for a structure with the optional tag field looks like this:

```
struct tag_field {
  member_type member1;
  member_type member2;
  member_type member3;
```

```
          .
          .
          .
    member_type member n;
};
```

A semicolon terminates the structure definition because it is actually a C and C++ statement. Several of the example programs in this chapter use a structure similar to the following:

```
struct stboat {
   char sztype [iSTRING15 + iNULL_CHAR];
   char szmodel[iSTRING15 + iNULL_CHAR];
   char sztitle[iSTRING20 + iNULL_CHAR];
   int iyear;
   long int lmotor_hours;
   float fsaleprice;
};
```

The structure is created with the keyword **struct** followed by the tag field or type for the structure. In this example, *stboat* is the tag field for the structure.

This structure declaration contains several members; *sztype, szmodel*, and *sztitle* are null-terminated strings of the specified length. These strings are followed by an **integer**, *iyear*, a **long integer**, *lmotor_hours*, and a **float**, *fsaleprice*. The structure will be used to save sales information for a boat.

So far, all that has been defined is a new hypothetical structure type called *stboat*. However, no variable has been associated with the structure at this point. In a program, you can associate a variable with a structure by using a statement similar to the following:

```
struct stboat stused_boat;
```

The statement defines *stused_boat* to be of the type **struct** *stboat*. Notice that the declaration required the use of the structure's tag field. If this statement is contained within a function, then the structure, named *stused_boat*, is local in scope to that function. If the statement is contained outside of all program functions, the structure will be global in scope. It is also possible to declare a structure variable using this syntax:

```
struct stboat {
   char sztype [iSTRING15 + iNULL_CHAR];
```

```
        char szmodel[iSTRING15 + iNULL_CHAR];
        char sztitle[iSTRING20 + iNULL_CHAR];
        int iyear;
        long int lmotor_hours;
        float fsaleprice;
} stused_boat;
```

Here, the variable declaration is sandwiched between the structure's closing brace
(}) and the required semicolon (;). In both examples, *stused_boat* is declared as structure
type *stboat*. Actually, when only one variable is associated with a structure type, the tag
field can be eliminated, so it would also be possible to write

```
struct {
   char sztype [iSTRING15 + iNULL_CHAR];
   char szmodel[iSTRING15 + iNULL_CHAR];
   char sztitle[iSTRING20 + iNULL_CHAR];
   int iyear;
   long int lmotor_hours;
   float fsaleprice;
} stused_boat;
```

Notice that this structure declaration does not include a tag field and creates what
is called an *anonymous structure type*. While the statement does define a single variable,
stused_boat, there is no way the application can create another variable of the same
type somewhere else in the application. Without the structure's tag field, there is no
syntactically legal way to refer to the new type. However, it is possible to associate
several variables with the same structure type without specifying a tag field, as shown
in the following listing:

```
struct {
   char sztype [iSTRING15 + iNULL_CHAR];
   char szmodel[iSTRING15 + iNULL_CHAR];
   char sztitle[iSTRING20 + iNULL_CHAR];
   int iyear;
   long int lmotor_hours;
   float fsaleprice;
} stboat1,stboat2,stboat3;
```

The compiler allocates all necessary memory for the structure members, as it does
for any other variable. To decide if your structure declarations need a tag field, ask
yourself the following questions: "Will I need to create other variables of this structure

type somewhere else in the program?" and "Will I be passing the structure type to functions?" If the answer to either of these questions is yes, you need a tag field.

C++ Structures: Additional Syntax and Rule Extensions

C++, in many cases, can be described as a superset of C. In general, this means that what works in C should work in C++.

Note *Using C design philosophies in a C++ program often ignores C++'s streamlining enhancements.*

The structure declaration syntax styles just described all work with both the C and C++ compilers. However, C++ has one additional method for declaring variables of a particular structure type. This exclusive C++ shorthand notation eliminates the need to repeat the keyword **struct**. The following example highlights this subtle difference:

```
/* legal C and C++ structure declaration syntax */
struct stboat stused_boat;

// exclusive C++ structure declaration syntax
stboat stused_boat;
```

Accessing Structure Members

Individual members can be referenced within a structure by using the **dot** or **member** operator (.). The syntax is

```
stname.mname
```

Here, *stname* is the variable associated with the structure type and *mname* is the name of any member variable in the structure.

In C, for example, information can be placed in the *szmodel* member with a statement such as

```
gets(stused_boat.szmodel);
```

Here, *stused_boat* is the name associated with the structure and *szmodel* is a member variable of the structure. In a similar manner, you can use a printf( ) function to print information for a structure member:

```
printf("%ld",stused_boat.lmotor_hours);
```

The syntax for accessing structure members is basically the same in C++:

```
cin >> stused_boat.sztype;
```

This statement will read the make of the *stused_boat* into the character array, while the next statement will print the *stused_boat* selling price to the screen:

```
cout << stused_boat.fsaleprice;
```

Structure members are handled like any other C or C++ variable with the exception that the dot operator must always be used with them.

Constructing a Simple Structure

In the following example, you will see a structure similar to the *stboat* structure given earlier in this chapter. Examine the listing to see if you understand how the various structure elements are accessed by the program:

```
/*
 *    struct.c
 *    C program illustrates how to construct a structure.
 *    Program stores data about your boat in a C structure.
 *    Copyright (c) Chris H. Pappas and William H. Murray, 1997
 */

#include <stdio.h>

#define iSTRING15 15
#define iSTRING20 20
#define iNULL_CHAR 1

struct stboat {
  char sztype [iSTRING15 + iNULL_CHAR];
  char szmodel[iSTRING15 + iNULL_CHAR];
  char sztitle[iSTRING20 + iNULL_CHAR];
  int iyear;
  long int lmotor_hours;
  float fsaleprice;
} stused_boat;

int main(void)
```

```
{
  printf("\nPlease enter the make of the boat: ");
  gets(stused_boat.sztype);

  printf("\nPlease enter the model of the boat: ");
  gets(stused_boat.szmodel);

  printf("\nPlease enter the title number for the boat: ");
  gets(stused_boat.sztitle);

  printf("\nPlease enter the model year for the boat: ");
  scanf("%d",&stused_boat.iyear);

  printf("\nPlease enter the current hours on ");
  printf("the motor for the boat: ");
  scanf("%ld",&stused_boat.lmotor_hours);

  printf("\nPlease enter the purchase price of the boat: ");
  scanf("%f",&stused_boat.fsaleprice);

  printf("\n\n\n");
  printf("A %d %s %s with title number #%s\n",
     stused_boat.iyear,stused_boat.sztype,
     stused_boat.szmodel,stused_boat.sztitle);
  printf("currently has %ld motor hours",
     stused_boat.lmotor_hours);
  printf(" and was purchased for $%8.2f\n",
     stused_boat.fsaleprice);

  return (0);
}
```

The output from the preceding example shows how information can be manipulated with a structure:

```
A 1952 Chris Craft with title number #CC1011771018C
currently has 34187 motor hours and was purchased for $68132.98
```

You might notice, at this point, that *stused_boat* has a global file scope since it was declared outside of any function.

Passing Structures to Functions

It is often necessary to pass structure information to functions. When a structure is passed to a function, the information is passed call-by-value. Since only a copy of the information is being passed in, it is impossible for the function to alter the contents of the original structure. You can pass a structure to a function by using the following syntax:

```
fname(stvariable);
```

If stused_boat was made local in scope to main( ), and if you move its declaration inside the function, it could be passed to a function named vprint_data( ) with the statement

```
vprint_data(stused_boat);
```

The vprint_data( ) prototype must declare the structure type it is about to receive, as you might suspect:

```
/* legal C and C++ structure declaration syntax */
void vprint_data(struct stboat stany_boat);

// exclusive C++ structure declaration syntax
void vprint_data(stboat stany_boat);
```

Passing entire copies of structures to functions is not always the most efficient way of programming. Where time is a factor, the use of pointers might be a better choice. If saving memory is a consideration, the malloc( ) function for dynamically allocating structure memory in C when using linked lists is often used instead of statically allocated memory. You'll see how this is done in the next chapter.

The next example shows how to pass a complete structure to a function. Notice that it is a simple modification of the last example. The next four example programs use the same basic approach. Each program modifies only that portion of the algorithm necessary to explain the current subject. This approach will allow you to easily view the code and syntax changes necessary to implement a particular language feature. Study the listing and see how the structure, *stused_boat*, is passed to the function vprint_data( ).

```
/*
 *  passst.c
 *  C program shows how to pass a structure to a function.
 *  Copyright (c) Chris H. Pappas and William H. Murray, 1997
 */
```

```c
#include <stdio.h>

#define iSTRING15 15
#define iSTRING20 20
#define iNULL_CHAR 1

struct stboat {
  char sztype [iSTRING15 + iNULL_CHAR];
  char szmodel[iSTRING15 + iNULL_CHAR];
  char sztitle[iSTRING20 + iNULL_CHAR];
  int iyear;
  long int lmotor_hours;
  float fsaleprice;
};

void vprint_data(struct stboat stany_boat);

int main(void)
{
  struct stboat stused_boat;

  printf("\nPlease enter the make of the boat: ");
  gets(stused_boat.sztype);

  printf("\nPlease enter the model of the boat: ");
  gets(stused_boat.szmodel);

  printf("\nPlease enter the title number for the boat: ");
  gets(stused_boat.sztitle);

  printf("\nPlease enter the model year for the boat: ");
  scanf("%d",&stused_boat.iyear);

  printf("\nPlease enter the current hours on ");
  printf("the motor for the boat: ");
  scanf("%ld",&stused_boat.lmotor_hours);

  printf("\nPlease enter the purchase price of the boat: ");
  scanf("%f",&stused_boat.fsaleprice);

  vprint_data(stused_boat);
```

```
    return (0);
}

void vprint_data(struct stboat stany_boat)
{
  printf("\n\n");
  printf("A %d %s %s with title number #%s\n",stany_boat.iyear,
      stany_boat.sztype,stany_boat.szmodel,stany_boat.sztitle);
  printf("currently has %ld motor hours",stany_boat.lmotor_hours);
  printf(" and was purchased for $%8.2f",
        stany_boat.fsaleprice);
}
```

In this example, an entire structure was passed-by-value to the function. The calling procedure simply invokes the function by passing the structure variable, *stused_boat*. Notice that the structure's tag field, *stboat*, was needed in the vprint_data( ) function prototype and declaration. As you will see later in this chapter, it is also possible to pass individual structure members by value to a function. The output from this program is similar to the previous example.

Constructing an Array of Structures

A structure can be thought of as similar to a single card from a card file. The real power in using structures comes about when a collection of structures, called an *array of structures*, is used. An array of structures is similar to a whole card file containing a great number of individual cards. If you maintain an array of structures, a database of information can be manipulated for a wide range of items.

This array of structures might include information on all of the boats at a local marina. It would be practical for a boat dealer to maintain such a file and be able to pull out of a database all boats on the lot selling for less than $45,000 or all boats with a minimum of one stateroom. Study the following example and note how the code has been changed from earlier examples:

```
/*
 *    stcary.c
 *    C program uses an array of structures.
 *    This example creates a "used boat inventory" for
 *    Nineveh Boat Sales.
 *    Copyright (c) Chris H. Pappas and William H. Murray, 1997
 */
```

```
#include <stdio.h>

#define iSTRING15 15
#define iSTRING20 20
#define iNULL_CHAR 1
#define iMAX_BOATS 50

struct stboat {
  char sztype [iSTRING15 + iNULL_CHAR];
  char szmodel[iSTRING15 + iNULL_CHAR];
  char sztitle[iSTRING20 + iNULL_CHAR];
  char szcomment[80];
  int iyear;
  long int lmotor_hours;
  float fretail;
  float fwholesale;
};

int main(void)
{
  int i,iinstock;
  struct stboat astNineveh[iMAX_BOATS];

  printf("How many boats in inventory? ");
  scanf("%d",&iinstock);

  for (i=0; i<iinstock; i++) {

    flushall( );      /* flush keyboard buffer */
    printf("\nPlease enter the make of the boat: ");
    gets(astNineveh[i].sztype);

    printf("\nPlease enter the model of the boat: ");
    gets(astNineveh[i].szmodel);

    printf("\nPlease enter the title number for the boat: ");
    gets(astNineveh[i].sztitle);

    printf("\nPlease enter a one line comment about the boat: ");
    gets(astNineveh[i].szcomment);
```

```
        printf("\nPlease enter the model year for the boat: ");
        scanf("%d",&astNineveh[i].iyear);

        printf("\nPlease enter the current hours on ");
        printf("the motor for the boat: ");
        scanf("%ld",&astNineveh[i].lmotor_hours);

        printf("\nPlease enter the retail price of the boat :");
        scanf("%f",&astNineveh[i].fretail);

        printf("\nPlease enter the wholesale price of the boat :");
        scanf("%f",&astNineveh[i].fwholesale);
      }

    printf("\n\n\n");

    for (i=0; i<iinstock; i++) {
      printf("A %d %s %s beauty with %ld low hours.\n",
             astNineveh[i].iyear,astNineveh[i].sztype,
             astNineveh[i].szmodel,astNineveh[i].lmotor_hours);
      printf("%s\n",astNineveh[i].szcomment);
      printf(
          "Grab the deal by asking your Nineveh salesperson for");
      printf(" #%s ONLY! $%8.2f.\n",astNineveh[i].sztitle,
             astNineveh[i].fretail);
      printf("\n\n");
    }

    return (0);
}
```

Here, Nineveh Boat Sales has an array of structures set up to hold information about the boats in the marina.

The variable *astNineveh[iMAX_BOATS]* associated with the structure, **struct** *stboat*, is actually an array. In this case, *iMAX_BOATS* sets the maximum array size to 50. This simply means that data on 50 boats can be maintained in the array of structures. It will be necessary to know which of the boats in the file you wish to view. The first array element is zero. Therefore, information on the first boat in the array of structures can be accessed with a statement such as

```
gets(astNineveh[0].sztitle);
```

As you study the program, notice that the array elements are accessed with the help of a loop. In this manner, element members are obtained with code, such as the following:

```
gets(astNineveh[i].sztitle);
```

The flushall( ) statement inside the **for** loop is necessary to remove the newline left in the input stream from the previous scanf( ) statements (the one before the loop is entered and the last scanf( ) statement within the loop). Without the call to flushall( ), the gets( ) statement would be skipped over. Remember, gets( ) reads everything up to and including the newline. Both scanf( ) statements leave the newline in the input stream. Without the call to flushall( ), the gets( ) statement would simply grab the newline from the input stream and move on to the next executable statement.

The previous program's output serves to illustrate the small stock of boats on hand at Nineveh Boat Sales. It also shows how structure information can be rearranged in output statements:

```
A 1957 Chris Craft Dayliner 124876 low hours.
A great riding boat owned by a salesperson.
Grab the deal by asking your Nineveh salesperson for
#BS12345BFD ONLY! $36234.00.

A 1988 Starcraft Weekender a beauty with 27657 low hours.
Runs and looks great. Owned by successful painter.
Grab the deal by asking your Nineveh salesperson for
#BG7774545AFD ONLY! $18533.99.

A 1991 Scarab a wower with 1000 low hours.
A cheap means of transportation. Owned by grandfather.
Grab the deal by asking your Nineveh salesperson for
#156AFG4476 ONLY! $56999.99.
```

When you are working with arrays of structures, be aware of the memory limitations of the system you are programming on—statically allocated memory for arrays of structures can require large amounts of system memory.

Using Pointers to Structures

In the following example, an array of structures is created in a similar manner to the last program. The arrow operator is used in this example to access individual structure members. The **arrow** operator can be used *only* when a pointer to a structure has been created.

```c
/*
 * ptrstc.c
 * C program uses pointers to an array of structures.
 * The Nineveh boat inventory example is used again.
 * Copyright (c) Chris H. Pappas and William H. Murray, 1997
 */

#include <stdio.h>

#define iSTRING15 15
#define iSTRING20 20
#define iNULL_CHAR 1
#define iMAX_BOATS 50

struct stboat {
  char sztype [iSTRING15 + iNULL_CHAR];
  char szmodel[iSTRING15 + iNULL_CHAR];
  char sztitle[iSTRING20 + iNULL_CHAR];
  char szcomment[80];
  int iyear;
  long int lmotor_hours;
  float fretail;
  float fwholesale;
};

int main(void)
{
  int i,iinstock;
  struct stboat astNineveh[iMAX_BOATS],*pastNineveh;
  pastNineveh=&astNineveh[0];

  printf("How many boats in inventory? ");
  scanf("%d",&iinstock);


    for (i=0; i<iinstock; i++) {
       flushall( );     /*  flush keyboard buffer */
       printf("\nPlease enter the make of the boat: ");
       gets(pastNineveh->sztype);
```

```
      printf("\nPlease enter the model of the boat: ");
      gets(pastNineveh->szmodel);

      printf("\nPlease enter the title number for the boat: ");
      gets(pastNineveh->sztitle);

      printf(
        "\nPlease enter a one line comment about the boat: ");
      gets(pastNineveh->szcomment);

      printf("\nPlease enter the model year for the boat: ");
      scanf("%d",&pastNineveh->iyear);

      printf("\nPlease enter the current hours on ");
      printf("the motor for the boat: ");
      scanf("%ld",&pastNineveh->lmotor_hours);

      printf("\nPlease enter the retail price of the boat: ");
      scanf("%f",&pastNineveh->fretail);

      printf(
          "\nPlease enter the wholesale price of the boat: ");
      scanf("%f",&pastNineveh->fwholesale);

      pastNineveh++;
   }

pastNineveh=&astNineveh[0];
printf("\n\n\n");

for (i=0; i<iinstock; i++) {
  printf("A %d %s %s beauty with %ld low hours.\n",
            pastNineveh->iyear,pastNineveh->sztype,
            pastNineveh->szmodel,pastNineveh->lmotor_hours);
  printf("%s\n",pastNineveh->szcomment);
  printf(
    "Grab the deal by asking your Nineveh salesperson for:");
  printf("\n#%s ONLY! $%8.2f.\n",pastNineveh->sztitle,
        pastNineveh->fretail);
        printf("\n\n");
        pastNineveh++;
```

```
    }

    return (0);
}
```

The array variable, *astNineveh[iMAX_BOATS]*, and the pointer, ***pastNineveh**, are associated with the structure by using the following statement:

```
struct stboat astNineveh[iMAX_BOATS],*pastNineveh;
```

The address of the array, *astNineveh*, is copied into the pointer variable, *pastNineveh*, with the following code:

```
pastNineveh=&astNineveh[0];
```

While it is syntactically legal to reference array elements with the syntax that follows, it is not the preferred method:

```
gets((*pastNineveh).sztype);
```

Because of operator precedence, the extra parentheses are necessary to prevent the dot (.) member operator from binding before the pointer, ***pastNineveh**, is dereferenced. It is better to use the arrow operator, which makes the overall operation much cleaner:

```
gets(pastNineveh->sztype);
```

While this is not a complex example, it does illustrate the use of the **arrow** operator. The example also prepares you for the real advantage in using pointers—passing an array of structures to a function.

Passing an Array of Structures to a Function

You learned earlier in the chapter that passing a pointer to a structure could have a speed advantage over simply passing a copy of a structure to a function. This fact becomes more evident when a program makes heavy use of structures. The next program shows how an array of structures can be accessed by a function with the use of a pointer:

```
/*
 *    psastc.c
 *    C program shows how a function can access an array
 *    of structures with the use of a pointer.
 *    The Nineveh boat inventory is used again!
 *    Copyright (c) Chris H. Pappas and William H. Murray, 1997
 */

#include <stdio.h>

#define iSTRING15 15
#define iSTRING20 20
#define iNULL_CHAR 1
#define iMAX_BOATS 50

int iinstock;

struct stboat {
  char sztype [iSTRING15 + iNULL_CHAR];
  char szmodel[iSTRING15 + iNULL_CHAR];
  char sztitle[iSTRING20 + iNULL_CHAR];
  char szcomment[80];
  int iyear;
  long int lmotor_hours;
  float fretail;
  float fwholesale;
};

void vprint_data(struct stboat *stany_boatptr);

int main(void)
{
  int i;
  struct stboat   astNineveh[iMAX_BOATS],*pastNineveh;
  pastNineveh=&astNineveh[0];

  printf("How many boats in inventory?\n");
  scanf("%d",&iinstock);

  for (i=0; i<iinstock; i++) {
```

```
    flushall( );      /*  flush keyboard buffer */
    printf("\nPlease enter the make of the boat: ");
    gets(pastNineveh->sztype);

    printf("\nPlease enter the model of the boat: ");
    gets(pastNineveh->szmodel);

    printf("\nPlease enter the title number for the boat: ");
    gets(pastNineveh->sztitle);

    printf("\nPlease enter a one line comment about the boat: ");
    gets(pastNineveh->szcomment);

    printf("\nPlease enter the model year for the boat: ");
    scanf("%d",&pastNineveh->iyear);

    printf("\nPlease enter the current hours on ");
    printf("the motor for the boat: ");
    scanf("%ld",&pastNineveh->lmotor_hours);

    printf("\nPlease enter the retail price of the boat: ");
    scanf("%f",&pastNineveh->fretail);

    printf("\nPlease enter the wholesale price of the boat: ");
    scanf("%f",&pastNineveh->fwholesale);

    pastNineveh++;
  }

  pastNineveh=&astNineveh[0];

  vprint_data(pastNineveh);

  return (0);
}

void vprint_data(struct stboat *stany_boatptr)
{
  int i;
```

```
  printf("\n\n\n");
  for (i=0; i<iinstock; i++) {
    printf("A %d %s %s beauty with %ld low hours.\n",
           stany_boatptr->iyear,stany_boatptr->sztype,
           stany_boatptr->szmodel,stany_boatptr->lmotor_hours);
    printf("%s\n",stany_boatptr->szcomment);
    printf(
       "Grab the deal by asking your Nineveh salesperson for");
    printf(" #%s ONLY! $%8.2f.\n",stany_boatptr->sztitle,
           stany_boatptr->fretail);
    printf("\n\n");
    stany_boatptr++;
  }
}
```

The first indication that this program will operate differently from the last program comes from the vprint_data( ) function prototype:

```
void vprint_data(struct stboat *stany_boatptr);
```

This function expects to receive a pointer to the structure mentioned. In the function, main( ), the array *astNineveh[iMAX_BOATS]*, and the pointer **pastNineveh** are associated with the structure with the following code:

```
struct stboat astNineveh[iMAX_BOATS],*pastNineveh;
```

Once the information has been collected for Nineveh Boat Sales, it is passed to the vprint_data( ) function by passing the pointer:

```
vprint_data(pastNineveh);
```

One major advantage of passing an array of structures to a function using pointers is that the array is now passed call-by-variable or call-by-reference. This means that the function can now access the original array structure, not just a copy. With this calling convention, any change made to the array of structures within the function is global in scope. The output from this program is the same as for the previous examples.

Structure Use in C++

The following C++ program is similar to the previous C program. In terms of syntax, both languages can handle structures in an identical manner. However, the example program takes advantage of C++'s shorthand structure syntax:

```cpp
//
//   struct.cpp
//   C++ program shows the use of pointers when
//   accessing structure information from a function.
//   Note:  Comment line terminates with a period (.)
//   Copyright (c) Chris H. Pappas and William H. Murray, 1997
//

#include <iostream.h>

#define iSTRING15 15
#define iSTRING20 20
#define iNULL_CHAR 1
#define iMAX_BOATS 50

int iinstock;

struct stboat {
  char sztype [iSTRING15 + iNULL_CHAR];
  char szmodel[iSTRING15 + iNULL_CHAR];
  char sztitle[iSTRING20 + iNULL_CHAR];
  char szcomment[80];
  int iyear;
  long int lmotor_hours;
  float fretail;
  float fwholesale;
};

void vprint_data(stboat *stany_boatptr);

int main(void)
{
  int i;
  char newline;
  stboat astNineveh[iMAX_BOATS],*pastNineveh;
  pastNineveh=&astNineveh[0];
```

```
    cout << "How many boats in inventory? ";
    cin >> iinstock;

    for (i=0; i<iinstock; i++) {
      cout << "\nPlease enter the make of the boat: ";
      cin >> pastNineveh->sztype;

      cout << "\nPlease enter the model of the boat: ";
      cin >> pastNineveh->szmodel;

      cout << "\nPlease enter the title number for the boat: ";
      cin >> pastNineveh->sztitle;

      cout << "\nPlease enter the model year for the boat: ";
      cin >> pastNineveh->iyear;

      cout << "\nPlease enter the current hours on "
           << "the motor for the boat: ";
      cin >> pastNineveh->lmotor_hours;

      cout << "\nPlease enter the retail price of the boat: ";
      cin >> pastNineveh->fretail;

      cout << "\nPlease enter the wholesale price of the boat: ";
      cin >> pastNineveh->fwholesale;

      cout << "\nPlease enter a one line comment about the boat: ";
      cin.get(newline);    // process carriage return
      cin.get(pastNineveh->szcomment,80,'.');
      cin.get(newline);    // process carriage return

      pastNineveh++;
    }

  pastNineveh=&astNineveh[0];
  vprint_data(pastNineveh);

  return (0);
}

void vprint_data(stboat *stany_boatptr)
```

```
{
  int i;
  cout << "\n\n\n";
  for (i=0; i<iinstock; i++) {
    cout << "A " << stany_boatptr->iyear << " "
         << stany_boatptr->sztype << " "
         << stany_boatptr->szmodel << " beauty with "
         << stany_boatptr->lmotor_hours << " low hours.\n";
    cout << stany_boatptr->szcomment << endl;
    cout << "Grab the deal by asking your Nineveh "
         << "salesperson for #";
    cout << stany_boatptr->sztitle << "ONLY! $"
         << stany_boatptr->fretail << "\n\n";
    stany_boatptr++;
  }
}
```

One of the real differences between the C++ and C programs is how stream I/O is handled. Usually, simple C++ **cout** and **cin** streams can be used to replace the standard C printf( ) and gets( ) functions. For example:

```
cout << "\nPlease enter the wholesale price of the boat: ";
cin >> pastNineveh->fwholesale;
```

One of the program statements requests that the user enter a comment about each boat. The C++ input statement needed to read in the comment line uses a different approach for I/O. Recall that **cin** will read character information until the first white space. In this case, a space between words in a comment serves as white space. If **cin** were used, only the first word from the comment line would be saved in the *szcomment* member of the structure. Instead, a variation of **cin** is used so that a whole line of text can be entered:

```
cout << "\nPlease enter a one line comment about the boat: ";
cin.get(newline);   // process carriage return
cin.get(pastNineveh->szcomment,80,'.');
cin.get(newline);   // process carriage return
```

First, cin.get(newline) is used in a manner similar to the flushall( ) function of earlier C programs. In a buffered keyboard system, it is often necessary to strip the newline character from the input buffer. There are, of course, other ways to accomplish this, but they are not more eloquent. The statement cin.get(newline) receives the newline character and saves it in *newline*. The variable *newline* is just a collector for the information and is not actually used by the program. The comment line is accepted with the following code:

```
cin.get(pastNineveh->szcomment,80,'.');
```

Here, cin.get( ) uses a pointer to the structure member, followed by the maximum length of the *szcomment*, 80, followed by a termination character (.). In this case, the comment line will be terminated when (n-1) or 80-1 characters are entered or a period is typed (the nth space is reserved for the null-string terminator, \0). The period is not saved as part of the comment, so the period is added back when the comment is printed. Locate the code that performs this action.

Additional Manipulations with Structures

There are a few points regarding structures that the previous examples have not illustrated. For example, it is also possible to pass individual structure members to a function. Another property allows the nesting of structures.

Passing Structure Members to a Function

Passing individual structure members is an easy and efficient means of limiting access to structure information within a function. For example, a function might be used to print a list of wholesale boat prices available on the lot. In this case, only the *fwholesale* price, which is a member of the structure, would be passed to the function. If this is the case, the call to the function would take the form

```
vprint_price(astNineveh.fwholesale);
```

In this case, vprint_price( ) is the function name and *astNineveh.fwholesale* is the structure name and member.

Nesting Structures Within Structures

Structure declarations can be nested. That is, one structure contains a member or members that are structure types. Consider that the following structure could be included in yet another structure:

```
struct strepair {
   int ioilchange;
   int iplugs;
   int iairfilter;
   int ibarnacle_cleaning;
};
```

In the main structure, the **strepair** structure could be included as follows:

```
struct stboat {
  char sztype [iSTRING15 + iNULL_CHAR];
  char szmodel[iSTRING15 + iNULL_CHAR];
  char sztitle[iSTRING20 + iNULL_CHAR];
  char szcomment[80];
  struct strepair strepair_record;
  int iyear;
  long int lmotor_hours;
  float fretail;
  float fwholesale;
} astNineveh[iMAX_BOATS];
```

If a particular member from *strepair_record* is desired, it can be reached by using the following code:

```
printf("%d\n",astNineveh[0].strepair_record.ibarnacle_cleaning);
```

Structures and Bit-Fields

Both C and C++ give you the ability to access individual bits within a larger data type, such as a byte. This is useful, for example, in altering data masks used for system information and graphics. The capability to access bits is built around the C and C++ structure.

For example, it might be desirable to alter the keyboard status register in a computer. The keyboard status register on a computer contains the following information:

	register bits
Keyboard Status:	76543210
Port(417h)	

where

bit 0 = RIGHT SHIFT depressed (1)
bit 1 = LEFT SHIFT depressed (1)
bit 2 = CTRL depressed (1)
bit 3 = ALT depressed (1)
bit 4 = SCROLL LOCK active (1)
bit 5 = NUM LOCK active (1)
bit 6 = CAPS LOCK active (1)
bit 7 = INS active (1)

In order to access and control this data, a structure could be constructed that uses the following form:

```
struct stkeybits {
  unsigned char
    ucrshift  : 1,        /* lsb */
    uclshift  : 1,
    ucctrl    : 1,
    ucalt     : 1,
    ucscroll  : 1,
    ucnumlock : 1,
    uccaplock : 1,
    ucinsert  : 1;        /* msb */
} stkey_register;
```

The bits are specified in the structure starting with the least significant bit (lsb) and progressing toward the most significant bit (msb). It is feasible to specify more than one bit by just typing the quantity (in place of the 1). Only **integer** data types can be used for bit-fields.

The members of the bit-field structure are accessed in the normal fashion.

Unions

A *union* is another data type that can be used in many distinctive ways. A specific union, for example, could be construed as an **integer** in one operation and a **float** or **double** in another operation. Unions have an appearance similar to structures. However, they are very dissimilar. Like a structure, a union can contain a group of many data types. In a union, however, those data types all share the same location in memory! Thus, a union can contain information on only one data type at a time. Many other high-level languages refer to this capability as a "variant record."

Unions: Syntax and Rules

A union is constructed by using the keyword union and the syntax that follows:

```
union tag_field {
  type field1;
  type field2;
  type field3;
    .
    .
```

```
     .
  type fieldn;
};
```

A semicolon is used for termination because the structure definition is actually a C and C++ statement.

Notice the declaration syntax similarities between structures and unions in the following example declaration:

```
union unmany_types {
  char c;
  int ivalue;
  float fvalue;
  double dvalue;
} unmy_union
```

The union is defined with the keyword **union** followed by the optional tag field, *unmany_types*. The union's optional tag field operates exactly the way its structure counterpart does. This union contains several members: a **character**, an **integer**, a **float**, and a **double**. The union will allow *unmany_types* to save information on any one data type at a time.

The variable associated with the union is *unmy_union*. If this statement is contained in a function, the union is local in scope to that function. If the statement is contained outside of all functions, the union will be global in scope.

As with structures, it is also possible to associate several variables with the same union. Also like a structure, members of a union are referenced by using the dot (.) operator. The syntax is simply

```
unname.mname
```

In this case, *unname* is the variable associated with the union type and *mname* is the name of any member of the union.

Constructing a Simple Union

In order to illustrate some concepts about unions, the following C++ program creates a union of the type just discussed. The purpose of this example is to show that a union can contain the definitions for many data types but can hold the value for only one type at a time.

```
//
//  unions.cpp
//  C++ program demonstrates the use of a union.
//  A union is created with several data types.
//  Copyright (c) Chris H. Pappas and William H. Murray, 1997
//

#include <iostream.h>

union unmany_types {
  char c;
  int ivalue;
  double fvalue;
  double dvalue;
} unmy_union;

int main(void)
{
  // valid I/O

  unmy_union.c='b';
  cout << unmy_union.c << "\n";

  unmy_union.ivalue=1990;
  cout << unmy_union.ivalue << "\n";

  unmy_union.fvalue=19.90;
  cout << unmy_union.fvalue << "\n";

  unmy_union.dvalue=987654.32E+13;
  cout << unmy_union.dvalue << "\n";

  // invalid I/O

  cout << unmy_union.c << "\n";
  cout << unmy_union.ivalue << "\n";
  cout << unmy_union.fvalue << "\n";
  cout << unmy_union.dvalue << "\n";

  // union size
```

PROGRAMMING
FOUNDATIONS

```
    cout << "The size of this union is: "
        << sizeof(unmany_types) << " bytes." << "\n";

    return (0);
}
```

The first part of this program simply loads and unloads information from the union. The program works because the union is called upon to store only one data type at a time. In the second part of the program, however, an attempt is made to output each data type from the union. The only valid value is the **double**, since it was the last value loaded in the previous portion of code.

```
b
1990
19.9
9.876543e+18
ÿ
-154494568
-2.05461e+033
9.87654e+018
The size of this union is: 8 bytes.
```

Unions set aside storage room for the largest data type contained in the union. All other data types in the union share part, or all, of this memory location.

By using the integrated debugger, you can get an idea of what is happening with storage within a union.

Miscellaneous Items

There are two additional topics that should be mentioned at this point: **typedef** declarations and enumerated types using **enum**. Both **typedef** and **enum** have the capability to clarify program code when used appropriately.

Using typedef

New data types can be associated with existing data types by using **typedef**. In a mathematically intense program, for example, it might be necessary to use one of the following data types: **fixed**, **whole**, **real**, or **complex**. These new types can be associated with standard C types with **typedef**. In the next program, two novel data types are created:

```
/*
 *   typedf.c
 *   C program shows the use of typedef.
 *   Two new types are created, "whole" and "real",
 *   which can be used in place of "int" and "double".
 *   Copyright (c) Chris H. Pappas and William H. Murray, 1997
 */
#include <stdio.h>

typedef int whole;
typedef double real;

int main(void)
{
  whole wvalue=123;
  real  rvalue=5.6789;

  printf("The whole number is %d.\n",wvalue);
  printf("The real number is %f.\n",rvalue);
  return (0);
}
```

Be aware that using too many newly created types can have a reverse effect on program readability and clarity. Use **typedef** carefully.

You can use a **typedef** declaration to simplify declarations. Look at the next two coded examples and see if you can detect the subtle code difference introduced by the **typedef** keyword:

```
struct stboat {
  char sztype [iSTRING15 + iNULL_CHAR];
  char szmodel[iSTRING15 + iNULL_CHAR];
  char sztitle[iSTRING20 + iNULL_CHAR];
  int iyear;
  long int lmotor_hours;
  float fsaleprice;
} stused_boat;
typedef struct {
  char sztype [iSTRING15 + iNULL_CHAR];
  char szmodel[iSTRING15 + iNULL_CHAR];
  char sztitle[iSTRING20 + iNULL_CHAR];
  int iyear;
```

```
    long int lmotor_hours;
    float fsaleprice;
} STBOAT;
```

Three major changes have taken place:

- The optional tag field has been deleted. (However, when using **typedef** you can still use a tag field, although it is redundant in meaning.)
- The tag field *stboat* has now become the new type *STBOAT* and is placed where structure variables have been defined traditionally.
- There now is no variable declaration for *stused_boat*.

The advantage of **typedef**s lies in their usage. For the remainder of the application, the program can now define variables of the type *STBOAT* using the simpler syntax

```
STBOAT STused_boat;
```

The use of uppercase letters is not syntactically required by the compiler; however, it does illustrate an important coding convention. With all of the possible sources for an identifier's declaration, C programmers have settled on using uppercase to indicate the definition of a new type, constant, enumerated value, and macro, usually defined in a header file. The visual contrast between lowercase keywords and uppercase user-defined identifiers makes for more easily understood code since all uppercase usually means, "Look for this declaration in another file."

Using enum

The enumerated data type **enum** exists for one reason only, to make your code more readable. In other computer languages, this data type is referred to as a user-defined type. The general syntax for enumerated declarations looks like this:

```
enum op_tag_field { val1,. . .valn } op_var_dec ;
```

As you may have already guessed, the optional tag field operates exactly as it does in structure declarations. If you leave the tag field off, you must list the variable or variables after the closing brace. Including the tag field allows your application to declare other variables of the tag type. When declaring additional variables of the tag type in C++, it is not necessary to repeat the keyword **enum**.

Enumerated data types allow you to associate a set of easily understood human symbols—for example, Monday, Tuesday, Wednesday, and so on—with an integral data type. They also help you create self-documenting code. For example, instead of having a loop that goes from 0 to 4, it can now read from Monday to Friday:

```
enum eweekdays { Monday, Tuesday, Wednesday, Thursday, Friday };

/* C enum variable declaration   */
enum eweekdays ewToday;

/* Same declaration in C++        */
eweekdays ewToday;

/* Not using the enumerated type */
for(i = 0; i <= 4; i++)

    .

    .

    .

/* Using the enumerated type    */
for(ewToday = Monday; ewToday <= Friday; ewToday++)
```

C compilers, historically speaking, have seen no difference between the data types **int** and **enum**. This meant that a program could assign an integer value to an enumerated type. In C++ the two types generate a warning message from the compiler without an explicit type cast:

```
/* legal in C not C++ */
ewToday = 1;

/* correcting the problem in C++ */
ewToday = (eweekdays)1;
```

The use of **enum** is popular in programming when information can be represented by a list of integer values such as the number of months in a year or the number of days in a week. This type of list lends itself to enumeration.

The following example contains a list of the number of months in a year. These are in an enumeration list with a tag name *emonths*. The variable associated with the list is *emcompleted*. Enumerated lists will always start with zero unless forced to a different integer value. In this case, January is the first month of the year.

```
/*
 *   enum.c
 *   C program shows the use of enum types.
```

```
*    Program calculates elapsed months in year, and
*    remaining months using enum type.
*    Copyright (c) Chris H. Pappas and William H. Murray, 1997
*/

#include <stdio.h>

enum emonths {
  January=1,
  February,
  March,
  April,
  May,
  June,
  July,
  August,
  September,
  October,
  November,
  December
} emcompleted;

int main(void)
{
  int ipresent_month;
  int isum,idiff;

  printf("\nPlease enter the present month (1 to 12): ");
  scanf("%d",&ipresent_month);

  emcompleted = December;
  isum = ipresent_month;
  idiff = (int)emcompleted - ipresent_month;

   printf("\n%d month(s) past, %d months to go.\n",isum,idiff);

  return (0);
}
```

The enumerated list is actually a list of integer values, from 1 to 12, in this program. Since the names are equivalent to consecutive integer values, integer arithmetic can be performed with them. The enumerated variable *emcompleted*, when set equal to December, is actually set to 12.

This short program will just perform some simple arithmetic and report the result to the screen:

```
Please enter the current month (1 to 12): 4
4 month(s) past, 8 months to go.
```

The next chapter completes the coverage of standard C and C++ programming features. After completing Chapter 14, you will be ready to investigate the fundamentals of object-oriented programming, which are presented in Chapter 15.

Chapter 14

Advanced Programming Topics

This chapter deals with advanced programming concepts common to both C and C++. Many of the topics discussed, such as type compatibility and macros, will illustrate those areas of the language where caution must be used when designing an algorithm. Other topics discussed, such as compiler-supplied macros and conditional preprocessor statements, will help you create more streamlined applications. The chapter ends by examining the concepts and syntax necessary to create dynamic linked lists.

Once you have completed Chapters 5 through 14, you will have enough knowledge of C and C++ to make a jump to the world of object-oriented programming. That topic occupies the bulk of the remainder of this book.

Type Compatibility

You have learned that C is not a strongly typed language. C++ is only slightly more strongly typed (for example, enumerated types). You have also learned how C can perform automatic type conversions and explicit type conversions using the cast operator. The following section highlights the sometimes confusing way the compiler interprets compatible types.

ANSI C Definition for Type Compatibility

The ANSI C committee is chiefly responsible for the discussion of and solution to compatible types. Many of the committee's recommendations added features to C that made the language more readily maintained, such as function prototyping. The committee tried to define a set of rules or coded syntax that nailed down the language's automatic behind-the-scenes behavior.

The ANSI C committee decided that for two types to be compatible, they either must be the same type or must be pointers, functions, or arrays with certain properties (as described in the following sections).

What Is an Identical Type?

The term "composite type" is associated with the subject of compatibility. The composite type is the common type that is produced by two compatible types. Any two types that are the same are compatible, and their composite type is the same type.

Two arithmetic types are identical if they are the same type. Abbreviated declarations for the same type are also identical. In the following example, both *shivalue1* and *shivalue2* are identical types:

```
short shivalue1;
short int shivalue2;
```

Similarly, the type **int** is the same as **signed int** in this next example:

```
int sivalue1;
signed int sivalue2;
```

However, the types **int**, **short**, and **unsigned** are all different. When dealing with character data, the types **char**, **signed char**, and **unsigned char** are always different.

The ANSI C committee stated that any type preceded by an access modifier generates incompatible types. For example, the next two declarations are not compatible types:

```
int ivalue1;
const int ivalue2;
```

In this next set of declarations, see if you can guess which types are compatible:

```
char *pc1, * pc2;
struct {int ix, iy;} stanonymous_coord1, stanonymous_coord2;
struct stxy {int ix, iy;} stanycoords;
typedef struct stxy STXY;
STXY stmorecoords;
```

Both *pc1* and *pc2* are compatible character pointers since the additional space between the * symbol and *pc2* in the declaration is superfluous.

You are probably not surprised that the compiler sees *stanonymous_coord1* and *stanonymous_coord2* as the same type. However, the compiler does not see *stanycoords* as being the identical type to the previous pair of variables. Even though all three variables seem to have the same two integer fields, *stanonymous_coord1* and *stanonymous_coord2* are of an anonymous structure type, while *stanycoords* is of tag type *stxy*.

Because of the **typedef** declaration, the compiler does see *struct stxy* as being identical type to *STXY*. For this reason, *stanycoords* is identical to *stmorecoords*.

It is important to remember that the compiler sees **typedef** declarations as being synonymous for types, not totally new types. The following code segment defines a new type called **MYFLOAT** that is the same type as **float**:

```
typedef float MYFLOAT;
```

Enumerated Types

The ANSI C committee initially stated that each enumerated type be compatible with the implementation-specific integral type; this is not the case with C++. In C++, enumeration types are not compatible with integral types. In both C and C++, no two enumerated type definitions in the same source file are compatible. This rule is analogous to the tagged and untagged (anonymous) structures. This explains why *ebflag1* and *ebflag2* are compatible types, while *eflag1* is not a compatible type:

```
enum boolean {0,1} ebflag1;
enum {0,1} eflag1;
enum boolean ebflag2;
```

Array Types

If two arrays have compatible array elements, the arrays are considered compatible. If only one array specifies a size, or neither does, the types are still compatible. However, if both arrays specify a size, both sizes must be identical for the arrays to be compatible. See if you can find all of the compatible arrays in the following declarations:

```
int imax20[20];
const int cimax20[20];
int imax10[10];
int iundefined[];
```

The undimensioned integer array *iundefined* is compatible with both *imax20* and *imax10*. However, this last pair is incompatible because they use different array bounds. The arrays *imax20* (element type **int**) and *cimax20* (element type **const int**) are incompatible because their elements are not compatible. If either array specifies an array bound, the composite type of the compatible arrays has that size also. Using the code segment above, the composite type of *iundefined* and *imax20* is **int[20]**.

Function Types

There are three conditions that must be met in order for two prototyped functions to be considered compatible. The two functions must have the same return types and number of parameters, and the corresponding parameters must be compatible types. However, parameter names do not have to agree.

Structure and Union Types

Each new structure or union type introduces a new type that is not the same as, nor compatible with, any other type in the same source file. For this reason, the variables *stanonymous1*, *stanonymous2*, and *stfloat1* in the following code segment are all different.

However, a reference to a type specifier that is a structure, union, or enumerated type is the same type. You use the tag field to associate the reference with the type declaration. For this reason, the tag field can be thought of as the name of the type. This rule explains why *stfloat1* and *stfloat2* are compatible types:

```
struct {float fvalue1, fvalue2;} stanonymous1;
struct {float fvalue1, fvalue2;} stanonymous2;
struct sttwofloats {float fvalue1, fvalue2} stfloat1;
struct sttwofloats stfloat2;
```

Pointer Types

Two pointer types are considered compatible if they both point to compatible types. The composite type of the two compatible pointers is the same as the pointed-to composite type.

Multiple Source File Compatibility

The compiler views each declaration of a structure, union, or enumerated type as being a new non-compatible type. This might raise the question, "What happens when you want to reference these types across files within the same program?"

Multiple structure, union, and enumerated declarations are compatible across source files if they declare the same members, in the same order, with compatible member types. However, with enumerated types, the enumeration constants do not have to be declared in the same order, although each constant must have the same enumeration value.

Macros

In Chapter 6, you learned how to use the **#define** preprocessor to declare symbolic constants. You can use the same preprocessor to define macros. A macro is a piece of code that can look and act just like a function.

The advantage of a properly written macro is in its execution speed. A macro is expanded (replaced by its **#define** definition) during preprocessing, creating inline code. For this reason, macros do not have the overhead normally associated with function calls. However, each substitution lengthens the overall code size.

Conversely, function definitions expand only once no matter how many times they are called. The trade-off between execution speed and overall code size can help you decide which way to write a particular routine.

There are other subtle differences between macros and functions that are based on when the code is expanded. These differences fall into three categories:

- In C, a function name evaluates to the address of where to find the subroutine. Because macros sit inline and can be expanded many times, there is no one address associated with a macro. For this reason, a macro cannot be used in a context requiring a function pointer. Also, you can declare pointers to functions, but you cannot declare a pointer to a macro.

■ The compiler sees a function declaration differently from a **#define** macro. Because of this, the compiler does not do any type checking on macros. The result is that the compiler will not flag you if you pass the wrong number or wrong type of arguments to a macro.

■ Because macros are expanded before the program is actually compiled, some macros treat arguments incorrectly when the macro evaluates an argument more than once.

Defining Macros

Macros are defined the same way you define symbolic constants. The only difference is that the *substitution_string* usually contains more than a single value:

```
#define search_string substitution_string
```

The following example uses the preprocessor statement to define both a symbolic constant and a macro to highlight the similarities:

```
/* #define symbolic constant */
#define iMAX_ROWS 100

/* #define macro              */
#define NL putchar('\n')
```

The **NL** macro causes the preprocessor to search through the source code looking for every occurrence of **NL** and substituting it with **putchar**('\n'). Notice that the macro did not end with a semicolon. The reason for this has to do with how you invoke a macro in your source code:

```
int main(void)
{
    .
    .
    .
   NL;
```

The compiler requires that the macro call end with a semicolon if the *substitution_string* of the macro ends with a semicolon:

```
#define NL putchar('\n');
```

After the macro expansion has taken place, the compiler would see the
following code:

```
int main(void)
{
    .
    .
    .
  putchar('\n');;
```

Macros and Parameters

Both C and C++ support macros that take arguments. These macros must be defined
with parameters, which serve a purpose similar to that of a function's parameters. The
parameters act as placeholders for the actual arguments. The following example
demonstrates how to define and use a parameterized macro:

```
/* macro definition */
#define READ_RESPONSE(c) scanf("%c",(&c))
#define MULTIPLY(x,y) ((x)*(y))

int main(void)
{
  char cresponse;
  int a = 10, b = 20;
    .
    .
    .
  READ_RESPONSE(cresponse); /* macro expansions */
printf("%d",MULTIPLY(a,b));
```

In this example *x*, *y*, and *c* serve as placeholders for *a*, *b*, and *cresponse*, respectively.
The two macros, **READ_RESPONSE** and **MULTIPLY**, demonstrate the different ways
you can invoke macros in your program. For example, **MULTIPLY** is substituted
within a printf( ) statement, while **READ_RESPONSE** is stand-alone.

Problems with Macro Expansions

Macros operate purely by substituting one set of characters, or tokens, with another. The
actual parsing of the declaration, expression, or statement invoking the macro occurs

after the macro expansion process. This can lead to some surprising results if care is not taken. For example, the following macro definition appears to be perfectly legal:

```
#define SQUAREIT(x) x * x
```

If the statement is invoked with a value of 5, as in:

```
iresult = SQUAREIT(5);
```

the compiler sees the following statement:

```
iresult = 5 * 5;
```

On the surface, everything still looks okay. However, the same macro invoked with this next statement:

```
iresult = SQUAREIT(x + 1);
```

is seen by the compiler as:

```
iresult = x + (1 * x) + 1;
```

instead of:

```
iresult = (x + 1) * (x + 1);
```

As a general rule, it is safest to always parenthesize each parameter appearing in the body of the macro, as seen in the previous **READ_RESPONSE** and **MULTIPLY** macro definitions and under those circumstances where the macro expansion may appear in a cast expression; for example:

```
dresult = (double)SQUAREIT(x + 1);
```

It is best to parameterize the entire body of the macro:

```
#define SQUAREIT(x) ((x) * (x))
```

Most of the time, the compiler is insensitive to additional spacing within standard C and C++ statements. This is not the case with macro definitions. Look closely at this next example and see if you can detect the error:

```
/* incorrect macro definition */
#define BAD_MACRO (ans) scanf("%d",(&ans))
```

Remember that the **#define** preprocessor searches for the *search_string* and substitutes it with the *substitution_string*. These two strings are delineated by one or more blanks. The definition above, when expanded, will appear to the compiler as:

```
(ans) scanf("%d",(&ans));
```

This creates an illegal statement. The problem has to do with the space between the macro name BAD_MACRO and *(ans)*. That extra space made the parameter list part of the *substitution_string* instead of its proper place in the *search_string*. To fix the BAD_MACRO definition, remove the extra space:

```
#define BAD_MACRO(ans) scanf("%d",(&ans))
```

To see if you really understand the hidden problems that you can encounter when using macros, see if you can determine what the following statement evaluates to:

```
int x = 5;
iresult = SQUAREIT(x++);
```

The situation gets worse when using certain C and C++ operators like **increment**, ++, and **decrement**, $--$. The result of this expression may be 30, instead of the expected 25, because various compilers may evaluate the expression in several different ways. For example, the macro could be expanded syntactically to read:

```
/* iresult = x * x; */
iresult = 5 * 5;
```

or

```
/* iresult = x * (x+1); */
iresult = 5 * 6;
```

Creating and Using Your Own Macros

Macros can include other macros in their definitions. This feature can be used to streamline your source code. For example, look at the following progressive macro definitions:

```
#define NL putchar('\n')
#define TAB putchar('\t')
#define FORMAT1 NL, NL, TAB
#define FORMAT2 NL, TAB, TAB
#define BEGIN_PROMPT FORMAT1, printf("Want to begin?"); \
                              printf("\nType 1 for yes, 0 for no")
#define READ_RESPONSE FORMAT2,scanf("%d",(&c))
#define FORMAT_PRINT(ccontrol,ivalue,fvalue) \
        printf("\n%c\t%d\t%8.2f",(ccontrol),(ivalue),(fvalue))
```

Now, instead of seeing all of the code defined in the macro, your program code takes on the following appearance:

```
int main(void)
{
  char cresponse;
  int ivalue = 23;
  float fvalue = 56.78;
     .
     .
     .
  BEGIN_PROMPT;
  READ_RESPONSE(cresponse);
  FORMAT_PRINT(cresponse,ivalue,fvalue);
```

Remember, however, that you trade off automatic compiler type checking for source code readability, along with possible side effects generated by invoking the statement's syntax.

Macros Shipped with the Compiler

The ANSI C committee has recommended that all C compilers define five special macros that take no arguments. Each macro name begins and ends with two underscore characters as listed in Table 14-1.

Macro Name	Meaning
__LINE__	A decimal integer constant representing the line number of the current source program line
__FILE__	A string constant representing the name of the current source file
__DATE__	A string constant representing the calendar date of the translation in the form "mmm dd yyyy"
__TIMESTAMP__	A string constant representing the date and time of the last modification of the source file in the form "Ddd Mmm hh:mm:ss yyyy"
__STDC__	Represents a decimal 1 if the compiler is ANSI C compatible

Table 14-1.   *Predefined Macros*

Predefined macros are invoked the same way user-defined macros are invoked. For example, print your program's name, date, and current line number to the screen with the following statement:

```
printf("%s | %s | Line number: %d",__FILE__,__DATE__,__LINE__);
```

Advanced Preprocessor Statements

There are actually 12 standard preprocessor statements, sometimes referred to as directives, shown in the following listing:

```
#define
#else
#elif
#endif
#error
#if
#ifdef
#ifndef
```

```
#include
#line
#pragma
#undef
```

You are already familiar with two of them, **#include**, and **#define**.

Recall that the preprocessor processes a source file before the compiler translates the program into object code. By carefully selecting the correct directives, you can create more efficient header files, solve unique programming problems, and prevent combined files from crashing in on your declarations.

The following sections explain the unique function of each of the ten new preprocessor directives not previously discussed. Some of the examples will use the code found in STDIO.H to illustrate the construction of header files.

#ifdef and #endif Directives

The **#ifdef** and **#endif** directives are two of several conditional preprocessor statements. They can be used to selectively include certain statements in your program. The **#endif** directive is used with all of the conditional preprocessor statements to signify the end of the conditional block. For example, if the name LARGE_CLASSES has been previously defined, the following code segment will define a new name called MAX_SEATS:

```
#ifdef LARGE_CLASSES
#define MAX_SEATS 100
#endif
```

Whenever a C++ program uses standard C functions, use the **#ifdef** directive to modify the function declarations so that they have the required **extern** "C" linkage, which inhibits the encoding of the function name. This usually calls for the following pair of directive code segments to encapsulate the translated code:

```
/*  used in GRAPH.H  */

#ifdef __cplusplus
extern "C" {          /* allow use with C++ */
#endif

/* translation units */

#ifdef __cplusplus
```

```
    }
#endif
```

#undef Directive

The **#undef** directive tells the preprocessor to cancel any previous definition of the specified identifier. This next example combines your understanding of **#ifdef** with the use of **#undef** to change the dimension of MAX_SEATS:

```
#ifdef LARGE_CLASSES
#undef MAX_SEATS 30
#define MAX_SEATS 100
#endif
```

The compiler will not complain if you try to undefine a name not previously defined. Notice that once a name has been undefined, it may be given a completely new definition with another **#define** directive.

#ifndef Directive

Undoubtedly, you are beginning to understand how the conditional directives operate. The **#ifndef** preprocessor checks to see if the specified identifier does not exist, and then performs some action. The code segment that follows is taken directly from STDIO.H:

```
#ifndef _SIZE_T_DEFINED
typedef unsigned int size_t;
#define _SIZE_T_DEFINED
#endif
```

In this case, the conditionally executed statements include both a **typedef** and **#define** preprocessor. This code takes care of defining the type *size_t*, specified by the ANSI C committee as the return type for the operator sizeof( ). Make sure that you read the section titled "Proper Use of Header Files" later in this chapter to understand what types of statements can be placed in header files.

#if Directive

The **#if** preprocessor also recognizes the term **defined**:

```
#if defined(LARGE_CLASSES) && !defined (PRIVATE_LESSONS)
#define MAX_SEATS 30
#endif
```

The code shows how the **#if** directive, together with the **defined** construct, accomplishes what would otherwise require an **#ifndef** nested in an **#ifdef**:

```
#ifdef LARGE_CLASSES
#ifndef PRIVATE_LESSONS
#define MAX_SEATS 30
#endif
```

The two examples produce the same result, but the first is more immediately discerned. Both **#ifdef** and **#ifndef** directives are restricted to a single test expression. However, the **#if** combined with **defined** allows compound expressions.

#else Directive

The **#else** directive has the expected use. Suppose a program is going to be run on a VAX computer and a PC operating under DOS. The VAX may allocate 4 bytes, or 32 bits, to the type **integer**, while the PC may allocate only 2 bytes, or 16 bits. The following code segment uses the **#else** directive to make certain that an integer is seen the same on both systems:

```
#ifdef VAX_SYSTEM
#define INTEGER short int
#else
#define INTEGER int
#endif
```

Of course, the program will have to take care of defining the identifier VAX_SYSTEM when you run it on the VAX. As you can readily see, combinations of preprocessor directives make for interesting solutions.

Note   *This type of directive played a major role in the development of Windows applications that were to be source code compatible among Windows 3.x, Windows 95, Windows 98, and Windows NT. Windows 3.2 applications were 16-bit, while Windows 95, Windows 98, and NT applications were essentially 32-bit.*

#elif Directive

The **#elif** directive is an abbreviation for "else if" and provides an alternate approach to nested **#if** statements. The following code segment checks to see which class size is defined and uniquely defines the **BILL** macro:

```
#if defined (LARGE_CLASSES)
    #define BILL printf("\nCost per student $100.00.\n")
```

```
    #elif defined (PRIVATE_LESSONS)
        #define BILL printf("\nYour tuition is $1000.00.\n")
      #else
        #define BILL printf("\nCost per student $150.00.\n")
#endif
```

Notice that the preprocessors don't have to start in column 1. The ability to indent preprocessor statements for readability is only one of the many useful recommendations made by the ANSI C committee and adopted by Visual C++.

#line Directive

The **#line** directive overrides the compiler's automatic line numbering. You can use it to help in debugging your program. Suppose that you have just merged a 50-line routine into a file of over 400 statements. All you care about are any errors that could be generated within the merged code.

Normally, the compiler starts line numbering from the beginning of the file. If your routine had an error, the compiler would print a message with a line number of, say, 289. From your merged files point of view, where is that?

However, if you include a **#line** directive in the beginning of your freshly merged subroutine, the compiler would give you a line error number relative to the beginning of the function:

```
#line 1
int imy_mergefunction(void)
{
    .
    .
    .
}
```

#error Directive

The **#error** directive instructs the compiler to generate a user-defined error message. It can be used to extend the compiler's own error-detection and message capabilities. After the compiler encounters an **#error** directive, it scans the rest of the program for syntax errors but does not produce an object file. For example:

```
#if !defined( _CHAR_UNSIGNED )
#error /J option required.
#endif
```

This code prints a warning message if **_CHAR_UNSIGNED** is undefined.

#pragma Directive

The **#pragma** directive gives the compiler implementation-specific instructions. The Visual C++ compiler supports the pragmas shown in the following list:

```
alloc_text
auto_inline
check_pointer
check_stack
code_seg
comment
data_seg
function
hdrstop
init_seg
inline_depth
inline_recursion
intrinsic
linesize
loop_opt
message
native_caller
optimize
pack
pagesize
skip
subtitle
title
warning
```

Conditional Compilation

Preprocessor statements aren't always found in header files. Preprocessor directives can be used in a program's source code to generate efficient compilations. Look at this next code segment and see if you can detect the subtle difference (hint: executable code size):

```
/* compiled if statement */
if(DEBUG_ON) {
  printf("Entering Example Function");
  printf("First argument passed has a value of %d",ifirst_arg);
```

```
}

/* comparison statement  */
#if defined(DEBUG_ON)
  printf("Entering Example Function");
  printf("First argument passed has a value of %d",ifirst_arg);
#endif
```

The first **if** statement is always compiled. This means that the debugging information is perpetually reflected in the executable size of your program. But what if you don't want to ship a product with your intermediate development cycle code? The solution is to conditionally compile these types of statements.

The second portion of the code demonstrates how to selectively compile code with the **#if**-defined directive. To debug your program, you simply define DEBUG_ON. This makes the nested **#if...#endif** statements visible to the compiler. However, when you are ready to ship the final product, you remove the DEBUG_ON definition. This makes the statements invisible to the compiler, reducing the size of the executable file.

Try the following simple test to prove to yourself how invisible the **#if...#endif** directives make the printf( ) statement pair. Copy the previous code segment into a simple C program that does nothing else. Include all necessary overhead (**#include**, main( ), {, and so on). Do not define DEBUG_ON. Make certain that when you compile the program, there are no error messages. Now, remove the **#include** <stdio.h> statement from the program and recompile.

At this point, the compiler stops at the first printf( ) statement nested within the if...printf( ) block statement. The message printed is "Function '**printf**' should have a prototype." You would expect this since the printf( ) statement within the **if** is always visible to the compiler. Now, simply remove or comment out the if...printf( ) block statement and recompile.

The compiler does not complain about the printf( ) statements nested within the **#if...#endif** preprocessors. It never saw them. They would only become visible to the compilation phase of the compiler if DEBUG_ON is defined. You can use this selective visibility for more than executable statements. Look at this next code streamlining option:

```
#if defined(DEBUG_ON)
  /****************************************/
  /* The following code segment performs  */
  /* a sophisticated enough solution step  */
  /* to require a comment and debug output */
  /****************************************/
  printf("    debug code goes here        ");
#endif
```

This example not only has a conditional output debug statement, but it also provides room for an explanatory comment. The little extra time it takes to write conditionally compiled code has its trade-off in easily debugged code and small executable code size.

Preprocessor Operators

There are three operators that are only available to preprocessor directives. These are the **stringize**, **#**, **concatenation**, **##**, and **charizing**, **#@**, operators.

Stringize Operator

Placing a single # in front of a macro parameter causes the compiler to insert the name of the argument instead of its value. This has the overall effect of converting the argument name into a string. The operator is necessary because parameters are not replaced if they occur inside string literals that are explicitly coded in a macro. The following example demonstrates the syntax for the **stringize** operator:

```
#define STRINGIZE(ivalue) printf(#ivalue " is: %d",ivalue)
        .
        .
        .
int ivalue = 2;
  STRINGIZE(ivalue);
```

The output from the macro will appear as:

```
ivalue is: 2
```

Concatenation Operator

The **concatenation** operator is useful when building variable and macro names dynamically. The operator concatenates the items, removing any white space on either side, forming a new token. When ## is used in a macro, it is processed after the macro parameters are substituted and before the macro is examined for any additional macro processing. For example, the following code shows how to create preprocessed variable names:

```
#define IVALUE_NAMES(icurrent_number) ivalue ## icurrent_number;
        .
```

```
    .
    .
    .
int IVALUE_NAMES(1);
```

The compiler sees the previous listing as the following declaration:

```
int ivalue1;
```

Notice that the preprocessor removed the blanks so that the compiler didn't see *ivalue1* as *ivalue 1*. The operator can be combined with other preprocessor directives to form complex definitions. The following example uses the concatenation operator to generate a macro name, which causes the preprocessor to invoke the appropriate macro:

```
#define MACRO1 printf("MACRO1 invoked.")
#define MACRO2 printf("MACRO2 invoked.")

#define MAKE_MACRO(n) MACRO ## n
    .
    .
    .
MAKE_MACRO(1);
```

The output from the example will appear as:

```
MACRO1 invoked.
```

#@ Charizing Operator

The charizing preprocessor precedes formal parameters in a macro definition. This causes the actual argument to be treated as a single character with single quotation marks around it. For example:

```
#define CHARIZEIT(cvalue) #@cvalue
    .
    .
    .
cletter = CHARIZEIT(z);
```

PROGRAMMING
FOUNDATIONS

The compiler sees the previous code as:

```
cletter = 'z';
```

The Proper Use of Header Files

Since header files are made up of syntactically correct C and C++ ASCII text, and are included in other files at the point of the **#include** directive, many beginning programmers misuse them. Sometimes they are incorrectly used to define entire functions or collections of functions. While this approach does not invoke any complaints from the compiler, it is a logical misuse of the structure.

Header files are used to define and share common declarations with several source files. They provide a centralized location for the declaration of all external variables, function prototypes, class definitions, and inline functions. Files that must declare a variable, function, or class **#include** header files.

This provides two safeguards. First, all files are guaranteed to contain the same declarations. Second, should a declaration require updating, only one change to the header file need be made. The possibility of failing to update the declaration in a particular file is removed. Header files are frequently made up of the following:

- **const** declarations
- enumerated types
- function prototypes
- preprocessor directives
- references to **externs**
- structure definitions
- **typedef**s

Caution should be exercised when designing header files. The declarations provided should logically belong together. A header file takes time to compile. If it is too large or filled with too many disparate elements, programmers will be reluctant to incur the compile-time cost of including them.

A second consideration is that a header file should never contain a nonstatic definition. If two files in the same program include a header file with an external definition, most link editors will reject the program because of symbols defined multiple times. Because constant values are often required in header files, the default linkage of a **const** identifier is static. For this reason, constants can be defined inside header files.

Making Header Files More Efficient

The compiling of header files is made more efficient by using combinations of preprocessor directives. The best way to learn how to construct an efficient header file is to look at an example:

```
#ifndef _INC_IOSTREAM
#define _INC_IOSTREAM

#if !defined(_INC_DEFS )
#include <_defs.h>
#endif

#if !defined(_INC_MEM )
#include <mem.h>     // to get memcpy and NULL
#endif
#endif  /* !_INC_IOSTREAM */
```

Before looking at the individual statements in the example, you need to know that passing one of the compiler builds a symbol table. One of the entry types in a symbol table is the mangled names of header files. Mangling is something that the compiler does to distinguish one symbol from another. The C compiler prepends an underscore to these symbols.

The easiest way to control the compiled visibility of a header file is to surround the code within the header file with a tri-statement combination in the form:

```
#ifndef _INC_MYHEADER
#define _INC_MYHEADER   /* begin _INC_MYHEADER visibility */
 .

    .
    .

#endif /* end of conditional _INC_MYHEADER visibility */
```

This is exactly what was done with the previous coded example where _INC_IOSTREAM was substituted for _INC_MYHEADER. The first time the compiler includes this header file, _INC_IOSTREAM is undefined. The code segment is included, making all of the nested statements visible. From this point forward, any additional **#include** <iostream.h> statements found in any of the other files used to create the executable bypass the nested code.

Precompiled Header Files

Writing efficient header files is one method of speeding up the compiling of a program. Another technique is to use precompiled header files. Precompilation is most useful for compiling a stable body of code for use with another body of code that is under development.

Creating Precompiled Headers

When working in the development environment, the compiler is set, by default, to automatically use precompiled header files. To create such files, use the Project menu and select the Settings menu item. Click the mouse on the C/C++ tab and select Precompiled Headers in the Category box. You will then be able to set the Create precompiled header file (.PCH) option from this folder.

A similar action can be achieved from the command line. The compiler's command-line option, /Yc, instructs the compiler to create a precompiled header (.PCH) file. The syntax looks like:

```
/Yc[yourfile]
```

No space is allowed between /Yc and [yourfile]. The /Yc switch causes the compiler to compile the entire source file, including any and all included header files. The precompiled file is saved with the *yourfile* name of the source file and a .PCH extension.

> **Note** *Precompiled header files are often quite large. When developing multiple projects, keep an eye on how many of these files you are willing to store on your hard disk.*

Using Precompiled Headers

You must follow a certain procedure to create a project that uses precompiled headers. The use of such headers in a project makefile has certain restrictions. First, there can only be one precompiled header *yourfile*.PCH file for each source language in the project (C and/or C++).

Second, all files for a given language must use the identical precompiled header. Additionally, each source file must include the same set of **include** files, in the same order, up to the **include** file that you specify. The same path must be specified with the **include** file in each source file.

The following steps ensure that a project uses precompiled headers:

1. Start by creating a normal project, making sure that you add at least one source file to the project file list. You can specify the source file from which the .PCH file will be generated by selecting this file in the list of files visible in the FileView window.

2. Next, choose the appropriate compiler options from the Project menu by selecting the Settings menu item and then the C/C++ tab.

At this point, select the Precompiled Header option in the Category box. Make sure the Automatic use of precompiled headers option is selected.

LIMITS.H and FLOAT.H

The ANSI C committee requires that all C compilers document the system-dependent ranges of integer and floating-point types in order to help you write portable code. Table 14-2 contains a listing of the ANSI C-required integral definitions found in the LIMITS.H header file.

Defined Type	Size	Description
#define CHAR_BIT	8	Number of bits in a **char**
#define CHAR_MAX	SCHAR_MAX	Maximum **char** value
#define CHAR_MIN	SCHAR_MIN	Minimum **char** value
#define INT_MAX	2147483647	Maximum (**signed**) **int** value
#define INT_MIN	(-2147483647 – 1)	Minimum (**signed**) **int** value
#define LONG_MAX	2147483647L	Maximum (**signed**) **long** value
#define LONG_MIN	(-2147483647L – 1)	Minimum (**signed**) **long** value
#define SCHAR_MAX	127	Maximum **signed char** value
#define SCHAR_MIN	(–128)	Minimum **signed char** value
#define SHRT_MAX	32767	Maximum (**signed**) **short** value
#define SHRT_MIN	(–32768)	Minimum (**signed**) **short** value
#define UCHAR_MAX	0xff	Maximum **unsigned char** value
#define UINT_MAX	0xffffffff	Maximum **unsigned int** value
#define ULONG_MAX	0xffffffffUL	Maximum **unsigned long** value
#define USHRT_MAX	0xffff	Maximum **unsigned short** value

Table 14-2. *Values defined in LIMITS.H (ANSI C)*

Program code can use these ranges to make certain that data will fit in the specified data type. For example, a VAX integer may be 4 bytes, while an older DOS-based integer is only 2. To solve this problem, the following code might be used:

```
if (PROGRAM_NEEDED_MAX > INT_MAX)
  pvoid = new llong_storage;
else
  pvoid = new iinteger_storage;
```

Table 14-3 shows the ANSI C-required floating-point definitions.

Handling Errors—perror( )

One of the many interesting functions prototyped in STDIO.H is a function called perror( ). The function prints to the *stderr* stream the system error message for the last library routine called that generated an error. It does this by using *errno* and *_sys_errlist*, prototyped in STDLIB.H. The *_sys_errlist* value is an array of error message strings. The *errno* value is an index into the message string array and is automatically set to the index for the error generated. The number of entries in the array is determined by another constant, –*_sys_nerr*, also defined in STDLIB.H.

The function perror( ) has only one parameter, a character string. Normally, the argument passed is a string representing the file or function that generated the error condition. The following example demonstrates the simplicity of the function:

```
/*
 *  perror.c
 *  A C program demonstrating the function perror( )
 *  prototyped in stdio.h
 *  Copyright (c) Chris H. Pappas and William H. Murray, 1998
 */

#include <stdio.h>

void main(void)
{
   FILE *fpinfile;
   fpinfile = fopen("input.dat", "r");

   if (!fpinfile)
     perror("Could not open input.dat in file main( ) :");
}
```

Definition	Value	Comment
#define FLT_RADIX	2	Exponent radix
#define FLT_ROUNDS	1	Addition rounding: near
smallest such that 1.0+FLT_EPSILON != 1.0 #define FLT_EPSILON	1.192092896e–07F	
smallest such that 1.0+DBL_EPSILON != 1.0 #define DBL_EPSILON	2.2204460492503131e–016	
smallest such that 1.0+LDBL_EPSILON != 1.0 #define LDBL_EPSILON	DBL_EPSILON	
#define FLT_DIG	6	# of decimal digits of precision
#define DBL_DIG	15	# of decimal digits of precision
#define LDBL_DIG	DBL_DIG	# of decimal digits of precision
#define FLT_MIN	1.175494351e–38F	Min positive val
#define DBL_MIN	2.2250738585072014e–308	Min positive val
#define LDBL_MIN	DBL_MIN	Min pos val
#define FLT_MIN_EXP	(–125)	Min binary exponent
#define DBL_MIN_EXP	(–1021)	Min binary exponent
#define LDBL_MIN_EXP	DBL_MIN_EXP	Min binary exponent
#define FLT_MIN_10_EXP	(–37)	Min decimal exponent
#define DBL_MIN_10_EXP	(–307)	Min decimal exponent
#define LDBL_MAX_10_EXP	DBL_MIN_10_EXP	Max decimal exponent

Table 14-3.   *Values Defined in FLOAT.H (ANSI C)*

Definition	Value	Comment
#define FLT_MAX	3.402823466e+38F	Max value
#define DBL_MAX	1.7976931348623158e+308	Max value
#define LDBL_MAX	DBL_MAX	Max value
#define FLT_MAX_EXP	128	Max binary exponent
#define DBL_MAX_EXP	1024	Max binary exponent
#define LDBL_MAX_EXP	DBL_MAX_EXP	Max binary exponent
#define FLT_MAX_10_EXP	38	Max decimal exponent
#define DBL_MAX_10_EXP	308	Max decimal exponent
#define LDBL_MAX_10_EXP	DBL_MAX_10_EXP	Max decimal exponent

Table 14-3.   *Values Defined in FLOAT.H (ANSI C) (continued)*

The output from the program looks like the following:

```
Could not open input.dat in file main( ) : No such file or directory
```

Dynamic Memory Allocation—Linked Lists

Linked lists are often the best choice when trying to create memory-efficient algorithms. Previous programs involving arrays of structures (see Chapter 9 and 13, for example) have all included definitions for the total number of structures used. For example, MAX_BOATS might be set to 25. This means that the program can accept data for a maximum of 25 boats. If 70 or 100 boats are brought into the marina, the program itself will have to be altered and recompiled to accommodate the increased number. This is because the structure allocation is *static* (do not confuse this with the storage class modifier—static). Static used in this sense means a variable that is created by the compiler at compile time. These types of variables exist for their normal scope and the programmer cannot create more of them, or destroy any of them, while the program is executing. The disadvantage of *static* allocation should be immediately clear.

One way around the problem is to set the number of structures higher than needed. If MAX_BOATS is set to 10000, not even Nineveh Boat Sales could have a marina that large. However, 10000 means that you are requiring the computer to set aside more than 400 times more memory than before. This is not a wise or efficient way to program.

A better approach is to set aside memory dynamically, as it is needed. With this approach, memory allocation for structures is requested as the inventory grows. Linked lists allow the use of dynamic memory allocation.

A linked list is a collection of structures. Each structure in the list contains an element or pointer that points to another structure in the list. This pointer serves as the link between structures. The concept is similar to an array, but enables the list to grow dynamically. Figure 14-1 shows the simple linked list structure for the Nineveh Boat Sales Program.

The linked list for this example includes a pointer to the next boat in the inventory:

```
struct stboat {
  char sztype[15];
  char szmodel[15];
  char sztitle[20];
  char szcomment[80];
  int iyear;
  long int lmotor_hours;
  float fretail;
  float fwholesale;
  struct stboat *nextboat;
} Nineveh, *firstboat,*currentboat;
```

The user-defined structure type *stboat* is technically known as a self-referential structure because it contains a field that holds an address to another structure just like itself. The pointer, *nextboat*, contains the address of the next related structure. This allows the pointer, **nextboat*, in the first structure to point to the second structure, and so on. This is the concept of a linked list of structures.

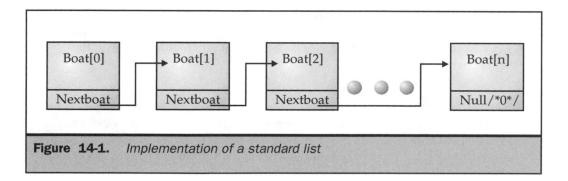

Figure 14-1.   *Implementation of a standard list*

Considerations when Using Linked Lists

To allow your program to dynamically reflect the size of your data, you need a means for allocating memory as each new item is added to the list. In C, memory allocation is accomplished with the malloc( ) function while in C++ new( ) is used. In the section below titled "A Simple Linked List," the complete program allocates memory for the first structure with the code:

```
firstboat=new (struct stboat);
```

The following code segment demonstrates how you can use a similar statement to achieve subsequent memory allocation for each additional structure. The **while** loop continues the entire process while there is valid data to be processed:

```
while (datain(&Nineveh) == 0) {
  currentboat->nextboat = new (struct stboat);
  if (currentboat->nextboat == NULL) return(1);
  currentboat=currentboat->nextboat;
  *currentboat=Nineveh;
}
```

To give you some experience with passing structures, the **while** loop begins by sending datain( ), the address of the *stboat* structure, &*Nineveh*. The function datain( ) takes care of filling the structure with valid data or returns a value of 1 if the user has entered the letter "Q" indicating that he or she wants to quit. If datain( ) does not return a 1, the pointer *currentboat->nextboat* is assigned the address of a dynamically allocated *stboat* structure. The **if** statement checks to see if the function call to new( ) was successful or not (new( ) returns a NULL if unsuccessful).

Since the logical use for *currentboat* is to keep track of the address of the last valid *stboat* structure in the list, the statement after the **if** updates *currentboat* to the address of the new end of the list, namely, *currentboat*'s new *nextboat* address.

The last statement in the loop takes care of copying the contents of the *stboat* structure *Nineveh* into the new dynamically allocated structure pointed to by **currentboat*. The last structure in the list will have its pointer set to NULL. Using NULL marks the end of a linked list. See if you can tell where this is done in the complete program that follows.

A Simple Linked List

The following program shows how to implement the Nineveh Boat Sales example using linked lists. Compare this program with the one in Chapter 13 under the section titled "Constructing an Array of Structures." The C example in Chapter 13 is similar except that it uses a static array implementation. Study the two listings and see which items are similar and which have changed.

```cpp
//
//      C++ program is an example of a simple linked list.
//      Nineveh used boat inventory example is used again
//      Copyright (c) Chris H. Pappas and William H. Murray, 1998
//

#include <stdlib.h>
#include <iostream.h>

struct stboat {
  char sztype[15];
  char szmodel[15];
  char sztitle[20];
  char szcomment[80];
  int iyear;
  long int lmotor_hours;
  float fretail;
  float fwholesale;
  struct stboat *nextboat;
} Nineveh, *firstboat,*currentboat;

void boatlocation(struct stboat *node);
void output_data(struct stboat *boatptr);
int datain(struct stboat *Ninevehptr);

main( )
{
  firstboat=new (struct stboat);

  if (firstboat==NULL) exit(1);

  if (datain(&Nineveh) != 0) exit(1);

  *firstboat=Nineveh;
  currentboat=firstboat;

  while (datain(&Nineveh)==0) {
  currentboat->nextboat=
    new (struct stboat);
```

PROGRAMMING
FOUNDATIONS

```
      if (currentboat->nextboat==NULL) return(1);
      currentboat=currentboat->nextboat;
      *currentboat=Nineveh;
    }

    currentboat->nextboat=NULL; // signal end of list

    boatlocation(firstboat);

    return (0);
}


void boatlocation(struct stboat *node)
{
  do {
    output_data(node);
  } while ((node=node->nextboat) != NULL);
}

void output_data(struct stboat *boatptr)
{
  cout << "\n\n\n";
  cout << "A " << boatptr->iyear << " "
   << boatptr->sztype << boatptr->szmodel << " "
   << "beauty with " << boatptr->lmotor_hours << " "
   << "low miles.\n";
  cout << boatptr->szcomment << ".\n";
  cout << "Grab the deal by asking your Nineveh salesperson for";
  cout << " #" << boatptr->sztitle << " ONLY! $"
   << boatptr->fretail << ".\n";
}

int datain(struct stboat *Ninevehptr)
{
  char newline;

  cout << "\n[Enter new boat information - a Q quits]\n\n";
  cout << "Enter the make of the boat.\n";
  cin >> Ninevehptr->sztype;

  if (*(Ninevehptr->sztype) == 'Q') return(1);
```

```
cout << "Enter the model of the boat.\n";
cin >> Ninevehptr->szmodel;

cout << "Enter the title number for the boat.\n";
cin >> Ninevehptr->sztitle;

cout << "Enter the model year for the boat.\n";
cin >> Ninevehptr->iyear;

cout << "Enter the number of hours on the boat motor.\n";
cin >> Ninevehptr->lmotor_hours;

cout << "Enter the retail price of the boat.\n";
cin >> Ninevehptr->fretail;

cout << "Enter the wholesale price of the boat.\n";
cin >> Ninevehptr->fwholesale;

cout << "Enter a one line comment about the boat.\n";
cin.get(newline);     // process carriage return
cin.get(Ninevehptr->szcomment,80,'.');

cin.get(newline);     // process carriage return
return(0);
}
```

Notice that the three functions are all passed pointers to an *stboat* structure:

```
int datain(struct stboat *Ninevehptr)
void boatlocation(struct stboat *node)
void output_data(struct stboat *boatptr)
```

The function boatlocation( ) checks the linked list for entries before calling the function output_data( ). It does this with a **do...while** loop that is terminated whenever *node* pointer is assigned a NULL address. This is only true when you have tried to go beyond the last *stboat* structure in the list. The output_data( ) function formats the output from each linked list structure.

Note   *As you test this application, don't forget to add a period (.) at the end of the comment regarding each boat. Failure to do this will cause the program to hang.*

PROGRAMMING
FOUNDATIONS

In most high-level languages, linked lists provide the most efficient use of memory, but are often the most difficult to debug. You will learn in Chapter 16 that the use of object-oriented C++ classes can improve efficiency even more.

Chapter 15

Power Programming: Tapping
Important C and C++ Libraries

Programmers rely heavily on functions built into C and C++ compiler libraries. These built-in functions save you from "reinventing the wheel" when you need a special routine. Both C and C++ offer extensive support for character, string, math, and time and date functions. Most library functions are portable from one computer to another and from one operating system to another. There are some functions, however, that are system or compiler dependent. Using these functions efficiently requires you to know where to locate the library functions and how to call them properly.

Many C and C++ functions have already been heavily used in earlier chapters. These include, for example, functions prototyped in the STDIO.H and IOSTREAM.H header files. It is difficult to do any serious programming without taking advantage of their power. This chapter does not repeat a study of their use; rather, it concentrates on new functions that will enhance character, string, and math work.

Important C and C++ Header Files

If you do a directory listing of your Visual C++ INCLUDE subdirectory, the frequently used header files shown in Table 15-1 should be present.

Header File	Description
CONIO.H	Console and port I/O
CTYPE.H*	Character functions
IO.H	File handling and low-level I/O
MATH.H*	Math functions
STDIO.H	Stream routines for C
STDLIB.H*	Standard library routines
IOSTREAM.H	Stream routines for C++
STRING.H*	String functions
TIME.H*	Date and time utilities

Table 15-1.   *Important Header Files for C and C++*

There will be others, too, but these are the header files you will use repeatedly. Since these files are in ASCII format, you may want to print a copy of their contents for a reference. You will find that some header files are short, while others are quite long. All contain function prototypes, and many contain built-in macros.

This chapter will illustrate a use for many popular functions prototyped in the header files marked with an asterisk in the preceding table. These include the system-independent functions prototyped in STDLIB.H, CTYPE.H, MATH.H, STRING.H, and TIME.H. Other functions contained in STDIO.H, IOSTREAM.H, and so on, have already been used throughout the book.

Standard Library Functions (STDLIB.H)

The standard library macros and functions comprise a powerful group of items for data conversion, memory allocation, and other miscellaneous operations. The most frequently encountered macros and functions are shown in Table 15-2. The prototypes are found in STDLIB.H.

As you examine Table 15-2, notice that almost half of the functions shown perform a data conversion from one format to another.

Macro or Function	Description
_exit( )	Terminates a program
_lrotl( )	Rotates an **unsigned long** to the left
_lrotr( )	Rotates an **unsigned long** to the right
_rotl( )	Rotates an **unsigned integer** to the left
_rotr( )	Rotates an **unsigned integer** to the right
abort( )	Aborts program; terminates abnormally
abs( )	Absolute value of an **integer**
atexit( )	Registers termination function
atof( )	Converts a string to a **float**
atoi( )	Converts a string to an **integer**
atol( )	Converts a string to a **long**

Table 15-2.   *Popular Standard Library Functions*

Macro or Function	Description
bsearch( )	Binary search on an array
calloc( )	Allocates main memory
div( )	Divides **integer**s
_ecvt( )	Converts a **float** to a string
exit( )	Terminates a program
_fcvt( )	Converts a **float** to a string
free( )	Frees memory
_gcvt( )	Converts a **float** to a string
getenv( )	Gets a string from the environment
_itoa( )	Converts an **integer** to a string
labs( )	Absolute value of a **long**
ldiv( )	Divides two **long integer**s
_ltoa( )	Converts a **long** to a string
malloc( )	Allocates memory
_putenv( )	Puts a string in the environment
qsort( )	Performs a quick sort
rand( )	Random number generator
realloc( )	Reallocates main memory
srand( )	Initializes random number generator
strtod( )	Converts a string to a **double**
strtol( )	Converts a string to a **long**
strtoul( )	Converts a string to an **unsigned long**
_swab( )	Swaps bytes from s1 to s2
system( )	Invokes DOS COMMAND.COM file
_ultoa( )	Converts an **unsigned long** to a string

Table 15-2. *Popular Standard Library Functions* (continued)

You'll make use of many of these functions and macros as you develop your own C and C++ programs.

Performing Data Conversions

The first important group of functions described in STDLIB.H are the data converting functions. Their principal job is to convert data from one data type to another. For example, the atol( ) function converts string information to a **long**.

The syntax of each function is shown in the following list of function prototypes:

```
double atof(const char *s)
int atoi(const char *s)
long atol(const char *s)
char *ecvt(double value,int n,int *dec,int *sign)
char *fcvt(double value,int n,int *dec,int *sign)
char *gcvt(double value,int n,char *buf)
char *itoa(int value,char *s,int radix)
char *ltoa(long value,char *s,int radix)
double strtod(const char *s,char **endptr)
long strtol(const char *s,char **endptr,int radix)
unsigned long strtoul(const char *s,char **endptr,int radix)
char *ultoa(unsigned long value,char *s,int radix)
```

In these functions, *s points to a string, *value* is the number to be converted, *n* represents the number of digits in the string, and *dec* locates the decimal point relative to the start of the string. The variable *sign* represents the sign of the number, *buf* is a character buffer, *radix* represents the number base for the converted value, and *endptr* is usually null. If not a null value, the function sets it to the character that stops the scan.

The use of several of these functions is illustrated in the following programs.

Changing a float to a String

The fcvt( ) function converts a **float** to a string. It is also possible to obtain information regarding the sign and location of the decimal point.

```
/*
 *   fcvt.c
 *   Demonstrating the use of the fcvt( ) function.
 *   Copyright (c) Chris H. Pappas and William H. Murray, 1998
 */

#include <stdio.h>
#include <stdlib.h>
```

```
main( )
{
  int dec_pt,sign;
  char *ch_buffer;
  int num_char=7;


  ch_buffer = fcvt(-234.5678,num_char,&dec_pt,&sign);
  printf("The buffer holds: %s\n",ch_buffer);
  printf("The sign (+=0, -=1) is stored as a: %d\n",sign);
  printf("The decimal place is %d characters from right\n",
         dec_pt);
  return (0);
}
```

The output from this program is shown here:

```
The buffer holds: 2345678000
The sign (+=0, -=1) is stored as a: 1
The decimal place is 3 characters from right
```

Changing a String to a long integer

The strtol( ) function converts the specified string, in the given base, to its decimal equivalent. The following example shows a string of binary characters that will be converted to a decimal number:

```
/*
 *   strtol.c
 *   Demonstrating the use of the strtol( ) function.
 *   Copyright (c) Chris H. Pappas and William H. Murray, 1998
 */

#include <stdlib.h>
#include <stdio.h>

main( )
{
  char *s="101101",*endptr;
  long long_number;
```

```
long_number=strtol(s,&endptr,2);
printf("The binary value %s is equal to %ld decimal.\n",
       s,long_number);
return (0);
}
```

In this example, "101101" is a string that represents several binary digits. The program produces the following results:

```
The binary value 101101 is equal to 45 decimal.
```

This is an interesting function since it allows a string of digits to be specified in one base and converted to another. This function would be a good place to start if you wanted to develop a general base change program.

Performing Searches and Sorts

The bsearch( ) function is used to perform a binary search of an array. The qsort( ) function performs a quick sort. The lfind( ) function can be used to perform a linear search for a key in an array of sequential records. The lsearch( ) function performs a linear search on a sorted or unsorted table. Examine the function syntax shown in the following listing:

```
void *bsearch(const void *key,const void *base,
   size_t nelem,size_t width,int(*fcmp)(const void *,
   const void *))

void qsort(void *base,size_t nelem,size_t width,
   int(*fcmp)(const void *,const void *))

void *lfind(const void *key,const void *base,
   size_t *,size_t width,int(*fcmp)
   (const void *,const void *))

void *lsearch(const void *key, void *base,
   size_t *,size_t width,int(*fcmp)
   (const void *,const void *))
```

Here, *key* represents the search key, *base* is the array to search, *nelem* contains the number of elements in the array, *width* is the number of bytes for each table entry, *fcmp* is the comparison routine used, and *num* reports the number of records.

The next application shows the use of two of the search and sort functions just described.

Using qsort( ) to Sort a Group of Integers

In C and C++, as in any language, sorting data is very important. Visual C++ provides the qsort( ) function for sorting data. The following example is one application in which qsort( ) can be used.

```c
/*
 *   qsort.c
 *   Demonstrating the use of the qsort( ) function.
 *   Copyright (c) Chris H. Pappas and William H. Murray, 1998
 */

#include <stdio.h>
#include <stdlib.h>

int int_comp(const void *i,const void *j);

int list[12]={95,53,71,86,11,28,34,53,10,11,74,-44};

main( )
{
  int i;

  qsort(list,12,sizeof(int),int_comp);

  printf("The array after qsort:\n");
  for(i=0;i<12;i++)
    printf("%d ",list[i]);
  return (0);
}

int int_comp(const void *i,const void *j)
{
  return ((*(int *)i)-(*(int *)j));
}
```

The original numbers, in the variable *list*, are signed **integers**. The qsort( ) function will arrange the original numbers in ascending order, leaving them in the variable *list*. Here, the original numbers are sorted in ascending order:

```
The array after qsort:
--44 10 11 11 28 34 53 53 71 74 86 95
```

Can qsort( ) be used with **float**s? Why not alter the previous program and see?

Finding an Integer in an Array of integers

You use the bsearch( ) function to perform a search in an **integer** array. The search value for this example is contained in *search_number*.

```c
/*
 *   bsearch.c
 *   Demonstrating the use of the bsearch( ) function.
 *   Copyright (c) Chris H. Pappas and William H. Murray, 1998
 */

#include <stdlib.h>
#include <stdio.h>

int int_comp(const void *i,const void *j);

int data_array[]={100,200,300,400,500,
                  600,700,800,900};

main( )
{
  int *search_result;
  int search_number=400;

  printf("Is 400 in the data_array? ");
  search_result=bsearch(&search_number,data_array,9,
                        sizeof(int),int_comp);
  if (search_result) printf("Yes!\n");
    else printf("No!\n");
  return (0);
}

int int_comp(const void *i,const void *j)
{
  return ((*(int *)i)-(*(int *)j));
}
```

This application sends a simple message to the screen regarding the outcome of the search, as shown next.

Is 400 in the data_array? Yes!

You can also use this function to search for a string of characters in an array.

Miscellaneous Operations

There are several miscellaneous functions, listed in Table 15-3 and described in this section, that perform a variety of diverse operations. These operations include calculating the absolute value of an **integer** and bit rotations on an **integer**.

Bit rotation functions give you the ability to perform operations that were once just in the realm of assembly language programmers.

Function	Description
Abort or End:	
void abort(void)	Returns an exit code of 3
int atexit(atexit_t func)	Calls function prior to exit
void exit(int status)	Returns zero for normal exit
int system(const char * command)	Command is a DOS command
void_exit(int status)	Terminates with no action
Math:	
div_t div(int number,int denom)	Divides and returns quotient and remainder in *div_t*
int abs(int x)	Determines absolute value of x
long labs(long x)	Determines absolute value of x
ldiv_t ldiv(long numerator,long denominator)	Similar to div( ) with **long**s
int rand(void)	Calls random number generator
void srand(unsigned seed)	Seeds random number generator

Table 15-3. *Miscellaneous Functions*

Function	Description
Rotate:	
unsigned long_lrotl(unsigned long val,int count)	Rotates the **long** *val* to the left
unsigned long_l lrotr(unsigned long val,int count)	Rotates the **long** *val* to the right
unsigned _rotl(unsigned val,int count)	Rotates the **integer** *val* to the left
unsigned _rotr(unsigned val,int count)	Rotates the **integer** *val* to the right
Miscellaneous:	
char * getenv(const char * name)	Gets environment string
int putenv(const char * name)	Puts environment string
void _swap(char * from, char * to,int nbytes)	Swaps the number of characters in nbytes

Table 15-3. *Miscellaneous Functions* (continued)

Using the Random Number Generator

Visual C++ provides a random number function. The random number generator can be initialized or seeded with a call to srand( ). The seed function accepts an **integer** argument and starts the random number generator.

```c
/*
 *   rand.c
 *   Demonstrating the use of the srand( ) and rand( ),
 *   random number functions.
 *   Copyright (c) Chris H. Pappas and William H. Murray, 1998
 */

#include <stdlib.h>
#include <stdio.h>

main( )
{
```

```
    int x;

    srand(3);

    for (x=0;x<8;x++)
      printf("Trial #%d, random number=%d\n",
             x,rand( ));
    return (0);
}
```

An example of random numbers generated by rand( ) is shown here:

```
Trial #0, random number=48
Trial #1, random number=7196
Trial #2, random number=9294
Trial #3, random number=9091
Trial #4, random number=7031
Trial #5, random number=23577
Trial #6, random number=17702
Trial #7, random number=23503
```

Random number generators are important in programming for statistical work and for applications that rely on the generation of random patterns. It is important that the numbers produced be unbiased—that is, that all numbers have an equal probability of appearing.

Rotating Data Bits

C and C++ provide a means of rotating the individual bits of **integer**s and **long**s to the right and to the left. In the next example, two rotations in each direction are performed:

```
/*
 *   rotate.c
 *   Demonstrating the use of the _rotl( ) and _rotr( )
 *   bit rotate functions.
 *   Copyright (c) Chris H. Pappas and William H. Murray, 1998
 */
```

```
#include <stdio.h>
#include <stdlib.h>

main( )
{
 unsigned int val = 0x2345;

 printf("rotate bits of %X to the left 2 bits and get %X\n",
        val,_rotl(val,2));
 printf("rotate bits of %X to the right 2 bits and get %X\n",
        val,_rotr(val,2));
 return(0);
}
```

Here are the results:

```
rotate bits of 2345 to the left 2 bits and get 8D14
rotate bits of 2345 to the right 2 bits and get 400008D1
```

Note that the original numbers are in hexadecimal format.

The use of the bit rotation functions and the use of logical operators such as **and**, **or**, **xor**, and so on, give C and C++ the ability to manipulate data bit by bit.

The Character Functions (CTYPE.H)

Characters are defined in most languages as single-byte values. Chinese is one case where 2 bytes are needed. The character macros and functions in C and C++, prototyped or contained in CTYPE.H, take **integer** arguments but utilize only the lower byte of the **integer** value. Automatic type conversion usually permits character arguments to also be passed to the macros or functions. The macros and functions shown in Table 15-4 are available.

These macros and functions allow characters to be tested for various conditions or to be converted between lowercase and uppercase.

Checking for Alphanumeric, Alpha, and ASCII Values

The macros shown in Table 15-5 allow ASCII-coded **integer** values to be checked with the use of a lookup table.

Macro	Description
isalnum( )	Checks for alphanumeric character
isalpha( )	Checks for alpha character
isascii( )	Checks for ASCII character
iscntrl( )	Checks for control character
isdigit( )	Checks for decimal digit (0–9)
isgraph( )	Checks for printable character (no space)
islower( )	Checks for lowercase character
isprint( )	Checks for printable character
ispunct( )	Checks for punctuation character
isspace( )	Checks for white-space character
isupper( )	Checks for uppercase character
isxdigit( )	Checks for hexadecimal digit
toascii( )	Translates character to ASCII equivalent
tolower( )	Translates character to lowercase
toupper( )	Translates character to uppercase

Table 15-4. *Character Macros Available in C and C++*

Macro	Description
int isalnum(ch)	Checks for alphanumeric values A–Z, a–z, and 0–9. ch0 is an **integer**
int isalpha(ch)	Checks for alpha values A–Z and a–z. ch0 is an **integer**
int isascii(ch)	Checks for ASCII values 0–127 (0–7Fh). ch is an **integer**

Table 15-5. *Three Important Macros*

The following program checks the ASCII integer values from zero to 127 and reports which of the preceding three functions produce a TRUE condition for each case:

```
/*
 *    alpha.c
 *    Demonstrating the use of the isalnum( ), isalpha( ),
 *    and isascii( ) library functions.
 *    Copyright (c) Chris H. Pappas and William H. Murray, 1998
 */

#include <stdio.h>
#include <ctype.h>

main( )
{
  int ch;
  for (ch=0;ch<=127;ch++) {
    printf("The ASCII digit %d is an:\n",ch);
    printf("%s",isalnum(ch) ? "  alphanumeric char\n" : "");
    printf("%s",isalpha(ch) ? "  alpha char\n" : "");
    printf("%s",isascii(ch) ? "  ascii char\n" : "");
    printf("\n");
  }
  return (0);
}
```

A portion of the information sent to the screen is shown here:

```
The ASCII digit 0 is an:
  ascii char

The ASCII digit 1 is an:
  ascii char
            .
            .
            .
The ASCII digit 48 is an:
  alpha-numeric char
  ascii char

The ASCII digit 49 is an:
  alpha-numeric char
```

PROGRAMMING
FOUNDATIONS

```
    ascii char
          .
          .
          .
The ASCII digit 65 is an:
  alpha-numeric char
  alpha char
  ascii char

The ASCII digit 66 is an:
  alpha-numeric char
  alpha char
  ascii char
```

These functions are very useful in checking the contents of string characters.

Checking for Control, White Space, and Punctuation

The routines shown in Table 15-6 are implemented as both macros and functions.

Routine	Description
int iscntrl(ch)	Checks for control character
int isdigit(ch)	Checks for digits 0–9
int isgraph(ch)	Checks for printable characters (no space)
int islower(ch)	Checks for lowercase a–z
int isprint(ch)	Checks for printable character
int ispunct(ch)	Checks for punctuation
int isspace(ch)	Checks for white space
int isupper(ch)	Checks for uppercase A–Z
int isxdigit(ch)	Checks for hexadecimal value 0–9, a–f, or A–F

Table 15-6.   *Routines Implemented as Both Macros and Functions*

These routines allow ASCII-coded **integer** values to be checked via a lookup table. A zero is returned for FALSE and a nonzero for TRUE. A valid ASCII character set is assumed. The value *ch* is an **integer**.

The next application checks the ASCII **integer** values from zero to 127 and reports which of the preceding nine functions give a TRUE condition for each value:

```c
/*
 *   contrl.c
 *   Demonstrating several character functions such as
 *   isprint( ), isupper( ), iscntrl( ), etc.
 *   Copyright (c) Chris H. Pappas and William H. Murray, 1998
 */

#include <stdio.h>
#include <ctype.h>

main( )
{
  int ch;
  for (ch=0;ch<=127;ch++) {
    printf("The ASCII digit %d is a(n):\n",ch);
    printf("%s",isprint(ch) ? "  printable char\n" : "");
    printf("%s",islower(ch) ? "  lowercase char\n" : "");
    printf("%s",isupper(ch) ? "  uppercase char\n" : "");
    printf("%s",ispunct(ch) ? "  punctuation char\n" : "");
    printf("%s",isspace(ch) ? "  space char\n" : "");
    printf("%s",isdigit(ch) ? "  char digit\n" : "");
    printf("%s",isgraph(ch) ? "  graphics char\n" : "");
    printf("%s",iscntrl(ch) ? "  control char\n" : "");
    printf("%s",isxdigit(ch) ? "  hexadecimal char\n" : "");
    printf("\n");
  }
  return (0);
}
```

A portion of the information sent to the screen is shown here:

```
The ASCII digit 0 is a(n):
  control char
```

```
The ASCII digit 1 is a(n):
  control char
          .
          .
          .
The ASCII digit 32 is a(n):
  printable char
  space char

The ASCII digit 33 is a(n):
  printable char
  punctuation char
  graphics char

The ASCII digit 34 is a(n):
  printable char
  punctuation char
  graphics char
          .
          .
          .
The ASCII digit 65 is a(n):
  printable char
  uppercase char
  graphics char
  hexadecimal char

The ASCII digit 66 is a(n):
  printable char
  uppercase char
  graphics char
  hexadecimal char
```

Conversions to ASCII, Lowercase, and Uppercase

The macros and functions shown in Table 15-7 allow ASCII-coded **integer** values to be translated.

The macro toascii( ) converts *ch* to ASCII by retaining only the lower 7 bits. The functions tolower( ) and toupper( ) convert the character value to the format specified. The macros _tolower( ) and _toupper( ) return identical results when supplied proper ASCII values. A valid ASCII character set is assumed. The value *ch* is an **integer**.

Macro	Description
int toascii(ch)	Translates to ASCII character
int tolower(ch)	Translates *ch* to lowercase if uppercase
int _tolower(ch)	Translates *ch* to lowercase
int toupper(ch)	Translates *ch* to uppercase if lowercase
int _toupper(ch)	Translates *ch* to uppercase

Table 15-7.   *Functions Used to Translate ASCII-Coded Integer Values*

The next example shows how the macro toascii( ) converts **integer** information to
correct ASCII values:

```
/*
 *   ascii.c
 *   Demonstrating the use of the toascii( ) function.
 *   Copyright (c) Chris H. Pappas and William H. Murray, 1998
 */

#include <stdio.h>
#include <ctype.h>

int ch;

main( )
{
  for(ch=0;ch<=512;ch++) {
    printf("The ASCII value for %d is %d\n",
           ch,toascii(ch));
  }
  return (0);
}
```

Here is a partial list of the information sent to the screen:

```
The ASCII value for 0 is 0
The ASCII value for 1 is 1
The ASCII value for 2 is 2
```

```
                    .
                    .
                    .
The ASCII value for 128 is 0
The ASCII value for 129 is 1
The ASCII value for 130 is 2
                    .
                    .
                    .
The ASCII value for 256 is 0
The ASCII value for 257 is 1
The ASCII value for 258 is 2
                    .
                    .
                    .
The ASCII value for 384 is 0
The ASCII value for 385 is 1
The ASCII value for 386 is 2
```

The String Functions (STRING.H)

Strings in C and C++ are usually considered one-dimensional character arrays terminated with a null character. The string functions, prototyped in STRING.H, typically use pointer arguments and return pointer or **integer** values. You can study the syntax of each command in the next section or, in more detail, from the help facility provided with the Visual C++ compiler. Additionally, buffer-manipulation functions such as memccpy( ) and memset( ) are also prototyped in STRING.H. The functions shown in Table 15-8 are the most popular ones in this group.

Function	Description
memccpy( )	Copies from source to destination
memchr( )	Searches buffer for first *ch*
memcmp( )	Compares *n* characters in buf1 and bufs
memcpy( )	Copies *n* characters from source to destination
memicmp( )	Same as memcmp( ), except case sensitive
memmove( )	Moves one buffer to another

Table 15-8.   *Popular String Functions*

Function	Description
memset( )	Copies *ch* into *n* character positions in buf
strcat( )	Appends a string to another string
strchr( )	Locates first occurrence of a *ch* in a string
strcmp( )	Compares two strings
strcmpi( )	Compares two strings (case insensitive)
strcoll( )	Compares two strings (local specific)
strcpy( )	Copies string to another string
strcspn( )	Locates first occurrence of a character in string from a given character set
strdup( )	Replicates the string
strerror( )	System-error message saved
stricmp( )	Same as strcmpi( )
strlen( )	Length of string
strlwr( )	String converted to lowercase
strncat( )	Characters of string appended
strncmp( )	Characters of two strings compared
strncpy( )	Characters of a string copied to another
strnicmp( )	Characters of two strings compared (case insensitive)
strnset( )	String characters set to a given character
strpbrk( )	First occurrence of character from one string in another string
strrchr( )	Last occurrence of character in string
strrev( )	Reverses characters in a string
strset( )	All characters in string set to given character
strspn( )	Locates first substring from given character set in string
strstr( )	Locates one string in another string
strtok( )	Locates tokens within a string
strupr( )	Converts string to uppercase
strxfrm( )	Transforms local-specific string

Table 15-8.   *Popular String Functions (continued)*

The memory and string functions provide flexible programming power to C and C++ programmers.

Working with Memory Functions

The memory functions, discussed in the previous section, are accessed with the syntax shown in the following listing:

```
void *memccpy(void *dest,void *source,int ch,unsigned count)

void *memchr(void *buf,int ch,unsigned count)

int memcmp(void *buf1,void *buf2,unsigned count)

void *memcpy(void *dest,void *source,unsigned count)

int memicmp(void *buf1,void *buf2,unsigned count)

void *memmove(void *dest,void *source,unsigned count)

void *memset(void *dest,int ch,unsigned count)
```

Here, ***buf**, ***buf1**, ***buf2**, ***dest**, and ***source** are pointers to the appropriate string buffer. The **integer** *ch* points to a character value. The **unsigned** *count* holds the character count for the function.

The next section includes a number of examples that show the use of many of these functions.

Find a Character in a String

In this example, the buffer is searched for the occurrence of the lowercase character "f," using the memchr( ) function:

```
/*
 *   memchr.c
 *   Demonstrating the use of the memchr( ) function.
 *   Finding a character in a buffer.
 *   Copyright (c) Chris H. Pappas and William H. Murray, 1998
 */

#include <string.h>
#include <stdio.h>
```

```
char buf[35];
char *ptr;

main( )
{
  strcpy(buf,"This is a fine day for a search." );
  ptr=(char *)memchr(buf,'f',35);
  if (ptr != NULL)
    printf("character found at location: %d\n",
           ptr-buf+1);
  else
    printf("character not found.\n");
  return (0);
}
```

For this example, if a lowercase "f" is in the string, the memchr( ) function will report the "character found at location: 11."

Compare Characters in Strings

This example highlights the memicmp( ) function. This function compares two strings contained in *buf1* and *buf2*. This function is insensitive to the case of the string characters.

```
/*
*    memcmp.c
*    Demonstrating the use of the memicmp( ) function
*    to compare two string buffers.
*    Copyright (c) Chris H. Pappas and William H. Murray, 1998
*/

#include <stdio.h>
#include <string.h>

char buf1[40],
     buf2[40];

main( )
{
  strcpy(buf1,"Well, are they identical or not?");
  strcpy(buf2,"Well, are they identicle or not?");
  /* 0 - identical strings except for case */
```

```
/* x - any integer, means not identical */

printf("%d\n",memicmp(buf1,buf2,40));
/* returns a nonzero value */
return (0);
}
```

If it weren't for the fact that "identical" (or is it "identicle"?) was spelled incorrectly in the second string, both strings would have been the same. A nonzero value, −1, is returned by memicmp( ) for this example.

Loading the Buffer with memset( )

Often, it is necessary to load or clear a buffer with a predefined character. In those cases, you might consider using the memset( ) function, shown here:

```
/*
*    memset.c
*    Demonstrating the use of the memset( ) function
*    to set the contents of a string buffer.
*    Copyright (c) Chris H. Pappas and William H. Murray, 1998
*/

#include <stdio.h>
#include <string.h>

char buf[20];

main( )
{
  printf("The contents of buf: %s",memset(buf,'+',15));
  buf[15] = '\0';
  return (0);
}
```

In this example, the buffer is loaded with 15 + characters and a null character. The program will print 15 + characters to the screen.

Working with String Functions

The prototypes for using several string-manipulating functions contained in STRING.H are shown in Table 15-9.

Function	Description
int strcmp(const char * s1, const char *s2)	Compares 2 strings
size_t strcspn(const char * s1, const char * s2)	Finds a substring in a string
char * strcpy(char * s1, const char * s2)	Copies a string
char * strerror(int errnum)	ANSI-supplied number
char * _strerror(char * s)	User-supplied message
size_t strlen(const char * s)	Null-terminated string
char * strlwr(char * s)	String to lowercase
char * strncat(char * s1, const char *s2, size_t n)	Appends *n* **char** s2 to s1
int strncmp(const char * s1, char * s2, size_t n)	Compares first *n* characters of two strings
int strnicmp(const char * s1, const char * s2, size_t n)	Compares first *n* characters of two strings (case insensitive)
char * strncpy(char * s1, const char * s2, size_t n)	Copies *n* characters of s2 to s1
char * strnset(char * s, int ch, size_t n)	Sets first *n* characters of string to **char** setting
char * strpbrk(const char * s1, const char * s2)	Locates character from **const** s2 in s1
char * strrchr(const char * s, int ch)	Locates last occurrence of *ch* in string
char * strrev(char * s)	Converts string to reverse
char * strset(char * s, int ch)	String to be set with *ch*
size_t strspn(const char * s1, const char * s2)	Searches s1 with char set in s2
char * strstr(const char * s1, const char * s2)	Searches s1 with s2
char * strtok(char * s1, char * s2)	Finds token in s1. S1 contains token(s), s2 contains the delimiters
char * strupr(char * s)	Converts string to uppercase

Table 15-9.   *String Manipulating Functions*

Here, ***s** is a pointer to a string, while ***s1** and ***s2** are pointers to two strings. Usually, ***s1** points to the string to be manipulated and ***s2** points to the string doing the manipulation. *ch* is a character value.

Comparing the Contents of Two Strings

The following program uses the strcmp( ) function and reports how one string compares to another.

```
/*
 *   strcmp.c
 *   Demonstrating the use of the strcmp( ) function
 *   to compare two strings.
 *   Copyright (c) Chris H. Pappas and William H. Murray, 1998
 */

#include <stdio.h>
#include <string.h>

char s1[45] = "A group of characters makes a good string.";
char s2[45] = "A group of characters makes a good string?";
int answer;

main( )
{
  answer = strcmp(s1,s2);
  if (answer>0) printf("s1 is greater than s2");
    else if (answer==0) printf("s1 is equal to s2");
      else printf("s1 is less than s2");
  return (0);
}
```

Can you predict which of the preceding strings would be greater? Can you do it without running the program? The answer is that **s1** is less than **s2**.

Searching for Several Characters in a String

The next program searches a string for the first occurrence of one or more characters:

```
/*
 *   strspn.c
 *   Demonstrating the use of the strcspn( ) function to find
 *   the occurrence of one of a group of characters.
 *   Copyright (c) Chris H. Pappas and William H. Murray, 1998
```

```
*/

#include <stdio.h>
#include <string.h>

char s1[35];
int answer;

main( )
{
  strcpy(s1,"We are looking for great strings." );
  answer=strcspn(s1,"abc");
  printf("The first a,b,c appeared at position %d\n",
         answer+1);
  return (0);
}
```

This program will report the position of the first occurrence of an "a," a "b," or a "c." A 1 is added to the answer since the first character is at index position zero. This program reports an "a" at position 4.

The First Occurrence of a Single Character in a String

Have you ever wanted to check a sentence for the occurrence of a particular character? You might consider using the strchr( ) function. The following application looks for the first blank or space character in the string.

```
/*
 *   strchr.c
 *   Demonstrating the use of the strchr( ) function to
 *   locate the first occurrence of a character in a string.
 *   Copyright (c) Chris H. Pappas and William H. Murray, 1998
 */

#include <stdio.h>
#include <string.h>

char s1[20] = "What is a friend?";
char *answer;

main( )
{
```

PROGRAMMING
FOUNDATIONS

```
answer=strchr(s1,' ');
printf("After the first blank: %s\n",answer);
return (0);
}
```

What is your prediction on the outcome after execution? Run the program and see.

Finding the Length of a String

The strlen( ) function reports the length of any given string. Here is a simple example:

```
/*
 *    strlen.c
 *    Demonstrating the use of the strlen( ) function to
 *    determine the length of a string.
 *    Copyright (c) Chris H. Pappas and William H. Murray, 1998
 */

#include <stdio.h>
#include <string.h>

char *s1="String length is measured in characters!";

main( )
{
  printf("The string length is %d",strlen(s1));
  return (0);
}
```

In this example, the strlen( ) function reports on the total number of characters contained in the string. In this example, there are 40 characters.

Locating One String in Another String

The strstr( ) function searches a given string within a group (a string) of characters, as shown here:

```
/*
 *    strstr.c
 *    Demonstrating the use of the strstr( ) function to
 *    locate a string within a string.
 *    Copyright (c) Chris H. Pappas and William H. Murray, 1998
 */
```

```
#include <stdio.h>
#include <string.h>

main( )
{
  char *s1="There is always something you miss.";
  char *s2="way";

  printf("%s\n",strstr(s1,s2));
  return (0);
}
```

This program sends the remainder of the string to the printf( ) function after the first occurrence of "way". The string printed to the screen is "ways something you miss."

Converting Characters to Uppercase

A handy function to have in a case-sensitive language is one that can convert the characters in a string to another case. The strupr( ) function converts lowercase characters to uppercase, as shown here:

```
/*
 *    strupr.c
 *    Demonstrating the use of the strupr( ) function to
 *    convert lowercase letters to uppercase.
 *    Copyright (c) Chris H. Pappas and William H. Murray, 1998
 */

#include <stdio.h>
#include <string.h>

char s1[]="Uppercase characters are easier to read.";
char *s2;

main( )
{
  s2=strupr(s1);
  printf("The results: %s",s2);
  return (0);
}
```

This program converts each lowercase character to uppercase. Note that only lowercase letters will be changed.

The Math Functions (MATH.H)

The functions prototyped in the MATH.H header file permit a great variety of mathematical, algebraic, and trigonometric operations.

The math functions are relatively easy to use and to understand for those familiar with algebraic and trigonometric concepts. The most popular math functions are shown in Table 15-10.

Note *Functions accept and return **double** values except where noted.*

Note *Functions ending in "l" accept and return **long double** values.*

Many of these functions were demonstrated in earlier chapters. When using trigonometric functions, remember that angle arguments are always specified in radians.

Programmers desiring complex number arithmetic must resort to using **struct complex** and the _cabs( ) function described in MATH.H. Following is the only structure available for complex arithmetic in Visual C++:

```
struct complex {double x, double y}
```

This structure is used by the _cabs( ) function. The _cabs( ) function returns the absolute value of a complex number.

Building a Table of Trigonometric Values

Since math functions have already been used extensively in this book, the only example for this section involves an application that will generate a table of sine, cosine, and tangent values for the angles from zero to 45 degrees.

This application also takes advantage of the special C++ formatting abilities. Study the following listing to determine how the output will be sent to the screen:

```
//
//  math.cpp
//  A program that demonstrates the use of several
//  math functions.
//  Copyright (c) Chris H. Pappas and William H. Murray, 1998
```

Function	Description
abs( )	Returns absolute value of **integer** argument
acos( ), acosl( )	Arc cosine
asin( ), asinl( )	Arc sine
atan( ), atanl( )	Arc tangent
atan2( ), atan2l( )	Arc tangent of two numbers
ceil( ), ceill( )	Greatest **integer**
cos( ), cosl( )	Cosine
cosh( ), coshl( )	Hyberbolic cosine
exp( ), expl( )	Exponential value
fabs( ), fabsl( )	Absolute value
floor( ), floorl( )	Smallest value
fmod( ), fmodl( )	Modulus operator
frexp( ), frexpl( )	Split mantissa and exponent
hypot( ), hypotl( )	Hypotenuse
labs( )	Returns absolute value of **long** argument
ldexp( ), ldexpl( )	x times 2 to the *exp* power
log( ), logl( )	Natural log
log10( ), log10l( )	Common log
modf( ), modfl( )	Mantissa and exponent
pow( ), powl( )	x to y power
pow10( ), pow10l( )	x raised by power of 10
sin( ), sinl( )	Sine
sinh( ), sinhl( )	Hyperbolic sine
sqrt( ), sqrtl( )	Square root
tan( ), tanl( )	Tangent
tanh( ), tanhl( )	Hyperbolic tangent

Table 15-10. *Popular Math Functions*

PROGRAMMING FOUNDATIONS

```
//

#include <iostream.h>
#include <iomanip.h>
#include <math.h>

#define PI 3.14159265359

main( )
{
  int i;
  double x,y,z,ang;

  for (i=0;i<=45;i++) {
    ang=PI*i/180;  // convert degrees to radians
    x=sin(ang);
    y=cos(ang);
    z=tan(ang);
    // formatting output columns
    cout << setiosflags(ios::left) << setw(8)
         << setiosflags(ios::fixed) << setprecision(6);
    // data to print
    cout << i << "\t" << x << "\t" <<
            y << "\t" << z << "\n";
  }
  return (0);
}
```

This application uses the sin( ), cos( ), and tan( ) functions to produce a formatted trigonometric table. The angles are stepped from zero to 45 degrees and are converted to radians before being sent to each function. This particular C++ formatting is discussed in more detail in Chapter 18.

Following is a partial output from this application:

```
0 0.000000 1.000000 0.000000
1 0.017452 0.999848 0.017455
2 0.034899 0.999391 0.034921
.    .       .        .
.    .       .        .
```

```
 .    .      .        .
28 0.469472 0.882948 0.531709
29 0.484810 0.874620 0.554309
30 0.500000 0.866025 0.577350
31 0.515038 0.857167 0.600861
32 0.529919 0.848048 0.624869
 .    .      .        .
 .    .      .        .
 .    .      .        .
43 0.681998 0.731354 0.932515
44 0.694658 0.719340 0.965689
45 0.707107 0.707107 1.000000
```

The Time Functions (TIME.H)

Table 15-11 shows some of the time and date function found in TIME.H.

These functions offer a variety of ways to obtain time and/or date formats for programs. A discussion of the syntax for each function is included in the next section.

Names	Description
asctime( )	Converts date and time to an ASCII string and uses tm structure
ctime( )	Converts date and time to a string
difftime( )	Calculates the difference between two times
gmtime( )	Converts date and time to GMT using tm structure
localtime( )	Converts date and time to tm structure
strftime( )	Allows formatting of date and time data for output
time( )	Obtains current time (system)
tzset( )	Sets time variables for environment variable TZ

Table 15-11. *Time and Date Functions*

Time and Date Structures and Syntax

Many of the date and time functions described in the previous section use the *tm* structure defined in TIME.H. This structure is shown here:

```
struct tm  {
  int   tm_sec;
  int   tm_min;
  int   tm_hour;
  int   tm_mday;
  int   tm_mon;
  int   tm_year;
  int   tm_wday;
  int   tm_yday;
  int   tm_isdst;
};
```

The syntax for calling each date and time function differs according to the function's ability. The syntax and parameters for each function are shown in Table 15-12.

The TZ environment string uses the following syntax:

```
TZ = zzz[+/-]d[d]{lll}
```

Here, zzz represents a three-character string with the local time zone—for example, "EST" for eastern standard time. The [+/-]d[d] argument contains an adjustment for the local time zone's difference from GMT. Positive numbers are a westward adjustment, while negative numbers are an eastward adjustment. For example, a five (5) would be used for EST. The last argument, {lll}, represents the local time zone's daylight savings time—for example, EDT for eastern daylight savings time.

Several of these functions are used in example programs in the next section.

Working with the localtime( ) and asctime( ) Functions

Many times it is necessary to obtain the time and date in a programming application. The next program returns these values by using the localtime( ) and asctime( ) functions:

```
/*
 *   asctim.c
 *   Demonstrating the use of the localtime( ) and asctime( )
 *   functions.
 *   Copyright (c) Chris H. Pappas and William H. Murray, 1998
```

Function	Description
char * ASCTIME(CONST STRUCT TM * TBLOCK)	Converts the structure into a 26-character string
	For example: Sun June 1, 10:18:20 1998\n\0
char * CTIME(CONST TIME_T *TIME)	Converts a time value, pointed to by * time into a 26-char string (see asctime( ))
double difftime(time_t time2, time_t time1)	Calculates the difference between *time2* and *time1* and returns a **double**
struct tm * GMTIME(CONST TIME_T * TIMER)	Accepts address of a value returned by the function time( ) and returns a pointer to the structure with GMT information
struct tm * LOCALTIME(CONST TIME_T * TIMER)	Accepts address of a value returned by the function time( ) and returns a pointer to the structure with local time information
size_t strftime (char * S, size_t maxsize, const char * fmt, const struct tm * t)	Formats date and time information for output. *s* points to the string information, *maxsize* is maximum string length, *fmt* represents the format, and *t* points to a structure of type **tm**. The formatting options include:
	%a Abbreviate weekday name
	%A Full weekday name
	%b Abbreviate month name
	%B Full month name
	%c Date and time information
	%d Day of month (01 to 31)
	%H Hour (00 to 23)
	%I Hour (00 to 12)
	%j Day of year (001 to 366)
	%m Month (01 to 12)

Table 15-12.   *Time and Date Function Parameters*

Function	Description
	%M Minutes (00 to 59)
	%p AM or PM
	%S Seconds (0 to 59)
	%U Week number (00 to 51), Sunday is first day
	%w Weekday (0 to 6)
	%W Week number (00 to 51), Monday is first day
	%x Date
	%X Time
	%y Year, without century (00 to 99)
	%Y Year, with century
	%Z Time zone name
	%% Character %
time_t time(time_t *timer)	Returns the time in seconds since 00:00:00 GMT, January 1, 1998
void _tzset (void)	Sets the global variables *daylight*, *timezone0*, and *tzname0* based on the environment string

Table 15-12.   *Time and Date Function Parameters* (continued*)*

```
*/

#include <time.h>
#include <stdio.h>

struct tm *date_time;
time_t timer;

main( )
```

```
{
  time(&timer);
  date_time=localtime(&timer);

  printf("The present date and time is: %s\n",
  asctime(date_time));
  return (0);
}
```

This program formats the time and date information in the manner shown here:

```
The present date and time is: Sat May 31 13:16:20 1998
```

Working with the gmtime( ) and asctime( ) Functions

There are other functions that you can also use to return time and date information. The next program is similar to the last example, except that the gmtime( ) function is used.

```
/*
 *   cmtime.c
 *   Demonstrating the use of the gmtime( ) and asctime( )
 *   functions.
 *   Copyright (c) Chris H. Pappas and William H. Murray, 1998
 */

#include <time.h>
#include <stdio.h>

main( )
{
  struct tm *date_time;
  time_t timer;

  time(&timer);
  date_time=gmtime(&timer);

  printf("%.19s\n",asctime(date_time));
  return (0);
}
```

The following date and time information was returned by this program:

```
Sat May 31 14:13:25
```

Working with the strftime( ) Function

The strftime( ) function provides the greatest formatting flexibility of all the date and time functions. The following program illustrates several formatting options.

```c
/*
 *    strtm.c
 *    Demonstrating the use of the strftime( ) function.
 *    Copyright (c) Chris H. Pappas and William H. Murray, 1998
 */

#include <time.h>
#include <stdio.h>

main( )
{
  struct tm *date_time;
  time_t timer;
  char str[80];

  time(&timer);
  date_time=localtime(&timer);
  strftime(str,80,"It is %X on %A, %x",
           date_time);
  printf("%s\n",str);
  return (0);
}
```

Here is a sample of the output for this program:

```
It is 17:18:45 on Saturday, 05/31/98
```

You may find that the strftime( ) function is not portable from one system to another. Use it with caution if portability is a consideration.

Working with the ctime( ) Function

The following C++ program illustrates how to make a call to the ctime( ) function. This program shows how easy it is to obtain date and time information from the system.

PROGRAMMING
FOUNDATIONS

```
//
//  ctime.cpp
//  Demonstrating the use of the ctime( ) function.
//  Copyright (c) Chris H. Pappas and William H. Murray, 1998
//

#include <time.h>
#include <iostream.h>

time_t longtime;

main( )
{
  time(&longtime);
  cout << "The time and date are " <<
          ctime(&longtime) << "\n";
  return (0);
}
```

The output, sent to the screen, would appear in the following format:

```
The time and date are Sat May 31 14:23:27 1998
```

Creating a Time Delay Routine

Usually it is desirable for programs to execute as quickly as possible. However, there are times when slowing down information makes it easier for the user to view and understand. The time_delay( ) function in the following application delays program execution. The delay variable is in seconds. For this example, there is a two-second delay between each line of output to the screen.

```
/*
 *   tdelay.c
 *   A C program that demonstrates how to create a delay
 *   function for slowing program output.
 *   Copyright (c) Chris H. Pappas and William H. Murray, 1998
 */

#include <stdio.h>
#include <time.h>
```

```
void time_delay(int);

main( )
{
  int i;

  for (i=0;i<25;i++) {
    time_delay(2);
    printf("The count is %d\n",i);
  }
  return (0);
}

void time_delay(int t)
{
  long initial,final;
  long ltime;

  initial=time(&ltime);
  final=initial+t;

  while (time(&ltime) < final);
  return;
}
```

What other uses might the time_delay( ) function have? One case might be where the computer is connected to an external data-sensing device, such as a thermocouple or strain gauge. The function could be used to take readings every minute, hour, or day.

What's Coming

The next chapter begins a new section of this book dealing with object-oriented programming. You'll find that many of the library functions discussed in this chapter can be extended to object-oriented programming techniques.

Part III

Foundations for Object-oriented Programming in C++